D0841585

ON
NARROW
GROUND

SUNY series in
Urban Public Policy

James Bohland and Patricia Edwards, editors

ON
NARROW
GROUND

Urban Policy and Ethnic Conflict in Jerusalem and Belfast

SCOTT A. BOLLENS

STATE UNIVERSITY OF NEW YORK PRESS

Published by
State University of New York Press, Albany

© 2000 State University of New York

All rights reserved

Printed in the United States of America

No part of this book may be used or reproduced in any manner
whatsoever without written permission. No part of this
book may be stored in a retrieval system or transmitted
in any form or by any means including electronic,
electrostatic, magnetic tape, mechanical, photocopying,
recording, or otherwise without the prior permission in
writing of the publisher.

For information, address State University of New York Press,
State University Plaza, Albany, N.Y., 12246

Cover photo by Meir Zarovsky
Production by Ruth Fisher
Marketing by Nancy Farrell

Library of Congress Cataloging-in-Publication Data

Bollens, Scott A.
    On narrow ground : urban policy and ethnic conflict in Jerusalem
and Belfast / Scott A. Bollens.
        p.   cm.—(SUNY series in urban public policy)
    Includes bibliography references and index.
    ISBN 0-7914-4413-9 (alk. paper).—ISBN 0-7914-4414-7 (pb. : alk.
paper)
        1. Urban policy—Jerusalem.   2. Jerusalem—Ethnic relations.
3. Urban policy—Northern Ireland—Belfast.   4. Belfast (Northern
Ireland)—Ethnic relations.   I. Title.   II. Series.   III. Series:
SUNY series on urban public policy.
HT169.I82 J473   2000
307.76'0956952—dc21   99-039693
                                                                CIP

10 9 8 7 6 5 4 3 2 1

To Yehonathon Golani, Ibrahim Dakkak,
Jackie Redpath, and the young pursuers of Short Strand

Shalom, Salaam, Peace, Siochain

To Damon and Denali
Children are the eyes of the world

Contents

Figures

Tables

Preface

I ask in this book whether a city functioning in the midst of a nationalistic conflict influences the processes and outcomes of that conflict. The book explores the role of policy and planning in contested urban environments and the effects these urban strategies have on the magnitude and manifestations of ethnonational conflict. I explore whether there are lessons for regional and national political negotiations that come from polarized cities regarding how to produce more mutually tolerable multiethnic living environments.

This work is the result of five years of research and analysis first started in summer 1993; the idea for this investigation was initiated in early 1987 when I met several community leaders from politically contested cities in a seminar in Salzburg, Austria. The research reported here is based on multiple sources—analysis of published and unpublished academic articles and government reports, quantitative urban data, and interviews with seventy-four current and former policymakers, nongovernmental organization officials, and academics in the polarized cities of Jerusalem (Israel/West Bank) and Belfast (Northern Ireland) conducted from October 1994 to March 1995. An integrative analytic approach combining the perspectives of four disciplines—political science, urban planning, geography, and social psychology—is utilized to study the complex social and ecological aspects of urban ethnic conflict. This study of urban policy connects broader political and ethnic ideologies to urban strategies and their specific territorial outcomes. These urban outcomes, in turn, have significant effects on group identity and deprivation, and thus ultimately on the extent and manifestations of urban unrest and violence.

I explore the proposition that a city amidst intense conflict is not a reflective mirror of those broader parameters, but instead an active mediating influence implicated in whether conflict is ameliorated or exacerbated. The city introduces a set of characteristics—proximate ethnic neighborhoods, territoriality, economic interdependency, symbolism, and centrality—that can bend or distort the relationship between ideological disputes and the manifestations of ethnic conflict. Urban policy decisions regarding land use, housing, economic development, urban services, and citizen involvement can independently harden or mollify intergroup cleavages. Two roles of urban policymaking are evident in the case studies—partisan and neutral. *Partisan* policymaking by Israel in Jerusalem seeks domination and subjugation which, paradoxically, produces urban and regional instability corrosive of Israel's genuine control over the city and its Palestinian residents. *Neutral* policymaking by the Northern Ireland government in Belfast over the past three decades has sought abstinence from violence, but is insufficient in a city of dysfunctional sectarian territoriality, shifting demographics, and differential needs across Protestant and Catholic communities. In both cities, a semi-autonomous role of urban policymaking amidst larger ethnic conflict results from the inherent difficulties of defining on a concrete level the operative forms of often abstract ideology or public goals pertaining to security, control, or stability. Urban operationalization can generate unforeseen consequences and contradictions that endanger the ideological policy goals themselves.

This book is most literate concerning events in these two regions that occurred from the middle of 1993 through the middle of 1996. The field research in Jerusalem occurred October 1994–January 1995. This was a period of time about one year after the signing of the Oslo Declaration of Principles (D.O.P.) and famous White House handshake, which established a process toward which Israel and the Palestinian National Authority would work toward peace. The Cairo Agreement signed about five months before my interviews outlined in greater detail how the D.O.P. was to be implemented, including the transfer in the next month of the Gaza Strip and Jericho to Palestinian control. In Jerusalem, Likud politician Ehud Olmert was completing his first year as mayor, after ending Teddy Kollek's twenty-eight-year reign. During the three months of interviews and field research, bombings by Hamas and Islamic Jihad took Israeli lives in Jerusalem, Tel Aviv, and Gaza. Members of these two Palestinian opposition groups clashed with Palestinian police in the Gaza Strip subsequent to Israeli demands that the Palestinian National Authority crack down on them. And, Israel and Jordan signed a peace treaty. The interviews occurred about nine months before the Oslo II agreement and the beginning of Israeli withdrawal and Palestinian empowerment in major West Bank population centers. Just less than one year later, Yitzhak Rabin was assassinated. About one and one-half years later, Binyamin Netanyahu was elected as prime minister of Israel.

The interviews in Belfast occurred January to March 1995, about five months after the ceasefires announced first by the Provisional Irish Republican Army (IRA), then subsequently by loyalist paramilitaries. Within the month of my arrival, British Army troops were pulled from the streets of Belfast, no longer backing up Royal Ulster Constabulary police. During my research stay, the British and Irish governments released their Joint Framework Documents, intended to move political discussions toward some mutually agreeable solution. About ten months after my visit, after multiparty negotiations had been consistently delayed over the issue of the decommissioning of IRA weapons, the IRA declared the end of their ceasefire with the bombing of a Docklands office building in London. In May 1998, seventy percent of Northern Ireland voters approved the creation of a new democratic Northern Ireland Assembly with executive and legislative powers and a new Ministerial Council to encourage island-wide cooperation. In addition, the Republic of Ireland to its south now agrees that Northern Ireland will remain part of the United Kingdom for as long as a majority of Northern Ireland voters are in support. Although this historic vote promises to significantly alter some of Northern Ireland's governing arrangements described in this book, the fundamental challenge of how to govern a splintered city remains as problematic today as when my field research was undertaken.

I document several inherent limitations of urban policy approaches in advancing peace in polarized cities. Nevertheless, I assert that reconceptualized urban policymaking can make a constructive difference not only in improving on-the-ground ethnic relations, but in contributing to, or reinforcing, political settlements at national and international levels. Tangible urban-level efforts and diplomatic national-level negotiations must be combined to create multifaceted peacemaking efforts. Urban accommodation without a national peace would leave the city vulnerable and unstable, but a national peace without urban accommodation would be one unrooted in the practical and explosive issues of intergroup and territorial relations. Progressive and ethnically sensitive urban strategies can operationalize and anchor formal national and local agreements over power, fostering urban ethnic interaction and political compromise. The narrow ground of urban policy does not need be a dire straits.

Acknowledgments

This project, and the many extraordinary people I have had the pleasure of interviewing, has enriched me personally and professionally. This experience has made me more human, and less patient with research done from a safe theoretical or analytical distance. We learn about difficult circumstances not through grand theorizing or simplistic generalizations, but by absorbing the views, concerns, and joys of people whose lives are intimately connected with them. Aldous Huxley said it well, that "there is all the difference in the world between believing academically, with the intellect, and believing personally, intimately, with the whole living self."

I extend my gratitude to the interviewees, who graciously provided me access into the sophisticated mind and tortured soul of the polarized city. Reflecting back on these individuals makes me want to both cry over our ability to hurt one another, and celebrate the human soul and its ability to persevere amidst the trials of hatred. I now have greater faith in the human spirit, and less confidence in the ability of elected political leaders. Specific appreciation is extended in Jerusalem to Israel Kimhi, Elinoar Barzacchi, Ibrahim Dakkak, Mahdi Abdul Hadi, and Yehonathan Golani; and in Belfast to Brendan Murtagh, Michael Graham, Bill Morrison, Colm Bradley, and Billy Hutchinson. I would like to acknowledge the hospitality and assistance of Professor Arie Shachar and the Institute of Urban and Regional Studies, Hebrew University of Jerusalem (Mt. Scopus campus); and Professor Frederick Boal and the School of Geosciences, Queen's University of Belfast.

One person whose ideas have been preeminent throughout the project is Meron S. Benvenisti, prolific writer and former Director of the West Bank Data Base Project, whom I initially met in 1987 at a seminar on "divided cities" in Salzburg, Austria. I thank Jonathan Howes, University of North Carolina, Chapel Hill, for providing me the opportunity to attend that stimulating seminar while I was a Ph.D. student there. At that seminar, Mustafa Akinci, former mayor of the Turkish Municipality of Nicosia, and Lellos Demetriades, mayor of the Greek Municipality of Nicosia, showed me that ethnic relations is between people as well as between peoples. Others have helped me develop research proposals and prepare logistically for field research, including Jay Rothman (Hebrew University and Haverford College), Craig Murphy (Wellesley College), Rachelle Alterman (Technion Institute), Mike McDonald (Williams College), James H. Wolfe (University of Southern Mississippi), Anthony Johnston (University of Ulster, Magee College), and Luis Suarez-Villa (University of California, Irvine).

Institutional and foundation support for this project have come from multiple sources, each of which I deeply appreciate: the United States Institute of Peace (Timothy Sisk, now at University of Denver, was particularly helpful); the Social Science Research Council—Near and Middle East Program; the Institute on Global Conflict and Cooperation and the Education Abroad Program, both at the University of California; and the Global Peace and Conflict Studies research unit and the School of Social Ecology, both at the University of California, Irvine.

I thank David Gorman for opening up the West Bank to me, Shaul Sapir for peeling back the historical layers of Jerusalem, an anonymous Hebrew-speaking assistant for interpreting the volatile Israeli press, and Ms. Daphna Oren for invaluable administrative support and hospitality. I thank Maura Pringle for castle and church, the Reverend Thabo Makgoba for his interpretation of the role of spirituality in contested societies, and Toby Nippel for sharing the joy of the path. I express my unending appreciation to Claudia for her support, care giving, and sharing of Hatsfira, Torr Head, and Linksfield.

Responsibility for errors lies solely with the author.

PART I

City and Sovereignty

1

Urban Arenas of Ethnic Conflict

A city is a product of both hegemonic and subordinate cultures, and, at the same time, the site for their production.

—J. Agnew, J. Mercer, and D. Sopher,
The City in Cultural Context (1984)

A disturbing number of cities across the world are susceptible to intense intercommunal conflict and violence reflecting ethnic or nationalist fractures. Cities such as Jerusalem, Belfast, Johannesburg, Nicosia, Montreal, Algiers, Sarajevo, New Delhi, Beirut, and Brussels are urban arenas penetrable by deep intergroup conflict associated with ethnic or political differences. In some cases, a city is the target or focal point for unresolved nationalistic ethnic conflict. Jerusalem is at the spatial epicenter of Israeli-Palestinian conflict which during the five years of the *intifada* cost more than 1,600 lives (Human Rights Watch 1993a). In other cases, a city is not a primary cause of intergroup conflict, but a platform for the expression of conflicting sovereignty claims or for tensions related to ethnic group relations. Belfast is the capital and the most important stage for conflict in contested Northern Ireland, a province that has borne witness to more than three thousand Protestant and Catholic deaths over the twenty-five years of civil war. New Delhi is the site of Hindu-Muslim tension and violence as separatist campaigns concerning Kashmir and Khalistan penetrate this center of Indian population and culture. And urban centers in Germany are platforms for right-wing groups in their

3

displays of hostility toward Mediterranean labor migrants and political refugees.[1]

In other cases, the management of war-torn cities holds the key to sustainable coexistence of warring ethnic groups subsequent to cessation of overt hostilities. In the former Yugoslavia, the cities of Sarajevo and Mostar are critical elements in whether enemies can spatially coexist in a workable reconstruction of a war-torn Bosnia that has suffered more than 200,000 dead and 1.7 million refugees.[2] Johannesburg is the economic powerhouse and largest urban region in the new democratic South Africa, a country where more than 15,000 people have been killed since the mid-1980s in political violence between the former white government and blacks, with thousands more dead from black-on-black hostilities (Human Rights Watch 1993a). The physically partitioned city of Nicosia is the focal point of the United Nations–managed settlement between Greek and Turkish Cypriots who engaged in a civil war that cost more than 10,000 lives in the 1960s and 1970s. The Lebanese political capital and cultural center of Beirut is undergoing physical and social reconstruction after a fifteen-year civil war that cost more than 15,000 Muslim, Christian, and Druze lives. And in the new Baltic countries of the former Soviet Union, native and Russian populations now coexist uneasily in the urban centers of Estonia, Latvia, and Lithuania. Yet, in other cities such as Brussels and Montreal, there have been effective efforts to defuse nationalistic conflict through cooperative communal governance and lawmaking.

Common to many of these cities is that ethnic identity[3] and nationalism[4] combine to create pressures for group rights, autonomy, or territorial separation. Such ethnic nationalism is often exclusive and fragmentary, and may constitute a threat to an existing state when an ethnic group aspires to create a nation-state different than currently exists.[5] In ethnically polarized cities, the machinery of government is often controlled by one ethnic group and used to discriminate against competing and threatening groups. In other cases, a third-party mediator may be brought in to govern the urban setting. In either case, the very legitimacy of a city's political structures and its rules of decisionmaking and governance are commonly challenged by ethnic groups who either seek an equal or proportionate share of power (such as blacks in South Africa) or demand group-based autonomy or independence (such as Palestinians in Jerusalem or the Quebecois in Montreal). In the most intense cases, these cities are battlegrounds between "homeland" ethnic groups, each proclaiming the city as their own (Esman 1985).

As we witness changes since the 1960s in the scale of world conflict from international to intrastate, urban centers of ethnic proximity and diversity assume increased salience to those studying and seeking to resolve contemporary conflict. Sixty-nine of the ninety-four wars recorded between 1945 and 1988 (INCORE 1994) have been intrastate conflicts killing an estimated 17–30 million people and displacing millions from their home countries. Eighty percent of all war deaths since World War II have been internal to national states (Russett and Starr 1989; Brogan 1990). Of the thirty-seven major armed conflicts in the world in 1991, twenty-five of them were intrastate conflicts between ethnic groups or between an ethnic group and a government (Eriksen 1993). Gurr and Harff (1994, 6) document forty-nine "protracted communal conflicts" in the world today that are confrontations between "ethnic groups and governments over fundamental issues of group rights and identity" and "usually involved recurring episodes of intense violence."[6]

Within ethnically tense and fragmenting states, urban management of ethnic competition has profound consequences for the national, and ultimately, international level (Ashkenasi 1988a). Urban areas and their civilian populations are "soft, high-value" targets for broader conflict (Brown 1993). They can become important military and symbolic battlegrounds and flashpoints for violence between warring ethnic groups seeking sovereignty, autonomy, or independence. Cities are fragile and vulnerable organisms subject to economic stagnation, demographic disintegration, cultural suppression, and ideological and political excesses violent in nature. They are focal points of urban and regional economies dependent on multi-ethnic contacts, social and cultural centers and platforms for political expression, and potential centers of grievance and mobilization. They provide the locus of everyday interaction where ethnicity and identity can be created and re-created (Erikson 1993). They are suppliers of important religious and cultural symbols, zones of intergroup proximity and intimacy, and arenas where the size and concentration of a subordinate population can present the most direct threat to the state. Much more than at larger geographic scales where segregation of ethnic communities is possible, the proximity of urban living means that contested cities can be located on the fault line between cultures—between modernizing societies and traditional cultures; between individual-based and community-based economies and societal ethics; between democracy and more authoritarian regimes; and/or between old colonial governments and native populations.

Polarized cities are characterized by "narrow ground" (Stewart 1977) where antagonistic parties encounter one another spatially and functionally.[7] In many cases, the proximate and contentious ethnic territoriality found in the residential fabric of a contested city constricts and dichotomizes urban living. A city is a site where belligerent peoples come together—if not due to intergroup competition over urban space, then to the economic interdependencies inherent to urban living. The narrow ground is also felt by city policymakers because ethnic polarization circumscribes policy options. Penetration of the city by extralocal conflict requires urban management not only of city services, but of ideological or religious expression and other correlates of intergroup tension and hostilities.

This study examines how nationalistic ethnic conflict penetrates the building of cities and explores whether urban policies and their effects may independently influence, for better or worse, the shape and magnitude of that conflict. In other words, it explores how urban policy is affected by the conditions imposed by deep-rooted nationalistic conflict, but also how local decisions may affect the dynamics of the conflict. It tests the proposition that cities are not simple mirrors of broader ethnic conflict, but instead capable of channeling, modifying, or disrupting broader imperatives and governing ideologies. Urban arenas of national conflict are not necessarily passive receptacles. Rather, as Friedland and Hecht (1996) suggest, national and religious conflict may be worked out, and modulated, in urban space. Through their shaping and control of ethnic territorial expression, city governing regimes may independently intensify or moderate the level of interethnic tension and the coherency of mobilization by a subordinated "out-group." Urban policy and administrative strategies related to spatial organization, demographic allocation, service delivery and spending, and economic development may have direct links to ethnic groups' feelings of psychological security and fairness in the urban milieu. Urban policies also may influence political organization on the part of an aggrieved group (McAdam, McCarthy, and Zald 1996; Tarrow 1994). If these expectations that cities matter amidst conflict are accurate, the urban region becomes an essential analytical scale for studying the contemporary intrastate patterns and processes of ethnic conflict, violence, and their management.

It is not evident whether a major city in the midst of nationalistic ethnic conflict will constitute a flashpoint for intergroup tension or a buffer against it. A city presents a subordinate ethnic group with the "often-contradictory forces of state assimilation and discrimination" (A. Smith 1993). On the one hand, the economic centrality and/or religious symbolism of a city within a national hierarchy and the close juxtaposition of antagonistic neighborhoods would lead one to anticipate exacerbation of the general level of interethnic tension and the increasing frequency of violent actions. Intergroup proximity and interaction characteristic of urban areas might provide sparks to unresolved and long-simmering ethnic fires. To the extent that a city is a flashpoint, it can act as a major and independent obstruction to the success of larger regional and national peace processes.[8] Yet the same features of urban closeness and interdependency may lead local political leaders and elites to engage in workable ethnic compromises not politically possible at a larger geographic scale. Ashkenasi (1988a) suggests that the pragmatic needs of communal government will influence city leadership and intergroup relations in a more affirmative fashion than it does national-level ethnic relations. In addition, the realities of urban interdependence may make it more difficult for ethnic groups to live in their own "purified" communities insulated by myths of sameness and communal solidarity (Sennett 1970). Cities may then be buffers against the strong winds of sectarianism and ethnicity. In these cases, the possibility exists that urban-based ethnic compromises may, under certain conditions, radiate outward to help pacify conflict at national and international levels.

*   *   *

This research project investigates city and regional conflicts that reflect deep ethno-ideological divisions, focusing on the relationship in ethnically polarized cities between urban policy strategies and the magnitude and manifestations of local and regional ethnic conflict. Specifically, it asks whether cities matter amidst conflict—is urban planning and policy capable of independently affecting relations between ethnic groups or are local actions derivative of fundamental governing ideologies and thus irrelevant? The study explores two case studies—Jerusalem (Israel and West Bank) and

Belfast (Northern Ireland)—through the analysis of published and unpublished academic articles and government reports, evaluation of quantitative urban data, and the undertaking of numerous interviews. Field research involved three months in each location during the October 1994 to March 1995 period. During this time, I undertook seventy-four face-to-face interviews with a diverse collection of persons involved in, or affected by, the city policymaking process. Throughout all research tasks, I examine whether there exists a semiautonomous, meaningful role for urban policymaking amidst conflict, and whether the effects of local decisions on ethnic relations facilitate or obstruct the goals of the governing regime.

If cities matter amidst conflict, urban management of ethnic strife may possibly provide lessons—either positive or adverse—for ethnic governance at national and cross-national scales. One of the greatest challenges facing many world cities today is to facilitate the expression of ethnic and cultural diversity that enriches city life while at the same time working against the physical and psychological barriers, hostility, and violence that can paralyze and impoverish it. Applied research in this area will provide to practitioners and officials a better understanding of the complexities of urban policymaking amidst uncertainty and strife.[9] Government practices and public policy are viewed here not as inconsequential to ethnic conflict. This is consistent with cross-national analyses of ethnic conflict which reveal that today's ethnic violence stems as much from actions by political elites and ethnic entrepreneurs as from traditional community antagonisms (Pesic 1996; Esman and Telhami 1995; Snyder 1993). Ethnic tension and violence at the urban level provides an important microcosm of intergroup dynamics at more encompassing geographic scales. Thus, applied urban research may provide to policy officials at local, national, and cross-national scales a keener awareness of how government authority and its expression affects the dynamics of ethnic nationalism.

This work is organized in the following fashion. The remainder of chapter 1 describes the extraordinary nature of societal division that exists within contested cities and asserts that diverse perspectives on the management of ethnic conflict must be utilized to effectively study the complexities of cities amidst conflict. Chapter 2 constructs a conceptual framework that connects the governing ideology of the urban state, urban policy strategies, ethnic conditions in the city (both objective and perceptual), and urban intergroup stability or volatility. Chapter 3 explains the selection of Jerusalem and Belfast for study and locates the field research within the larger and evolving peacemaking processes enveloping Israel/Palestine and Northern Ireland. The next three chapters comprise a case study of Jerusalem, exploring the key aspects of Israeli urban policy in chapter 4, the internal dynamics of partisan policymaking and its effect on Palestinians in chapter 5, and the effect of urban policy on intergroup ethnic relations in the city, metropolitan region, and West Bank in chapter 6. A case study of Belfast comprises the next three chapters. In chapter 7, the neutral intentions of British urban policy are described; in chapter 8, the effects of this approach on government action and on Belfast's residents and neighborhoods are analyzed; in chapter 9, the rudiments of an alternative urban policy approach more consistent with the advancement of peace are portrayed. Finally, in chapter 10, I explore the connecting and distinguishing themes culled from the two case studies, draw conclusions regarding the effects of urban policy on conflict, and suggest that cities (and urban policies) have an indispensable role to play in fostering and deepening national peace and reconciliation.

Divided and Polarized Cities

Ethnically polarized cities host a deeper, more intransigent type of urban conflict than is found in most cities. Cities are frequently divided geographically by ethnicity, race, income, and age (Massey and Denton 1993; Goldsmith and Blakely 1992). In most cities, conflicts focus on issues of service delivery (such as housing), land use compatibility, and facility siting. Yet conflicts in these *divided* cities are addressed within accepted political frameworks. Questions of what constitutes the public good are debated but largely within a sanctioned framework. For example, African Americans in the 1960s protested for a greater share of economic benefits, but did so within a political framework they largely accepted.[10] After the 1992 Los Angeles riots, issues of service distribution dominated those of territoriality and sovereignty. Gurr (1993) labels these as "ethnoclass" conflicts involving quests for political and economic equality and for cultural rights. In such divided cities, coalition building remains possible across ethnic groups and cross-cutting cleavages defuse and moderate intergroup conflict (Nordlinger 1972). One of the major roles of urban planning in such circumstances is to ameliorate urban conflict through an acceptable allocation of urban services and benefits across ethnic groups and their neighborhoods.

In contrast, urban *polarization* occurs in cases where ethnic and nationalist claims combine and impinge significantly and consistently on distributional questions at the municipal level (Boal and Douglas 1982; Benvenisti 1986a). Polarized cities host "alternative and directly opposing cultures that are 'contestable'" (Agnew, Mercer, and Sopher 1984). Such conflicts are "ethnonational" wherein one group seeks autonomy or separation (Gurr 1993). In such a circumstance, a strong minority of the urban population may reject urban and societal institutions, making consensus regarding political power sharing impossible (Douglas and Boal 1982; Romann and Weingrod 1991). The severity and intractability of intergroup conflict in polarized cities can overwhelm the adversary politics between government and opposition common in modern democratic states. Political means are seen as incapable of effectively resolving urban ethnic differences. While doctrines of collective rights, pluralism, or autonomy are invoked by those on the outside, the politically dominant *in-group* views resistance by a historically subordinated *out-group* as an obstacle to "natural" processes of city building and assimilation (Gurr 1993; Horowitz 1985).

Whereas in most cities there is a belief maintained by all groups that the existing system of governance is properly configured and capable of producing fair outcomes, assuming adequate political participation and representation of minority interests,[11] governance in "polarized" cities is often viewed by a not insubstantial segment of the ethnic minority population as artificial, imposed, or illegitimate. In those cases where an ethnic minority acknowledges the authority of city governance, it deeply mistrusts its intrinsic capability to respond to calls for equal, or group-based, treatment. A "combustible mixture" of distributive and political grievances can then combine to turn the attention of subordinated ethnic leaders from urban reform of the existing system to, next, radical restructuring or to, finally, separation and autonomy.[12]

The occurrence of intergroup tension and violence in polarized cities can be qualitatively different than in divided cities. Many polarized cities are the sites of enduring and consistent interethnic violence laden with political meaning, capable of destabilizing both city life and larger peace processes. The potential for explosiveness in many polarized cities is more catastrophic and politically salient than the individual criminally based actions of divided cities.[13] In settings where antagonistic sides view each other as threats to physical, cultural, or social survival, violence can be "rational" in that it is viewed as the only way for an aggrieved ethnic group to change intractable institutions and circumstances (Sisk 1995). Such circumstances, however, can produce "hurting stalemates" where the status quo is mutually damaging and neither side can impose its solution upon the other (Touval and Zartman 1985).

Urban Policy amidst Polarization

This study of the relationship between urban policy and broader ideological conflict seeks to integrate political science, urban planning, geographic, and social-psychological perspectives on the management of ethnic conflict. Models and theories from multiple disciplines are utilized because no single perspective is likely to capture fully the complex social and ecological aspects of urban ethnic conflict. I now discuss each disciplinary strand and its contributions and limitations to the study of city-based nationalistic conflict.

Political science models of conflict management focus on political and legal arrangements and mechanisms at the level of the nation-state that might diffuse or moderate conflict. By de-emphasizing applications to city governance and management, these models limit their utility regarding how city officials are to operate in ethnically polarized cities. Micropolitical, or smaller scale, forms of conflict management in urban areas—such as discrimination and segregation, demographic policies, or community relations—are seen simply as tools of larger macropolitical objectives operating at national and international levels (O'Leary and McGarry 1995). The city is assumed to reflect at a concrete level the playing out of broader imbalances of power. Or, as Rothman (1992) points out, the "low politics" of groups and how they pursue the fulfillment of human needs for their constituents is dismissed as unimportant compared to the "high politics" of states and their promotion and protection of national interests.

Notwithstanding their dismissal of city-based dynamics, political science models of conflict management have important implications for urban management. O'Leary and McGarry (1995) outline two

types of methods—those that would eliminate ethnic differences
and those that would manage such differences.[14] Methods that seek
to eliminate differences include forced mass population transfers,
partition or secession, and integration or assimilation. Ethnic
cleansing in Sarajevo (Bosnia-Herzegovina) and apartheid in Johannesburg (South Africa) illustrate the application at the urban
and regional scale of forced population transfers. More commonly,
city administrations manipulate demographic proportions and spatially fragment an antagonistic ethnic group in order to achieve the
same political objectives as forced relocations. Political partitioning
of urban space (as in Nicosia, Cold War Berlin, and Jerusalem from
1948 to 1967) can be an important feature of national-level agreements regarding territorial separation. At the same time, urban
partitioning introduces practical problems not found at a national
scale. Finally, integration or assimilation strategies in many ways
have greater salience at the smaller-scale urban level than they do
at more dispersed national scales. Cities can seek integration
through the attempted creation of a civic identity that would transcend ethnic identity. Assimilation takes this one step farther in attempting to create a common cultural identity derived through a
melting pot process.

Methods for managing, rather than eliminating, ethnic differences
include hegemonic control, third-party intervention, cantonization or
federalization, and consociation or power sharing. Political stability
is achieved by hegemonic control at the cost of democracy. One side
dominates the state apparatus and channels in a partisan way decisionmaking outcomes toward the favored ethnic group (Lustick 1979;
Smooha 1980). However, the proximity and interdependence of
urban ethnic populations may necessitate in hegemonically controlled cities greater cooperation or co-optation between political
leaders than would be found at national levels. Third-party intervention relies on there being an arbiter whose claim of neutrality
must be broadly accepted by contending ethnic groups. At the urban
scale, this perceived joint neutrality can be difficult because historic
imbalances and inequalities are highlighted by a relative deprivation
effect induced by physical proximity. Even well-intended policies by
a third party can be seen as reinforcing these inequalities if root
causes of urban disparities are not addressed.

Cantonization and federalization involve, in the first case, devolution of some government authority to homogeneous ethnonational

territories; and, in the second, separate domains of formal authority between levels of government. Urban applications of these concepts include, in the first case, the creation of community or neighborhood-based groups that would advise or decide on local issues. In the second case, there would be the creation of a metropolitan government and subordinate municipal governments. The last model of ethnic management is consociation or power sharing. At the national level, this has been the most closely scrutinized option for deeply divided societies. Lijphart's (1968, 1977) "consociational" democracy and Nordlinger's (1972) "conflict-regulating practices" focus on the role of cooperative efforts by political leaders in creating government structures and rules (such as proportional representation and minority veto power) that can overcome and diffuse societal fragmentation. Horowitz (1985) recommends the creation of incentives that would encourage politicians and voters to consider interests beyond their communal segments.[15] Although power sharing is usually studied exclusively at the national governmental level, it has relevance to the governance of cities split by ethnic nationalism (O'Leary and McGarry 1995).

Another line of political investigation—exemplified by McAdam, McCarthy, and Zald (1996), Gurr and Harff (1994), Tarrow (1994), Gurr (1993), and Weitzer (1990)—explores the cause and dynamics of communal conflict and ethnic group mobilization. Although applied to national settings, its focus on whether relative conditions of deprivation or aspects of an ethnic group's political organization and leadership primarily cause community protest and rebellion has direct salience to urban settings. In the first case, the origins of protest and resistance are found in a sense of injustice and grievance widely shared across out-group members. In the second case, resistance is a function of the actions and skills of ethnic group leaders, organizations, and networks. Targeting relative deprivation as the culprit, city governments could potentially try to ameliorate nationalistic claims and protests by an antagonistic ethnic group through betterment of objective urban conditions. Because cities may be either platform or palliative for community protest, the intensity of urban opposition may be different than, and be able to affect, the quality of national-level opposition.

Models and theories of *urban planning* have more directly addressed local policymaking and administration. However, a major limitation of this literature is that much of planning prescription and theory has been dependent upon there being legitimate sources of power and control (Friedmann 1987). Traditional planning practice is rooted in assumptions of the maintenance of a stable state (Morley and Shachar 1986). In contrast, urban planning in ethnically polarized cities must act within conditions of instability and uncertainty that call into question the very basis of its traditional practice. Traditional planning is linked to societal guidance, urban reform, and the pursuit of a general "public interest" within the largely consensual policymaking environments characteristic of Western democracies. In contrast, the "public interest" in polarized cities is either fragile or impossible under contested conditions.

Urban planning has tended to focus on technical aspects of land use and development and avoided discussions concerning values and social justice (Thomas 1994; Thomas and Krishnarayan 1994). Equity-based approaches to planning exist that are based on notions of social justice (Davidoff 1967; Krumholtz and Clavel 1994). Yet their emphasis on increasing the representation of disadvantaged groups' interests during decisionmaking does not appear to be generalizable to situations where politics is segmented and antagonistic. The role of urban planning amidst ethnic polarization is problematic. Benvenisti (1986a) states that planning's use of pragmatic, process-oriented approaches aimed at urban symptoms, not root causes, legitimizes the status quo and institutionalizes the dual, unequal conditions common to urban polarization. Planners' definition of urban problems in universal, civil-libertarian terms can reach a "manageable" solution by a convenient perception of the problem, yet a solution that has little importance when sovereignty and autonomy are the leading issues. The compatibility between dominant forms of power and the exercise of urban planning bears a resemblance to structuralist and neo-Marxist critiques of urban planning policy. These have castigated the profession for its subservience to the economic powers of advanced urban capitalism (Dear and Scott 1981). In its extreme, urban planning can be instrumental in the exercise of state repression and coercion (Yiftachel 1995). In contrast, two models of planning policy described by Friedmann (1987) have potentially more productive roles in the management and reconstruction of polarized cities. A "social learning" model of urban planning allows for the profession to learn from action and practice in ethnically polarized environments, and could be at the forefront in grassroots efforts to accommodate antagonistic ethnicities within the urban milieu. A "social mobilization" or "empowerment" model of urban planning is more radical and seeks emancipation of working people, women, and oppressed ethnic groups (Friedmann 1987, 1992).

Geographic analyses of ethnically polarized environments provide insight into the spatial and territorial aspects and dynamics of such contest. Sack's (1981, 55) definition of territoriality is illuminating:

> [T]he attempt to affect, influence, or control actions and inter-actions (of people, things, and relationships) by asserting and attempting to enforce control over a specific geographical area.

A dominant ethnic government in a contested city can seek to contain an antagonistic group's territorial expression (Yiftachel 1995). This can be done through the intentional expansion of the dominant group's urban space or the restriction of subordinate group space. There is the effort to prevent the emergence of a powerful, regionally-based, counterculture which may challenge the ethnic state (Yiftachel 1995.) Territorial policies can displace attention away from the root causes of social conflict to conflicts among territorial spaces themselves (Sack 1986). In the urban setting, this means that international issues of sovereignty and autonomy become reducible to issues over neighborhoods and suburban growth. Urban territoriality can also become worthy of endless defense, no matter its realistic functionality in meeting the defending ethnic group's objective needs. In such a setting, even a well-intentioned urban government's sensitivity toward ethnic territoriality can help sustain and promote ethnic social cleavages (Murphy 1989).

The proximity of urban living introduces problematic effects of territoriality that must be faced by a dominant ethnic group. To control an antagonistic ethnic population, a dominant ethnic group in many cases will try to penetrate it geographically in order to establish a physical presence and to fragment the opposing group's sense of community. Yet such penetration forces the protagonist to give up some of the security provided by ethnic separation (Romann 1995).[16] Thus, efforts at territorial control can paradoxically reduce group security. Spatial competition brings antagonistic groups closer together, establishing conditions for further conflict. In other cases, achievement of territorial control at one geographic scale (for instance, that of the city) may expose the dominating group to demographic and physical threats at the next broader geographic scale (for instance, the urban or metropolitan region). Thus, territoriality may engender further efforts at territorial control in a self-fulfilling cycle (Sack 1986). Yet it has been suggested that in contested areas the greater the land area under territorial control, the less the control over the subordinated population (Akenson 1992, Williams 1994). Administrative control over land and political control over people are not necessarily the same.

Other urban geographic treatises have examined the relationship between urban space and social justice. Harvey's (1973) territorial distributive justice implies a spatial form that fulfills basic needs, contributes to the common good as well as private needs, and allocates extra resources to areas of extreme environmental or social difficulty. To D. Smith (1994), a socially just geography is one that reduces inequality. And Barry (1989, 146) connects the concept of spatial distributive justice to its institutional basis, highlighting the "institutions that together determine the access (or chances of access) of the members of a society to resources that are the means to the satisfaction of a wide variety of desires." This last comment highlights the need in ethnically polarized cities to connect geographic strategies and outcomes to the motivating ideologies and institutional rationales underlying them. How political goals are connected to specific territorial policies, and the effect these territorial outcomes have in turn on these goals, is a topic that geographic analyses have de-emphasized. We need to connect the spatial to the political.

The *social psychology* of urban intergroup conflict is a final important consideration when studying urban ethnic conflict. Social-psychological studies of intergroup conflict and urban aggression indicate the immediate sources of ethnic conflict that must be addressed in efforts at accommodation. Ethnic conflicts of the type found in polarized cities are only marginally over material interests, but rather touch deeply on human needs for security, identity, and recognition, fair access to political institutions, and economic participation (R. Cohen 1978; Burton 1990; Kelman 1990; Azar 1991). The proximity of urban living can exacerbate these felt needs through the effect of relative deprivation and the psychology of imbalance. The threatened loss of group identity and security amidst conditions of urban conflict—due in particular to urban territorial changes—can be a prime motivator of antagonism and unrest. To a threatened subgroup, psychological needs pertaining to community and cultural viability (measured through the survival, for instance, of ethnic schools or religious institutions in a neighborhood) can be as important as objective needs pertaining to land for housing and economic activities. Recognition and maintenance of group identity would seem to be an essential building block for peacemaking efforts at urban and national levels.[17]

Psychologists trained in intergroup conflict resolution emphasize not the promotion and preservation of political interests, but the non-negotiable values of each side associated with human needs and identity needs. As Burton (1991, 81) states, "there can be no resolution of a conflict unless it takes into account as political reality the perceptions and values of those who are represented in facilitated discussions." Without addressing core human needs such as identity, security, and economic access, conflicts may be managed for awhile by political leaders but seldom resolved, since core human needs are often bypassed by political negotiations. Social-psychological, needs-based approaches to conflict resolution focus on locally based intergroup conflict and thus have salience to urban conflict. However, these techniques are usually not directly linked to formal policy processes. Indeed, such intergroup deliberations, to be effective, need to be free of the power relations and vested interests of formal politics and policymaking (Kelman and Cohen 1976; Burton 1990; Fisher 1990; Rothman 1992). The current study attempts to highlight the social-psychological effects of urban policy on both subordinate and dominant ethnic groups. It seeks to explain the debilitating effects of urban strategies on group perceptions of security, identity, and cohesiveness, and to hopefully indicate directions whereby future urban actions can accommodate and respect human needs as part of a larger peace.

Psychologists have also examined the physical ecology (environmental factors) and social ecology (personal characteristics) of aggression. Absent resolution of root causes underlying urban violence, policymakers can seek attenuation of overt hostile acts by either designing physical environments to dissuade aggression or providing opportunities for conflict-reducing intergroup conflict (Goldstein 1994). The former category of environmental design interventions includes access control, formal surveillance by security personnel, and the creation of environments that facilitate natural surveillance by residents engaged in day-to-day activities (Wood 1991; Clarke 1992). "Defensible space," for example, is designed so that multiple "eyes on the street" dissuade criminal behavior (Newman 1975). A more hardened approach to environmental crime prevention is described by M. Davis (1990) in his account of a "militarization of urban space" aimed at protecting against urban aggressors or unwanteds. Social ecological interventions, in contrast, seek to facilitate intergroup contact that will overcome stereotyping and hatred. This assumes that group insularity and prejudice are at the roots of intergroup conflict. Yet intergroup encounters may actually increase conflict if the groups are not of equal status or do not share some common goals (Allport 1954; Goldstein 1991). This is problematic because in ethnically polarized cities, status—actual or perceived—is commonly not equivalent between groups, but is usually of a dominant-subordinate nature. Identity-enhancing and confidence-building community development initiatives on both sides of the urban divide may be necessary for intergroup contact to have any measurable positive effect.

*   *   *

Each analytical perspective on the management of ethnic conflict—political science, urban planning, geographic, and social-psychological—offers penetrating insights into the dynamics, management, and possible resolution of urban-based ethnic conflict. Yet, because each tends to have a different target of analysis—national political, urban strategic, territorial/spatial, and individual or group-based, respectively—it becomes necessary to integrate their perspectives to more fruitfully learn about the multifaceted interplay of urban management and ethnic nationalism. A synthesis of several perspectives provides the opportunity to connect broader political ideologies to urban strategies and their specific territorial outcomes. These, in turn, have significant effects on group identity and deprivation, and thus ultimately on the extent and manifestations of urban unrest and violence.

2

Cities as Catalysts

C ities exist between the ideological and historical bases of ethnic conflict and the interpersonal or intergroup dynamics of ethnic relations. Such an intermediary role, however, does not necessarily imply that cities are inert and passive reflectors of larger societal tensions and dynamics. Rather, cities may be capable through their physical and political qualities of exerting independent effects on ethnic tension, conflict, and violence (A. Shachar, Hebrew University of Jerusalem, interview). Urban policy and planning approaches, and their effects, are not essentially predetermined by ideological goals and parameters in this view. Rather, there are qualities of the urban system—intergroup proximity, social interaction, and economic interdependency—that can bend or distort the relationship between ideological disputes and the manifestations of ethnic conflict. Depending upon how a polarized city is governed, the urban arena can be a catalyst either toward intergroup tension or toward tolerance.

A city, while not the primary cause of ethnonational strife, constitutes nonetheless an active mediating channel through which ideological and ethnic conflicts may be either enhanced or lessened. The physical and political structures of a city may modify the cause-effect relationship between the broader causes of ethnic strife—political disempowerment and cultural deprivation—and the forms and level of ethnic strife. Rather than a physical container which passively reflects larger societal processes, a city is an active social and political agent capable of moving a society toward either disruptive unrest or ethnic accommodation.

Cities are salient in a world of intrastate conflict, ethnic group identity, unprecedented migration, and postcolonialism. There is an emerging consensus in the study of ethnic conflict that political leaders play a key role in either inflaming or attenuating the ancient hatreds of antagonistic ethnic groups (Pesic 1996; Esman and Telhami 1995; Snyder 1993). Pesic (1996, 19) concludes that "The principal mechanism for escalating interethnic conflicts in a multinational state begins when political elites in tenuous positions of power successfully portray their ethno-nation as being threatened by another." Thus, deliberate policy decisions can play key roles in stimulating or stifling group antagonisms. In this study, I look at the intentions of national and local policymakers pertaining to cities having great symbolic and/or economic centrality, and how these actions intensify, suspend, or moderate community hatreds. The catalytic urban arena of conflict is worthy of attention because urban policy provides a lever that is more understandable to public officials, nongovernmental advocates, and the public at large than the higher-level and less tangible political negotiations carried out by government ministers and foreign diplomats. To the extent that broader extralocal political negotiations are stalled or nonproductive, the tangible, on-the-ground strategies at the urban level pertaining to physical structure and empowerment may make the difference between mutual tolerance and armed urban conflict.[1]

Figure 2.1 presents a diagram outlining the hypothesized relationships between broader ethnonationalist conflict, the city, and the stability or volatility of ethnic relations.

Governing Ideology and Urban Policy

An ideology is a comprehensive political belief system that embraces an inner logic and seeks to guide and justify organized political and social actions (Bilski and Galnoor 1980). In this study, I focus on the ideology adopted by *governments* regarding their desired urban outcomes in a society of conflicting ethnic groups. I emphasize governing ideologies because public authorities operating amidst ethnic unrest must adopt an explicit doctrine that justifies and defends their policies amidst societal fragmentation. A primary issue facing government in polarized cities is how its ideology of urban governance will interact with the highly salient ethnonationalist ideologies of its competing populations. The governing ideology in a polarized city constitutes an intake or gatekeeper function,

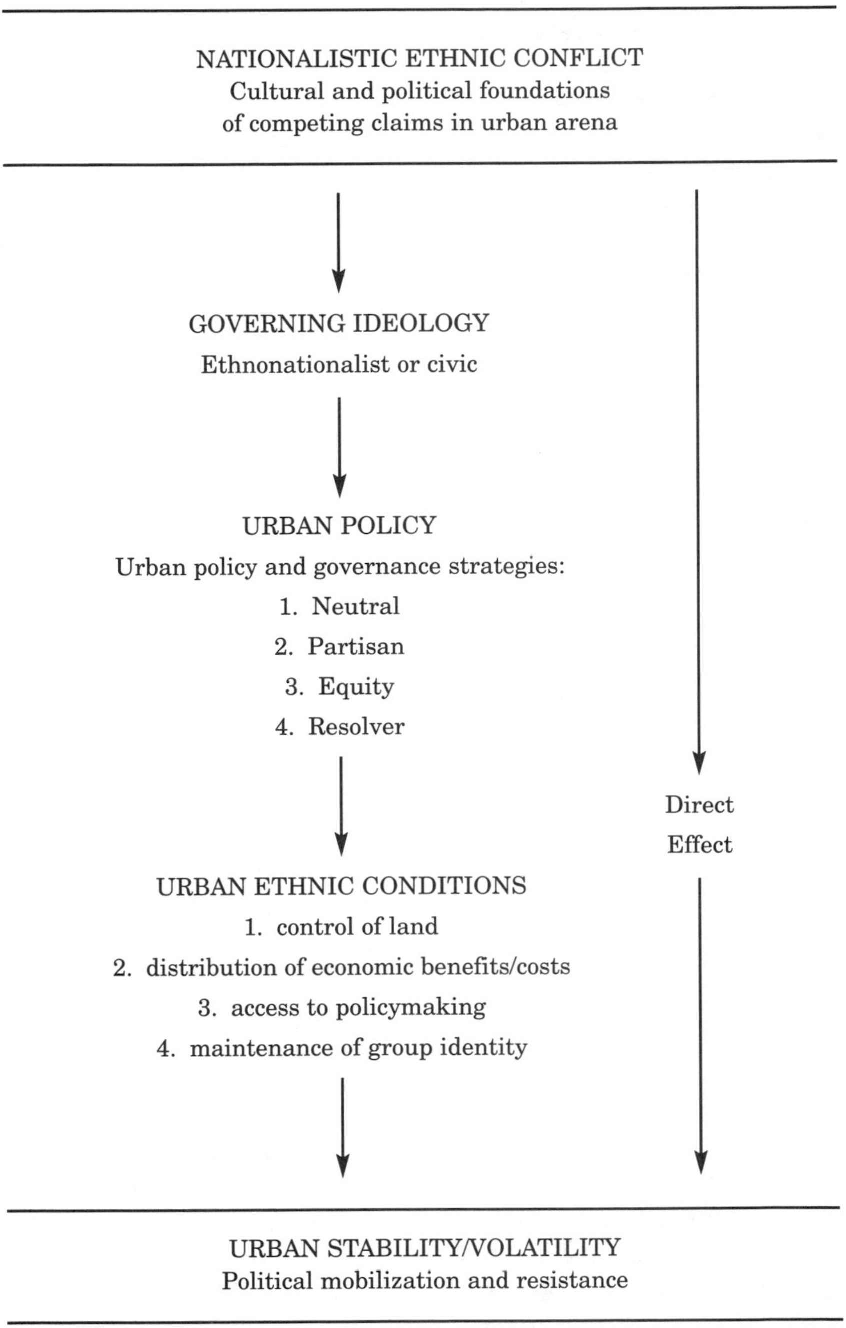

NATIONALISTIC ETHNIC CONFLICT
Cultural and political foundations
of competing claims in urban arena

GOVERNING IDEOLOGY
Ethnonationalist or civic

URBAN POLICY
Urban policy and governance strategies:

1. Neutral

2. Partisan

3. Equity

4. Resolver

Direct
Effect

URBAN ETHNIC CONDITIONS

1. control of land

2. distribution of economic benefits/costs

3. access to policymaking

4. maintenance of group identity

URBAN STABILITY/VOLATILITY
Political mobilization and resistance

Figure 2.1   Ideology, Urban Policy, and Ethnic Relations

Source: Adapted from Yiftachel 1992 and Gurr 1993

either allowing or barring a single ethnic group's claim to penetrate and frame public policy. A state's urban governing ideology can either be ethnonationalist or civic.[2] When there is a single dominating ethnic group in control of the government apparatus, the morally based doctrines of that ethnonational group regarding sovereignty and cultural identity will merge with the state's urban policy. In cases where a third party overseer may govern the city, or after the resolution of political conflict, government goals may pursue a civic ideology that seeks to accommodate or transcend ethnonational ideologies.

The translating of governing *ideology* into urban *policy* is not straightforward. Ideology must be translated into technical prescriptions that seek to move a society, or in this case a city, toward those final goals or vision. Yet ideology is fraught with ambiguity that may engender multiple interpretations as to which actions are appropriate to achieve chosen ends. The moral and implementation dimensions of ideology have been identified as "fundamental" and "operative," respectively (Seliger 1970). The problem for societies, and political leaders, is that operative ideology does not automatically proceed from the grand visions or moral ends asserted by fundamental ideology. For example, both liberal economies and communism espouse liberty and equality, yet propose drastically different means as the way to achieve them (Seliger 1970). In other circumstances, equality between ethnic groups may be espoused as the best way to resolve polarization, yet how it should be achieved in societies where there are significant historic imbalances does not proceed automatically from such overall moral agreement.[3]

Fundamental ideology in an urban system is implemented primarily through urban planning and policy decisions. City planners and administrators seek to give concrete meaning to goals pertaining to fairness and ethnic accommodation (in the case of civic ideology) or political control (in the case of ethnonationalist ideology). Fundamental ideology, however, may not be easily translatable onto the urban landscape. The exercise of urban policy and planning may highlight difficulties in the implementation of a morally based fundamental ideology in a contested society. Whether a government is pursuing an ethnonationalist or civic agenda, the urban arena can constitute an obstacle to the achievement of regime goals. In the case of a partisan regime, an ethnonationalist ideology espousing urban separation and ethnic segregation can be at odds with the centripetal and interdependent dynamics of urban areas. Politically and emotionally salient overtures to nationalist ideology may become diluted as they are operationalized at the more pragmatic level of urban management. On the other hand, in those cases in which a government seeks to accommodate ethnic differences and implement a civic ideology, the achievement of goals can be obstructed by the strict territoriality or community contentiousness emblematic of polarized cities, or by more mundane barriers such as economic and budgetary limitations.

In this study, I examine the extent of use, and impacts, of four *urban policy strategies* discussed in the literatures of public administration and urban planning. These models, identified in Table 2.1, differ in their substantive goals, in the extent to which they address root causes or urban symptoms of intergroup conflict, and in the degree to which they incorporate ethnic criteria.

A *neutral* urban strategy employs technical criteria in allocating urban resources and services, and distances itself from issues of ethnic identity, power inequalities, and political exclusion. Residents are treated within local planning processes as individuals rather than members of ethnic groups (M. Smith, 1969). Thus, planning acts as an ethnically neutral, or "color-blind," mode of state intervention responsive to individual-level needs and differences. This is the traditional style of urban management and planning rooted in an Anglo-Saxon tradition and commonly applied in liberal democratic settings (Yiftachel 1995). In a polarized city, a government espousing a civic ideology of ethnic accommodation or transcendence would likely utilize this reform tradition. A neutral urban strategy

Table 2.1   Models of Urban Policy Strategies*

Strategy	Tactics
Neutral	Address urban symptoms of ethnic conflict at *individual level*
Partisan	Maintain/increase disparities
Equity	Address urban symptoms of ethnic conflict at *ethnic group level*
Resolver	Address root causes/sovereignty issues.

*Adapted from Benvenisti 1986a.

of benevolent reform would seek to depoliticize territorial issues by framing urban problems as value-free, technical issues solvable through planning procedures and professional norms (Torgovnik 1991; Forester 1989; Nordlinger 1972). It would seek to avoid and prevent urban civil war through professional methods responsive to individual needs on both sides in a fair way. Disagreements and negotiations between ethnic groups would likely be channeled by government toward day-to-day service delivery issues and away from larger sovereignty considerations (Rothman 1992). Despite its appeal to governing regimes seeking legitimacy amidst conflict, the social conservatism and technical emphasis on land use and development characteristic of the neutral strategy tends to limit its utility in addressing issues of race and ethnic relations (Thomas and Krishnarayan 1994; Davidoff 1967). Even in consensual societies, the "color-blind" approach of much planning has been criticized for being "insensitive to the systematically different needs and requirements of the population and, in particular, . . . some black and ethnic communities" (Thomas and Krishnarayan 1994, 1899).

A *partisan* urban strategy, in contrast, chooses sides and is a regressive agent of change (Yiftachel 1995). It furthers an empowered ethnic group's values and authority and rejects claims of the disenfranchised group. The city's governing ideology merges with the empowered group's ethnonationalist ideology. Domination strategies are applied to land use planning and regulation in order to entrench and expand territorial claims or enforce exclusionary control of access (Lustick 1979; Sack 1981). Public policies are endorsed which substantially restrict out-group economic, political, and land-based opportunities. Methods of "institutionalized dominance" provide monopoly or preferential access to the urban policymaking machinery for members of the dominant group (Esman 1973). City residents are identified through their ethnic group affiliation, the main lens through which urban policy is directed (M. Smith 1969).

There are cases where the tools used by partisan urban strategies have been explicitly repressive, such as apartheid South Africa. In most cases, however, the important difference between partisan and neutral urban strategies lies not in their visible tools, but more covertly in the goals pursued and their handling of urban ethnicity. In other words, partisan planners may use many of the same tools as ethnically neutral strategists and speak a common language of objectivity and rationality. Nonetheless, these tools operationalize a fundamental ideology dominating of the urban landscape. Indeed, many urban planning tools emphasize regulation and control of land use and thus supply important means to implement partisan goals of territorial control and subjugation (Yiftachel 1995). Planning may also provide a mask of objectivity behind which discriminatory intent can be hidden. For example, seemingly neutral land development and ownership requirements applied by a dominating government can lead to unfair outcomes given contrasting cultural notions of basic urban resources such as land. Partisan planners act foremost as trustees or representatives of the state, and secondarily as urban managers. At certain times, planning may be needed to address some of the urban contradictions created by ideologically led city building. Urban planning may then even appear to run at cross-currents with the broader ideology in seeking to preserve certain urban qualities in the face of ideological imperatives. Nevertheless, this is more an issue of how to implement the fundamental ideology with a gentler face than it is an assault on the guiding ideology itself—a disagreement over means, not of partisan goals.

The third model, the *equity* strategy, gives primacy to ethnic affiliation in order to decrease, not perpetuate, intergroup inequalities. The administrator uses equity-based criteria, such as an ethnic group's relative size or need, in allocating urban services and spending (Nordlinger 1972; Esman 1973). Because they seek remediation and compensation for past hurts and wrongs, equity-based criteria will often be significantly different from the functional and technical criteria used by the ethnically neutral professional planner (Davidoff 1965; Krumholz and Forester 1990). An equity planner is more aware than a neutral planner of group-based inequalities and political imbalances in the city, and will recognize the needs for remediation and affirmative action policies based on group identity. In its purest form, the equity urban strategy posits that city planners and administrators should be advocates for those local groups whose interests are traditionally neglected in the formulation and implementation of urban policy (Davidoff 1965). This model is "one infinitely more politicized, committed, and relevant than that offered by the pseudo-professionalism of contemporary practice" (Kiernan 1983, 85). Progressive planning targeted at positive discrimination is employed to lessen urban inequalities in efforts to create a more just city and society. Basic human needs—public services, human rights, employment opportunities, food and shelter, and participation in decisionmaking—would be assured by urban development and planning policy.[4]

Equity planning applied to politically polarized cities assumes that the causes of ethnic conflict and tension reside, at least partially, in the objective economic disparities of the urban landscape. Since equity policies attempt to improve the out-group's urban existence and well-being, they may affect the outcome of larger political processes (Yiftachel 1989). This could occur through the incorporation of urban claims dealing with basic needs and fairness into larger negotiations concerning sovereignty and territoriality. Equity planning may also be used by an empowered group in a less accommodating spirit as a way to defer the need to engage in broader sovereignty and political discussions. While a strategy of conflict attenuation through greater urban fairness and service distribution may improve the material conditions of the out-group, it nonetheless utilizes a conception of justice separated from its institutional and political foundations. In addition, targeting of resources to the out-group may actually mobilize or radicalize the subordinate population, which, in turn, can precipitate opposition from within the in-group to such special considerations and a call for reimposition of coercive rule (Weitzer 1990).[5] In this sense, urban equity strategies that are disconnected from sovereignty and territorial negotiations may be bounded by the political dynamics of the opposing ethnic communities and may act as a flashpoint for urban unrest and state repression. Equity-based targeting may have to wait until the resolution of core political claims to the city.

The final model—a *resolver* strategy—is the most demanding. It seeks to connect urban issues to the root political causes of urban polarization—power imbalances, subordination, and disempowerment. It is the only strategy of the four that attempts to resolve the conflict, as opposed to managing it. In the resolver model, urban policy and planning is positioned as an innovating public policy arena having the potential to empower subordinate urban groups and address root issues of conflict (Friedmann 1992, 1987). This model seeks not incremental reform of basic parameters, but rather emancipation and basic structural change that can confront and contradict neutral and partisan urban strategies. It goes beyond the equity-based allocation of urban resources—with its focus on urban symptoms—to pursue urban empowerment for all ethnic groups in the city.

Urban professionals can play a significant role in connecting city issues and policymaking to root political and territorial issues by documenting and validating each side's territorial and resource needs required for coexistent community vitality. Planning arguments can be brought to bear to outline the basic parameters of a sustainable and peaceful urban system, one that meets each side's needs for territorial jurisdiction, control of population movement, and access to resources and to adequate supplies and distribution of labor. The development of alternative physical plans that refute and challenge government intent (known as "counter-planning"), lobbying, and legal challenges at national or international levels are some forms of resistance that can benefit most significantly from urban professional input. Here, urban specialists seek to overcome the systematic and structural distortions of overriding ideologies (Forester 1989), pointing out the unequal outcomes of seemingly "neutral" and "professional" techniques. The resolver urban strategy is essentially confrontational of the status quo in its attempts to link scientific and technical knowledge to processes of system transformation. Such a strategy will not likely come initially from within a bureaucratic state, but would be created through the actions of nongovernmental planners, cross-ethnic political groups, and urban professionals within the subordinated out-group. It demands much change from urban professionals, asking them to transcend each of the stances—neutral professionalism, narrow partisanship, and urban equalization—of the previous three strategies. The most advanced strategy in terms of its conciliatory potential, it requires that locally based planners engage in constructive intergroup dialogue in circumstances where there are no perceived outsiders.

Urban Policy and Ethnic Conflict

Figure 2.2 focuses on the last two stages illustrated earlier in Figure 2.1—how *urban policy* may affect (1) *ethnic conditions*, and (2) *urban stability/volatility*. *Urban ethnic conditions* relate to social, cultural, and economic deprivation and the unfulfillment of basic human needs for identity and purpose; four types of urban conditions are identified in Figure 2.2. The relative deprivation theory of ethnic conflict posits such unjust disparities and unmet human needs as a primary motivational force of political action (Gurr 1993;

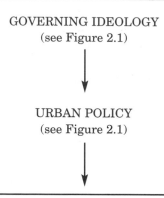

GOVERNING IDEOLOGY
(see Figure 2.1)

URBAN POLICY
(see Figure 2.1)

URBAN ETHNIC CONDITIONS

CONTROL OVER LAND/TERRITORIAL JURISDICTION
Settlement of vacant lands; control of settlement patterns; dispossession from land; control of land ownership; determination of planning boundaries; ethnic boundaries and identities

DISTRIBUTION OF ECONOMIC BENEFITS AND COSTS
Allocation of "externalities"; magnitude and geographic distribution of urban services and spending

ACCESS TO POLICYMAKING
Formal and informal participation processes; inclusion /exclusion from political process; influence of nongovernmental organizations

MAINTENANCE OF GROUP IDENTITY AND VIABILITY
Maintenance or threat to collective ethnic rights and identity; education, religious expression, cultural institutions

URBAN STABILITY / VOLATILITY

POLITICAL MOBILIZATION AND RESISTANCE
Actual and potential organization for and commitment to joint action in pursuit of group interests

Figure 2.2   Urban Ethnic Conditions and Urban Stability/Volatility

Burton 1990). I investigate how urban policy affects each type of urban ethnic condition—territoriality, economic distribution, policy-making access, and group identity. Then, I discuss how city policy and governance, and the urban conditions they create, may dampen or energize political mobilization and resistance by the aggrieved "out-group," the key measure used here to measure the *stability or volatility* of the urban system.

Urban policy most concretely affects the ethnic conditions of the urban environment through its significant influence on *control of land and territoriality* (Murphy 1989; Yiftachel 1992; Gurr 1993; Williams 1994). Urban territorial policies seek to reify power and enforce control (Sack 1986). Two common techniques of territorial control amidst ethnic tension aim to (1) alter the spatial distribution of ethnic groups and (2) manipulate jurisdictional boundaries to politically incorporate or exclude particular ethnic residents (Coakley 1993). The combination of a government's regulatory and developmental efforts can significantly affect in a polarized city the demographic ratios between the two sides, change the scale of focus of planning efforts, and reinforce or modify the ethnic identity of specific geographic subareas. An urban government involved in active territorial policies may seek penetration or dispersal of an opposing ethnic group in order to diminish its group coherence and ability to coalesce politically (Murphy 1989). Penetration involves placing members of the dominant ethnicity into areas having an opposing group majority. Such a strategy seeks to fragment or contain the opposition group geographically and to increase the dominant party's surveillance of the out-group. This technique is likely used by a dominating group when an opposing group's consolidation of ethnic territory in or near a polarized city is viewed by the empowered group as a threat to urban and regional political stability. In contrast, a dispersal territorial strategy seeks to spatially displace and disconnect the out-group from the urban system. In this case, separation of ethnic groups, rather than commingling, is viewed by the governing regime as more politically stabilizing and capable of excluding the subordinate group from a city's system of electoral and material benefits.

Urban policy also substantially shapes the *distribution of economic benefits and costs* and the allocation of urban service benefits (Yiftachel 1992; Stanovcic 1992; Gurr 1993). Urban land use and growth policies affect such aspects as the accessibility and proximity of residents and communities to employment, retail, and recreation; the distribution of land values; and the economic spin-offs (both positive and negative) of development. The planning and siting of economic activities can significantly influence both the daily urban behavior patterns and residential distributions of ethnic groups. Economic nodes have the ability to either integrate or separate the ethnic landscape. For example, major employment or commercial centers could be placed along ethnic territorial interfaces as a way to turn formerly "no-man's land" into mutually beneficial spaces of intergroup economic and social interactions. In contrast, economic development can be encouraged amidst a subordinate group's territory as a way to solidify or reinforce intergroup separation. Urban service and capital investment decisions—related to housing, roads, schools, and other community facilities—may be used to consolidate intergroup inequalities across a polarized city's ethnic geography by distributing benefits and advantages disproportionately to the ethnic in-group. Alternatively, urban spending can be directed disproportionately in favor of the subordinate group in an effort to remedy past inequalities.

Urban policy and planning processes can have substantial effects on the distribution of local political power and *access to policymaking* (Yiftachel 1992; Stanovcic 1992; Gurr 1993). Unequal access to policymaking is a common ingredient of ethnically polarized cities which translates into unequal urban outcomes dealing with local communities and their built environments. Usually, there is limited access to the formal machinery of city government by one of the ethnic antagonists (or by both, in the case of a third-party intervenor). Along with poor or no representation in legislative deliberations, an ethnic group is concurrently marginalized in terms of access to urban planning processes and administrative rule setting. "Hegemonic control" by one ethnic group occurs when the opposing group is fully excluded from the political decisionmaking process (as in apartheid Johannesburg). This exclusion can result from direct actions of the empowered group or through the out-group's own decision not to cooperate with an authority it does not recognize as legitimate.

Alternatives to hegemonic political control in a contested city include the use of an overseer regime, decentralized authority, and power sharing. "Third-party intervention" removes contentious local government functions such as housing, employment, and services from control by *either* of the warring parties and empowers a third-party overseer to manage the urban region. Sometimes, as in the case of Nicosia (Cyprus), the overseer may be the United Nations; in other cases, such as Belfast (Northern Ireland), the urban manager has been a distant, intentionally benign government—Great Britain. Urban "cantonization" occurs when there is devolution of some municipal powers to neighborhood-based community councils or boroughs, which advise the city government on "own-community" affairs. Finally, "consociationalism" (Lijphart 1968; Nordlinger 1972) is based on accommodation or agreement between political elites over a governance arrangement capable of managing ethnic differences. Elements of urban consociational democracy can be found in Brussels (Belgium) and Montreal (Canada). Particularly useful appear the use of power-sharing arrangements as a municipal jurisdiction shifts toward majoritarian democracy, and the use of ethnic proportionality standards in decreasing the bias commonly seen in the police forces of contested cities. Even in the midst of sovereignty conflict, some collaboration between sides may occur due to mutual practical and political benefits. The in-group gains insight into the dynamics of the out-group and may be able to dampen potential inflammatory problems, while the out-group elites' participation may be due to their desire to maintain control within their own communities through the extension of patronage benefits or to improve their followers' living conditions and thus the sustainability of out-group perseverance under hegemonic control.

In circumstances where access to formal policymaking is substantially curtailed for one urban ethnic group, pressure for change often is redirected through nongovernmental channels. The web of nongovernmental and voluntary associations that deal with urban issues such as community development, land and housing, cultural identity, social service delivery, and human rights protection constitutes a polarized city's "civil society" (Weitzer 1990; Friedman 1991; Partrick 1994). This organizational web can be an important source of glue holding together a threatened or disempowered minority, providing access to international organizations and their funding, and advocating for change in the urban system through documentation, demonstrations, and protests. A city government may affect positively the development and maintenance of such a civil society through the granting of direct funding or technical assistance to minority community organizations, or negatively through intimidation and restrictions on the receipt of capacity-building international funding for organizations operating within the contested city's boundaries.

The *maintenance of group identity*—the final aspect of urban ethnic conditions affectable by urban policy and planning in Figure 2.2—is critical to the nature of interethnic relations in a polarized city. Collective ethnic rights such as education, language, press, cultural institutions, and religious beliefs and customs are connected to potent ideological content. Exercise of these rights is viewed as a critical barometer by an out-group of an urban government's treatment of their rights. For an urban subgroup that feels threatened, these psychological needs pertaining to group viability and cultural identity can be as important as territorial and material needs. The social-psychological content of urban group identity can be enhanced or disrupted through urban policy and planning actions. Public policy can affect important forms of ethnic expression through its influence on public education (particularly dealing with language) or through its regulatory control over the urban side effects (such as noise) of religious observances. Urban service delivery decisions dealing with the location of proposed new religious, educational, and cultural institutions, or the closing down of ones deemed obsolete, can indicate to urban residents the government's projected ethnic trajectories of specific neighborhoods and can substantially threaten ethnic group identity. For there to be attenuation of ethnic conflict, the governing regime of a polarized city will commonly need to address not only the material, but also the psychological and identity-related, conditions of its antagonistic sides. The challenge facing urban planners and their political leaders is to incorporate the nontechnical and subjective aspects of community and group identity into planning processes traditionally biased toward objective and often quantifiable distributive criteria.

These urban ethnic conditions—land control, economic distribution, policymaking access, and group identity—can influence *urban stability/volatility* (see Figure 2.2). City conditions affectable through urban policy may inflame or moderate interethnic tension and conflict at the urban scale. An indicator of a city's stability or volatility is the magnitude and prevalence of *political mobilization* and resistance on the part of the subordinated group. Mobilization refers to an ethnic group's capacity—in terms of organization and commitment—to engage in political action and resistance (Tilly

1978). Such actions run the gamut from nonviolent actions such as verbal opposition, demonstrations, strikes, and rallies, to violent protests such as symbolic destruction of property, sabotage, and rioting, to active rebellion in the forms of terrorism, guerrilla activity, and protracted civil war (Gurr 1993).

Urban policies are capable of both producing a widely-shared sense of deprivation conducive to sustained communal resistance and providing a platform for the purposeful and rational actions of inflammatory ethnic group leaders. In the early stages of organized political resistance, objective urban conditions related to deprivation may be critical causes (Gurr 1993; Gurr and Lichbach 1986). However, once collective political action is underway, these objective conditions can pale in significance to factors related to group organization and leadership (Gurr 1993). In other words, political organization related to ethnic conflict can reach a point beyond which betterment of objective conditions through urban policy would have only marginal effects on the amelioration of urban ethnic tension. This means that the internal political dynamics and needs of the out-group's political organization, as well as the urban needs of its city residents, must be accommodated in efforts to secure urban stability. State urban policies can structure the local political system in ways that either restrict or enable out-group political opportunities, and they can frustrate or cultivate the development of out-group organizations and networks that comprise the collective building blocks of political capacity (McAdam, McCarthy, and Zald 1996; Tarrow 1994; Tilly 1978). Urban policies can forcefully repress political resistance, as well as internally fragment the out-group's urban political community, through planning regulations that spatially separate out-group neighborhoods and through the preferential channeling of urban benefits to more "moderate" subgroups. Alternatively, urban policies can provide political opportunities for the out-group through electoral representation, provision of multiple and decentralized layers of local governance, or by nurturing nongovernmental organizations aligned with the out-group.

Because material grievance and political disenchantment can both contribute to urban instability, urban policies seeking stability will likely need to address both the physical city and the political relationships within it. Accordingly, I seek in this study to detail the effects of government policies on the material and psychological states of urban residents, as well as on the characteristics of the out-group's community organization and coherency of its political expression.[6]

This chapter has outlined a process whereby nationalistic ethnic conflict is filtered through an urban system. A state's governing ideology regarding the urban arena is either derived from one group's political claims, or seeks to transcend or integrate competing ethnic visions. This constitutes an important gatekeeper function that influences the extent that ethnic bias will or will not penetrate governmental goals and actions. Urban policies that operationalize a governing ideology then affect the spatial, economic, social, and political dimensions of urban space. This urban effect can intensify or lessen intergroup hostility through its impacts on material urban conditions, social-psychological aspects of urban group identity, and place-specific forms and dynamics of political resistance and mobilization.

Whether urban policy moderates, exacerbates, or simply mirrors the broader historical conflict is expected to be dependent upon the policy strategies chosen, the spatial, economic, and psychological conditions and contradictions they generate in the built landscape, and how these affect the organization and mobilization of urban opposition groups. Urban policy operates at a distinctive level of interaction, having dynamics, participants, and consequences potentially different than those found at regional or national levels. A city may thus be an important contributor to the intensification or lessening of ethnic tension among antagonistic peoples.

3

Investigating Urban Policy and Conflict

Jerusalem and Belfast

I selected the ethnically polarized cities of Jerusalem and Belfast for study for three reasons. First, each city is the most populated within its country and encapsulates deep-rooted cleavages based on competing nationalisms and arguments over sovereignty or state legitimacy. In Jerusalem, Jewish-Muslim religious tension is intertwined with Israeli-Palestinian nationalist conflict. In Belfast, Protestant unionist and Catholic republican aspirations regarding political control have left little room for compromise. Second, both provide multidecade accounts of urban planning and management in contested bicommunal environments. In many polarized cities in other countries, the existence of unstable governing regimes prevents analysis of the long-term planning function. Third, since the study relies strongly on face-to-face interviews, the case study cities were chosen to minimize communication difficulties owing to language. In both cities, the urban system functions as a physically unpartitioned whole while the perceived environment is one of polarization. Such a contradiction is played out daily because no impassable physical boundaries are present to separate the conflicting parties.[1] Although both cities are central urban regions, a fundamental difference is that Jerusalem is also a sacred or holy city. Because of this status, Jerusalem city constitutes an additional layer of difficulty to the negotiations over Israeli and Palestinian sovereignty. In contrast, there is no Belfast problem independent of the larger Northern Ireland problem. Nevertheless, because it is by far the most populated city of Northern Ireland and its capital, Belfast constitutes an important focal point for the broader national conflict.

A compelling thread that connects these two cities is that both were engrossed during my research in a transition process tied to progress on a broader political front. The Jerusalem interviews occurred about twelve months after the signing of the Oslo I Declarations in September 1993, which established a process toward which Israel and the Palestinian National Authority would work toward peace. The interviews occurred subsequent to Palestinian empowerment in the Gaza Strip and Jericho, but prior to the start of the gradual withdrawal of Israeli troops from other parts of the West Bank. Negotiations over the status and political control of Jerusalem were to commence no later than May 1996, about eighteen months after field research. As of 1998, such negotiations had been obstructed by disagreements over the appropriate size of Israeli troop withdrawals and the ability of the Palestinian Authority to control extremists.

The Belfast interviews occurred about five months after the ceasefires announced first by the Provisional Irish Republican Army, then subsequently by the loyalist paramilitaries. During my research stay, the British and Irish governments released their Joint Framework Documents, which were intended to move political discussions toward some mutually agreeable solution. Ideas in these Documents supportive of democratic provincial government and cross-border institutions were eventually incorporated, after three years of on-again, off-again ceasefires and political negotiations, into the April 1998 "Agreement Reached in the Multi-Party Negotiations." This agreement, approved by Northern Ireland voters in May 1998, is an attempt to restructure Northern Ireland governance in a way mutually agreeable to both sides. Monumental challenges remain in terms of how to put this agreement into effect and how provincial and local government in Northern Ireland, no matter how they may be configured, can formulate and implement public policy that accommodates the needs and perceptions of both Protestants and Catholics.

The larger transitions within which the two urban systems existed provide a unique opportunity to look not just backward at the effects of urban policy, but also forward toward possible different urban futures and the role government policy might play in them. I believe that this transitional mood added greatly to the rich and oftentimes self-critical evaluation by those interviewed of the role—past and potential—of government policy amidst ethnic contest.

One delimiting factor in the examination of the two cities is the time periods that I chose to study. In the Jerusalem case, I focus on urban policy and issues in the period from 1967, when Israel assumed control of Jerusalem and the West Bank. In the Belfast case, I concentrate on the period from 1972, when Britain assumed direct rule over Northern Ireland. I discuss earlier periods during the twentieth century in each city in terms of the legacies and dilemmas they produce for urban policymakers in the periods of study focus. Thus, for Jerusalem, the British Mandate (1920–1948) and partitioned city (1948–1967) periods are discussed. For Belfast, the legacy of Unionist-majority Northern Irish governance (1920–1972) is examined. Although these earlier phases constitute important and essential background, they are not the main stories of this investigation. Rather, I am concerned with how *current regimes* approach and utilize urban policy in the context of such historically based ethnic conflict.

It was not possible to address each ethnic or racial conflict in its full richness. To do so would require accounting of Jewish-Muslim relations in Palestine over the last 1,300 years, and Catholic-Protestant relations since the Protestant plantations in Ulster province more than 450 years ago. I suggest that full portrayals of each conflict's complexities would divert attention away from my true focus and purpose—urban policy under current regimes during the last three decades. At the same time, I assert that current urban policy circumstances can be studied effectively under their own terms, not those of the historic past, however much those historical antecedents affect what the "city" is today. Indeed, part of the solution to these intractable urban conflicts seems to require an "intentional forgetfulness," or more majestically stated, a forgiveness, concerning past injustices and harms. For instance, Jerusalem is so difficult an urban issue because, as stated by current city mayor Olmert, debate over its control concerns not just the present and future, but the past as well. A disentangling of the past from current and future urban strategies appears a requisite to successfully negotiating these cities of polarized hostilities.

Research Methods

This comparative project seeks to add to the body of knowledge about the differing contexts within which urban policy and planning practice operates cross-nationally. The case study research method was employed because it is most appropriate for the cross-national study of policy processes (Masser 1986; Cropper 1982). For each case study, I bring together multiple forms of evidence—analysis of academic articles, writings in the popular press, and published and classified government reports; evaluation of urban quantitative data; and the undertaking of interviews with government and community leaders. I aim to document the anatomy and effect of policy strategies that may transcend particular urban and ideological contexts, while acknowledging the unique national contexts of the two cities. I suspect that there are aspects of professional planning and policy processes that can be inherently harmful or beneficial to urban intergroup relations in ethnically polarized environments.

The primary phase of the five-year scholarly endeavor was field research, which consisted of three months of in-country research in each city.[2] Seventy-four interviews were conducted and are used to construct an account of urban policymaking amidst political strife. In addition to documenting the complex objective realities and influences in these cities, I was interested in how interviewees made sense of their everyday activities and professional roles. I sought to observe and understand the organizational, cultural, and historical context within which governmental and nongovernmental planners operate. In particular, I observed closely the interplay between the professional norms and values of many planning roles and the more emotion-filled ideological imperatives that impinge daily upon the professional's life. The distortions, the omissions, the emphases on some issues and not others, and how urban issues and constituents are defined are all part of the story I wish to tell of urban policymaking amidst contested ethnicities. In addition to allowing for face-to-face interviewing, in-country residence allowed me to immerse myself in the intriguing day-to-day conditions and concerns of "polarized" urban life, as expressed by public officials and people on the street and through popular media. Collaboration with academic institutions was an essential part of each research stay and further deepened the research experience.[3] They provided research hospitality, a valuable set of initial community contacts, and an academic base of office support which facilitated my interview scheduling.

I investigate the influence of ethnic polarization on urban policy and the effects these policies have had on the nature and level of ethnic conflict. I also seek to develop recommendations, regarding policy goals and implementation means, that would increase the ability of urban policy strategies to lessen deep-rooted ethnic conflict in meaningful and long-term ways. Because polarized cities are important microcosms, the usefulness of this work is expected to transcend local contexts and extend to regional and national debates over ethnic conflict management. A set of research issues provided a framework for interview and secondary research. These issues are outlined in Table 3.1 and described more fully in Appendix 1.

I analyze the influence of ethnic polarization on the city's institutional context, formulation of development goals, public agenda setting and decisionmaking, and policy implementation. I concurrently evaluate how city policies that are enacted and implemented affect the nature and level of ethnic conflict and community opposition, and explore whether, and why, governing regimes change ethnic strategies. Throughout, the focus is on how ethnicity permeates the goals and processes of urban management and control, and how urban decisions in turn constrain or open opportunities for conflict alleviation.

Contextual factors institutionally and legally structure the decisionmaking environment. Legal frameworks and city and neighborhood organizational arrangements may condone institutional differentiation or seek to integrate or unify ethnic groups within a common public domain. In defining *policy issues and goals* in an ethnically polarized city, urban policymakers and administrators must take a position on ethnicity. Such a position can run the gamut from acknowledging explicitly the presence and effects of ethnic fractures, to seeking to depoliticize ethnicity by emphasizing universalism and an overarching public interest. Policy goals articulate the city's governing ideology as ethnonationalist or civic. *Urban decisionmaking* is composed initially of public agenda setting, wherein local policy and planning alternatives to be considered can be restricted by ethnonational and political realities. For those alternatives evaluated, decisionmaking rules—such as technical, partisan, or equity—are applied that can expose most directly a government's role within,

Table 3.1 Guiding Research Issues[a]

CONTEXTUAL FACTORS
Ethnicity and legal frameworks
Urban institutional differentiation
Basic values

POLICY ISSUES AND GOALS
Urban ethnic issues
Treatment of ethnic conflict
The city's interest—policy goals and objectives
Citizen participation—processes

URBAN DECISIONMAKING
Agenda setting
Decisionmaking rules
Planning/policymaking roles
Territorial policies

POLICY OUTCOMES
Implementation
Results
National-local intergovernmental relations

CONFLICT OUTCOMES AND MECHANISMS
Patterns of conflict intensification (amelioration)
Formal mechanisms for reducing conflict
Informal mechanisms for reducing conflict
Intra-ethnic effects; Cross-cutting cleavage patterns

COMMUNITY DYNAMICS AND ORGANIZATION
Intersection of national and local interests
Community organization in a controlled environment
Re-structuring community

CHANGE AND EVOLUTION
Changes in planning strategies
Change—underlying factors
Change—effect on ethnic conflict

---

[a] See Appendix 1 for expanded outline of issues.

and position toward, ethnic polarization. The next set of research questions—*policy outcomes*—explores the implementation of policy by administrative agents, and constitutes an important lens through which to evaluate the relationship between the guiding ideology and its urban operationalization. I examine on-the-ground outcomes of urban policymaking in terms of the distribution of costs and benefits across ethnic communities.

Questions focused on *conflict outcomes and mechanisms* do not evaluate the direct on-the-ground outcomes of urban policy decisions, but how particular policies effect the nature and level of ethnic conflict and tension in the city. Objective and political-psychological outcomes of policy can be significantly different in polarized cities. For example, extension of public authority premised on a criterion of urban fairness may be deemed as illegitimate and may thus be actually stimulative of resistance and conflict. Accordingly, assessment by government of policy implementation may include ways to contain conflict resulting from it, so as to avoid breakdown of the planning policy. Such mechanisms for coping with ethnic conflict during policy implementation may utilize governmental channels of interethnic mediation or informal contacts between government and minority elites. Also salient within this line of questioning is the fact that public policy can not only exacerbate friction between ethnic communities, but also internally divide ethnic groups or create communities of interests that cut across the ethnic divide. The next set of issues—*community dynamics and organization*—explores survival techniques used by the subordinated population and the forms of community mobilization that result. Questions also concern how ethnic community groups can shift from being solely organs of protest and resistance to constructive co-participants in the creation of alternative urban scenarios. The intersection of national and local interests is also a salient point when dealing with the internal coherency of each ethnic group. Urban-based interests and initiatives may act either to reinforce or inhibit national political interests and strategies.

The final set of inquiries explores issues of actual or potential *change and evolution* in the relationship between urban policy strategies and ethnicity. Planning goals and strategies may shift over time due to changes in economic, political, or ideological factors, or due to feedback documenting previous policy's effects on the urban out-group and intergroup coexistence. Change may be either progressive, moving the urban system closer to political resolution or at least social accommodation, or regressive, tightening further the opportunities for coexistent viability of antagonistic urban communities. In other cases where urban operationalization of fundamental ideology highlights internal contradiction, I am interested in how urban actors respond in terms of policy and the arguments they use to buttress their efforts. Amidst urban turbulence and uncertainty, it is significant whether urban policymakers and planners adopt a narrow vision of their roles or a position more conducive to problem re-framing and social learning.

In this study, I focus on urban planning because this function of government, through its direct and tangible effects on ethnic geography, can reveal the intent and effects of municipal actions in a polarized city. Plans and decisionmaking procedures are in effect formalizations of often unwritten patterns of power, actualizing abstract notions of control and territoriality. The label *urban planner*, in this project, encompasses all officials (government and nongovernmental) involved in the anticipation of a city's or urban community's future and preparation for it.[4] The category thus includes, within government, town and regional planners, urban administrators and policymakers, and national and regional-level urban policy officials. Outside government, it includes community spokespeople, project directors and staff within nongovernmental, community, or voluntary sector organizations, scholars of urban and ethnic studies, and business community participants.

The primary urban public policies examined have direct and tangible influences on ethnic geography and group identity.[5] They are:

- land use planning

- promotion of real estate development

- economic development

- housing construction and unit allocation

- capital facility planning

- social service delivery

- community participation and empowerment

- municipal government organization.

Land use planning by government, through its designation and regulation of activities, identifies areas that are to be devoted to different types and densities of urban activities, such as residential, commercial, and industrial. *Promotion of real estate development* positions government as a developer that sponsors, subsidizes, and enters into partnerships with the private sector to build new housing projects, redevelop deteriorated inner city areas, or stimulate economic activities. *Economic development* policies include government actions that help develop sites for economic activities, and numerous other public actions—such as transportation improvements, labor force training, and provision of public subsidies—that seek to create urban environments attractive to private investment. In terms of *housing*, government becomes involved in delivery and regulation to assure its quality and affordability and to maintain neighborhood stability. Government can be the full owners and operators of housing (in the case of public housing), can help subsidize the private production of low-cost housing, or otherwise regulate development to assure that housing is delivered at appropriate quantities and prices.

Capital facility planning involves decisions dealing with the prioritization, funding, size, and location of major public investments such as highways and roads, and water and sewer infrastructure. The *social service delivery* function of government is instrumental in providing to urban residents services such as education, health, recreation, and cultural facilities. The urban policymaking process commonly articulates government's view of the proper role of *community participation* and empowerment. A city government can delegate or devolve a genuine degree of citizen power through the creation of community councils or neighborhood associations which have some impact on policy formulation or implementation. Alternatively, city governments can pay lip service to citizen participation, engaging in token forms of citizen consultation or outright manipulation of citizen consent through cooptation (Arnstein 1969). Finally, *municipal government organization* involves both how a city bureaucracy is internally organized and how jurisdictional and electoral boundaries are drawn. The structure of city bureaucracies can influence how government addresses the complex issues of urban ethnicity—either vertically through the lenses of individual line departments; or laterally based on the experiences and viewpoints of multiple departments. Boundary drawing defines city electoral wards that can politically empower or marginalize ethnic communities, and the "city" itself through municipal border gerrymandering that can include or exclude ethnic neighborhoods.

Each of the urban policies has substantial potential effects on those urban ethnic conditions portrayed in Figure 2.2 as conducive to ethnic stability or volatility. For instance, land use planning and regulation can produce uneven patterns of advantage and disadvantage across ethnic neighborhoods, government facilitation of development can reinforce or modify the ethnic identity of specific areas, housing policies have substantial potential impacts on solidifying or changing the demographic ratio between ethnic groups, and social service delivery becomes intertwined with collective group rights related to language, education, and culture. The policies have the ability to mediate between the broader and nonurban ideological influences and the magnitude and manifestations of city interethnic conflict. These policies can maintain or disrupt territorial claims, they can distribute economic benefits fairly or unfairly, they can provide or discourage access to policymaking and political power, they can protect or erode collective ethnic rights, and they can stifle or galvanize political urban-based opposition.

* * *

Field research included forty interviews in Jerusalem and thirty-four in Belfast. Appendix 2 lists the interviewees and their institutional affiliations. The in-person interview was selected over other research techniques because it permits greater depth, enables probing to obtain greater data, and makes it possible to establish rapport with the respondent (Isaac 1971). I used an interview guide that structured and customized the set of topics for each discussant, while at the same time allowing discretion on my part in the ordering and phrasing of questions. Questions were open-ended. This allowed interviewees flexibility and depth in responding and facilitated responses not anticipated by the research design (Mayer and Greenwood 1980). Most frequently, interviews were conducted with individuals currently in policymaking and implementation positions at national, regional, and municipal levels of government. Former government officials were also a rich source of information, providing a longitudinal perspective on current urban issues and problems. I also interviewed representatives (official and unofficial) of opposition ethnic groups who for various reasons were operating outside of formal governmental channels. Some of these representatives worked for nongovernmental organizations (NGOs) that advocated either a single ethnic group's cause or bridge building between antagonistic ethnicities. Next to current government officials, NGO analysts represented the second largest pool of interviewees. Finally, I talked with several university-based scholars and a number of individuals with private sector or commercial interests in the contested city.

Core interview lists were developed for each city prior to arrival. They were constructed based on contacts made initially at a 1987 Salzburg Seminar on divided cities, from subsequent correspondences with practitioners and scholars, and from research and professional literatures. A strong majority of interviewees was identified after arrival based upon word-of-mouth referrals from initial discussants and academics at my host institution, and through local media, primarily newspapers. Because ethnic affiliation and government employment may influence interviewees' judgments, strong efforts were made to interview individuals so that there would be a fair distribution across ethnic groups, and across government and nongovernmental officials. Identification of interviewees by pertinent characteristics is portrayed in Table 3.2. Interview samples are likely biased toward individuals with moderate, centrist views on urban ethnic conflict and its management. This sample feature is due to my intention to study possibilities in which urban policy can contribute constructively to urban and regional peace. Nonetheless, more extreme attitudes toward these ethnic conflicts can be found within each of the interview samples. In addition, I use secondary sources (government reports and written statements) to help construct the more hard-line positions of right-wing Israelis, Palestinian militant rejectionists, and those aligned with paramilitary causes in Northern Ireland. Together, I believe the pool of interviewees and secondary sources in each city represents adequately and broadly the complexities, arguments, and emotions of working and living in a politically contested city. At the same time, however, my emphasis was on that part of the political spectrum potentially more supportive of peacemaking efforts.

Three months of intensive interviewing in each locale allowed me to contact and successfully carry out discussions with more than eighty percent of those individuals identified for potential interviews. Of those potential interviewees who were contacted by phone

Table 3.2   Classification of Interviewees by Nationality and Affiliation

JERUSALEM

Nationality	
Israeli	24
Palestinian	15
Other	1
Affiliation	
Governmental (Israel)[a]	12
Academic	11
Nongovernmental organization[b]	17

BELFAST

Ethnicity	
Protestant	16
Catholic	12
Not reported	6
Affiliation	
Governmental	19
Academic	7
Nongovernmental organization	8

[a] Includes both current and former government officials.
[b] This category includes interviewees who worked for the then-emerging Palestinian National Authority.

and letter, only one refused to be interviewed. Because of the moderate, centrist nature of my samples, politically inspired rhetoric and misrepresentations are felt to be minimal. Many interviewees were professionally and personally introspective concerning the momentous changes each society was undergoing, and appeared to present honest, even self-critical, appraisals of their group's tactics. I used secondary literature and data to check the accuracy of respondent perceptions, as well as cross-checking with other interviewees. In those cases when interviewees clearly brought political messages and agendas to the discussion, I present them as important components of how a governing regime or opposition group portrays itself amidst contentiousness.

All interviews were face-to-face discussions. On average, each lasted about one and one-half hours. More than ninety percent of the interviews were audiotaped and then transcribed. Because of this procedure, misquotations and misinterpretations are felt to be minimal. The audiotaped record also helped to clarify particular sentences where different linguistic habits may have otherwise obfuscated the meaning.[6] Audiotaping did not appear to act as an obstacle to candid, full-bodied responses on the part of discussants. Many interviewees seemed to want their concerns and issues to be "on the record." When interviewees did not want to be quoted directly, I fulfilled this wish in all cases.

In addition to direct interviews, I investigated during both field research and over the five-year research span published and unpublished city, regional, and national plans and policy documents, implementing regulations, and laws and enabling statutes in terms of how they address urban issues of localized and national ethnic conflict. In cases where material on a particular subject was classified or undocumented, interviews were conducted during field research with policy practitioners and scholars familiar with the policy or project history. In many cases, I was able to obtain copies of such sensitive and provocative material after these interviews. In the case of Jerusalem, it was necessary to hire a Hebrew-language student to review and take notes on relevant Hebrew-language articles and reports. Quantitative data concerning growth and housing trends and budgetary spending were tapped to supplement interview-based conclusions. Finally, a rich reservoir in each country of published analytic reports and academic articles provided critical foundations from which to evaluate the subjective content of interviews.

PART II

Jerusalem— The Fallacy of Partisan Policy

The air above Jerusalem is filled with
prayers and dreams.
Like the air above cities with heavy industry,
hard to breathe.

—Yehuda Amichai,
"Jerusalem Ecology," 1980

Figure 4.1   Jewish Quarter, Old City Jerusalem

Source: Scott A. Bollens

4

Israel's "Jerusalem"

Background

Jewish-Muslim religious, and Israeli-Palestinian nationalist, tensions intertwine in a city that defies exclusivity (I. Matar, American Near East Refugee Aid, interview; Elon 1989). The result on the ground is the creation of "intimate enemies" and a life of encounters, proximity, and interaction, yet simultaneously remote, extraneous, and alienated (Benvenisti 1995; Benvenisti 1986a). The meaning behind what Jerusalem represents, and the importance people attach to control over it, is such that "People will kill, shed tears, and write poems" (E. Barzacchi, former city engineer, Jerusalem Municipality, interview). It is a site of demographic and physical competition between two populations aiming at substantive achievements with clear political purposes of control and sovereignty.

Just since the end of World War II, the social and political geography of Jerusalem has dramatically changed. From a multicultural mosaic under the 1917–1948 British Mandate emerged a two-sided physical partitioning of Jerusalem into Israeli and Jordanian-controlled components during the 1949–1967 period. Since 1967, it has been a contested Israeli-controlled municipality three times the area of the pre-1967 city (due to unilateral, and internationally unrecognized, annexation) and encompassing formerly Arab east Jerusalem. Despite Israel's political claim, the international status of east Jerusalem today is as "occupied" territory. It is this post-1967 period that is the focus of this analysis. From an urban policy and planning perspective, it has had the most significant effects on today's urban and regional landscape.

Physical and Demographic Setting

The estimated 1996 population of 603,000 within the disputed post-1967 Israeli-defined municipal boundaries is composed of 70 percent Jews and 30 percent Arabs (Palestinians),[1] who are either Muslim or Christian in religiosity (Jerusalem Municipality 1997; Mazor and Cohen 1994). This is more than twice the 267,000 residents that resided in Jerusalem upon Israel's assuming full political control in 1967. Due to the addition of an average of 12,000 new residents each year for twenty-five years, the city by the 1980s had overtaken the city of Tel Aviv-Yafo in terms of both population and geographic size.[2] Despite the speed of total population change, the relative distribution of Jews and Arabs in the Israeli-defined city since 1967 has remained remarkably constant. At no time in thirty years has the Jewish majority gone below 70 percent (Jerusalem Municipality 1997). This constancy of Jewish demographic advantage has occurred despite a higher rate of natural increase for the city's Arabs than for its Jews.[3]

Spatially, Jerusalem is dominated demographically by Jews to the west of the former "Armistice line," while the Jewish/Arab population proportion on the former Jordanian side of the 1949–1967 partition was about 50/50 in 1996 (see Figure 4.2). The Old City, east of the former "Armistice line," is composed of four quarters—Jewish, Muslim, Christian, and Armenian. Within the Old City lie the extraordinary and sacred sites of the three great monotheistic religions—the Jewish western, or wailing, wall of the Temple Mount; Islam's Al Aqsa Mosque and the Dome of the Rock; and Christianity's Church of the Holy Sepulchre containing the sites of Christ's crucifixion, burial, and resurrection. Although Jews are now a large presence in formerly Arab east Jerusalem, there is complete segregation of the two groups there with no mixed neighborhoods. Within the city's Jewish population, segregation exists between the orthodox neighborhoods of Mea She'arim, Tel Arza, and Romema and secular/nonorthodox neighborhoods. Growth in the orthodox population is necessitating outward expansions of their living areas, including the building of a new neighborhood—Shu'afat Range—adjacent to an Arab neighborhood.[4]

Pursuant to the 1967 War, Israel occupied three identifiable parts of Palestine—the West Bank, east Jerusalem, and the Gaza Strip (see Figure 4.3). The Israeli-occupied West Bank territory surrounds on three sides the municipal boundaries of formerly east

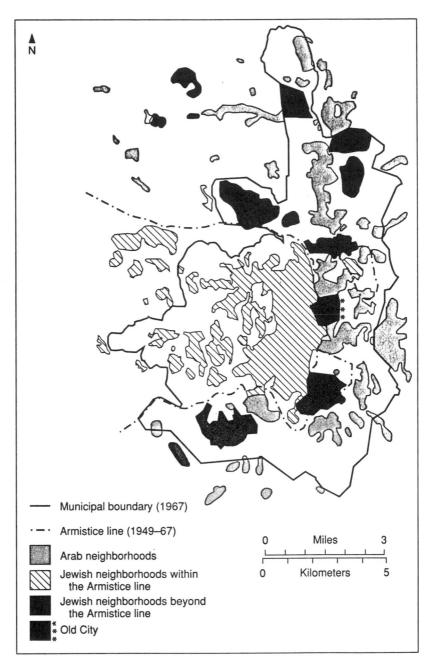

Figure 4.2 Jewish and Arab Neighborhoods in Israeli-Defined City of Jerusalem, 1991

Source: Meron Benvenisti. *City of Stone: The Hidden History of Jerusalem.* Copyright © 1996 The Regents of the University of California. Berkeley, CA: University of California Press, p. 188.

Figure 4.3   Israel, Occupied Territories, and the Region

Source: Adapted from State of Israel. Central Bureau of Statistics. 1984. *Census of Population and Housing 1983*. Jerusalem: CBS.

Jerusalem.[5] Jerusalem thus sits at a geographic point of nexus between the country of Israel (approximately 5.9 million population in 1997; 80 percent Jewish) and occupied east Jerusalem and West Bank. Table 4.1 presents the approximate population distributions in the areas occupied by Israel in 1967.

Table 4.1   Estimated Mid-1990s Population in Territories Occupied[a] by Israel in 1967

"OCCUPIED" TERRITORY[a]	POPULATION (estimated)	
	PALESTINIAN	JEWISH
West Bank (excluding east Jerusalem)	1.7 million[b]	150,000[c]
East Jerusalem[e]	180,000[d]	166,000[d]
Gaza Strip	1.0 million[b]	6,000[c]
TOTAL	2.9 million	322,000

[a] "Occupied" according to international law.
[b] Palestinian Central Bureau of Statistics. 1998. *Palestinian Population, Housing and Establishment Census—1997.*
[c] Source: Peace Now. 1997. *Settlement Watch-Report No. 9.* www.peace-now.org.
[d] Jerusalem, Municipality of. 1997. *Statistical Yearbook 1996.* Jerusalem: The Jerusalem Institute for Israel Studies.
[e] Municipality as defined by Israel.

There are more than 140 Jewish settlements in the West Bank and Gaza Strip, in addition to ten Jewish neighborhoods created within the disputed borders of east Jerusalem. Some of the largest Jewish settlements in the West Bank (such as Maale Adumin, Benjamin, and Givat Zeev) occur within commuting range of either Jerusalem or Tel Aviv. Unlike east Jerusalem, the West Bank and Gaza Strip have been subject, pursuant to the 1993 Declaration of Principles, to various degrees of Palestinian political empowerment since 1993.

It is within this complex pattern of political geography that the city and urban region of Jerusalem is overlaid. Because the municipal boundaries of Jerusalem are contested, it is informative to examine the demographic characteristics of the region at large before the demographic makeup of the politically demarcated city space. Mazor and Cohen (1994) delineate the metropolitan area of Jerusalem based on commuting patterns.[6] One conclusion was that it was, "much more an Arabic metropolitan area than a Jewish one"

Table 4.2 Ethnic Distribution of 1991 Population for Metropolitan
Region of Jerusalem

Jews:	525,000	46%
Arabs:	610,000	54%
Total:	1,135,000	100%

Source: Mazor, A., and S. Cohen. 1994. Metropolitan Jerusalem Master and Development Plan.

(A. Mazor, co-author of Metropolitan Jerusalem Master and Development Plan, interview). Table 4.2 displays early 1990s population figures for this metropolitan region, and Table 4.3 classifies the region into three distinguishable political components.

Although a strong Jewish majority dominates the Israeli-defined city jurisdiction, the functional urban system has a not insubstantial Palestinian majority. The metropolitan region that is outside Israeli Jerusalem, which contains more than one-half of total metropolitan population, is approximately 70 percent Palestinian. Concentrations of Palestinian population occur in such places as Bethlehem and Beit Sahor to the south, Hebron further to the south, and Ramallah to the north. With the exception of the Arab center of Jericho to the far east, the Palestinian presence in the region has a north-south orientation. Just outside the Israeli municipal borders, communities such as A-Ram, E-Azariya, and Abu Dis fill in this north-south axis. The Jewish presence, in contrast, has more of a west-east orientation, with Bet Shemesh and Modiin to the west and Maale Adumin to the east. The functionally defined metropolitan region of Jerusalem thus constitutes an intersection between east-west and north-south axes (Y. Golani, director of Planning Administration, Israel Ministry of Interior, interview).

Economically, Jerusalem in many ways remains peripheral to the financial and commercial economy of Tel-Aviv. Its employment base has traditionally been biased instead toward public and government services and tourism. Fully 41 percent of employed persons working in the city in 1992 were in public and community services (compared with 29.5 percent in Israel; 20.8 percent in Tel-Aviv). This highlights Jerusalem as the capital of the State of Israel, and as a main center of education and culture; national, academic, and reli-

Table 4.3 Political Components of Jerusalem Metropolitan Region

POLITICAL PARTS OF METROPOLITAN AREA	POPULATION % OF TOTAL METRO POP. (1990)	DEMOGRAPHIC MAKEUP
Jerusalem city (Israeli-defined)	47	72% Jewish
Remainder of Jerusalem district (in Israel)	5	91% Jewish
Judea/Samaria (West Bank)	48	90% Arab

Source: Mazor, A., and S. Cohen. 1994. Metropolitan Jerusalem Master and Development Plan.

gious institutions; and health services. But the industrial sector in Jerusalem is weak, with only 12 percent of the city's employees in that sector (compared to 21 percent in Israel overall). And Jerusalem's 11 percent employment in financial and business service jobs pales in comparison to Tel-Aviv's 24 percent. These economic weaknesses of the city are owing to the lack of nearby natural resources and the problems of transportation and market access created by Jerusalem's geographical location vis-à-vis the rest of Israel. To Palestinians, the city is the economic and commercial focal point for the West Bank, providing a central marketing and distribution center for the string of primarily north-south Palestinian towns. Access by West Bank Palestinians to Jerusalem and the rest of Israel has been commonly inhibited, though, by security-motivated closures of the West Bank by the Israeli government.[7]

Political Control

What is considered "Jerusalem" and who controls its resources has for many generations had significant political, emotive, and symbolic importance. Twentieth-century Jerusalem has been, except for the 1948–1967 period, an unpartitioned and functionally integrated urban system. During the British Mandate period from 1917 to

1948, Jewish and Arab residential patterns were representative of a multisector mosaic more than an integrated city. There were clearly identifiable Arab neighborhoods throughout the city, including Lifta, Ein Kerem, Katamon/Baka, and Talbiya to the west of what was to become the Armistice Line in 1949. Segregation was largely voluntary and was the outcome of mutual and symmetrical exclusionary attitudes between Jews and Arabs (Benvenisti 1986a). Jews were in a majority during this phase, constituting 54 percent of city population in 1922 and 60 percent in 1947 (Bahat 1990). Municipal administration was difficult due to constant intercommunal political tension. Outbursts of violence included deadly 1929 rioting that cost 133 Jewish lives in and around Jerusalem and stimulated the development of a Jewish defense underground (Irgun Bet). From 1930 to 1945, the municipality and city council barely functioned, with local elections able to be held during this period only in 1934. Political tension and rioting during the 1930s was, in part, over Jewish demands that the Jewish majority be reflected more fairly in city governance.[8] By 1945, the city council was abolished and replaced with a British ad hoc committee to run the city.

Under the control of the British government during this period, ethnic relations was not emphasized by urban policymakers. Rather, the focus was on design aspects and establishing appropriate identities for the newer parts of the city relative to the Old City. The British government saw planning as a way to neutralize ethnic conflict (B. Hyman, director of local planning, Israel Ministry of Interior, interview). Like any other urban problem, ethnic tension was seen as solvable through a planning approach based on logic and reason. In this way, ethnic conflict was viewed as having an objective solution; rationality was perceived as capable of overcoming the political. Each side of the ethnic divide—Jewish and Arab—had the luxury of blaming the Britons for bias in the formulation and implementation of urban policy (A. Shachar, professor, Hebrew University, interview).

When the British Mandate over Palestine drew to an end in 1948, the State of Israel was established and Jerusalem became a battleground between Israeli, Transjordan (now Jordan), and Egyptian armies. Intense warfare that centered on the Holy City turned to shambles an earlier United Nations resolution that the city of Jerusalem be a demilitarized and neutral *corpus separatum* (a separate entity) governed by a special international regime and administered by the U.N.[9] This separate entity would have included

Bethlehem to the south, Ein Kerem to the west, Abu Dis to the east, and Shuafat to the north. When the War ended, Jordanian forces were in control of the eastern parts of the city, while Israeli forces controlled the west. In early 1949, an armistice agreement was concluded between Israel and Jordan that divided jurisdictionally the city. This partition separated from their homes about sixty thousand Arab inhabitants who had been dislocated from their villages in west Jerusalem (Matar 1983). These villages included Lifta, Deir Yassin, Ein Karem, Baka, Katamon, and Talbieh (Khalidi 1993). For Jews, the partition separated them from the Western Wall, the Temple Mount, Mount of Olives cemetery, and institutions such as the Hebrew University on Mount Scopus,[10] now all within Jordanian-held east Jerusalem. Another United Nations resolution—this time in 1949[11]—called for Jerusalem to be an international city. But by then Israel was focused on staking its claim to Jerusalem through the movement of its Prime Minister's office and the Knesset. Prime Minister Ben-Gurion, four days before the U.N. action, had stated that "Jewish Jerusalem is an organic and inseparable part of the State of Israel."[12]

For almost twenty years, Jerusalem was a physically divided city separated by a "green line." The borderline was, in reality, between 98 and 131 feet wide, and it included entire buildings and even whole streets. Many areas became "no-mans land," with concrete barriers constructed to protect against sniping (Bahat 1990). During these years of physical partition, sovereignty conflict influenced planning decisions and the spatial form of the metropolitan area. Because the Israeli city was surrounded on three sides by Arab-controlled territory, Israeli urban planners, out of necessity, had a westward orientation and Israeli Jerusalem expanded into the western hills. The first Israeli plan for Jerusalem, done in 1948 by Rau, and the subsequent 1956 plan by Shviv, moved the city's center of gravity from its historic position—the Old City—to the western parts of the city. Determined to assert their claim to half of Jerusalem, urban planners established a new Hebrew University, government center, and Parliament Building in the western sector. At the same time, the city's Old City and commercial center were largely abandoned (Benvenisti 1976). Growth on the Arab-controlled side of Jerusalem, meanwhile, was constrained by desert conditions east of the city and sprawled along the hilltops to the north (Shepherd 1988). The 1964 Jordanian plan derived from the 1944 Kendall plan thus zoned most of the Old City's landscape—hills, slopes, and valleys—for residential development (Kutcher 1975). East Jerusalem lagged behind the west as the Hashemite Kingdom of Jordan neglected Palestinian community and economic development and focused its attention on the development of its capital, Amman (Bahat 1990; Friedland and Hecht 1996).[13] The legacy of "Armistice line" constraints on planning are apparent today in unpartitioned Jerusalem. Growth outward from the Old City and border "seam" area during the twenty years of partition perpetuated city divisions, lessened the functional importance of the Old City, and intensified the geographic separation of Jewish and Arab neighborhoods (Shepherd 1988; Efrat and Noble 1988).

The Six Day War in 1967 produced a new political landscape in Palestine. The Israel Defense Forces conquered and "united" east Jerusalem, Judea and Samaria (the "West Bank"), the Golan Heights, and the Sinai desert. Soon after the war, Israeli policymakers undertook a threefold geographic expansion of Jerusalem's municipal borders from 9,400 to 26,800 acres (Bahat 1990). This municipal border expansion allowed Israel to control many strategic geographic points in the region and establish a large reserve of buildable land, while excluding several Arab-populated neighborhoods—such as Abu Dis, A Ram, and Beit Hanina—within the functional urban system (Benvenisti 1976). More than five thousand acres were expropriated by Israel as part of this areal enlargement for the purposes of constructing new Jewish neighborhoods (Bahat 1990). Under these new borders, the "city" of Jerusalem in 1967 had a 74-26 Jewish-Arab population distribution. At the same time as enlarging the city, Israel also extended the application of its law, jurisdiction, and administration to all of this larger city and its formerly Jordanian-held portions.[14]

These measures of areal enlargement and annexation by Israel pursuant to military actions met with fierce criticism from the United Nations. International law considers formerly Jordanian-controlled "east" Jerusalem as occupied territory similar to the West Bank. U.N. Security Council Resolution 242, adopted on November 22, 1967, states the international position unequivocally, "emphasizing the inadmissibility of the acquisition of territory by war" and calling for the "withdrawal of Israel armed forces from territories occupied in the recent conflict" (*1967 War*).[15] Nonetheless, since 1967 Israel has exerted and maintained political control over all of its defined city of Jerusalem, including the approximately 180,000 Palestinian residents living there in 1996. The Jewish demographic advantage within the Israeli "Jerusalem" has translated into Jewish control of the city council and mayor's office. This Jewish control is further magnified due to Arab resistance to participating in municipal elections.[16] Most Arabs boycott municipal elections. Since 1969, no more than twenty-one percent of Arabs have ever voted for Jerusalem's mayor (Romann and Weingrod 1991). In November 1993, Teddy Kollek, Jewish mayor of Jerusalem for twenty-eight years and a public advocate for Jewish-Arab peaceful coexistence, lost the mayoral election to Ehud Olmert of the right-wing Israeli Likud party. Less than 5 percent of the city's Arab residents voted.

The *Declaration of Principles on Interim Self-Government Arrangements* ("The Oslo I agreement") was signed by Israel and the Palestine Liberation Organization (PLO) on September 13, 1993, and contains a set of mutually agreed-upon general principles and phases regarding a five-year "interim" period of self-rule. The philosophy guiding these negotiations, says F. Husseini (Jerusalem leader—Palestinian National Authority),[17] was that Israel and Palestinian leaders could move beyond a zero-sum (I win, you lose) understanding of the situation. Land and political autonomy for Palestinians would be exchanged for enhanced security for Israelis and regional stability. The agreement states, in Article V (3), that the status of Jerusalem was not to be discussed in the negotiations for the interim arrangements but should be one of the subjects left for "permanent status" negotiations originally scheduled to occur no later than May 1996. The stages anticipated by the agreement were:

- *Gaza-Jericho*: self-rule by the Palestinian National Authority (PNA), and withdrawal of Israeli forces from Gaza and Jericho, was the first step implemented.

- *Early Empowerment*: in the rest of the West Bank, five specific spheres—education and culture, health, social welfare, direct taxation, and tourism—were transferred to the PNA. Additional spheres were transferred, as agreed by both sides.

- *Interim Agreement and Elections*: The "Oslo II agreement," signed September 28, 1995, by Israel and the PLO, detailed the self-government arrangements in the West

Bank; it also specified the structure and powers, and election procedures, regarding a Palestinian Council. The agreement map demarcated three areas of the West Bank: Area A (seven of the major Palestinian cities where Arabs are to enjoy full territorial and security control); Area B (village areas where the PNA would have territorial control, but security control would be shared); and Area C (areas whose status had not yet been determined and where Israel maintained full control; includes areas Israel deems to be of strategic security value).[18] The Israeli army redeployed away from Areas A and B in phases. Palestinian national elections occurred in April 1996.

- *Permanent Status*: Negotiations on the permanent status—to determine the nature of the final settlement between the two sides—were to begin by May 1996. The Declaration of Principles states that negotiations will cover the issues of Jerusalem, refugees, settlements, security arrangements, and borders. As of 1998, these negotiations were obstructed by serious disagreements over the size and timing of Israeli withdrawals from the West Bank, Israeli building plans in east Jerusalem, and the PNA's ability to constrain extremists.[19]

Despite the engagement by both sides in this staged peace process, the rhetoric concerning Jerusalem and its future status remains derisive and inflammatory. The positions today echo those in the Camp David accords of 1978, when Prime Minister Menachem Begin stated that "Jerusalem is one city, indivisible, the Capital of the State of Israel," and Egyptian president Anwar el-Sadat stated that "Arab Jerusalem is an integral part of the West Bank," and "should be under Arab sovereignty."[20] Upon the signing of the 1993 Declaration agreement, the late Prime Minister Yitzhak Rabin stated that "Jerusalem is the ancient and eternal capital of the Jewish people." An undivided Jerusalem under Israeli sovereignty is and remains a fundamental Israeli position embraced both by former Prime Minister Benyamin Netanyahu and his successor, Ehud Barak, elected May 1999. Palestinian chairman Yasser Arafat, meantime, speaks of Jerusalem as the capital of the state of Palestine, staking claim to formerly Jordanian-controlled parts of Jerusalem that are now home to some 160,000 Jews.

Jewish-Arab Relations

> The explosive potential is always there—it is like a flame; some-
> times bright, sometimes dim, but it is not going to vanish. We have
> to accept that this explosiveness is an integral part of the urban
> situation.
>
> —Avi Melamed,
> Deputy Advisor on Arab Affairs of the
> Municipality of Jerusalem, in an interview

Although lacking a physical partition since 1967, Jerusalem is a city functionally and psychologically divided. Romann and Weingrod (1991) describe this as "living together separately." Neighborhood-level residential segregation is almost total.[21] Separate business districts, public transportation systems, and educational and medical facilities are maintained. Functionally and psychologically, there are no grey areas where either Jewish or Arab identity is not apparent (Romann 1989). Interactions that do occur indicate an interdependency that is asymmetric and reflective of the political power imbalance in the city (M. Romann, professor, Tel Aviv University, interview). There is a spatial dependence of some Arabs on west Jerusalem (for employment and public services, such as bus transportation) that is not present for Jews and east Jerusalem. Because the Jewish sector is much larger and more commercially developed, Arabs are often required to visit Jewish west Jerusalem to obtain needed income, goods, or city services (Romann 1989).

For many residents of Jerusalem, ethnic relations are psychologically ambiguous[22] because the city is in the unclear middle between two less complicated situations: 1) Arab-Jewish relations of some mutual coexistence and acceptance within cities of Israel proper (such as Nazareth or Tel Aviv/Yafo); and 2) relations of open hostility and confrontation between the two sides in the West Bank outside Israeli Jerusalem. Attempting to coexist in the contested Jerusalem region, on the other hand, presents residents with boundaries of communal identity that are permeable and shifting. There is not the tacit acceptance by Arabs of Israeli sovereignty, as occurs within a Tel Aviv or Nazareth. At the same time, because the two sides are forced to coexist and function as urban residents within a metropolitan system, open hostility seen in the West Bank can become moderated in Jerusalem because its effects on the urban system can be detrimental to the economic and social well-being of both sides. Communal identity, viewed by N. Friedland (interview) as the key in conflict situations, is at its most unclear in Jerusalem. Because the city has experienced such significant political change over the years, little in the city is seen in a stable frame of reference that could solidify such communal identity.

The *intifada* that began in 1987 shattered the illusion that coexistence in Jerusalem was possible (Romann 1992). Jewish-Arab violence in Jerusalem was of a different quality than in the West Bank. Street battles were less fierce and less frequent than in West Bank cities such as Ramallah, Hebron, and Nablus. However, although the manifestations of the *intifada* were less visible in Jerusalem than elsewhere, it was in the city that Palestinian political elites created the Unified Leadership of the Intifada, a grouping that brought together competing strains within Palestinian society to organize political actions (Friedland and Hecht 1996). Jewish casualties during the *intifada* were disproportionately higher in the city of Jerusalem than elsewhere, with many political murders occurring along the old boundary "seam" (Friedland and Hecht 1996). On the other hand, Israel's use of police rather than the military in the city has meant a more moderate and disciplined Israeli reaction than in the West Bank, where indiscriminate beatings and open firing by soldiers were more characteristic (Friedland and Hecht 1996; Human Rights Watch 1993b; Shalev 1991; Schiff and Ya'ari 1990; Cohen and Golan 1991). E. Felner, researcher of the human rights organization B'TSELEM (interview), explains that the use of force by Israeli authorities has been moderated in east Jerusalem by the needs to present the "facade of a unified city" to the international community, and to maintain civility to not dissuade tourists from visiting the city. Since the end of the *intifada* in 1993, violence in Jerusalem has assumed more dramatic and violent forms that have traumatized the city. Suicide bombings of municipal buses and bus stops in Jerusalem by Hamas and the Islamic Jihad have cost hundreds of Jewish lives, heightened security measures in the city, led to the frequent closing of Israel and Jerusalem to West Bank Palestinians, and paralyzed the Middle East peace process engendered by the 1993 Declaration of Principles. Principles of Jewish-Arab coexistence have been subordinated to calls by Israeli political leaders to separate or contain the ethnic groups for the purposes of security. Yet Jerusalem, with all its intermingled complexity, appears immune to such seemingly simple solutions.

The contemporary vulnerability and instability of Jerusalem can not be understood without an understanding of the urban spatial and social structure created by Israel since it assumed full political control in 1967. I now explore in detail the goals, implementation techniques, and physical outcomes of Israeli urban policy since 1967.

Israeli Urban Policy Since 1967

Let there be no mistake. I do not want to enhance the Arab population in Jerusalem. It should not grow . . . I wish that the Arab minority in Jerusalem will shrink.

—Ehud Olmert, Mayor of Jerusalem
(as told to Yediot Aharonot),
Los Angeles Times May 13, 1995

Once you have determined the planning of Jerusalem, everything else is only commentary.

—Meron S. Benvenisti,
Former Deputy Mayor of Jerusalem,
in an interview

Urban Goals

Since Israel assumed control over the eastern side of the Jerusalem region in 1967, Israeli planning and development policies have consistently been directed at enhancing Israeli control over the urban region. Of particular note are goals pertaining to Israeli *unification*, or political control, of Jerusalem and the assurance of *security* to Jewish people collectively. The director of the Department of Local Planning, Ministry of the Interior (B. Hyman, interview), explains that urban goals seek to:

- extend the Jewish city geographically and demographically;

- control the heights for military security;

- reconnect the formerly partitioned areas by building a Jewish development bridge from west to east;

- build Jewish neighborhoods so that division of the city in terms of political control and sovereignty is never again possible.

Urban policymakers and planners have pursued political "unification" or control through policies that entrench a Jewish majority within the Israeli-defined city. These strategies involve: (1) stabilization of Jewish-Arab demographic proportions; (2) location of new Jewish neighborhoods; and (3) expansion of the economic base of the city. These three strategies are linked and build one upon the other. New neighborhoods have to be constructed to facilitate and accommodate Jewish population growth. This stabilization of Jewish demographic dominance assures continued local political control should Palestinians end their boycott of local elections. The clearest articulation of this Israeli urban strategy was Prime Minister Golda Meir's proclamation in the early 1970s that Israel should do all that is necessary to maintain the numerical ratio of 73 percent Jewish/27 percent Arab population then existing within the municipal borders (interviews: B. Hyman, director, department of local planning, Ministry of the Interior; and I. Kimhi, former Jerusalem city planner).[23] Second, Jewish neighborhoods need to be built in locations that establish a Jewish presence throughout the city while at the same time guarding the security of Jewish residents vis-à-vis Arab villages and residents in the city. This geographic reach is important in establishing "facts on the ground" that make a potential political re-division of the city problematic. Third, economic growth has to occur that will facilitate continued Jewish population growth in Jerusalem, both through attraction of Jewish labor from elsewhere in Israel and a reduction of labor outflow to job-rich urban areas such as Tel Aviv. Economic planners in Jerusalem thus pursue government-sponsored industrial park development and the improvement of transport networks connecting Jerusalem to the rest of Israel in terms of goods and labor.

Israeli political control is linked to the "security" of Jerusalem and its Jewish inhabitants. Two operational forms of security are evident. "Military" security focuses on the defensibility of the urban system and concentrates on the location and expansion of military installations and the ability of the road network to provide access to defense units. Jewish neighborhoods have intentionally been built on or near strategic hilltops in order to secure them militarily. And military considerations influenced the substantial enlargement of

Jewish municipal borders in 1967. Yet it has been more "political" security which has guided urban policy and planning since 1967 (Shachar interview). This type of security—associated with political control—can be affected by government actions pertaining to growth and development, in particular those policies influencing the demographic dominance and geographic reach of the Jewish population in Jerusalem, the potential for friction between proximate Jewish and Arab neighborhoods within the municipality, and the economic security of the city. Maintaining or enhancing Jewish demographic dominance within the municipal borders, in the eyes of Israeli policymakers, decreases the chances that political control will be wrested away from Israel. The potential for friction can be minimized at the same time through the safe placement of new Jewish neighborhoods and the building of road networks that will be minimally exposed to Arab towns and villages. Economic development and the provision of job opportunities, meanwhile, can help solidify the Jewish presence in the urban region.

Structure of Israeli Planning

Before explaining in greater detail the specific means by which Israel has pursued political control and security in Jerusalem, it is necessary to describe the Israeli planning system's major participants and its intergovernmental (national-regional-local) allocation of authority.

The Town Planning Ordinance of 1936 and the Planning and Building Law of 1965, together, establish the contemporary planning framework for Israel. After 1948, national comprehensive planning was deemed as vitally important by the young and vulnerable country. A National Planning Office was established and for three years (1950–1953) resided in the Prime Minister's Office. Subsequently, the planning system was lodged in the Ministry of the Interior, where it is today (Alexander, Alterman, and Law-Yone 1983). The early years of the country saw the development of several large-scale plans, including agricultural settlement, desert colonization, the national water system, and the planning of a set of development towns. These large-scale national plans were linked to two defining goals of early Israeli planning: dispersal of the population; and settlement in frontier and border regions to thicken the Jewish presence across the new country (Hill 1980; Yiftachel 1992). It became

apparent, however, that more was needed than a planning framework which tended to be passive and regulatory-based (Alexander,
Alterman, and Law-Yone 1983). Regulation of proposed activities
was not sufficient for a young country with strong ambitions. The
result was the ad hoc creation of more active development-oriented
institutions and organizations. Ministries other than Interior were
granted powerful developmental roles and large supportive budgets.

Thus, today the "planning" system can be described as a "parallel" one composed of (1) a statutory system hosted by the Ministry of
the Interior that is reactive, passive, and regulatory; and (2) a developmental system characterized by organizational complexity and
pragmatic, proactive, and dynamic strategies (Alexander, Alterman,
and Law-Yone 1983; Yiftachel 1992; Hill 1980). It is the latter set of
participants who have been intimately involved in the creation of
"facts on the ground."

The regulatory, statutory planning system is a highly centralized one consisting of three levels—national, district (regional),
and local. Its intergovernmental framework is composed of a national planning board, six district planning commissions across
the country, and approximately 110 local planning commissions.
The National Planning Board, chaired by the head of Interior and
composed of representatives of government ministries and local
government, is responsible for preparing national "outline" (statutory) plans dealing with infrastructure of national significance
(airports and national roads, for instance), areas of particular environmental significance (Lake Kinnerret, for example), and the
land development needs related to immigrant absorption (Gabbay
1994). It also sets standards and guidelines concerning national
population distribution and reviews regional outline plans to assure consistency. Significantly, there also is at the national level a
twelve-member Ministerial Committee on Jerusalem, which helps
formulate government policy pertaining to the city. Convened by
the Prime Minister, this high-level committee makes important
land-use decisions, such as in February 1997 when it approved a
controversial six thousand-unit Jewish housing development
called Har Homa in southeast Jerusalem.

The six district planning commissions, of which the Jerusalem
district body is one, are dominated by representatives of central
government ministries. Reflecting the centralized nature of Israeli
statutory planning, they are more administrative agents of the cen-

tral government than a separate level of planning. The Jerusalem district planning commission prepares a district outline plan, sets population distribution targets and oversees matters of region-wide significance (sites for urban development; industrial development; open space and recreation). Importantly, it also has strong oversight power over local outline plans prepared by municipalities, approval power over most local building permits, and hears appeals on local rejection. In sum, the Jerusalem district planning commission is the major decisionmaking body about most day-to-day planning and permit granting problems in the city (Alexander, Alterman, and Law-Yone 1983). Most of the national government strategies pertaining to Jerusalem can easily be taken through the district commission without consultation with the municipal government (I. Kimhi, interview).

Local planning commissions, in Jerusalem constituted as a subcommittee of the city council, have powers that are largely conditional on approval by the district commissions. They have review powers over proposed projects; however, often their decisions are not the final word but are then considered at the district commission where they can be overridden. Local commissions prepare local outline plans but these must be approved by the district commission. And local planning commissions prepare or review "detailed" plans that are similar to "subdivision" plans in the United States, specifying at a project-level land uses, building sizes, and infrastructure layout (Alexander, Alterman, and Law-Yone 1983). In addition to statutory "outline" and "detailed" plans, master plans have been done sporadically for the Jerusalem area. These plans, unlike the others, are conceptual and not statutory; in other words, they do not have the force of law unless a subsequent outline plan is done based on the master plan. The 1968 Master Plan for Jerusalem done by Hashimshoni, Schweid, and Hashimshoni, for example, was never approved as an outline plan, so it does not have the force of law today.

There are two powers of land expropriation for public purposes in Israeli law that have critical importance to Jerusalem planning. These powers are more extensive in Israel than in any Western country (Alexander, Alterman, and Law-Yone 1983). The first power is rooted in the Planning and Building Law and allows local government to expropriate without compensation up to 40 percent of private land in the course of implementing a detailed plan. Such land is to be used for public uses, such as schools, roads, and religious institutions. The planner also has the ability to "reparcel" without landowner consent, which is a means to reconfigure ownership boundaries to overcome problems of fragmented ownership. The second, and more significant, power of land expropriation allows whole areas to be expropriated for public purpose with compensation. Based on Ministry of Treasury powers, this procedure occurs outside the planning regulatory system and can appropriate large areas of land for public purposes as defined by the Minister of Finance. Wholesale taking of land by the Israeli government, as we shall see, has played a critical role since 1967 in establishing a Jewish presence throughout Israeli-defined Jerusalem.

The second component of Israeli planning—the developmental planning system—involves a maze of agencies and organizations, each having specific charges. Yiftachel (1992) classifies these entities into governmental, semi-governmental, and quasi-governmental. Governmental bodies consist entirely of elected and appointed officials. The most important one from the viewpoint of urban growth and development in the Jerusalem region is the Ministry of Housing and Construction, involved with the development of housing, infrastructure, and roads. Other significant players are the Ministry of Defense, which can influence land use along borders; and the Ministry of Trade and Industry, which oversees the development of industrial estates. Semi-governmental bodies, in contrast, are a mixture of governmental and nongovernmental involvement that are governed by state legislation but are only partially accountable. Of note here is the Israeli Lands Authority (ILA), which controls the extensive public land holdings and influences development through the release of such land for residential, industrial, and afforestation purposes. Recently, the ILA has been incorporated into the Ministry of Housing and Construction, adding to the strength of this ministry. Lastly, quasi-governmental bodies exist based on "compacts" with government that endow these bodies with powers and responsibilities on behalf of government. The Jewish National Fund played a key role pre-1948 in purchasing land in Palestine on behalf of the Jewish people. All such land was subsequently transferred to the ILA. Another such body is the Jewish Agency, which has exclusive authority to deal with the absorption and settlement of immigrants to Israel.

The relationship between the two Israeli planning systems—regulatory and developmental—is critical when examining the formulation and implementation of Israeli urban policy in and around Jerusalem. Generally, the degree of compliance with regulatory plans and procedures is relatively low as formal regulations are frequently ignored or overridden in the name of the national interest (Alexander, Alterman, and Law-Yone 1983). Later, I explore the land-use and growth strategies incorporated into the regulatory system and how such policies are modified when they intersect with the developmental planning system and immediate national interests.

Operationalizing "Unification" and "Security"

> From the very first, all major development represented politically and strategically motivated planning.
>
> —Israel Kimhi,
> City Planner of Jerusalem (1963–1986),
> in an interview

In pursuing goals of unification and security, the Israeli government has utilized land-use planning mechanisms as a territorial tool to extend the reach of its disputed public authority. Urban growth and development policies, equating land with political control, have spurred territorial extensions that have penetrated and diminished Arab land control. This approach to planning is clearly identifiable as the *partisan* approach to urban planning and administration.[24] These growth policies, in combination with selective extension of the municipal border after 1967, have increased both Jewish spatial and demographic claims to disputed territory. Urban policies have been designed that further the desire of Israel to maintain sole political control of the city. According to I. Kimhi, city planner during this time, the basic assumption when work started in 1963 on what was to become the 1968 Master Plan of Jerusalem (the "Hashimshoni, Schweid, and Hashimshoni" [H/S/H] plan) was reunification of the city. This is significant because it shows that reunification was a planning assumption four years *prior* to the eradication of the city's physical partitions. The goal of this plan was to physically express a united Israeli Jerusalem (Kutcher 1975).

Political unification has been pursued since 1967 through two chief means: (1) boundary drawing, and (2) demographically-based planning. The threefold territorial expansion (from 14.5 square miles to 42)[25] by the Israeli government of the municipal borders of Jerusalem soon after the 1967 War had three major effects—inclusion, exclusion, and legitimation. First, because the new borders encompassed "maximum land with minimal population," it provided a large land supply for subsequent Israeli development of Jewish neighborhoods. The "unification" of Jerusalem far transcended the simple connecting of west Jerusalem and Jordanian east Jerusalem (2 square miles) and absorbed more than 25 square miles of West Bank territory into Jerusalem and thus Israel. In the short term, this impulse toward territorial aggrandizement actually came at the expense of demographic goals (Amirav 1992; Layish 1992). The large-scale annexation brought twenty-eight Arab villages and settlements into the domain of Israeli control. Schmelz (in Layish 1992) estimates that annexation of the additional 25 square miles (beyond Jordanian east Jerusalem) increased the non-Jewish percentage in the "city" by 7 percent.[26] In the longer term, however, the threefold areal expansion allowed Israel to control many strategic geographic points in the Jerusalem region, and established a large reserve of buildable land upon which it could practice partisan planning and reinforce demographic dominance.

A second effect of boundary drawing was an exclusionary one. Where it was possible to exclude Arab populations from the greatly expanded new "Jerusalem," Israel did so. The new border was intentionally drawn to exclude several Arab nodes of population well within the urban sphere. As Figure 4.4 displays, boundary drawing left out such villages as A-Ram in the north, and e-Azariya and Abu Dis to the east. These and other population agglomerations adjacent to "Jerusalem" today have a combined population of approximately 85,000 (K. Tufakji, Arab Studies Society, interview). Third, by extending municipal borders, Israel provided a grounds whereby they argue that growth and development issues in the region are of municipal, not international, concern. Controversy and instability are dealt with by attempting to place contested actions within a framework of routine management (Dror 1989). This municipalization of controversial action can be traced back to 1967, when the Knesset decided that territorial enlargement should occur through municipal legislation, not through its own declarative acts (Amirav 1992).[27] Today, a common legit-

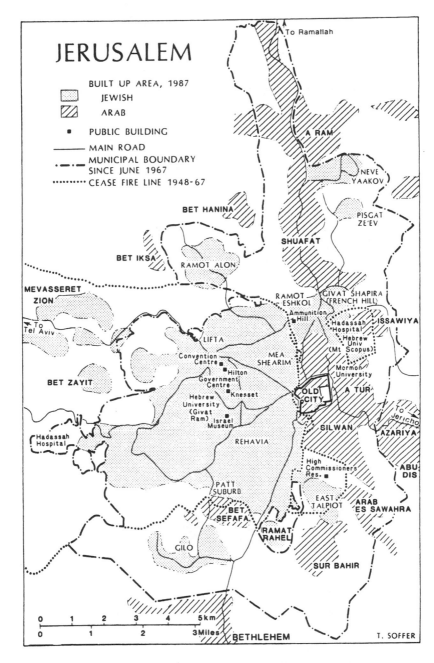

Figure 4.4 Post-1967 Municipal Boundary and Ethnic Residential Distribution

Source: Naomi Shepherd. 1988. *Teddy Kollek, Mayor of Jerusalem.* New York: Harper and Row.

73

imization of Israeli development plans in east Jerusalem suggests that they are being done to accommodate "natural urban growth."

According to E. Barzacchi, (former City Engineer, Municipality of Jerusalem, interview), the re-drawing of municipal borders in 1967 was the most important urban policy in the thirty years of Israeli control because it defined the "scale of preference" and the approach that government would take in the subsequent years—namely, dispersal of the Jewish population within the newly delineated city-space. Former city planner I. Kimhi (interview) described the boundary modification process as "generals going on the hills and making lines." The new municipal borders were influenced strongly by military needs to control access to the city and locations at the top of hills. Both these officials lamented the lack of sacredness of new municipal borders, establishing instead a border that has little to do with what Jerusalem is in the minds of Jews, Arabs, and Christians. Ms. Barzacchi asks a question that illuminates Israel's new dilemma: "Is an area annexed to Jerusalem now holy and are we then to shed our blood over it?"

Boundary drawing established the playing field upon which a land-use competition has been played out over the past thirty years. However, it only drew lines on a map; it did not create facts on the ground. It was left to the second means toward unification—demographically based planning—to give form to the Jewish territorial presence in this expanded Jerusalem. By "demographically based planning," I refer to growth strategies that consciously take into account the goal of maintaining or increasing the ratio of Jews to Arabs within municipal borders. B'Tselem (1995), an Israeli human rights organization, concludes that Israeli urban policy "is based, first and foremost, on creating a demographic and geographic reality that will preempt every future effort to question Israeli sovereignty in east Jerusalem." Such planning differentiates between Jewish growth and Arab growth, facilitating the former and restricting the latter.

It is not the statutory planning framework that illuminates these Israeli urban growth strategies. There is not a single plan or document that comprehensively provides guidance for the city as a whole. B. Hyman (Israeli Ministry of the Interior, interview) states that there is little chance of ever having one because of the political complexities. He states, "It would be political dynamite having one statutory plan for all of Jerusalem. You are stepping on mine fields, no matter what you put on it." Since Israeli urban strategies are controversial, there are advantages to not having them spelled out in statutory plans. The last statutory plan covering west Jerusalem is the 1959 one and it only covers the west side and the area then within the municipal borders (pre-annexation). For areas annexed in 1967, there is no outline plan. Only in the last five years, and after many delays, have outline plans been prepared for some parts of Arab east Jerusalem, although problems of implementation here are numerous, as explained later.

Instead of planning documents, it is the utilization of a set of implementation tools that reveals Israeli urban growth goals and strategies. The tools of greatest importance here are (1) expropriation; (2) the Jewish community development process; and (3) the use of restrictive "green area" zoning, and passive planning, in Arab areas of Jerusalem. These tools have been used to pursue three main goals related to unification and security:

1. facilitate the *pace* and increase the *magnitude* of Jewish development to maintain demographic advantage;

2. influence the *location* of new Jewish development in annexed areas to create an obstacle to "re-division" of the city;

3. restrict Arab growth and development to weaken their claims to reunified Jerusalem.

Magnitude. Figure 4.4 displays the growth and development patterns in Israeli-defined Jerusalem. It illustrates the decision by Israeli planners to build large communities since 1967 inhabited exclusively by Jews in strategic locations throughout the annexed municipal area. I. Kimhi (interview) describes this as, "basically, building new small towns within Jerusalem's outskirts." Because Jewish security has been an overriding concern, the establishment of a "critical mass" of Jews after 1967 was essential to Jewish feelings of safety and confidence (interviews: Y. Golani, director of planning administration, Ministry of the Interior; B. Hyman). The Jewish neighborhoods constructed since 1967 are:

- Ramot Eshkol, Givat Hamivtar, Maalot Dafna, and Givat Shapira (French Hill). Built 1968–1970 and containing, together, about 5,500 units.

- Neve Yaakov, Ramot Allon, Gilo, and East Talpiot. Built 1970–1980 and containing a total of 27,000 housing units (accommodating about one-quarter of the city's entire population).

- Pisgat Zeev. Built beginning in the 1980s, planned to contain 12,000 housing units.

- Har Homa (approved in 1997). Would be built in southeast Jerusalem proximate to Arab village of Um Tuba. Planned number of housing units is 6,500 (Trounson 1997; Keinon 1997).

Land has been consistently expropriated in order to build these new communities. As stated earlier, Israeli law enables the Ministry of Treasury to expropriate whole areas for public purpose with compensation. This procedure occurs outside the planning regulatory system and can appropriate large areas of land for public purposes as defined by the Minister of Finance. Table 4.4, compiled by K. Tufakji (interview) and found in Palestinian National Authority (1995), itemizes these expropriations.

Of the approximately 27 square miles of area annexed after the 1967 War, approximately 9 square miles have been expropriated by the Israeli government (B'Tselem 1995; Palestinian National Authority 1995). This represents 33 percent of the annexed land area. A vast majority of this land had been owned by Arabs (B'Tselem 1995). These expropriations by the Israeli government were done for "public purposes"; yet, as Benvenisti (1996a) observes, this is "a unique conception of the concept 'public.'" As of early 1995, neighborhoods built by Israel on these lands hold about 38,500 residential units, homes to approximately 160,000 Jewish residents (B'Tselem 1995).[28] No housing units have been built on these expropriated lands for Palestinians. Such manipulation of demographic proportions on land whose control was achieved militarily is against international law, which states that "The occupying power shall not deport or transfer parts of its own civilian population into the territory it occupies."[29]

Table 4.4   Israeli Expropriations of Land in Annexed Jerusalem since
1967 (as of 11/94)

DATE	LAND AREA EXPROPRIATED Acres	LOCATION/SUBSEQUENT DEVELOPMENT
1967	29	old city
1968	836	Ramot Eshkol/Givat Hamivtar/ Maalot Dafna/French Hill
1970	118	Neve Yaakov
1970	1218	Ramot Allon
1970	675	Gilo
1970	560	East Talpiot
1980	1100	Pisgat Zeev
	25	near old city
	33	miscellaneous
	300	road construction
1990	462	Har Homa (planned)

When expropriation of private Arab property has occurred,
compensation is required but is almost always not pursued by
Arabs because they view the process as illegal. To pursue and accept compensation for these lands would be to validate Israeli
claims of sovereignty (Interviews: I. Dakkak, Palestinian Economic Council for Development and Reconstruction; K. Tufakji,
Arab Studies Society; M. Abdul-Hadi, Palestinian Academic Society for the Study of International Affairs). More common, however, is Israeli expropriation of areas it considers "state land."
These are areas with no clearly defined private ownership in that
they were owned by the Jordanian government pre-1967 or because privately owned land was not formally registered under
previous governments. Using Western standards to define "private ownership," Israel has conveniently used this apparent void
to legitimize massive expropriations in Jerusalem over the green
line, without even the legal need for compensation. Also targeted
for expropriation and takeover by Israel are properties considered
"absentee," which means they are owned by a Palestinian who
now lives outside Jerusalem.

Jewish community development is facilitated by an active network of developmental agencies that are "positive, dynamic, and innovative" (Alexander, Alterman, and Law-Yone 1983). This planning ideology has been needed by the country in its nationwide efforts at settlement planning, land colonization, and the creation of security borders. The application of these developmental tools in the Jerusalem region has pursued similar goals, creating new settlements (neighborhoods) in the Israeli-demarcated city in areas that were unpopulated. State agencies with extensive powers can propose, and shepherd through, large new Jewish communities. The Israeli Lands Authority (ILA) performs a critical land banking role after expropriation, and influences development through the release of this land for residential, industrial, and afforestation purposes. The Ministry of Housing and Construction, involved with the development of housing, infrastructure, and roads, is the active development agent that creates "facts on the ground" in efficient and significant ways. The building styles of these large-scale neighborhoods in annexed Jerusalem, rather than blending in with the surrounding hilltops, dominate the landscape and skyline as symbols reaffirming the Jewish presence in unified Jerusalem (Seelig and Seelig 1988) (see Figure 4.5).

Location. In addition to the pace and magnitude of Jewish development, the location of the new communities is significant. Much of the new growth could have occurred in west Jerusalem locations not as controversial under international law. Under this scenario, the demographic ratio could still have been maintained in Israeli-defined Jerusalem. However, as B. Hyman (interview) explains, "How many Jews you put in the western corridor increases numbers in the city on paper, but it doesn't strengthen the Jewish hold on Jerusalem." New neighborhoods were thus located to expand the geographical reach of Israeli authority within the post-1967 municipal boundary and spatially fragment Jerusalem's Arab neighborhoods from one another and from the West Bank (see Figure 4.6). Post-1967 Jewish communities have established a Jewish presence throughout the unified Jerusalem municipality, supported by infrastructure policies that have connected these communities to each other functionally through road building.

Israeli development policies have created consolidated and interconnected complexes of Jewish neighborhoods in strategic areas

Figure 4.5   Jewish Neighborhood of Neve Yaakov in North Jerusalem

Source: Scott A. Bollens

throughout annexed Jerusalem. The initial phase of Jewish development connected west Jerusalem to Mount Scopus and the Hebrew
University so as to assure a physical link. These neighborhoods—
Ramot Eshkol, Givat Hamivtar, Maalot Dafna, and French Hill—
were built in and adjacent to the Arab Sheikh Jarrah quarter. The
second phase of development created four huge residential complexes that encircled the urban core and claimed strategic hilltops—
Ramot Allon (northwest), Neve Yaakov (northeast), East Talpiot
(southeast) and Gilo (southwest). Fully one-quarter of the city's population lived in these four communities in the early 1990s (Bahat
1990). The third phase of construction was in the 1980s, when Pisgat Zeev connected Neve Yaakov to French Hill (Givat Shapira), reinforced through a north-south connector highway. The planned Har
Homa neighborhood in southeast Jerusalem, if built in the 1990s,
would tighten and complete the Jewish residential encirclement of
Jerusalem's urban core, and disconnect Jerusalem from Palestinian
Bethlehem to the south. The geography of these post-1967 Jewish
communities creates substantial obstacles to any possible future re-
division of the city politically or physically.[30] If Jerusalem ever were

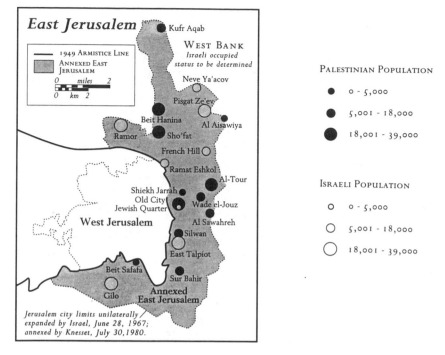

Figure 4.6   Location of Jewish Neighborhoods in Annexed Jerusalem

Source: Edward Said. 1994. *The Politics of Dispossession: The Struggle for Palestinian Self-Determination, 1969–1994.* New York: Pantheon.

to be split politically into Israeli and Palestinian components, what would be done with the substantial Jewish population of more than 160,000 in areas contestable under international law? Psychologically, such construction has affected the Israeli public's view of what is Jerusalem. As E. Felner (B'Tselem, interview) describes, "West Jerusalem has been re-accommodated conceptually according to the political view of the Israelis. Gilo and East Talpiot are seen as part of west Jerusalem."

This Israeli locational strategy is not without risks, however. In building up such a significant Jewish presence in annexed areas, Israeli planners were faced with the practical limits imposed by urban coexistence. M. Romann (Hebrew University, interview) and Sack (1981) speak of the increase in vulnerability to tension and violence caused when one side seeks to control territory inhabited by the other. Quickening the pace and enhancing the magnitude of Jewish development in east Jerusalem runs the real risk of increasing the vulnerability of Jews living there to Palestinian threats, tension, and urban violence near the interfaces of Palestinian and Israeli communities. Thus, there was attention paid to the location of new Jewish communities relative to Arab areas. Efforts were made to control areas through Jewish facts on the ground while maintaining some degree of spatial separation between Jewish and Arab communities. This combined effort aimed at territorial control and security through separation is a difficult task because control and separation are often not mutually compatible (M. Romann, interview). The pattern selected by Israeli planners was to penetrate, but not integrate, annexed Jerusalem. The goal was macro-scale penetration at the level of community, not a micro-scale integration at the level of neighborhood or street. In this pattern, penetration has occurred while maintaining buffer areas between the two communities. Few efforts were made to integrate the two sides at the level of neighborhood. As Y. Golani, Ministry of the Interior planner (interview), states, "One of the most important roles of urban planning in a contested city is to not try to push together side-by-side the two parties." Israeli development patterns in annexed areas utilize both natural (valleys or *wadis*) and man-made barriers (roads) in minimizing contact between antagonistic parties. For example, a valley separates Jewish Neve Yaakov from Arab A-Ram, and a road separates Jewish East Talpiot from Arab Jebel Mukabber. The old "seam area" itself that separated the two sides 1949–1967 has been transformed into a multilane boulevard that physically separates Jewish and Arab neighborhoods.

Restrictions. Israeli facilitation of Jewish growth is one part of the picture; restriction of Palestinian growth is the other. The natural increase of the Palestinian population within Israeli-demarcated Jerusalem presents a problem to Israeli demographically based planning. From 1967 to 1996, the average annual growth rate in the city of the non-Jewish population has been 3.3 percent, compared to 2.6 percent for the Jewish (Jerusalem Municipality 1997). This is owing, in part, to higher rates of natural increase among non-Jews. As Figure 4.7 shows, the non-Jewish population has been a younger one, on average. In 1992, its median age was 19.1 years compared to 25.9 years for Jews (Jerusalem Municipality 1994a).

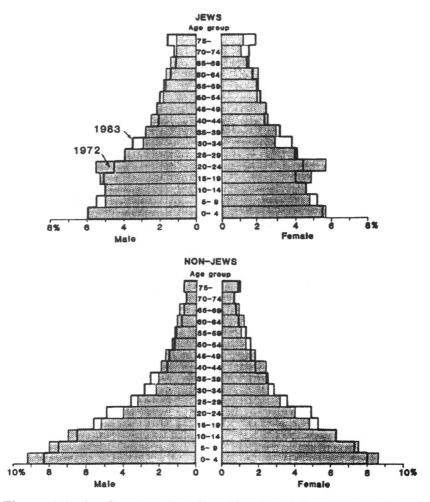

Figure 4.7   Age Structure Jewish vs. Non-Jewish Population in City of Jerusalem, 1972 and 1983

Source: Benjamin Hyman, Israel Kimhi, and Joseph Savitsky. 1985. *Jerusalem in Transition: Urban Growth and Change 1970's–1980's.* Jerusalem: Jerusalem Institute for Israel Studies and the Institute of Urban and Regional Studies, Hebrew University.

Accordingly, it has had a greater proportion of its population currently in, or approaching, child-bearing age brackets. In 1992, for instance, non-Jewish natural increase was 30/1,000 compared to 20.9/1,000 for Jews. For Israeli policymakers, this situation means that it is not sufficient in maintaining the city's demographic ratio to concentrate only on the facilitation of Jewish growth. Indeed, Palestinian population and growth is "perceived as a demographic threat to Israeli control of the city" (B'Tselem 1995). Palestinian internal growth could potentially outnumber Jewish population growth stimulated through Israeli-promoted new communities. Due to these demographic parameters, Israel must "run to stand still" in order to maintain its 70 percent majority (Dumper 1997).

Israeli planners have thus worked to restrict through the planning apparatus the growth potential of Palestinian communities within "Jerusalem."[31] This has been accomplished through: (1) the expropriation of land by Israel; (2) the restriction through "green area zoning" of Palestinian rights to development; (3) the use of road building to restrict and fragment Palestinian communities; (4) "hidden guidelines" within Israeli plans that restrict building volume in Palestinian areas; and (5) the intentional absence of plans for Arab areas that would be needed for infrastructure provision and community development. As described above, expropriation by Israel has removed from the Palestinians one-third of all annexed land for the purposes of Jewish residential development. Additional Israeli techniques further tighten Arab autonomy and rights regarding growth and development. I first examine green area zoning and road construction, then the obstacles imposed through Israeli plans.

"Green area" zoning is used by Israeli planners to restrict development potential for the purposes of maintaining areas in open space to protect views from the city outward to the desert and hills (N. Sidi, city planner, Municipality of Jerusalem, interview). Such zoning is used throughout the city, including on the west side. However, the magnitude of its use in annexed areas severely restricts the horizontal expansion of existing Arab communities there. In addition, the fact that such zoning has been overridden at times to build new Jewish communities calls into question the true motivations beyond such land-use regulation. This indirect control of Palestinian growth has closed off approximately 40 percent of annexed Jerusalem to Palestinians (K. Tufakji interview; Palestinian National Authority 1995). These regulations draw tight borders around existing Arab communities. For example, the built-up area of Shuafat to the north is approximately two square miles; yet the allowable building area for the village not zoned "green area" is less than one-half square mile. Similarly, the built-up area of the village of Issawiya (near Mount Scopus) is four square miles compared to its allowable built area of .2 square miles. This practice has been described by S. Kaminker (interview), former city planner, as "liberally covering existing houses with green paint," resulting in the restriction of Arab growth to small urban ghettos unconnected to each other. Similarly disturbing from an equity perspective is the fact that such "green areas" at times have been used to restrict Arab growth at first, then subsequently to facilitate the creation of new Jewish communities. A recent case of this is the development of the new ultra-orthodox Jewish community of Shuafat Ridge.

Together, the direct control through expropriation and the indirect control through "green area" zoning has resulted in about 73 percent of annexed east Jerusalem being off-limits to Palestinian development (K. Tufakji, interview). In addition to restricting new growth, such practices severely fragment existing Arab communities by discouraging horizontal connections between them. Road building by Israeli planners has taken an additional 6 percent of the land for annexed Jerusalem. These roads can, of course, be used by both parties. However, their placement has tended to divide existing Arab communities and constrain Arab growth while establishing links between Jewish communities. For example, in the Arab village of Beit Safafa in south Jerusalem, regional road building that connects the Jewish Gilo neighborhood to west Jerusalem has divided the village into four pieces.

Table 4.5 exhibits the cumulative impact of Israeli restrictions on Palestinian growth. Expropriation, green area zoning, and road building leaves 21 percent of annexed east Jerusalem for potential Palestinian development.[32] One-half of this (10 percent) represents already Palestinian built-up areas. Thus, at the most, 11 percent of annexed Jerusalem is vacant land where the Israeli government today allows Palestinian development (K. Tufakji, interview).

Restrictions on Arab development in Jerusalem have produced glaringly different development trajectories of the two ethnic groups. Since 1967, 88 percent of all housing units built in Jerusalem have been built for the Jewish population (B'Tselem 1995).[33] Data from the Statistical Yearbook of Jerusalem (compiled by the Municipality in association with the Jerusalem Institute for Israel Studies) detail the effects of such restrictions on Arab growth. In 1993, only 3.8 percent of the 2,720 housing units built that year in the city were in Arab neighborhoods. In 1992, 1,755 dwellings were started citywide;

Table 4.5 Israeli Restrictions on Palestinian Growth in Annexed
Jerusalem (as of 1995)

METHOD	PERCENT OF LAND IN ANNEXED JERUSALEM
Expropriated by Israel	33
Restricted through green area zoning	40
Off-limits due to road construction	6
Land remaining for development	21
Palestinian built-up areas	10
Vacant land available for Palestinian growth	11

only eighty-one (or 4.6 percent) of these dwelling starts occurred in Arab quarters. Similar patterns existed in 1990 and 1988 (4.9 and 3.7 percent of dwelling starts in Arab sub-quarters, respectively). In these years, the bulk of new dwelling starts was occurring in the newer large Jewish communities of Neve Yaakov and Pisgat Zeev (northeast), Ramot Allon (northwest), and Gilo (to the south). These restrictive policies applied to Palestinians have created a severe housing shortage among that population. Consensus estimates among planners and architects put the shortage at more than 20,000 residential units (B'Tselem 1995). In contrast, fewer than 10,000 units total have been built for the Palestinian population in the twenty-eight year period following Israeli control. Israeli development policy both restricts population growth of the Palestinians and increases housing density for those wishing to reside in Jerusalem. B'Tselem (1995) reports that almost one-third of Jerusalem's Palestinians (32.3 percent) lived in conditions of housing density of more than three persons per room, as opposed to only 2.4 percent among Jews. It is true that Arabs traditionally have more persons per housing unit. However, Israeli policy has intensified housing density well beyond what cultural factors could explain. Indeed, since the start of Israeli control over east Jerusalem in 1967, "the gap in housing density between the Palestinian population and the Jewish population doubled" (B'Tselem 1995).

Tight restrictions on Jerusalem "residency" for Palestinians assure that residential in-migration does not overshadow the effects of Israeli restrictions on Arab building in the city. Legal immigration by Palestinians from the West Bank and Gaza to Jerusalem is limited. Many of the thousands of Palestinians who left or were driven out of east Jerusalem due to the 1967 War have been denied the right to return and live in their homes (Krystall 1993; Abu Lughod 1984). Since 1991, non-Jerusalem Palestinians have been barred from entering the city without a permit.[34] If a Palestinian resident of Jerusalem decides to relocate to the West Bank or to elsewhere in the world in order to find work, he loses the right to return as an official resident. This Palestinian would become an "absentee" and his property in Jerusalem subject to dispossession and expropriation[35] (Krystall 1994 and 1993). Even Palestinians who marry a Jerusalemite but who live outside the city's borders will encounter difficulty establishing city residence.

"Yes, We Have Plans": The Mismatch between Israeli Planning and the Arab Community

Areas in annexed Jerusalem not obstructed through direct expropriation, green area zoning, and road construction constitute, at the most, 21 percent of the area, of which one-half is covered by existing Arab neighborhoods and villages. Palestinian development could be facilitated in the remaining vacant and underutilized areas if Israeli development (outline) plans accommodated the market dynamics and development processes inherent in the Arab community. Such, unfortunately, is seldom the case. Israeli urban policy and planning for Arab areas, both through its absence for many years and through its belated presence today, adds additional sources of constraint in areas where Palestinian development is not obstructed through expropriation, green area zoning, or road building. Only in the last five years has the Municipality of Jerusalem begun to prepare outline plans for Arab sectors of the city. A "politically conscious" decision in part (I. Kimhi interview), the lack of outline plans for decades made it extremely difficult for Palestinians to gain building permits because these plans are a necessary condition for permit approval. For more than two decades, the only approved outline plan pertaining to Arab growth in east Jerusalem was the

Sharon Plan, which dealt only with the area within and immediately adjacent to the Old City. Kimhi expresses shame that no statutory plans were developed for eastern Arab Jerusalem.

Without explicit decision-guides to development, the Israeli government can rely on nonstatutory mechanisms to curtail "legal" Palestinian growth. For instance, in the Arab village of Shuafat, the land supply could accommodate approximately 18,000 persons. Yet, owing mainly to Ministry of Housing decisions, development for only 7,000 persons has been allowed (Kimhi interview). In another case, in the Sawahra village, building permits were not allowed for many years because there was no approved plan, this despite an average 4 percent growth rate per year. Kaminker (interview), former city planner, spoke of "hidden guidelines" used to regulate Arab growth. Examples of these include intentionally wide road standards that closed off development opportunities for rows of building lots consumed by the road; tight restrictions on allowable floor area as a percentage of property size (15–25 percent of lot is common in Arab areas; compared to up to 200–300 percent in Jewish communities); and strict height standards. The result of these restrictions has commonly been the "illegal" building by Palestinians to accommodate their housing needs. The stamp of "illegality" then provides Israel the right under their laws to demolish buildings for lack of building permit. This is another example of the "municipalization" of what in reality are decisions with international ramifications. The demographic manipulation of populations in internationally contested east Jerusalem becomes transformed into the mundane arena of municipal regulation and building permit issuance. Israeli policymakers are keenly aware that they have much to gain from the acceptance of such actions as routinized and "municipal."

In the last few years, outline plans have been prepared for between 70 and 80 percent of the Arab sector, according to N. Sidi, director of urban planning policy for the Municipality. It took the district planning commission a long time to approve such plans. According to Sidi, "Such delays may well have been political." These plans project 15,210 new dwelling units for Arabs, a 67 percent increase over the 22,860 existing units (Jerusalem Municipality 1994b). City planner N. Sidi admits that the overriding demographic ratio goal of Israel does affect the capacity of the plans. At the same time, she claims that the growth allowed under the plans would be more than sufficient to meet Arab growth through the year 2010, based on a projected Arab growth rate of 2.5 percent a year. However, it is not clear whether such growth rates incorporate potential internal migration into Jerusalem from West Bank locations outside, or whether it is based only on natural increase. The 2.5 percent figure is described in the *Statistical Abstract of Jerusalem* as keeping with the needs of demographic growth "for the population existing in 1967." This implies that internal migration is not to be accommodated in Israeli plans for the Arab sectors. In contrast, internal migration of Jews to Jerusalem is not only to be accommodated, but stimulated.

Where Israeli outline plans exist, they are commonly tenaciously restrictive. In Sur Bahir village in south Jerusalem, for example, the outline plan draws a tight boundary around the built-up area of 670 dunams (one dunam = $\frac{1}{4}$ acre), whereas Arabs own approximately ten thousand dunams in the area (S. Kaminker, interview). Israeli planners use an argument here that the traditional low-density and scattered form of Arab development is not appropriate within a municipality. Golani of the Ministry of Interior (interview) states that such low-density development is "a way of building that we don't like very much, although Arabs want to build their own way." It must be noted that such a planning argument is a legitimate concern throughout urban areas of the world. However, in the Jerusalem case, much low-density development is found in traditionally rural villages in the south and is only considered worthy by planners of urban scale development because Israel expanded the pre-1967 borders to incorporate them into their new city. What are rural villages became overnight part of a large and contested city and its partisan urban planning apparatus.

Even if one concurs with the Municipality that its outline plans can accommodate adequate Arab population growth, a major obstacle is present that makes it highly improbable that this "allowable" growth will ever occur. This has to do with the ill fit between the Western standards incorporated into Israeli plans and the realities of non-Western Arab development processes and ownership patterns. According to Yiftachel (1983), "The cultural orientation of planning regulations are often at odds with the execution of traditional Arab building methods and designs." Or, as former city engineer E. Barzacchi (interview) proclaims, "The answers we town planners give to the Arab population are technically 'right' and interesting, but are absolutely irrelevant."

Development that occurs under the Israeli planning system must meet several conditions not often present in Palestinian society. After an outline plan is prepared that allocates land uses and densities, there must be clearly defined private ownership boundaries that are legally "registered" with the government. Such registration is needed because planners must reconfigure ("reparcellate") ownership boundaries for the purposes of creating areas for public institutions (like schools and religious institutions) and infrastructure (roads and utilities, for instance). A "detailed plan" is then put together that lays out in great specificity the placement of these institutions and infrastructure within the larger project. In Jewish developments, such reparcellation and detailed plans are relatively easy because the land is commonly in public ownership, and there exists a publicly supported process of community development—led by the Ministry of Housing and Construction—that takes the project to its ultimate fruition.

In Arab areas, unclear ownership patterns militate against development occurring under Israeli plans, in those cases where plans exist. About one-half of the Arab sector in Jerusalem has unregistered land ownership patterns, which makes it next to impossible for Israeli planners to reparcellate in anticipation of development. Arab ownership patterns are a legacy of much land being held in community or state ownership under British and then Jordanian control. In other cases, whole families own large areas of land with no intention to sell or develop. This, together with the fact that they do not view Israeli planning control as a legitimate exercise of power, means that "registration" will not be pursued. Thus, when Israeli planners attempt to reparcellate Arab land, "it is like working in the dark" (Sidi interview). Detailed plans, required for development under Israeli law and common for Jewish new communities, are frequently never put forth for Arab areas because of unclear land title. In addition, whereas Western world regulatory and development processes assume a responsive land market of buyers and sellers, little of this activity occurs in the Arab world. In the Western world, a piece of land where government allows growth will likely be built on, if not by the current landowner, then by another party which buys the property for that purpose. In Palestinian society, such selling is rare; rather, land can remain vacant and in one family's ownership for many years. This sluggish land market obviates against Arab development under Israeli control. This is so because when, as commonly occurs, the allocation of building rights by Israeli plans tends not to fit with Palestinian land owners' expectations regarding future land use, such land where growth is allowed can remain vacant for decades until time that the landowner feels his, or his extended family's, needs dictate development. The problem of lack of fit between public plans and private development ambitions is not uncommon to many countries. In those situations, though, the land market, and its usually responsive buying and selling, acts as a mechanism through which municipal planning goals and the meeting of private ambitions can occur over a much shorter time than in Palestinian society.

Another source of ill-fit between Israeli planning and Arab society is the Israeli planning system's use of its expropriation authority. This is not the wholesale expropriation of land discussed earlier, but the ability of local government to expropriate without compensation up to 40 percent of private land in the course of implementing a detailed plan. This land is to be used for public uses, such as schools, roads, and religious institutions. This idea of "confiscating land for your benefit" is foreign to Palestinian society. This concept becomes even more problematic when it is being done not by your own people, but by an "occupier" (E. Barzacchi interview). What is a logistical challenge in "normal" circumstances then becomes a "political challenge" in contested urban situations. Even when such expropriation is negotiated between parties, Israeli rigidity can create obstacles. For example, a negotiated amount of land was agreed upon by the Municipality and an Arab community which was to be expropriated and used for a community school. However, because the amount of land offered was below that required, the Israeli Ministry of Education did not provide funding because it did not meet its school size standard (I. Kimhi interview).

Finally, whereas Israel fully supports its new Jewish communities through a strong communal process of planning and building, the Palestinian society is not characterized by such collective development processes. Rather, it is an collection of urban villages characterized by individually pursued land development. Part of this is owing to the deteriorated state of Palestinian institutions under occupation; and part is attributable to qualities inherent to Palestinian, and most Arab, societies. One could make the claim here that, "Well, this is a Palestinian problem; not anything Israeli planning must worry about" (E. Felner, B'Tselem, interview). Yet the Israeli government in its claim of sole sovereignty over Jerusalem also then takes on the responsibility of caring for *all* its residents. This means that it has the moral obligation to use its strong communal development processes to benefit both Jews and Arabs. Yet the expropriation and community development processes have been used to overwhelmingly benefit Jews over Arabs.

In summary, a set of characteristics exists in Arab areas that militates against Palestinian development in those areas of Jerusalem not already restricted by more direct Israeli actions. These characteristics are unclear ownership patterns, the lack of a land market ethic, the hesitancy to accept a "confiscation for their own good" argument put forth by a government they view as illegitimate, and the absence of collective institutional development processes. These qualities allow the Israeli government and the Municipality to boast that, "Yes, we have plans" (N. Sidi, Jerusalem city planner, interview) for the Arab sector while knowing that most of the allowable growth will not come to fruition because the means and tools of implementation are not there due to cultural and political reasons. According to J. de Jong (planning consultant, St. Yves Legal Resource and Development Center, interview), Israel says, "Look, we gave you the possibilities. If you as a society don't make use of it, we have no responsibility." Former Deputy Mayor Benvenisti (interview) states that "Planning is meaningless without a system to implement it," and that "Israelis did not plan for the Arab community, but planned just so there would be a plan." Israeli planners, rather than taking proactive responsibility for making plans and reality meet, instead accept by default built-in mechanisms that disadvantage significantly the Palestinian community in Jerusalem. It is only when one gets beneath the surface level of Israeli claims that one realizes the difficulties faced by the Palestinian urban population in attempting to sustain itself under Israeli rule.

First through the absence of outline plans for the Arab areas, and subsequently through approved plans that do not fit the on-the-ground reality of Arab society, Israeli planners have restricted those areas not already foreclosed through wholesale expropriation, green area zoning, and road construction. The mismatch between Israeli planning and the Palestinian population adds an additional and more opaque layer of Israeli restrictions upon Arab development in Jerusalem, over and above the more transparent expropriation and restrictive zoning schemes. S. Kaminker (interview) points to these tools and states, "Planners have been doing their most in the municipality to restrict Arab growth and to make life miserable for Arabs through the planning process." In total, land-use and growth strategies undertaken by the Israeli government and the Jerusalem Municipality since 1967 have had significant and long-lasting effects on the urban system. They have increased both Jewish spatial and demographic claims to disputed territory, penetrated and fragmented Palestinian communities and villages, and changed forever the physical landscape of the Holy City. Because of their partisan approach, these strategies have irretrievably divided the social fabric of the urban system.

Urban Service Delivery in a Contested City

In addition to plan making and growth management by the Israeli government since 1967, another important facet of urban policy is the magnitude and allocation of urban spending and service delivery across Jewish and Palestinian neighborhoods of the city. Development of ethnically homogeneous neighborhoods had been under the Kollek administration (1967 to 1993) the official urban planning policy of Jerusalem's government. Municipal goals included the "preservation of the unity of Jerusalem by siting neighborhoods in a form that would create a nonpolarized mosaic of communities" (Shepherd 1988). And, indeed, ethnic segregation is the norm (Stern 1992). Jews or non-Jews constituted more than 95 percent of the population in twenty-nine of the thirty-five subquarters of the city (Jerusalem 1984; Central Bureau of Statistics 1983). This neighborhood mosaic policy, however, is associated with significant interethnic disparities in public expenditures and services. Ethnic and sectoral criteria appear to overshadow functional and geographic factors in the distribution of many urban services. Benvenisti (1986a), former deputy mayor, declares that 90 percent of public resources was invested in Jewish neighborhoods in Jerusalem. Interviewees in 1994 (both Israeli and Palestinian) consistently cited an approximately eight to one spending ratio by the Municipality in Jewish versus Arab communities within Israeli Jerusalem. In 1992, the Municipality spent about $900 per capita in Jewish areas, compared to about $150 in Arab areas (Benvenisti 1996a). Amirav (1992) documents that the municipality never provided more than 4 percent of its development budget for infrastruc-

ture—roads, sewage, water, electricity, schools—in Arab neighborhoods. These estimates provide a range of between 4 and 17 percent of
Municipality urban spending directed at Arab areas, far below what
their proportionate share of spending would be based on population
(30 percent). Factoring in an annual increment of spending over and
above proportionality to make up for huge initial differences in 1967
urban services, spending in Arab areas represents between 11 and 46
percent of what it would likely be in a "normal" city.[36] In addition,
these municipal figures underestimate the Jewish-Arab spending gap
because they do not include the significant central government sponsorship and subsidization of public housing, which almost never benefits the Arab population (Romann and Weingrod 1991).

Municipality spending that does occur in Arab neighborhoods has
been more guided by image concerns than by objective conditions. A
planning document (Jerusalem Municipality 1986) prioritizes infrastructure and public institution projects in Arab areas on the basis
of "degree of visibility" to residents and tourists. The report justifies
this approach by stating that development in the Arab sector has a
"picture window" effect. G. Baskin (director, Israel/Palestine Center
for Research and Information, interview) claims that a similar approach drives spending on Arab projects by the private Jerusalem
Foundation—"They are pet projects to show the world, but go off the
tourist paths and there is nothing." For services administered citywide that employ both Jewish and Arab workers (such as police and
fire fighting), employees are dispatched not on the basis of their geographic proximity, but according to their ethnic match with the
neighborhood requesting assistance. Complete separateness of other
service systems—such as electrical supply and education—further
perpetuates city divisions (Efrat and Noble 1988) and can entail an
"asymmetry in access to urban services" (Romann and Weingrod
1991). For example, the Arab bus system has a much more restricted service area than the Jewish bus system even though a significant number of Jerusalem Arabs travel daily to Jewish west
Jerusalem for work.

A 1994 report on East Jerusalem prepared by the Municipality
(*East Jerusalem: Conflicts and Dilemmas—Urban Coping in the
East of the City*) documents the huge gap in services between Jew-
ish and Arab neighborhoods found in 1967, and states that the city
since 1967 "has not done enough" (Jerusalem Municipality 1994b).
Documented 1994 service needs in Arab communities include:

- One-half of water lines in need of replacement. NIS 52 million needed to complete and improve water system.[37]

- One-half of neighborhoods have no sewage system. Serious drainage problems in several neighborhoods due to difficult topography. Estimated cost of needed sewerage and drainage improvements = NIS 79 million.

- Many areas have dirt roads with no sidewalks or proper lighting. Significant problems with local and arterial roads. Arab sector estimated to need 80 miles of new roads at cost of NIS 200 million for construction.

- Lack of public spaces because of inability of Municipality to appropriate land.

- Some neighborhoods suffer from inadequate cleaning and garbage collection due to inaccessibility.

These service inadequacies are not present in Jewish neighborhoods in west and east Jerusalem. There, communities are built in their entirety and include full and modern infrastructure, despite often building in difficult topographical areas. According to the 1992 Statistical Yearbook of Jerusalem, 11,365 properties existed in Jerusalem that either lacked part of conveniences entirely or had part of these conveniences outside the dwelling (Jerusalem Municipality 1994a). Whereas Arabs make up about 30 percent of the population, approximately 70 percent of these dwellings were in Arab neighborhoods. Arab neighborhoods having concentrations of inadequately serviced dwellings include the Moslem quarter of the Old City, the Silwan and Abu-Tor communities, Issawiya and Mount of Olives, and the areas of Arab es-Sawahra and Bet Safafa in southern Jerusalem.

Israeli administrators claim that one of the reasons behind service inadequacies is that Arabs do not pay their local taxes (called *arnona*). The 1994 city report states that arnona payment rates are 49.2 percent for dwellings and 43.8 percent for businesses in Arab eastern Jerusalem, compared to 78 and 74 percent, respectively, from west Jerusalem. As such, "Payments received from the east of the city cover only a small percentage of expenditures in different services to this sector" (Jerusalem Municipality 1994b). Independent analysis of Statistical Yearbook data confirms this pattern.

Whereas the 1992 citywide arnona nonpayment rate was 8.1 percent, rates in the six largest Arab sub-quarters range from 25.0 to 39.4 percent. Despite this disproportionality of payment, however, Jerusalem Arabs appear not be getting services equivalent to their payments. Amirav (1992), using special 1990 data from the municipal finance department, found that while Arabs paid 7.5 million U.S. dollars in municipal taxes that year, total expenditures in Arab sectors (from municipal and national governments combined) amounted to slightly greater than 3 million U.S. dollars. As such, arnona nonpayments by Arabs appear to provide a pretense under which the Municipality penalizes Arab communities far beyond what nonpayment might call for. In a sense, says Amirav (p. 40), "the Arabs have been required to bear the costs of Israeli domination without reaping equivalent benefits."

Urban Disparities and Political Strategy

The Israeli policy of promoting Jewish development and curtailing Arab growth in Jerusalem (since 1967) only weakens Israel's hold on the city.

—Amir Cheshin,
former advisor on Arab affairs
in the Municipality of Jerusalem

In a contested city such as Jerusalem, urban disparities are intimately connected to political claims. Wide intergroup disparities in Municipality of Jerusalem public spending supports the partisan approach to urban planning and administration. E. Barzacchi, former city engineer (interview), observes the huge spending differentials and states, "The (1967 green) line is still there, and that's our worst failure." In a similar vein, M. Warshawski, director of an Arab-Jewish collaborative nongovernmental organization (interview), declares, "The line in Jerusalem was never a physical border post-1967, but it was more real than the Berlin wall." Ethnic criteria have overshadowed functional factors in the distribution of urban services and approval of building permits. Planners and administrators have played an instrumental role in legitimizing and institutionalizing a dual, unequal system of public authority. This partisan approach might well be masked as technical and noncontroversial, as when the city's spending imbalances were concealed behind Mayor Kollek's seemingly benign policy of encouraging neighborhood mosaic patterns. Nonetheless, partisan planning has been pervasive, deepening polarization because the disenfranchised Arab minority views the planner as a guardian and perpetuator of disputed political structures.

Post-1967 urban policy in Jerusalem illustrates the type of dilemma faced by policymakers operating in ethnically polarized cities where sovereignty is contested. City spending disparities and the functional fragmentation of urban service delivery do consolidate advantages for the city's Jewish neighborhoods and residents. Yet paradoxically, the imposition of separateness resulting from such planning strategies will likely be an obstacle in the future to Israel's claim of sovereignty over the urban region. Partisan service delivery such as in Jerusalem since 1967 exacerbates sovereignty conflict. Service disparities provide telling evidence to the international community that Jerusalem Palestinians are treated as second-class residents and that the Israeli-defined city, in terms of functionality and urban service distribution, is not now unified.

Israeli policymakers and administrators are cognizant of the negative effects of uneven service delivery in the city on their political claims. However, significantly different strategies have been used to dampen these negative effects by the former Kollek administration (1967–1993) and the current Olmert administration (1993–). After reunification in 1967, a strategy of providing equal services to both Arab and Jewish residents was considered by policymakers. Amirav (1992) suggests that the goal would have been to encourage through fair treatment Arab acceptance of Israeli rule, and thereby to separate Arabs in Jerusalem from those in the West Bank outside Israeli-defined Jerusalem. The belief was that economic development and the extension of the Israeli welfare state to annexed residents would moderate nationalistic aspirations. Today, E. Barzacchi (interview), former city engineer, reflects:

> We should have treated Arabs as equal Israeli citizens. Give and take from them everything. You cannot be one-half citizen: resident of the city but not citizen of Israel. Full citizenship and bridging of the west-east gap should have been done quickly after 1967.

Such was not the case as partisan service delivery soon became the dominant mode of governance. Yet Benvenisti (1986a) doubts that equal service provision would have been effective anyway. By focusing on a convenient perception of the problem—resource allocation—Israeli planners would have reached a "manageable solution," premised on universal, civil-libertarian terms, to the problems of a polarized city. The urban symptoms, rather than the root cause, of the sovereignty conflict would be the target of public policy. However, since the Jerusalem conflict is not based on the distribution of sewerage, street lighting, or welfare benefits, but rather on deep-rooted conflicts of sovereignty, this liberal strategy of service provision would not have worked. Such an urban policy addressed to alleviating material inequalities between Jews and Arabs would do little to lessen, and may even have exacerbated, national sovereignty conflicts.

The twenty-seven years of the Teddy Kollek administration are full of contradictions. As a Labor politician, he publicly advocated fairness of treatment toward Arab residents and mutual coexistence of the two groups. In a highly centralized government structure, he skillfully carved out a niche for his administration through the creation of a coalition of local Jewish and Arab notables, grassroots advocates, liberals, and officials from the central government, particularly from the Housing and Foreign Affairs Ministries (S. Hasson, department of geography, Hebrew University, interview). In contrast to the central government's macrostrategy based on hegemony and control in Jerusalem, Hasson and Kouba (1994) suggest that Kollek used a "municipal micro-strategy based on elite accommodation, informal cooperation and enlightened paternalism." Together, these municipal policies were successful in "absorbing and containing the conflict within the dominant system of Israel's control over the city" (Hasson and Kouba 1994). Such paternalism helped mitigate the negative effects of uneven service delivery on Israel's claims to the city. R. Twite, in a similar vein (Hebrew University, interview), recounts that "Kollek created a better atmosphere, but in practice he carried out the Israeli stamp on Jerusalem." At the same time that Jewish-Arab spending ratios reflected gross inequalities, Kollek professed liberal beliefs in equal and fair treatment for all residents.

Kollek's municipal microstrategy relied on accommodative strategies with Arab local notables called *mukhtars*, heads of large clans who constituted the older leadership in the city. Kollek used the forty-five to sixty mukhtars in the city as mediators between the local Arab community and the municipal government. Through the rewarding of cooperative traditional leaders with the delivery of services to their neighborhoods, these leaders were coopted into the Israeli system of control. According to Hasson and Kouba, this fostered a certain Arab dependency on the Israeli system, maintained functional if not affective loyalty, and led to the maintenance of relatively peaceful relations between the ethnic groups. J. de Jong (interview) describes this as Kollek's effort to buy off the Palestinian middle class through the provision of benefits to compliant neighborhoods. Kollek also professed support for greater local autonomy for Arab communities through a system of self-administered neighborhood councils called *minhelot*. Despite this rhetoric, however, only two self-management councils were established in Arab communities and these had little independent power (Hasson 1992). M. Romann (interview) is informative regarding the Kollek strategy. He differentiates between two components of ethnic relations—a political one dealing with power relations and a cultural one dealing with language and customs. Kollek solidified the political component through his acceptance of Israeli expansionary policies regarding new Jewish settlements, while at the same time compromising on the cultural component, allowing flexibility, for example, regarding the allowable hours of Arab business operation during the Jewish sabbath and holidays.

The expansionary Israeli development policies since 1967 have required tremendous outlays from the municipal budget to provide roads, transportation, and water and sewer infrastructure to these often remotely located Jewish communities. As such, little was left and forthcoming to Arab neighborhoods. Because of this constrained municipal budget space, M. Benvenisti (interview) proclaims that "the city could not bear financially the Palestinians getting even one-half of what the Jews get." Thus, even if Kollek was genuine in his belief in equal treatment of Jews and Arabs in Jerusalem, he could not have achieved such equality without a significant inflow of funds from the central government to the municipal budget. And this did not occur. First, central government funds into Jerusalem were overwhelmingly used to support Jewish development. Second, such central government subsidies decreased through the years. Amirav (1992), using Municipality Finance Department data, shows that central government participation in the funding of municipal activities decreased from 40 percent of municipal budget to 10 percent from the early 1980s to the end of the decade.

In the end, the urban evidence of uneven service delivery patterns over almost thirty years became the enduring legacy of the Kollek administration. Less important, and still debatable, is whether Kollek's public stance advocating equality of treatment went unfulfilled because of lack of personal commitment or because of the absence of central government funds to take up the slack.

Ehud Olmert, a Likud politician and Jerusalem Mayor since November 1993, professes much more forcefully and adamantly than Kollek that Jerusalem is a Jewish city, albeit open to other religions. For example, in a November 1994 presentation,[38] he stated unequivocally that:

> Jerusalem was, never ceased to be, continues to be, and will forever remain the undivided capital of only the state of Israel and the Jewish people.

Despite this stern and unaccommodating stance, the Olmert administration is involved for the first time since 1967 in the documentation of Arab community service needs in the city.[39] The administration plans to use these figures to support their efforts to narrow Jewish-Arab spending differentials and to advocate for increased central government funding for Arab communities. What might at first appear to be a contradiction between rhetoric and reality is due to a rational connection made by the Olmert administration between the treatment of Jerusalem Arabs and Israel's political claims to the city. In anticipation of the final phase of Israeli-Palestinian negotiations over the status and sovereignty of Jerusalem, the Olmert administration has been cognizant of the potentially negative effects on Israel's political claims of the historic and current service and spending differentials. It sees increased spending in Arab neighborhoods as a way to secure continued Jewish control over the city. I. Cohen, (Jerusalem city manager, interview), admits that "imbalances make it harder for Israel to say 'the city is unified.'" As such, these municipal efforts must be seen as attempts to consolidate Israel's negotiating position over Jerusalem through the positioning of the Municipality as benign caretaker of its Arab residents.

This incremental narrowing of the service gaps between Jewish and Arab communities is a "political tactic" (U. Ben-Asher, district planner for Jerusalem, interview). The municipal government sees this strategy as capable of countering the Arab argument that the city is not truly unified because there are two types of citizens—one serviced and Jewish; the other underserviced and Arab. A. Melamed (Arab Advisor of the Municipality, interview), suggests that in these negotiations Israel will have to support its moral claim to the city, and that the city must treat its Arab residents as human beings or let them tend to their affairs. Service gap narrowing in this scenario makes sense both morally and politically. Regarding the Olmert administration's spending plan, J. Abu-Shakrah, formerly with the Palestine Human Rights Information Center (interview), states that provision of urban services is what moves people and that "This is what will make or break your sovereignty . . . your ability to govern."

In the end, both Kollek and Olmert bear witness to the complex relationship between political rhetoric and urban administrative realities. Kollek's benign gap widening and neglect can be contrasted with Olmert's symbolic gap narrowing in pursuit of political ends. In Kollek's case, his rhetoric about a peaceful and coexistent multicultural mosaic was in contrast to his administration's acceptance of, if not active participation in, Israeli partisan service delivery and planning. In Olmert's case, his strong interests in safeguarding a unified Jewish hegemony over Jerusalem has necessitated what on the surface appear to be equity-oriented urban strategies. The final status international negotiations over Jerusalem present Olmert with a political timeline never faced by Kollek and requires that Olmert select urban administrative tactics not necessarily consistent with his personal beliefs, but nonetheless essential for securing his government's ultimate goal of political control.

5

Partisanship and the Palestinians

The Internal Dynamics of Partisanship

The primary motivation behind my practice of urban planning has been the trauma of the Holocaust and the lesson it taught that we can not count on anybody but ourselves.

—Yehonathan Golani,
Director, planning administration,
Israeli Ministry of the Interior,
in an interview

To gain a deeper understanding of Israeli urban policy formulation and implementation regarding Jerusalem, one must go beyond the analysis of ideology and policy to study specific institutional contexts and individual participants. This section portrays the intergovernmental and psychological issues and tensions involved in creating and carrying out partisan planning policy.

The Intersection of National and Municipal Imperatives

Since 1967, the central government has shaped or preempted the goals and strategies of local planning as sovereignty issues penetrate the city landscape. National interests revolving around political, demographic, and security aspects have dominated municipal objectives aimed at liveability and sustainability. National goals have sought to extend the Jewish city geographically and demographically, control the heights for military security, reconnect formerly partitioned areas through building of a west-to-east Jewish development bridge, and build Jewish neighborhoods in ways that prevent political re-division of the city. In contrast, municipal-level interests in Jerusalem emphasized the maintenance of a city scale that would be sustainable in terms of transportation, liveability, and municipal finance. These municipal goals were obstructed by the development of satellite Jewish neighborhoods that stretched and stressed the urban system. Peripheral development of Ramot Allon and Gilo, for example, on the next ridge of hills away from the city center imposes severe urban service demands on the municipal fiscus.[1] Such satellite growth ran counter to city goals of consolidating the city scale so as to create a "definite city-site" identifiable as one city and one central business district. Municipal imperatives toward the condensation of city scale and attending to the needs of the inner city were cancelled out by central government's strategies of enlarging and widening Jerusalem to strengthen Israel's claims to the city.

In this intersection of national and municipal imperatives, national prerogatives have been dominant due to two main reasons. First, a national consensus was sufficiently intact regarding the political goal of city unification. This allowed the development and budgetary organs of the central state, and central planning system, to override the regulatory and municipal planning systems. R. Alterman, professor of planning at Technion University (interview), describes the planning system's ability to meet its goals as "an achievement not of regulatory planning, but due to a consensus between political parties and the capacity for budgeting and development." Second, the centralized structure of Israeli planning enables national government strategies to be implemented with minimal municipal influence. The Jerusalem district planning commission, which oversees local municipal plans and has approval power over most local building permits, is dominated by representatives of central government ministries. It is this body through which most national development goals and strategies are implemented, with or without Municipality agreement. For example, in the central government's desire to maintain Jewish-Arab demographic ratios, Uri Ben-Asher, district planner for the Jerusalem District (interview), states that:

If the Municipality allowed "too much" Arab growth, we cut them. This was done according to "central" government policy.

There was no need to rationalize on other criteria basis [*sic*] such as environmental.

Such "cutting" of Arab growth was done through the district commission's modification of local plans to lower allowable density or decrease the amount of land area allowed to be built upon.

Another example of national-level superiority involves the most active central government body in development—the national Ministry of Housing and Construction. Having both planning and implementation powers, it has the power to change outline plans and modify green area designations. The ministry does have to put its proposals before the local planning commission (Municipality-level), but if the local government does not approve a ministry project, the ministry will take its proposal to the district commission level, which can overturn local decisions. In this way, national urban policy bypasses and overrides municipal resistance, when it exists. The Israeli planning case points to a potentially generalizable conclusion. The implementation of fundamental national ideologies (such as city unification) appears to require a centralized planning and policy apparatus capable of bypassing municipal-level concerns about urban sustainability and quality of life.

As is, the hierarchical central-municipal government relationship involves a division of labor between the two levels. Central government strategies, frequently initiated by the Ministry of Housing and approved through a district planning commission, establish the basic parameters of Jerusalem development, including where growth will occur and at what magnitude. City planners then attempt to influence "bit" adjustments within the proposed neighborhoods, dealing with density, physical connections, school siting and provision, architectural design, and open space provision. N. Sidi, city planner (interview), states that in the proposals for new Jewish neighborhoods initiated by the Ministry of Housing in annexed east Jerusalem, the main role of the Municipality was to "work on the open space and service correlates of these development proposals." This division of labor between central and local government is analogous to a decisionmaking model referred to as "mixed scanning" by Etzioni (1968). Major or fundamental decisions are made by central government or its affiliates and shape Jerusalem development on a citywide or community scale. In contrast, minor or "bit" decisions are taken by the Municipality and affect development more on a neighborhood or micro-scale. These "bit" decisions by local government seldom reach to a level of deciding whether or not the project would be built, or what the size of the new neighborhood should be. In one case where it did, the Ramot Allon proposal, the city organized opposition to the proposal's size. A subsequent central-local government compromise decreased planned dwelling units from fifteen thousand to eight thousand and left the eastern part of the area as open space. Indicative of where the true planning power lies, part of this "green area" has subsequently been opened up due to internal political reasons for the development of the ultra-orthodox Jewish community of Shuafat Ridge.

It should not be deduced from this portrayal of central government hegemony, however, that there was a progressive Labor-led local planning apparatus that was crushed by Likud central government dictates. Indeed, the majority of Israeli planners interviewed felt that agreement between national and municipal officials was more prevalent than disagreement, and that any differences that did exist were more often form than substance. M. Benvenisti (interview) states adamantly that almost all major growth decisions were taken by central government, and that Kollek had little interest in land-use planning policy. In the end, Benvenisti states that "Kollek was not a fighter. He never fought for anything. He never said, 'now these are my instructions regarding the master planning of Jerusalem.'" Another insider at the time, S. Kaminker (interview), suggests that the Labor coalition that held together the Kollek regime for twenty-seven years "brought in non-ideological, liberal constituencies that facilitated the long-term maintenance of a strategic and ideologically-based planning approach." She feels that Kollek's "was not a liberal administration as far as the Arabs were concerned." At the same time that Kollek hid behind a liberal image, liberals participating in his governing coalition "closed off Arab east Jerusalem from their minds." In another account (E. Barzacchi, former city engineer, interview), municipal objections to central government proposals were based more on political maneuvering between Labor and Likud parties than on genuine substantive planning-based reasons.

Kollek did stand firm on one conviction, that regarding the juxtaposition of new Jewish development relative to Arab communities. The municipal administration effectively postponed central government desires to directly penetrate existing Arab communities through neighborhood-level integration. Kollek believed strongly in the two ethnic groups living side by side whereby a Jewish community may be next to an Arab one, but not individuals integrated on the neighborhood level.[2] Stressing a mosaic pattern of residential location as most desirable and in line with historic patterns of the city, Kollek's belief was that Jews and Arabs should "live near each other, not with each other" (E. Barzacchi, interview).

"This Was a Glorious Time": The Psychology of Israeli Planning

> One must understand conflicts that you can not resolve and see them as an inseparable part of our lives.
>
> —Y. Golani, Ministry of the Interior. Included in list of personal planning principles, prepared for ministry staff upon retirement from central government after thirty years of service

This section examines the perceptual and psychological characteristics of urban planners and policymakers practicing within such an ideological context, and draws primarily from the interviews conducted with Israeli planners. I ask the following questions. How do Israeli professional planners, trained in the objective and technical processes of information gathering, forecasting, and policy articulation, respond within an environment of partisan planning? To what extent are the personal preferences of practicing planners in line with the ideological stance of the planning apparatus within which they operate? What are the personal histories and beliefs that guide urban professionals in the performance of their work in a contested city? It is my belief that in Jerusalem, as in other cities of contested identity and political control, human emotions are an integral part of urban day-to-day living and professional practice. Leaving such emotional content out of this study of urban policy would unnecessarily sterilize a vibrant and emotion-laden landscape. Through attention to planners' and policymakers' *beliefs* and *perceptions* about their roles and functions, we may learn about the ability of individual planners to affect change in the operationalization of fundamental ideology in order to improve the living environment of Jerusalem and other contested urban systems.

Israeli planners interviewed were almost all aware of the partisan nature of their planning practice. Nor was there self-denial about the ultimate effects of planning actions on the city landscape. I. Kimhi (interview) asserts that:

> We planners have harmed the coexistence of the two nations and peoples. If planned the right way, then both nations can develop here in Jerusalem.

Y. Golani (interview) describes himself as an open-minded liberal; yet, "On this issue I cannot be indifferent. I can not speak objectively. You can not be about this situation." Indeed, one major motivation he cites that has driven his planning career is the trauma of the Holocaust and "that we can not count on anybody but ourselves; that we have to have our own territory and be able to control our own territory." B. Hyman, Director of Local Planning, Ministry of Interior (interview), jumps in his discussion of Jerusalem between functional planning arguments and political considerations and ultimately states, "it is hard to work out anything that resembles a 'natural solution.'" In making professional choices between planning and political criteria, he states:

> We are first of all Israelis and officers of the government of Israel. First and foremost.

Yet, within this ideological and political context, Israeli planners exert and utilize professional planning expertise. Morley and Shachar (1986) suggest that in dealing with issues that involve strong value conflicts, planners adopt nonideological postures and seek legitimation for an objective methodology of planning. Some interviewees spoke forthrightly about this legitimation function. S. Moshkovitz, Director of Central Planning Department, Civil Administration for Judea and Samaria (West Bank) [interview], explains that his goal is to assure "that political expression is done in the most professional way possible." Similarly, B. Hyman asserts that "We try to make the political decisions sensible from the professional planning point of view." And U. Ben-Asher, District Planner for Jerusalem District, Ministry of the Interior (interview), declares that his goal is to "maintain professional principles within this politically determined context." The function of these professional planning techniques applied to political decisions is seen by others interviewed to have less a legitimizing role than a humanizing effect on Jerusalem residents. This perception is brought forth by I. Kimhi, former city planner: "For the last twenty-seven years, we have made a very clear statement. Everything that was done, though, was done in a humane way. I know how it was done." Similarly, current city planner N. Sidi explains how she has learned to be "flexible and creative within this political environment." She recounts her distaste of efforts to penetrate Jewish growth into Arab sectors, and describes how "sometimes I can find an elegant solution" by proposing alternative sites for proposed Jewish development. This harkens back to the basic assumptions of town planning during the British Mandate period 1917–1948. Although conscious of Arab-Jew divisions, the British protectorates saw planning as a way of neutralizing ethnic conflict. Ethnic conflict could be ameliorated through a logical and reasonable planning approach in which the rational could diffuse the political.

It was striking how Israeli planners could live comfortably with the two worlds—one ideological; the other technical. Planning in a contentious environment presents planners and other urban professionals with a dichotomous professional identity which many planners interviewed did not seek to escape or hide from. Nevertheless, planners' personal relationship to the contentiousness of the political parameters within which they work is an ambiguous one. On the one hand, there is frustration and impotence; on the other hand, attraction and intrigue. Some interviewees were frustrated by the constant politicization of their work and sought psychological security through reliance on their professional niche and skills. Consistent with Morley and Shachar (1986), several planners compartmentalized their role through emphases on professional methodologies and arguments of functionality and practicality. This provided them with a "safe space" within which to address emotion-laden controversial topics. For instance, I. Kimhi asserts that the minute one talks about sovereignty, planning becomes impossible. Instead, there is the need to "postpone issues of sovereignty; instead, let's talk over the next five–ten years on a practical level—how we can live together." He relies on functional argument, recommending that "It's a matter of finding the right way of handling things." N. Sidi explained the difficulties of planning and project implementation in Arab sectors of the city in terms of "objective conditions, not political" even through these objective conditions only superficially account for the multiple constraints facing Palestinians.

The compartmentalization of a planner's expertise area within the political context came through most interestingly in the discussion with district planner and architect Uri Ben-Asher. When asked about the most important policy decision that has guided Jerusalem development, he first stated that it was the decision to preserve green areas in the region and to create a greenbelt around the city. He also was proud of the maintenance of architectural standards (pertaining to stone facades); since "even politicians accepted these rules, in the eye of the architect, most political decisions have had little effect." Yet, later in the interview, he forthrightly and in a non-self-contradictory way spoke of the dominating effect of demographic dictates on the composition of Jerusalem residents. Thus, at first he answered within a frame of reference provided by his architectural training and expertise. This seemed to provide him with a psychological security blanket or "safe space" within which to approach such a contentious topic as Jerusalem development policy. The compartmentalization of expertise relative to the political context appeared to provide many interviewees with the ability to cope with the larger politics and emotion-laden inquiries and issues.

Separation of the professional from the political becomes more problematic in planning that affects the West Bank territory that lies outside the Israeli-defined Jerusalem municipal borders. S. Moshkovitz (interview) was involved in the formulation of a regional road scheme in the West Bank (1991 Partial Regional Scheme for Roads #50). This network of "strategic roads" is to link Jewish settlements and bypass Palestinian population centers and play an instrumental role for Israel in the implementation of the Oslo 2 agreement signed late September 1995. These roads are key to increasing Jewish settlement security in what would otherwise be Palestinian-controlled West Bank areas and will include four hundred miles of new roads and bypasses (*Jerusalem Report* 1994; Meehan 1996). Moshkovitz, in the interview, detaches himself from the political and strategic labels by stating, "My duty is not to deal with strategic roads. I don't think politically." In addition, he considers that since congestion and topographical factors were the guiding criteria "the road network would be accepted in any country." When pressed further about the role of political considerations, he states that "I'm philosophically in the middle of the political debate, so I have no problem." Finally, he admits that "There are political aims expressed in these plans; but this doesn't mean that I give my political view." Another coping mechanism used by Israeli planners during interviews was a psychological separation of an administrative "me" from a political "them." In these instances, the planner attributes to the "other" (whether it be politicians or government officials) the blatantly political decisions. The planning professional in this case positions herself as acting within the decision-space created by others. This psychological separation was in part due to a certain reality. On the other hand, the tendency was so prevalent as to make the author believe that it also constituted a defense reaction against assuming responsibility for partisan policy and its outcomes.

At the same time that some planners separated themselves from the political through coping mechanisms, other planners (and frequently the same planners but at different times) showed a fondness and attraction toward their politically contentious environment. I. Kimhi, former city planner (interview), displays the excitement over planning's salience in recounting his involvement in planning for a newly unified (Israeli-controlled) Jerusalem after 1967:

> It was a most fortunate situation for a planner—that you are needed. We were needed by the politicians—what road to open, what wall to knock down, where is the sewerage, what to do. They simply came to us—we had all the information. We were prepared for this act of reunification. It was a glorious time.

N. Sidi refers in amazement to the "whole cosmos of planning in Jerusalem." Meanwhile, U. Ben-Asher, Jerusalem district planner, finds the political environment interesting and stimulating and describes how, "without any political constraints, my work would be too abstract. It would be too general unless tied to political realities." Because it plays an instrumental role in implementing fundamental ideology, the salience of urban planning increases and fulfills a basic need of urban professionals to feel important and necessary. The irony here is that planning salience increases in a partisan approach at the same time that such planning actions can do irreparable damage to the mutual coexistence of competing ethnic or racial groups.[3]

Not all urban planners interviewed bought into the partisan style of planning. These were either Israeli planners outside of government or other urban professionals advocating a greater Palestinian autonomy regarding development issues. S. Kaminker, former urban planner with the city, dealt with her frustration by leaving government: "If employed by government, you must be an agent of government. People did not vote for you to make policy. If you can't live within that framework, then you have to leave. Then, you can throw off your 'establishment character.'" In her provision of technical planning assistance to Arab communities since leaving government, she

> with a heavy heart, must give away at times the planning principles that I was raised on to meet the political needs (of Palestinians) that are greater today. I am not going to say "we have to protect the beauty of Jerusalem, but only when it comes to the Arabs."

In summary, Israeli planners working within the governmental system exhibit a mixture of beliefs and stances within the partisan planning apparatus. They tend to be aware of partisan planning and its outcomes and realize that their ability to be objective is limited. Some are conscious that their expertise results in little more than providing professional labels to otherwise political objectives. Others have greater confidence that their actions can humanize and moderate, but not significantly affect, the implementation of fundamental ideology. A strong majority cope with their politically volatile environment by psychologically separating from it. This can occur either through the compartmentalization of their expertise through reliance on the technical arguments of their training (those of functionality, practicality, and objective conditions) and/or through the separation of an administrative "me" from a political "them." At the same time, politically partisan planning significantly increases the salience of the profession. Thus, Israeli planners are ambivalent about their political environment—experiencing feelings of both frustration and attraction. I turn now to the Arab side of the ethnic divide, including an examination of the contributions of urban professionals to the maintenance and potential reconstruction of Palestinian society.

Palestinians and Israeli Urban Policy

An iron fist kills everything that grows underneath it.

—Robin Twite, Joint Director,
Project on Managing Political Disputes,
Hebrew University, in an interview

Palestinians in Jerusalem are seen as a problem, a historical mistake, as an unwanted child.

—Ibrahim Dakkak,
Palestinian Economic Council for Development
and Reconstruction (PECDAR),
A-Ram, West Bank, in an interview

I now focus on the Palestinians of the city and region of Jerusalem—their demographic and spatial characteristics, political beliefs, and their internal cohesiveness in the face of Israeli partisan actions. I then describe several tactics of resistance they have used since 1967, and explore whether more proactive counterstrategies are possible given the current imbalance in political and economic power. I find that obstacles to Palestinian capacity building come not just from Israeli impediments but also from internal differences within Palestinian society over the meaning and desirability of democracy and grassroots local action.

Jerusalem's Palestinians

The Palestinian population within the Israeli-defined municipal borders of Jerusalem constitutes about thirty percent of the city's population. The estimated 180,000 Palestinian residents of the city in 1996 lived spread among thirty neighborhoods (see Figure 4.4, page 73). Some areas—those closest to the former green line—are urban in feel and density, such as Abu-Tor, Sheikh Jarrah, and American Colony (which comprise the Arab commercial zones), Silwan, Beit Hanina, and the Moslem Quarter of the Old City. A significant number of Arab habitation zones within the municipal border, however, are rural in character, with scattered buildings and low levels of physical infrastructure and social services. Such areas include Arab es-Sawahra, Jebel Mukabber, Issawiya, and the refugee camp of Shuafat. Many of these villages were brought within the municipal borders upon the threefold expansion by Israeli authorities of the municipal borders after 1967. The vast majority of Arab population in the metropolitan region lives outside the Israeli-defined municipal borders, with particular concentrations just beyond and adjacent to the Israeli-defined city. These nodes of population include the urban clusters of Ramallah and Bethlehem (combined population approximately 100,000), and the semi-urban communities of A-Ram, e-Azariya, and Abu Dis (combined population approximately 41,000) [see Figure 5.1].[4] The Palestinian population outside the municipal borders more than compensates for the Arab minority status within the municipality, resulting in a metropolitan region that in the early 1990s was about 54 percent Palestinian (Mazor and Cohen 1994).

Many Arab communities, both inside and outside the Israeli municipal border, are separated from Jewish communities through natural features (valleys in the case of Issawiya and A-Ram) or man-made features, such as highways (such as Wadi Joz in inner east

Figure 5.1 Arab Neighborhood of A-Ram outside Israeli-Defined Jerusalem, Looking Northward from within Israeli-Defined Jerusalem

Source: Scott A. Bollens

Jerusalem). Other Arab communities (such as Abu Tor, American Colony, Beit Safafa, and Jebel Mukabber), however, are immediately adjacent to Jewish areas; Arab and Jewish neighborhoods in these cases are separated more psychologically than physically. Separation between Arab and Jewish communities is also created by the Israeli-defined municipal border and Israeli checkpoints, such as in the south between Jewish Gilo and Palestinian Bethlehem/Beit Jala and in the north between Jewish Neve Yaakov and Palestinian A-Ram. Thus, the residential geography of the Jerusalem region is an intricate mosaic web of distinct Arab and Jewish communities. No integration on a street or neighborhood level occurs. The old pattern of Jewish west and Arab east Jerusalem, solidified by the twenty years of physical partition, has been overtaken by significant Jewish development and population growth east of the old dividing line. Major Jewish communities such as Neve Yaakov, Pisgat Zeev, East Talpiot, and Givat Shapira (French Hill) exist in eastern areas annexed by Israel in 1967. Indeed, Jews in 1996 made up almost 48 percent of the population in the annexed part of the Israeli-defined city.

Restrictions on Arab development within the municipality have led to the stagnation of the Jerusalem Palestinian population and have deflected Arab growth to less restricted areas outside the city borders. Many well-trained and educated Palestinians who normally would comprise an important part of the Arab Jerusalem population now reside in the centers of Ramallah or Bethlehem. Israeli restrictive policies have also led to Arab growth in what would normally be considered unlikely areas, especially those of difficult terrain. Arab growth outside the borders, largely unplanned, is often carried out without coordination of basic service provision such as roads, sewage, water, and social services. The fabric of much Arab growth outside the city borders consists of scattered and widely dispersed sets of buildings.

The result of Israeli expansionary policies and restrictions on Arab growth has been to physically fragment Arab communities and to separate them from each other.[5] The road and highway system has been built to connect Jewish communities to each other; no such connective system exists to tie together Arab communities. J. de Jong, geographer working for a Christian legal resource center (interview), explains:

Israeli policies have disconnected Palestinians from the land in and around Jerusalem by turning many areas into Jewish habitation and industrial zones connected to the Israeli metropolitan area.

Intragroup differences and tensions inherent in Arab society have been reinforced through such physical separation and neighborhood atomization. Israeli physical development policies have had a distinct and significant influence on decreasing the potential cohesiveness of the Palestinian community in and around Israeli Jerusalem. J. Abu-Shakrah, formerly with a Palestinian human rights organization (interview) concludes that, "The decimation and breaking up of East Jerusalem has left no feeling of community, of common history, common future, common cause." With no "community of interests," internal conflicts among the Palestinians play themselves out; for example, between landowners and renters and between the oligarchical families and the younger professionals. This lack of commonality leads some to conclude, such as A. Aghazarian, public relations director for Birzeit University in Ramallah (interview), that, "We're more conquered than those in Gaza. They as least have an identification."

In examining the Jerusalem Palestinian population and its potential responses to Israeli expansionary policies, it is important to note that this population is socially heterogeneous. This is due in part to the incorporation of many different types of Arab villages into the municipal structure of the city post-1967. In some cases, intra-Arab differences in income and education are greater than Arab-Jewish differences (Ashkenasi 1988b). The richest subquarter of Beit Hanina, for example, can be contrasted with the poverty conditions of the depressed village conditions of Silwan. In terms of political orientation, the political moderation of Beit Safafa (which is on both sides of the old green line and contains a significant percentage of Israeli Arabs) is in marked contrast to the Islamic fundamentalist orientation of the poorest subquarter, the Shuafat refugee camp.

A survey of Jerusalem's Arab residents in 1987 found that a majority held a moderate political view[6] advocating a secular Palestinian state, one consistent with the Arafat/Fatah[7] position (Ashkenasi 1990). Concerning Jerusalem specifically, the sentiment supported division, not accommodation—there was twice as much support for an east-west political division of the city than there was for an "open city." Support for the creation of a secular Palestinian state was especially strong among established Jerusalemites, such as the self-employed, Christians, Muslims over thirty years old, and those in the larger subquarters of Beit Hanina, Al-Tur, and the Old City. However, according to Ashkenasi, this moderate group contains many disparate subgroups and has not crystallized politically. Due to Israeli restrictions, no formal structure of municipal or community governance exists to organize and hold these moderate groups together. Ominously, Ashkenasi (1990) declared that the lack of political reform and economic programs aimed at Arab Jerusalem will over time enable Islamic fundamentalism and political intolerance, especially among the Palestinian young, to take root and find expression in Jerusalem. One sign that such a shift in political allegiances is occurring in Jerusalem's Arab population is that elections for the East Jerusalem Chamber of Commerce, once a bastion of moderate Jordanian Hashemites, has been postponed for years for fear among the Israelis that the more extreme Hamas faction could win a majority.

There is a tension inherent in the effects of Israeli policies on the Palestinian community. Physical and social fragmentation have hindered the development of a cohesive Palestinian population and allowed the city government to administer the city with a minimum of friction and maximum benefit to Jewish residents. Contacts that did exist between the administration and Palestinians were neighborhood-based, and goods and services were made available on the basis of whether a particular neighborhood cooperated with the city administration. Several major Palestinian family units profited under this cooperative arrangement with the city administration. At the same time, however, this neighborhood-based cooptative arrangement leaves out noncooperating areas and those younger Palestinians not part of the traditional family-based oligarchic structure of Arab society. These frustrations create the conditions for the growth of religious fundamentalism and extremist actions. Ashkenasi (1988b) astutely states that, "the *intifada* was as much a revolt against Palestinian society that had led to fragmentation and relative docility as a revolt against Israeli occupation." In the end, Israeli urban policy that has facilitated Israeli domination of the urban political landscape may be creating the very conditions of Palestinian extremism and antagonism that it set out to suppress in the first place.

*   *   *

Given a situation where the internal differences within the Arab population are occurring in an environment of Israeli control that seeks to physically fragment and submerge it, Palestinian self-interest has tended to rise above public interest. R. Abdulhadi, Arab planner in the West Bank city of Ramallah (interview), states that:

Occupation, fragmentation, and the absence of a national authority have deprived the Palestinian people of the opportunity to develop a framework of public interest.

With no legitimate source of governance in Jerusalem and in a "community that is being constantly re-charged with anger and hatred,"[8] individual action increasingly occurs without accepted rules. Lacking vehicles for organized political expression, unorganized political activism can quickly cross over into criminal action. M. Warshawski, of an Arab-Jewish joint nongovernmental organization (interview), asserts that:

> In my nightmares, I see Jerusalem as a Jewish city with a Palestinian ghetto—depoliticized, demobilized, and criminalized.

Further adding to the splintering of the Jerusalem Palestinian population are two dynamics occurring regarding political leadership: 1) an uneasy relationship between local and national Palestinian leadership; and 2) shifts within local leadership away from reliance on traditional leaders. According to the Palestinian Academic Society for the Study of International Affairs (PASSIA 1993b), there are three schools of Palestinian thought concerning Jerusalem:

- Mainstream: consisting of professionals and Palestinian Liberation Organization (PLO) leadership and followers.

- Opposition: a) secular, which lack an alternative political agenda to the current Palestinian-Israel peace process; and b) religious, well organized and ideologically driven, existing outside the peace process.

- "Silent majority in the communities," who are critical of Palestinian leadership and fear the absence of a clear strategy for dealing with Jerusalem.

There is a local leadership within Palestinian Jerusalem that feels neglected or overshadowed by national political leader, Yasser Arafat, and his negotiations with Israel over West Bank autonomy. One leader,[9] for example, expresses the frustration in this way:

We look to the PLO, but they are outside. Palestinian leadership is too diffused, tending to the needs of Palestinians worldwide. When you go from generalities to particulars, like Jerusalem, you have a problem.

The problem is that national leadership is supplying little guidance to local Jerusalem leaders regarding how they should address day-to-day and longer-term city-based issues. J. Abu-Shakrah, formerly of a Palestinian human rights organization (interview), states:

Community mobilization from the bottom up that is needed to counteract Israeli actions is difficult because Palestinian people are used to it being a nationalist thing most properly in the hands of politicians. Yet, these national politicians are more interested in the symbolic level of Jerusalem, not the people that live there.

An additional complexity facing Jerusalem Palestinians are tensions internally between the traditional leadership, a younger generation raised in the *intifada*, and an emerging professional class. Since the *intifada* (1987–1993), the power of the old guard of local leadership (mukhtars and religious leaders) has been on the decline (I. Dakkak, interview). The problem, however, is that an alternative local leadership has not yet emerged. Much of the younger generation gained experience during the *intifada*, and thus they "don't know how to deal with local issues, but are interested in nationalist issues" (S. Hasson, Hebrew University, interview). I. Dakkak (interview) states that "The time is not yet right for the leadership from the *intifada*." He describes a grassroots feeling among Jerusalem Palestinians today that is very much alive, yet lacking in organization and sustainability of leadership. With this local vacuum of power, the potential is present for increased criminality based on individual behavior and a growing identification with Islamic fundamentalism, which is capable of supplying an identification for the young Palestinians they do not currently have.

The local leader in the Jerusalem Palestinian population is Faisal Husseini, who is Minister without portfolio in charge of Jerusalem Affairs for the Palestinian National Authority. He is aligned with the Hebronite branch of Palestinians in Jerusalem, a branch that has control over the Arab commercial center. Another branch, those born in Jerusalem, is not necessarily loyal to Husseini (Z. al Qaq, international director, Israel-Palestine Center for Research and Information, interview). At the same time, M. Abdul Hadi, president of the Palestinian Academic Society for the Study of International Affairs (interview), describes a tension between the old oligarchical familial lines and a professional class of local Palestinians. He explains:

> There are two sides to Palestinian society—are we seeing a change from the old guard to the new professionals? If so, in an emerging society, at what speed should this transition take place? After all, Husseini has the name. Can they be combined?

Thus, the Palestinian society in Jerusalem is a community amidst contest that exhibits tensions regarding appropriate leadership. These strains, inherent in many Arab societies, are exacerbated by Israeli policies that have extended the spatial reach of Jewish development and contracted and fragmented Palestinian habitation and commercial zones. As J. de Jong, geographer (interview), notes, "Israel makes effective use of the vacuum of no Palestinian state." However, such a vacuum also provides opportunities for the entry of Islamic fundamentalist ideas into Jerusalem Palestinian society. M. Doudi, project officer for the Society for Austro-Arab Relations (interview), claims that the Islamists can supply an important identification to the younger population, are highly educated, have a clear vision and a systematic approach, based on provision of basic human needs, to winning over followers.

The complex and splintered characteristics of Jerusalem Palestinian society have important implications for the coherency and effectiveness of both (1) short-term tactics of resistance to Israeli control in Jerusalem and (2) longer-term comprehensive counterstrategies. I evaluate these tactics and strategies in the next two essays.

Tactics of Resistance

Four tactics of Palestinian resistance to Israeli control over Jerusalem are evident: (1) electoral non-participation/ boycott; (2) *sumud* or steadfastness; (3) building and development outside Israeli control mechanisms; and (4) community activism and protests.

A consistent tactic since 1967 has been the Palestinian boycotting of municipal elections that they view as illegitimate. Since 1969, no more than 21 percent of Arabs ever voted for Jerusalem mayor (Romann and Weingrod 1991). In the November 1993 election, only 3 percent of the city's Arab residents voted as a consequence of a PLO-ordered boycott and despite pleas by moderate Israelis that such a low turnout would enable a Likud majority in the city council (Friedland and Hecht 1996).[10] This boycotting has two effects. First, Palestinians undoubtedly lose out in the distribution of urban services and spending because there are no Arab voices on the city council. It provides a rationale to Israeli leaders for service disparities because Palestinians are not playing the local politics game. Second, Arab boycotting gives support to their nonrecognition of what they, and the international community, consider an illegitimate claim of municipal authority.

I. Dakkak, member of PECDAR (interview) portrays the Palestinian view:

> The city council is a mechanism whereby I have to abdicate my rights because it considers past Israeli actions as fait accompli. Some have told me it was a mistake for Palestinians not to participate in municipal elections. They're right in a way, but wrong in many ways. We may have gotten more in urban services, but an implicit recognition of Israel's sovereignty would be tantamount to surrendering. Those from the Israeli left who say such things have the convenience of being an Israeli.

A minority view is held by J. Abu-Shakrah, formerly of a Palestinian human rights organization (interview):

> Palestinians should participate in the municipality and protest and object. This is how disparities can be highlighted, not by boycotting. This boycott mentality has been one of the worse effects of life in Jerusalem. Palestinians don't have to play by the municipality's rules, but they should know the rules and learn how to manipulate them. They should protest against them and show them for the baggage that they are.

H. Siniori, publisher of *Biladi-The Jerusalem Times* (interview), was one Palestinian who has advocated for Palestinian electoral participation. He states that Palestinians "misperceived that participation would mean giving up our claim of sovereignty. Yet, perceptions are more important than practicalities and you cannot preach something that people cannot accept."

A second important Palestinian practice has been that of *sumud* or steadfastness. Locally, this means "staying on the land" and protecting the status quo in terms of the Palestinian presence in and around Jerusalem. H. Siniori (interview) states that "Palestinian society has never given up regarding their self-sufficiency, their attachment to the land, their ability to survive and even grow in the face of occupation." Protest is through not moving, using the land, and maintaining Palestinian "facts on the ground." H. Law-Yone, planning professor at Technion (interview) describes how this tactic is consistent with Arabs' intimate view of the land as sustenance and life, as providing meaning, and as communal. In addition, he explains, "Arabs' view of the land is long-term. They feel it will come back to them; that all Jewish growth and development is reversible and temporary."

The steadfastness tactic is related to the third stratagem—building and development outside of Israeli control mechanisms. Such Arab building within Israeli-defined Jerusalem is frequently viewed as "illegal" building by Israeli authorities. House demolitions by Israeli authorities then can occur due to the lack of a building permit. E. Felner (B'TSELEM, interview) contends that the number of demolitions is low compared to the number of units built without a permit. Still, demolitions (often highly publicized) along with Israeli restrictions on Arab growth in the city force Palestinians needing living space to live in a "closed circle." They must either leave the city, live in inhumane conditions of overcrowding in the city, or build "illegally" under constant threat of demolition. A fourth channel is open—attempt to build consistent with Israeli regulatory and control mechanisms. I. Dakkak (interview) bitterly recalled the dilemma he faced in his unsuccessful effort:

> Should I go ahead with the detailed plan and development scheme as required by municipal authorities or should I stick with my political position not to do it. The outcome of my efforts? I feel like an unwanted baby. I am used to Israeli behavior.

One response to the tight Israeli controls in the city is to build outside municipal borders. Under less restrictive Israeli Civil Administration[11] land use requirements outside the city, Palestinian growth has occurred in areas such as E-Azariya (20,000 population) and Abu Dis (20,000) to the east, and A-Ram (45,000) to the north. This development pattern facilitates and reinforces spatial separation of Palestinians from Israeli-defined Jerusalem, a result not inconsistent with Israeli goals concerning the city's sovereignty. Nonetheless, it builds up the Palestinian presence in the metropolitan region at large and this may have important implications in future international negotiations.

A final tactic of Palestinian resistance relies on community activism and protest actions against Israeli development plans and projects (see Figure 5.2). This is problematic because such protests tend to be reactive to plans and projects that have progressed to the point where ground breaking is about to occur. The hope of such protests is to bring international attention to the issue of Israeli development strategies in annexed Jerusalem and in the "West Bank" part of the metropolitan region. However, community activism is not a normal part of many Arab societies, is restricted in the Jerusalem case by the legacy of disempowerment, and is further dampened locally by the national-level focus of many Palestinian politicians. Protesting Jewish development plans through community activism or legal action in the midst of negotiations over Jerusalem sovereignty poses a challenge to Palestinians. M. Warshawski (interview), an Israeli progressive activist, describes the Palestinian population in Jerusalem as less mobilized than those in the West Bank due to three factors: (1) they are better off in terms of socioeconomic conditions and thus have more to lose; (2) the atomization of Arab neighborhoods previously described; and (3) an unconscious adoption by Jerusalem Arabs of Israel's oft-repeated slogan that Jerusalem is their "eternal and undivided capital." He continues:

> There is a certain Palestinian passivity toward the whole of life, especially in Jerusalem. This is somewhat understandable since every concrete decision in Israeli courts concerning development goes against them. Their impression is that all will be negotiated in the future. Thus, there is the feeling that resistance today is unimportant or inefficient. Meanwhile, however, the world is changing around them.

Warshawski recounts protest actions against Israeli actions that drew far more Israeli progressive activists than Palestinian residents from neighborhoods that would be affected by Israeli plans.

Figure 5.2   Outside Jerusalem City Hall

Source: Scott A. Bollens

He concludes that, "Israeli progressive activists cannot be alone. The victims must be deeply involved in defending their own rights." In attempting to inform Palestinian residents of Israeli actions that will have profound effects on them, "We have discovered that Palestinians know very little about urban issues that will affect their livelihood." A case in point is the planned Har Homa Jewish neighborhood in southern Jerusalem. This planned neighborhood of more than six thousand housing units would link with Gilo to the west, closing out the connection between Bethlehem and Jerusalem. It would have major adverse effects on the Arab Bethlehem area, be two minutes from Arab homes, and would be built on "reserve land" of the Arab neighborhood of Beit Sahur. Yet, when Warshawski gave a lecture and tour of southern Jerusalem to make Palestinian activists aware of Israeli development plans, "It was like I was giving a report on Rwanda. I found apathy and unawareness."

The seeming Palestinian passivity in the face of Israeli partisan actions can be traced to three sources, in particular. First, the boycott mentality among Palestinians may have extended to encompass community-based protests against any municipal actions. In this view, community and legal protests may erroneously be seen by some Palestinians as recognizing the authority of Israel over Jerusalem. J. Abu-Shakrah (interview) is correct to point out, however, that "interacting with and fighting the municipality is recognition of de facto sovereignty, but not de jure sovereignty." Second, the debilitating effects on the Arab psyche of almost thirty years of disempowerment should not be underestimated. S. Kaminker (interview) states that tactics and technical assistance must be employed to help these communities gain confidence that they can affect change. Once this confidence is gained, "They can leap from being victims to being citizens with some form of empowerment." J. de Jong, trained geographer who has worked for a nongovernmental organization, describes the important role of "empowering groups that those in authority do not want empowered." He emphasizes the critical role of information gathering and provision in a Palestinian society he views as "exhausted and demoralized." Land-based information can stimulate a "realistic sense of urgency," make leadership on both sides of the contest accountable to the facts, and inform the international audience about the effects of Israeli partisan planning strategies. A third reason behind limited Arab community-based action is that there is the belief that it will not be concrete protests and legal actions that will solve the Jerusalem problem, but the "final status" negotiations concerning the city. Here, there is reliance on national leaders, not local actions, to resolve the Jerusalem conflict. This feeling is in part derived from the *sumud* stratagem, which seeks to maintain the status quo while waiting for a solution from the outside (either from the PLO or the international community). The problem with this view, though, is that while Palestinians have awaited the negotiations, Israel has been seeking to predetermine the parameters of such negotiations and to strengthen their position at the negotiation table through their ongoing housing and road construction plans in annexed Jerusalem.

Although Palestinian spokesmen such as Faisal Husseini state that the battle over Jerusalem has started, it is not a battle that has effectively used grassroots community-based activism. M. Warshawski (interview) asserts that "there needs to be a connection between the high, diplomatic actions of the PLO and 'on the ground' grassroots actions of the victims themselves."[12] Without national guidance, local actions are unrooted and unorganized. An obstacle faced by local activists is explained by J. Abu-Shakrah (interview):

People are afraid to move outside the "political frame" of the PLO, which they have relied on for years. If they move outside this frame to deal independently with urban issues, they are afraid to be labelled as "collaborator."

A troubling irony exists in this interplay between local and national Palestinian interests. That which appears necessary on the urban level to further Palestinian interests—community-based activism and protests against Israeli expansionary policies—may run counter to the more authoritarian propensities of national Palestinian leadership. J. de Jong, geographer for the Christian-based NGO (interview), asserts that, "Palestinian leadership does not want a local democratic surge even if it costs them Jerusalem." He witnesses an accommodation between national Palestinian leaders and locally-based Jerusalem leaders that "stifles political culture and destroys the capacity to mobilize." M. Benvenisti (interview) points to the inexperience of Arab societies with democratic political processes and the importance of developing a "civil society" of non-governmental activist and advocacy organizations. J. de Jong (interview) agrees with this assessment and describes its effect:

There is no "public political domain" in the Arab world. In Jordan, they can get away with this because there is not Israel next door to take advantage of the vacuum. For Palestinians, though, it is killing them.

Palestinians admit to this troubling attribute of Arab society and polity. One source[13] states that efforts to create a locally based Arab democratic city council in Jerusalem would likely be suppressed by Palestinian National Authority ministries and Fatah. Although such democratization of the local Palestinian community could potentially increase Israeli acceptance of Arab autonomy in Jerusalem, this appears unacceptable to national Arab politicians. As the source states, "We must eventually allow people to choose between Arafat power and people power." Another Arab source[14] describes Palestinian leadership as "popularistic, but not popular" and worries about the Arab world's propensity toward demagoguery. The source feels that the potential for local leadership is there, but is currently being suppressed by national leadership. This issue is a point of sensitivity among Palestinians. I asked

Z. Abu Zayyad (interview), experienced in high-level peace talks with the Israelis, about this issue. His answer reflected both a political sensitivity and posture.

> There are not leaders at the local level, but spokespeople. We are all cautious about the need for a single address for the Palestinian National Authority. We need to be represented as coherent, not fragmented. Local spokespeople "complete but not compete" with the national PNA.

Counterstrategies

> In the history of colonial invasion maps are always first drawn by the victors, since maps are instruments of conquest.
>
> —Edward Said,
> *Al-Hayat*, December 10, 1993

> A major weakness in almost all liberation struggles is the absence of proactive and alternative plans.
>
> —Miloon Kothari,
> Habitat International Coalition:
> United Nations Representative,
> in an interview

> We will use all possible means to enhance the Palestinian presence in Jerusalem.
>
> —Samir Abdallah,
> Director, Economic Policy and Project Selection,
> Palestinian Economic Council for Development
> and Reconstruction (PECDAR), in an interview

The resistance actions just discussed suffer from several limitations. They are either reactive and not sustainable (community protests), based on individual rather than collective actions (*sumud* and Arab building), or premised on a boycott mentality that does not pose an alternative future (electoral nonparticipation). M. Benvenisti (interview) observes that "Palestinians are not creating facts in the old Zionist fashion." What he means by this is that Arab building in and around Jerusalem is done individually, out of need, and often without basic services like roads and sewerage. Thus, in an Arab-Jewish land use war, Palestinians are unable to compete with the coherency, magnitude, and quality of Israeli Ministry of Housing projects. This section examines whether Palestinians can transcend these limitations of resistance tactics to develop a comprehensive, communally based and proactive set of strategies aimed at countering Israeli expansionary policies in and around Jerusalem.

Kothari's statement at the start of this section reflects a common difficulty among societies fighting for their freedom—the challenge of moving from resistance to an existing reality to the formulation of an alternative one based on vision and institution building.[15] J. Abu-Shakrah (interview) states that:

> Palestinians have not yet made the leap from resistance to community building—moving from threat and reaction to a proactive and sustainable framework for action. *Sumud*—staying on the land—is important; but there is no movement toward the next step—active initiation.

In her West Bank work, Abu-Shakrah has helped form ad hoc committees of villagers to counteract Israeli master plans. Yet, without thinking about the village proactively as a community, these counteractions (such as the filing of objections to Israeli authorities) remain solely reactive to planned Israeli actions. Thus, "The Palestinian Authority needs to provide a planning framework within which local communities can act." R. Abdulhadi, who has prepared "counterplans" for West Bank and Jerusalem villages, states (interview) that:

> Filing objections to Israeli actions and preparing counterplans, although such plans propose an alternative future, are still basically reactive to the dominant side's actions. We must move from reactive to proactive.

A Palestinian plan or strategy for Jerusalem would signify a move away from solely reaction, would likely counter more effectively Israeli control and actions, and would help coalesce people around a common goal. M. Warshawski (interview) suggests that legal and organizational tactics have to be tied to a broader campaign over the future long-term status of Jerusalem. Not insignificantly, a plan tied to action and concrete benefits to people would have significant political benefits. M. Doudi, project officer of an Arab nongovernmental group (interview), argues that PLO leaders must shift from revolutionaries to statesmen, asserting that:

> Flag waving will not put food on the table. High politics is not enough. Economic benefits, institution building, and helping the person on the street is what is important. It's not enough to have slogans. It is always economics that is important.

A 1993 report by a Palestinian academic society stated that there, "is no Palestinian agenda on the question of Jerusalem. There has been little mobilization to create groups or national bodies to carry out the responsibilities, to face the Israeli challenges or to negotiate on proposals" (Palestinian Academic Society for the Study of International Affairs [PASSIA] 1993b). The president of PASSIA, M. Abdul Hadi (interview), asserts that there has been "only slogans so far about 'two states, two capitals, open city' and not much specification beyond that." Z. Abu Zayyad confirms that this absence remained in 1995 and explains:

> There is no time to plan such a strategy regarding Jerusalem because the PNA is working on so many issues at so many levels. Our approach to wait until negotiations is now being sabotaged ahead of time through Israeli expansion. We are now thinking about a different way of looking at the problem.

Palestinians have been and still are faced with a difficult choice between two tracks—"get into the game" and work within and against the Israeli political system to create facts on the ground through counterplans, or "play outside" and build "illegally" and emphasize final political negotiations as the main moral avenue toward sovereignty and political empowerment. The first option would likely entail the presentation of Palestinian "counterplans" before Israeli municipal authorities for approval. One Palestinian planner (interview),[16] reasons that "we had no choice but to work with authorities" in designing alternative plans for villages just outside Israeli-defined Jerusalem. However, these alternative plans were simply subsumed into larger Israeli strategies and used as the basis for expropriation. Many in the Palestinian community thus objected to his role and saw him as a collaborator. H. Law-Yone (Israeli planning professor at Technion Institute) asserts that:

> Most Palestinians would not play this game of counterplanning, which gives Israeli control over the city legitimacy. Indeed, Israelis would love for the Palestinians to do counterplanning within the formal mechanisms of the Israeli planning process.

Some observers wonder why the role of the Palestinian urban professional has not been stronger in advocating their urban cause. Z. Baran, Jewish architect/urban planner, asks in Baskin and Twite (1993, 175), "Why didn't the Palestinian professional come twenty or thirty or forty years ago and demand a master plan for their neighborhoods and create facts and put plans on the table and create public opinion and go to the media?" Others in this edited volume describe well the two tracks. C. Beckerman, advocating greater Palestinian initiative, reflects:

> [P]erhaps we should proceed on two tracks: look at what might happen in terms of urban planning if Palestinians decide to take their political rights in the existing unequitable system; and on the other hand, what can we come up with assuming that the political obstacles (to involvement) on the Palestinian side prevent this. (Baskin and Twite 1993, 172)

In a similar way, M. Safier, from University College in London, recommends

> a multiple track approach—take advantage of the existing possibilities within the Israeli-controlled situation . . . working through the mechanisms; at the same time prepare an independent Palestinian capacity to plan and develop Jerusalem on their terms. (Baskin and Twite 1993, 181)

Although informative in portraying the dilemma, these observations may reflect a false choice in reality. K. Tufakji, in recounting the dividing up of the Arab village of Beit Safafa by Israeli roads, states, "If we make objections, nobody cares. If we draw a new master plan, nobody will agree to it" (Baskin and Twite 1993, 190).

* * *

The most critical sovereign power is planning. Every line you draw
on a map is a political decision.

—Sarah Kaminker,
former urban planner,
Municipality of Jerusalem,
in an interview

We cannot dissociate the urban planning question from the underlying political conflict because confiscation, building, boundaries,
all express unequal opportunity.

—Michael Romann,
Tel Aviv University,
in Baskin and Twite (1993)

The reality of power imbalances in contemporary Jerusalem calls
for a deeper examination of the potential of Safier's second track:
"preparing an independent Palestinian capacity to plan and develop
Jerusalem on their terms." I examine two strategies—a political/ge-
ographic one; and an institutional development one[17]—as potential
means toward increasing independent Palestinian capacity. The
first strategy—political-geographic—addresses the political nature
of land development and municipal borders in the area. It would
suggest spatial options for the coalescing of the Palestinian population in Jerusalem. K. Tufakji works for the Arab Studies Society and
has been the main resource person for the Palestinian negotiating
delegation on the question of Jewish settlements. In our interview,
he stated that, for mutual coexistence to occur, one identifiable part
of Jerusalem must have an Arab majority. One option would be to
recreate the Arab pre-1967 municipal borders of east Jerusalem; in
this configuration, Tufakji estimates that 50–70 percent of the population in the 2.5 square mile area would be Arab. A second option,
based on today's annexed boundaries of "east" Jerusalem, runs up
against the reality that a substantial proportion of residents in annexed Jerusalem are now Jewish. Thus, Tufakji's required Arab majority would need to be secured through one or more of these means:

- expand borders of Jerusalem to include Arab areas east
  and north (Abu Dis, E-Azariya, and A-Ram);

- recreate the old west-east separation of Jews and Arabs by transferring, with compensation, Jewish residents from east to west;

- allow Palestinians to live inside Israeli neighborhoods in eastern sectors (such as Pisgat Zeev and Neve Yaakov). Allow for sufficient Palestinian growth on east side.

Palestinian planner R. Abdulhadi (interview) states that "There is still enough room to create a viable Palestinian Jerusalem." Most of this room to grow is currently zoned as "green area" by Israeli authorities. S. Kaminker (interview) suggests that chances still remain for Arabs to spatially "finger in" to Jerusalem from outside the borders, such as from Abu Dis. This linking of Arab settlements in and outside the municipal border would thicken the Palestinian presence on a metropolitan scale.

The second strategy aimed at building independent Palestinian capacity—institutional development—seeks to create organizations in and around Jerusalem that can sustain the Palestinian presence. Three separate tracks are evident from interviews: (1) creation of governance structures for Jerusalem Arabs; (2) establishment of public and private entities to facilitate the development process; and (3) development and maintenance of Palestinian nongovernmental "civil society" organizations.

A group of local Palestinian leaders are trying to create an Arab representative structure in east Jerusalem so as to "re-establish the Arab municipality of Jerusalem" (interview).[18] This activity is against Israeli policy, which acts sternly against the creation of any organization in east Jerusalem that establishes a Palestinian governance function. In discussions among local Palestinians, there has been identification of the need to: (1) unite, mobilize, and coordinate all Palestinian activities locally; and (2) connect national and local leadership and geography. In one proposal, a locally elected "Jerusalem National Council" would seek to extend Palestinian political influence and authority to include, if not be centralized in, Jerusalem (Palestinian Academic Society for the Study of International Relations 1993b). A preparatory committee has been working under the auspices of PASSIA to develop and operationalize the idea of a local representative structure. One of the cornerstones to this political organizing has been to bring mosque and church leaders into the process. One source stated that "religion brings people into it," along with their deeply held feelings and driving emotion. The key has been to combine the religious, nationalist, and professional sides of Palestinian society (interview). Obstacles internal to Palestinian society remain, however; in particular, the tension between local and national prerogatives. A facilitator of the local discussions regarding a potential Arab municipal council explained that they must be disconnected from the broader Arafat-centered negotiation processes—"I can not raise the final-status negotiations with the group I am nurturing" (interview). The feeling among the work committee, this source states, is "we will work for Jerusalem; but we will not negotiate Jerusalem." Another obstacle is national leadership and Fatah resistance to the development of a locally elected democratic structure in Jerusalem. Should such a local council be created, an ironic and complex future may be possible—a locally elected Palestinian council of east Jerusalem in an otherwise hierarchical Palestinian state.

Democratically accountable Palestinian governance in Jerusalem would appear to be in the interests of both Arabs and Jews. It may help stem a more radical Islamic influence in the area through its ability to hold and attract a professional class and stimulate private investment (Interviews: M. Doudi, Society for Austro-Arab Relations; S. Abdallah, Palestinian Economic Council for Development and Reconstruction). At the same time, it would bring Palestinian local governance closer to the Western democratic norms acceptable to Israel. Any potential evolution of Palestinian society in and around Jerusalem toward a more democratically based polity, however, would likely be a fragile and tenuous one. A. Melamed, municipal Arab advisor (interview), sees a growing democratization of Jerusalem Palestinians occurring due to their proximity to, and awareness of, the Israeli political system. He observes a

> slow ongoing diffusion of Israeli influence on Palestinians in Jerusalem. Whereas the Arab tradition is not democratic and thus Arabs view municipal services as a "favor," here they are beginning to base their claims to municipal services on individual "rights."

Other interviewees caution against this interpretation, however. E. Barzacchi, former city engineer (interview), is elegant on this point:

Societies go through their own rates of change regarding their concepts of land, democratic values, their urban-ness. Israeli immigrants brought with them democratic values. Now, we think we can come to a people and teach them democracy and freedom. But, you don't implant concepts of right and wrong. Rather, the Palestinians have to find their own appropriate rates and kinds of societal change.

Barzacchi views Palestinian planners and other professionals as playing an instrumental role in taking their society through this complicated process of transformation. R. Abdulhadi, who helped develop *Master Planning the State of Palestine: Suggested Guidelines for Comprehensive Development* (Center for Engineering and Planning, 1992), sees his role as "helping Palestinians articulate a long-term vision of ourselves." In an emerging society, urban professionals can hold a longer-term, and more comprehensive, view of societal transformations than do politicians. Where the former see opportunities, the latter may see threats. Israeli paternalism will not work here; rather, as N. Carmon, planning professor at Technion University (interview) states, "Let them develop their own ideas and their self-confidence so that they can then sit at the table with Israelis as partners."

Local Palestinians are aware of the fragile movement toward democracy. Z. Abu Zayyad (co-editor, *Palestine-Israel Journal*, interview) feels strongly that Arabs must be educated about democracy—"I am afraid that some people might misunderstand what is meant by democracy. They need to be educated and guided, put in the right direction." In addition to this public education, there must be the development of traditional democratic institutions. In the end:

There are two challenges. One, a challenge to the leaders not to be tempted by power. Two, a challenge to the people to become educated about democracy so they can be watchdogs to help it grow.

An additional perspective on the importance of Palestinian democracy comes from S. Abdallah, economic development planner (interview), who declares that along with a proper investment climate, "Democracy and human rights are crucial to the holding and bringing back of sophisticated and skilled people to Palestine.

Authoritarianism is not the way to build a civil and modern economic society."

Institutional development, in addition to creating governance structures for Jerusalem Arabs, must also establish public and private organizations to facilitate Palestinian growth and investment in and around Jerusalem. For the West Bank and Gaza overall, the Palestinian Economic Council for Development and Reconstruction (PECDAR) was established pursuant to the September 1993 signing of the PLO-Israel Declaration of Principles. It was created because there were no Palestinian institutions for planning and development, urgent needs were building up, and there was the need for an institution to channel increasing amounts of external donations to implementing organizations (S. Abdallah, director of economic policy and policy section, PECDAR, interview). The need for an investment strategy had earlier been demonstrated by Palestinian building patterns in the Jerusalem region. During the boom Gulf oil economy of the early 1980s, Palestinians working there sent back considerable sums of money to the West Bank. This money financed large amounts of housing in the northern sections of the Jerusalem region stretching northward toward Ramallah. Little was invested, however, in job creation, capital production, and infrastructure—all backbones of a balanced regional economy. Thus, Palestinian development faced not only the obstacles of restrictive Israeli policy, but also internal organizational handicaps. In response, PECDAR was established to provide a framework to guide investment priorities and to review and coordinate implementing organizations' requests for funding. External donors' pledges for 1994–1998 amounted to about $2.3 billion; major donors included the European Union, United States, Japan, Norway, Saudi Arabia, Denmark, and the World Bank (PECDAR 1994). This money is to be used primarily on the rehabilitation, maintenance, and expansion of public infrastructure capacity, including water and sewerage, solid waste, transportation, education, health, and social welfare. The emphasis on infrastructure was premised on the belief that the public sector will need to play a major role in this area for some time to come (PECDAR 1994).

PECDAR, however, is not slated to be a major funder of projects in the Jerusalem area of the West Bank. Rather, its "framework for the allocation of investment funds by geographical location" targets 50 percent of funds to the Gaza Strip. Half of the remaining funds go to the districts of Hebron, Qualqilia, Jenin, and Jericho; only 5 percent of funds from 1994 to 1998 were slated to go to the Jerusalem area (PECDAR 1994). Thus, PECDAR is not being used as an instrument to implement a Jerusalem development counter-strategy. Rather, it seeks to target and consolidate economic bene-fits in those areas of the West Bank that are within Palestinian National Authority jurisdiction, or soon scheduled to be, under the PLO-Israel Declaration of Principles (S. Abdallah, interview). An important reason why Jerusalem funding through PECDAR is min-imal is the presence of restrictions put on PECDAR-channeled money by the United States and Israel. Donor country funding can-not be used to assist nongovernmental organizations (NGOs) or projects in Arab parts of Israeli-defined Jerusalem.[19]

PECDAR's inability to channel investment to Jerusalem is sig-nificant because there is a lack of a collective process of Palestinian development in the Jerusalem region that could, in Benvenisti's words, act in a Zionist fashion. Such an authority could, for in-stance, expropriate, re-parcel, and build large-scale Palestinian housing and commercial development not now possible. Benvenisti (interview) suggests that, unlike the Jewish community in the Mid-dle East, "Palestinians do not understand the need to organize as a 'minority' through institutions and volunteer support because they will not accept Israel's definition that they are a 'minority' in 'Jerusalem.'" Without such communal actions, Palestinians are left attempting to fight the Israeli growth machine through individual and unplanned actions in the face of multiple Israeli restrictions. J. Abu-Shakrah (interview) points to the strategic importance of a communal process of development:

> You cannot rely on private Palestinian investment alone be-cause they will not feel it is safe and secure. If you're going to wait until it is secure, who is going to liberate this place for you? This is why community people and leaders must come with a plan and investment to use Israeli-designated "green land."

This Palestinian collective development process could be done with strong PNA involvement (government-controlled land owner-ship and development) or through the provision of subsidies and partnerships to facilitate private investment (such as been done in support of the private Palestine Development and Investment Company). Either way, there needs to be "the creation of an indigenous set of institutions" (I. Dakkak, interview). Such institutions as a Housing Bank or Development Bank could be vehicles for outside investment; others, such as a Palestinian Housing Council, could be targeted at specific societal needs, such as provision of low-cost housing.

The final track of the institutional development strategy is the establishment and maintenance of a "civil society" of Palestinian nongovernmental organizations (NGOs) involved in education, health, human services, and human rights advocacy. Civil society acts both as a conduit for the articulation of individual and community needs and as a defense mechanism against excessive governmental power and abuses. As such, there is in the building of new institutions "the need to create and maintain space where nongovernmental organizations can work" (M. Kothari, U.N. Representative for Habitat International Coalition, interview). Yet the education, health, human service, and advocacy NGOs that operate in east Jerusalem face the difficult challenge of finding direct, non-PECDAR mediated, links with donors.[20] In addition, internal problems obstruct the development of an Arab civil society in Jerusalem. M. Kothari (interview) states that the "PLO is not responding or acknowledging human rights work." In addition, the "particularistic state" of the PNA works against the creation of civil institutions by rewarding political favorites, thus producing territorial and political infighting that has fractured Palestinian NGOs. At the same time, the Authority has felt threatened by the development of independent local organizations, especially those involved in human rights (M. Kothari, interview). In such difficult conditions for NGOs, both M. Kothari and J. Abu-Shakrah (interviews) argue for the establishment of an NGO coalition that could decrease political infighting and act as a defense mechanism against a potentially overreaching Palestinian national authority. Z. Abu Zayyad (interview) asserts that in the transition from occupation to self-authority, there is the need for coordination of real work, not perpetuation of political work.

The restrictions on funding of Palestinian institutional development and NGO assistance in Arab Jerusalem run counter to the creation of a vibrant and independent sector within Palestinian society.[21] Although this meets the short-term Israeli goals of "emptying the city of Palestinians" (M. Doudi, interview), it creates a civic vacuum within which either an authoritarian Palestinian state or an Islamic fundamentalist strategy can enter. Nongovernmental civic institutions are capable of bringing government to the people, both in terms of service delivery and responsiveness. M. Doudi asserts that "The various departments of PECDAR and the PLO have been too top-down, bureaucratic, and too removed. They have been *superstructural* (with politicians as heads), not *infrastructural* with benefits coming to the person on the ground." In addition, such locally based civil groups can be instrumental in supporting Palestinian demands for human rights under international law (J. Abu-Shakrah and M. Kothari, interviews). For example, there has been an effort to promote the Palestinians' right to adequate housing through the combined use of international human rights instruments and local activism and publicity (Habitat International Coalition and Palestine Human Rights Information Center, 1994). It relies both on claims to the United Nations that Israeli policy violates international law regarding housing rights[22] and the use of a set of local NGOs to monitor and document Israeli violations. Linking of international and local actions helps develop local NGO skills, interpersonal relations, and organizational capacity that have positive long-term benefits for educating people about their rights. Human rights action linking international and local NGO levels is also capable of breaching larger political sovereignty issues. Housing rights ("a place to live in security and dignity"), for example, can encompass ingredients such as access to civil services, livelihood, and planning and settlement decisions (M. Kothari, interview). At this point, human rights and sovereignty issues become connected. As Kothari (interview) suggests, "The subversive part of housing rights is a political agenda . . . trying to change the terms of decisionmaking."

In summary, there are difficulties facing Palestinians in developing a comprehensive, communally based, and proactive set of strategies aimed at countering Israeli expansionary policies in Jerusalem. The development of an independent Palestinian capacity—whether through political-geographic or institutional development strategies—to engage in Jerusalem affairs appears essential for there to be a mutual coexistence of the two sides. Yet, the challenge of moving from resistance to an existing reality, to the formulation of an alternative one based on vision and institution building, appears problematic. In the early stages of Palestinian empowerment, there appear to be obstacles facing each form of institution building—local governance, community and economic development, and civil society. They come both from Israeli restrictions and from splinters within Palestinian society itself. In the potential creation of local governance, Israeli limits on political organization in east Jerusalem combine with national-local differences within the Palestinian community concerning the question of democracy and accountability. In community development, external donor funding restrictions combine with an inherent Palestinian tendency toward individual land-based actions. And, in the creation of an Arab civil society in Jerusalem, the effects of funding restrictions attached by Israel to international aid are magnified by the Palestinian National Authority's lack of enthusiasm concerning grassroots advocacy and human rights work.

The establishment of Palestinian local democracy and civil society has the potential to both enhance Palestinian capacity and further Israeli interests because they would likely create a Jerusalem buffer against a possible authoritarian Palestinian state or a radical Islamic opposition. Local democracy could encourage moderation through its ability to hold and attract a professional middle class and encourage private investment. Seen in this light, unilateral Israeli actions that restrict local political organizing and civil institutional structures may squeeze too tightly and create the very conditions—an authoritarian or radicalized Palestinian presence—that they are seeking to avoid.

6

Jerusalem, the West Bank, and Peace

Thickening the Land-Use War

Which metropolitan area? We have two politically but one in terms of physical qualities.

—Khalil Tufakji,
Geographer, Arab Studies Society,
in an interview

U sing municipal borders as the scale of analysis and discussion, as I have done in chapters 4 and 5, uses the frame of reference and boundaries according to Israel. We must transcend these political boundaries, however, in order to examine the active re-shaping of the human landscape in the region at large, and to more effectively study the intertwining issues of Jerusalem and the West Bank. When we go beyond the politically constructed boundaries of Israeli Jerusalem, we traverse into a landscape that has its own set of opportunities and complexities. I now examine metropolitan Jerusalem and the regional connections between the city, the larger West Bank, and Israel.

Metropolitan Jerusalem

In 1992, a team of Israeli central, district, and municipal government planners was established to investigate the metropolitan region of Jerusalem. The "Metropolitan Jerusalem" project was led by a fifteen-person steering committee of government officials from the

Ministries of Housing and Interior, the Israel Land Authority, district (regional) planners and architects, Civil Administration (West Bank) planners, and former and current city planners and engineers. Architects A. Mazor and S. Cohen were hired to develop a Master Plan and Development Plan for the metropolitan region, the draft of which was produced June 1994 (Mazor and Cohen 1994). The following discussion is based on interviews with six of the principals involved on the Israeli side,[1] and with several non-Israeli urban professionals familiar with the project and its strategies.

Despite successful efforts to maintain a Jewish majority within the Israeli-defined municipal borders, Mazor and Cohen (1994) report that the metropolitan area in 1990 "was more an Arabic metropolitan area than a Jewish one."[2] Approximately 54 percent of the regional population was Arabic/Palestinian. The 90 percent majority Arab in the West Bank parts of the metropolitan area outside Israeli-defined Jerusalem more than counterbalanced the then 72 percent Jewish majority within the city borders.[3] Metropolitan Plan team member E. Barzacchi (interview) describes the Israeli reaction to such figures: "It's a reality. Maybe looking at a mirror is scary, but it doesn't change a thing by looking at it. We didn't invent anything." Three concentric rings outward from the central city each hold large Arab majorities (Mazor and Cohen 1994). An inner ring (outlined west to east by Neve Ilan to Mishor Adumin; north to south by Bet El and Bethlehem) contains approximately 270,000 persons, of which 82 percent are Arab. Concentrations of Arab towns and villages that are spread over the plateau at a high topography include Ramallah and El-Bireh (north), Bethlehem, Beit Jala, and Beit Sahor (south). A middle ring (Bet Shemesh to Mishor Adumin; Kfar Malach/Ateret to Gush Etzion) has 130,000 residents, 70 percent of whom are Arab. And, an outer ring (Bet Shemesh Forest/Modiin to Jericho; Shilo Valley/Male Lvona to Hebron) contains 161,000 people, 80 percent of whom are Arab.

The intricate and complicated ethnic spatial pattern evident in the region at large has been produced by a series of actions, reactions, then further reactions (B. Hyman, Israel Ministry of Interior, interview). New Jewish neighborhoods built within the Israeli-defined city stimulated Arab building immediately outside municipal borders, producing an explosion of Arab villages—uncoordinated, unplanned, and spread out—outside Jerusalem. On the one hand, Arab growth outside Jerusalem city borders is consistent with Israeli goals—it attracts Arabs from within more tightly restricted Jerusalem; and it "catches" migrants into the region (U. Ben-Asher, district planner, interview). On the other hand, such regional growth increases Arabs' ability to support political claims to land adjacent to Jerusalem city as part of a future state of Palestine. This Arab development then spawns Israeli actions seeking to produce spatial counterweights to Arab building (B. Hyman, interview). In the end, Jewish settlement patterns in the West Bank outside Israeli-delineated Jerusalem do not create a dominant Jewish presence in any direction,[4] but rather supply important counterweights to Arab growth—Jewish Givat Zeev and Givon to Arab Ramallah in the north; Maale Adumin to Abu Dis and e-Azariya in the east; and Efrat to Bethlehem/Beit Jala/Beit Sahur in the south (see Figure 6.1).

The challenge facing the Metropolitan steering committee was to approach from a regional planning perspective a region divided politically but unified physically. There are striking features of the Israeli metropolitan planning effort that inform us about the role of planning policy amidst ethnic polarization and political uncertainty. These are:

- Goals and aspirations of metropolitan planning

- Perceived separability of the functional from the political

- Professional techniques aimed at conflict alleviation

- Planning participants

- Planning outputs amidst political contest

Goals and Aspirations of Metropolitan Planning. There was the hope among several participants and observers that enlarging the geographic scale of investigation may produce opportunities for political solutions not available in the confined space of municipal Jerusalem. Trying to uncover political solutions in the tightly confined space of the Israeli-defined city appears to be a zero-sum game, where one side gains at the expense of the other. As M. Benvenisti (interview) asserts, "What Jews want must be taken from the Arabs because Jerusalem is densely populated." At the metropolitan scale, a different set of opportunities may become available. A. Gonen (Hebrew University, interview) states that, "Metropolitanizing the Jerusalem question leaves more room for

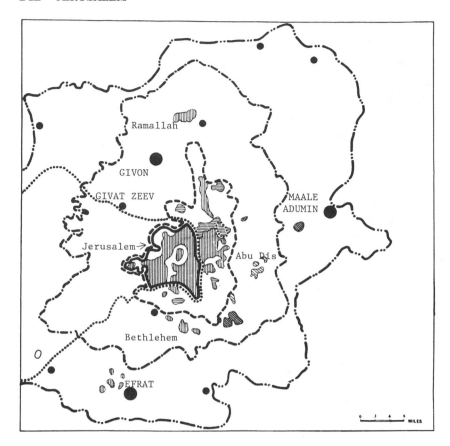

Figure 6.1   Israeli Spatial Counterweights outside Israeli-Defined Jerusalem

Note: The rings on the map are not exactly the same as those used in Metropolitan Jerusalem Plan.
Source: Elisha Efrat. 1988. *Geography and Politics in Israel Since 1967.* London: Frank Cass & Company Ltd, Newbury House, 890-900 Eastern Avenue, Iford, Essex IG2 7HH, England. Reprinted by Permission.

manipulation and possible solutions." Similarly, I. Kimhi (interview) describes that "Within the existing city borders, political solutions are limited and difficult. But if you approach the entire region, there is a set of solutions." Past Israeli-Jordan agreements over water rights and supply present an interesting parallel to this equating of metropolitanization with problem solving. It was when a series of new water development projects was incorporated into negotiations that the zero-sum battling over existing resources evolved toward mutual sharing of a newly enlarged water pie with positive sum outcomes, and solutions were reached (*Jerusalem Report*, November 17, 1994).

These positive-sum aspirations applied to metropolitan Jerusalem are associated with the expectation that an autonomous Palestinian area may be easier to define on a regional than a city scale. There is the hope among Israelis that a Palestinian capital could be located outside Israeli-defined Jerusalem but within the Jerusalem region. Areas for a Palestinian capital that apparently have been discussed include Abu Dis (east), Hizma (northeast), and Ramallah (north).[5] Under this scenario, both sides could claim victory—the Israelis because the capital was outside "Jerusalem"; the Palestinians because it was inside "Jerusalem." This "solution" would exploit the different meanings and geographies underlying the two groups' use of the word "Jerusalem." Similarly, Palestinian growth could be allowed and facilitated outside the city to meet Arab needs while not interfering with Jewish demographic requirements within the city. Even one Palestinian observer, S. Ghadban (architecture professor at Birzeit University in Ramallah, interview), suggests that metropolitanization may facilitate Palestinian political claims, something Arab development strategies within municipal borders are unlikely to do because of the strong Jewish majority. Independent of political implications, an open metropolitan region of increased economic scope and interdependencies is seen as mutually beneficial. To Israelis, a regional economy and labor pool would benefit the Jewish core and transform the "cul-de-sac" nature of Jerusalem at the edge of Israel's borders. To Palestinians, they would accrue the employment and income advantages of being the only Arabs in the Middle East to live in an advanced economy (A. Mazor, interview).

The 1994 draft metropolitan plan argues that regional planning is needed for spatial and economic reasons. First, interdependencies (especially commuting) and spatial connections exist on a scale much larger than the Israeli-defined city and should be planned for accordingly. Second, large-scale, region-wide service operations can produce economic efficiency, savings and increased quality. The draft Master Plan defines the main goals and principal targets to guide future growth and service delivery in the metropolitan region (p. 11). One goal is striking by its political content: *strengthening the special status of Jerusalem as Israel's capital* and as a "world city." The principal targets to achieve this goal include: (1) physical preservation and environmental suitability; (2) population balance; and (3) *reduction of friction between the populations* (italics by author). Another objective related to intergroup relations is the *closing of gaps, pluralism, and increased tolerance*. The goals and objectives in the report thus represent a seeming contradiction. Whereas the special status goal seeks to consolidate Israeli control over the city, the means to achieve this include accommodating strategies dealing with the reduction of intergroup tension, socioeconomic equalization, and increased tolerance. This dichotomy harkens back to the current Olmert Administration strategy of narrowing service gaps as a means of strengthening Israeli political goals.

The draft Development Plan for the metropolitan area identifies five areas outside the city that should be prepared, through service provision, for development. It plans for substantial Jewish population growth in politically contested West Bank sub-regions outside Israeli-defined Jerusalem. The five growth areas are Maale Adumin (east); Givat Zeev (northwest); Tsur Hadassa (southwest); the "green heart" area west of Jerusalem; and Bet Shemesh (west). The first two areas are clearly on the formerly Jordanian-controlled side of the 1967 green line. The Tsur Hadassa area, meanwhile, straddles the old dividing line, encompassing on the east the Palestinian villages of Bet Jala and Betar and the Jewish settlement block of Gush Etzion, and is proximate to the Arab city of Bethlehem. More striking than the politically controversial locations of anticipated metropolitan growth are the ethnic breakdowns of forecasted growth, as displayed in Table 6.1. Future growth favors Jewish development at a rate of at least nine to one over Arab development in Maale Adumin and Tsur Hadassa, and six to four in the Givat Zeev area. In these three growth areas in or straddling the politically contested West Bank, the 37 percent Jewish to 63 percent Arab population ratio in 1991 is expected to be 67 percent Jewish and 33 percent Arab when the areas are fully developed.[6] Whereas Jewish growth in these three areas is to increase 900 percent (from 36,700 to 192,000), Palestinian "expected" growth is to go from 62,700 to 96,000, a 53 percent increase.

The goals and population forecasts in the Metropolitan Plan expose planning more as a partisan strategy constraining of opportunities for mutual co-existence than as an accommodating one enabling of political solution in a positive-sum environment. Going

Table 6.1   Population (1991 and Expected) in Five Growth Areas of Metropolitan Jerusalem

		1991 POPULATION	EXPECTED POPULATION (CAPACITY)
Maale Adumin			
Jewish		17,000	65,000
Arab		35,000	41,000
Total		52,000	106,000
Jewish growth as % of total expected growth	89%		
Givat Zeev			
Jewish		8,200	42,000
Arab		22,200	45,000
Total		30,400	87,000
Jewish growth as % of total expected growth	60%		
Tsur Hadassa			
Jewish		11,500	85,000
Arab		5,500	10,000
Total		17,000	95,000
Jewish growth as % of total expected growth	94%		
"Green Heart"			
Jewish		28,000	73,000
Arab		0	0
Total		28,000	73,000
Jewish growth as % of total expected growth	100%		
Bet Shemesh			
Jewish		28,000	255,000
Arab		0	0
Total		28,000	255,000
Jewish growth as % of total expected growth	100%		

Source: Mazor, A. and S. Cohen, *Development Plan for Metropolitan Jerusalem.* June 1994. Sections 12.3.1–12.3.5

beneath the stated goals through interviews with policymakers and urban administrators helps to identify the deeper political motivations behind metropolitan planning in Jerusalem. There appear to be two main spatial methods of furthering Israel's claims to the city of Jerusalem—through the strengthening of the Jerusalem corridor so as to increase the functional connection to metropolitan Tel Aviv to the west; and through the thickening of the Jewish presence within the metropolitan area by creating spatial counterweights to Arab growth in the contested West Bank. In the first instance, growth is pushed to the west; in the second instance, to the east, north, and south.

The first strategy toward strengthening Jerusalem focused on the Jerusalem corridor would seek to increase interdependencies between the economically vibrant Tel Aviv and Jerusalem. Y. Golani (interview) speaks of the importance of creating a two-pole metropolitan area of Israel ("a Jerusalem D.C.") connected by improved rail and road links and integrated by the development of the new town of Modiin. This integration of Jerusalem with the rest of Israel is vitally important because the 1948 borders of the Israeli state left Jerusalem as a "dead-end" or "cul-de-sac" city, at the edge of the border and only minimally connected to the rest of the state by a narrow belt. To Israeli planners, this "cul-de-sac" nature of Jerusalem leaves it vulnerable economically and functionally, and thus politically. Modiin, the planned new city of between 61,000 and 106,000 housing units[7] to be located on land close to the old cease-fire line and about one-half hour commute west of Jerusalem, thus serves critical political-strategic objectives. It will serve as the hub of the main development axis between Jerusalem and Tel Aviv. Significantly, Modiin is a potential source of sophisticated high-technology jobs for Jerusalem residents and thereby can facilitate the continued Jewish residential expansion of the Jerusalem region. As reported in a government document (Israel Ministry of Construction and Housing 1992):

> Establishment of Modiin will serve the primary national interest of strengthening Jerusalem by creating a strong, solid spine that fortifies the Israeli capital.

In addition to this political strategy of strengthening Jerusalem's links westward, there is the desire to thicken the Jewish presence in the West Bank peripheries of the city. Here, the strategy focuses on the creation of facts on the ground to counter Palestinian claims of sovereignty in the city. Such Palestinian autonomy is viewed by many Israelis as damaging to Jerusalem (I. Cohen, Municipality city manager interview). Y. Golani (interview) similarly asserts that, "east Jerusalem as the capital of a Palestinian state would transmit a constant threat to Israel's sovereignty over Jerusalem." The creation of a Jewish "greater Jerusalem" is seen as able to create obstacles to such a Palestinian presence (I. Cohen, interview). A spatial counterweight strategy of suburban Jewish development is viewed as best able to facilitate future annexation by Israel of areas around the city. This would act as a buffer against a new Palestinian state and further complicate Palestinian political claims to east Jerusalem. K. Tufakji, the Palestinian geographer (interview), asserts that:

There is a difficulty in talking "region" when addressing a politically controversial city. "Metropolitan Jerusalem" is a functional or geographic concept. "Greater Jerusalem," on the other hand, becomes a political concept.

The spatial counterweights of Givat Zeev, Maale Adumin, and Efrat/Gush Etzion contained about 32,000 Jewish residents in 1993.[8] As Table 6.1 discloses, the Metropolitan Plan projects and plans for a total Jewish population of about 107,000 in the Maale Adumin and Givat Zeev areas, a fourfold increase over the 25,000 Jews there in 1991. Assuming conservatively that one-half of the Jewish population growth in the Tsur Hadassa planning area will be in Gush Etzion, the projected Jewish population in all three spatial counterweights will be about 155,000, a fivefold increase over 1991 conditions. The creation of this regional mosaic of Jewish development in the West Bank is important politically because it "makes it hard to have a political solution that is not more functional than geographic" (B. Hyman, Ministry of the Interior, interview). In other words, it would become hard to draw a political line in metropolitan Jerusalem that separates a potential Palestinian state from Israel. This connection between metropolitan planning and political goals leads S. Kaminker (interview) to declare that "This is not true metropolitanism; it is conquest in the guise of regional planning."

A basic assumption of the metropolitan planning project was that the functional issues and solutions stay the same no matter the political configuration.

—Uri Ben-Asher,
architect and member of steering committee,
Metropolitan Jerusalem, in an interview

Perceived Separability of the Functional from the Political. Many Israeli interviewees rationalized metropolitan planning as a way to focus on functional and technical issues free from the entanglements of organizational and political obstacles. A. Mazor (interview) curtly suggests that "The advantage of long-range planning is that you can get rid of the organizational distortions," and later asserts that "The first thing you do when you develop a metropolitan plan is to ignore all of the politics." Further, he states, "If you let political lines determine and split functional considerations, then you're no long considering it on a metropolitan level." Functional issues and solutions were the focus, while sovereignty and political issues were viewed as outside the scope of discussions (N. Sidi, interview). Similarly, A. Gonen (interview), in his working group, examined spatial interrelationships within the metropolitan region independent of political configuration possibilities. The basic assumption was that functional issues and solutions would stay the same no matter the political configuration. Many participants and observers proudly asserted that any political changes in the future would likely not affect the planners' functional proposals and strategies.[9]

This Israeli stance that the metropolitan plan separates the functional from the political appears disingenuous. The interplay of functional and political considerations represents a complex web in which one cannot be isolated from the other. Indeed, functional arguments and strategies often are derived from a politically constructed status quo, or have important political implications because of their effects on the location, timing, and size of growth. For example, there are strong functional arguments (economic and social) supportive of Israel's strategy to consolidate the settlement ribbon between Tel Aviv and Jerusalem. The development of Modiin can provide supplies of labor for Jerusalem economic interests or, conversely, jobs for Jerusalem residents. Either way, Jewish Jerusalem becomes strengthened economically and demographically. In contrast, metropolitan planners are prepared to accommodate for political reasons more than 150,000 new Jewish residents east, north, and south of the city. The result, says U. Ben-Asher (interview) is a "distorted cityscape being pushed in all directions figuratively and literally." In the end, the Jerusalem region assumes a less functional, more inefficient, urbanscape. Environmental planning also becomes entangled with political considerations. Environmental groups, fearful of losing open space to growing development pressures, want more green area zoning in the western sectors. Yet, the political needs for restrictive land use regulations are greater in the eastern sectors (U. Ben-Asher, interview). In this case, functional arguments are distorted and bent by political considerations.

A second example illustrating the inseparability of functionality and politics involves the Maale Adumin settlement east of Israeli-defined Jerusalem. The most functionally optimal Jewish settlement pattern in the West Bank, according to S. Moshkovitz, architect for the Civil Administration (interview), is a suburban pattern of settlements within the commuting spheres of Jerusalem and Tel Aviv. Yet such functionally based strategies create a complex and combustible puzzle of Arab-Jewish spatial patterns. With sole reference to functional and efficiency arguments, the new city of Maale Adumin (65,000 population capacity) and the adjoining industrial park of Mishor Adumin (750 acres) should be connected spatially and administratively to the city of Jerusalem. Yet to do so would be to automatically annex a swath of the West Bank, counter to international law and potentially inflammatory to Arab-Jewish relations and negotiations. In this case, functional planning has significant and inseparable political consequences. A final example involves the construction of a new regional highway. Highway #45 is planned to connect Tel Aviv to Jerusalem, increase access to Jerusalem, and thus improve economic development. Yet the road would cross areas of the West Bank expected to come under Palestinian authority in the future. Problematic to Israeli planners is that the road would likely attract settlements along it that take advantage of improved access; these growth nodes would likely be Palestinian and within the metropolitan area. Thus, Israeli efforts to strengthen the Jewish claim to the city through economic development ultimately could stimulate Palestinian growth in, and political claims to, the metropolitan region. Again, functional and political aspects of planning are intertwined.

Far from being separable from political considerations, functional planning arguments are capable of defining the urban system parameters (connection lines; activity networks; points) of political negotiations dealing with political control and sovereignty. They transform political strategies into urban functional issues dealing with the management of interdependent, seemingly ethnically neutral, flows of economic and demographic change. In reality, however, functional planning arguments take as given current political arrangements and thus tend to reinforce and strengthen, not reconsider or disrupt, politically disputed ethnic spatial distributions.

Professional Techniques Aimed at Conflict Amelioration. There is a belief among Israeli planners that professional planning techniques of activity allocation can effectively address and alleviate intergroup conflict. As mentioned earlier, Morley and Shachar (1986) assert that in dealing with value-laden issues, planners "base their proposals on a discourse that avoids viewing them from a particular ideological perspective. This approach becomes a strategy to create legitimation for the objective methodology of planning." The planning profession's search for identity becomes all the more dire because, as stated by H. Law-Yone (planning professor, Technion University), "There is no methodology that we can use to deal with a politically uncertain future." Co-author A. Mazor (interview) summarized the approach to planning metropolitan Jerusalem as "the use of technical and professional measures to try to resolve conflict." The team used territorial and geographic tools in efforts to attenuate tension. A technical planning tool—called the "potential model"—was used to identify areas of conflict in the region that both ethnic groups—Jewish and Palestinian—desire. The land-use competition within the region was viewed as a "kind of game," wherein each side wants to connect spatially with its other zones of habitation and activity in order to increase its territory, while avoiding the creation of enclaves surrounded by the other side's territory.[10] Resulting areas of conflict identified, for example, included the Jewish French Hill neighborhood penetration of the north-south Arab growth pattern; and areas where Israeli efforts to link Neve Yaakov and Pisgat Zeev have been complicated by Arab development and land holdings.

The spatial distribution of ethnic conflict potential was then overlaid upon a map of the relative magnitude and geographic distribution of functional/service needs of each side. The goal was to, as much as possible, plan for activities of mutual interest in those areas of highest potential for conflict. These activities would include services that both sides need: markets, free industrial zones, an international university campus, or infrastructure such as a regional highway. Such activities would establish "everyman's land" in an area of conflict, so that each side sees the land use as a continuity of their own side's land. Each side can directly use the activity, or pass through the land to get to an area of like ethnicity. The location of these mutually beneficial land uses would create porous activities and continuities, not borders, ethnic frontiers, or enclaves. A. Mazor (interview) speaks of a river whose banks are on separate sovereignties. Rather than being seen as a dividing line, the river can be viewed as providing mutual benefit, wherein "we can row together in the river without being regarded as crossing the border."

Using this approach, 93 to 95 percent of the region was delineated as areas for one ethnic group or the other;[11] about 7 percent was designated as areas of mutual interest. An important assumption underlies this approach—that increased Arab-Jewish interaction will attenuate ethnic conflict. Without this assumption, A. Mazor states, "the metropolitan Jerusalem plan will not work." Yet such efforts at mutual interaction have not worked in the past. Safdie (1986) recounts the idea of creating an north-south "urban boulevard" in northern Jerusalem that would bring Arabs from the west together with Jews from the east. The outcome, however, was the creation of a regional highway that acted as a separator and barrier between ethnic groups, rather than a "river" of interaction. Today, two other north-south roads are clearly identifiable as an "Arab road" serving a string of Arab communities (Ramallah Road) and a "Jewish road" serving the communities of Pisgat Zeev and Neve Yaakov (Route 13).

Metropolitan planners also advocated the use of technical and allocational means to locate politically sensitive activities in a way that would meet the emotional and political requirements of both sides. For example, land uses of particularly emotional impact—synagogues and mosques—would be located well away from these areas of mutual interest and deep within their own ethnic territories. Even the question of where a possible Palestinian capital might be located was seen as potentially amenable to such allocational procedures. A. Mazor (interview), for example, suggests that "On the professional level, you can find a place—close enough that in the eyes of Arabs it will be regarded as Jerusalem but, from the

Israeli view, it will not be within the heart of Jerusalem." Here, the shaky foundations of the functionality paradigm are exposed because political and emotional factors become the primary criteria in the allocation equations.

If their recommendations are implemented, these planning techniques used by Jerusalem metropolitan planners would represent a significant shift of Israeli planning from partisan to neutral. Yet neutrality by Israeli planners is insufficient to overcome, and may actually legitimize, the spatial pattern created by partisan planning and its effects on Palestinian disempowerment and community fragmentation. Identification of conflict areas solely at places of intergroup interfaces necessarily assumes consensus over noninterface ethnic areas of continuity and size. In this way, such geographic tools help solidify Jewish large-scale communities in politically disputed territory. At the same time, seemingly objective locational techniques, when applied to the siting of activities of high emotional-political content, expose the shallowness of the functionality paradigm.

> We tried to be scholars, but we were all Israelis. And, I don't think you can be objective. You can try to be scientific; you cannot be objective.

> —Elinoar Barzacchi,
> Director of Steering Committee,
> Metropolitan Jerusalem,
> in an interview

Planning Participants. A striking feature of the Jerusalem metropolitan planning process is the exclusion of Palestinians (either Israeli or non-Israeli) from the process.[12] This is the most damaging aspect because, as A. Gonen (interview) avows, "We broke a cardinal rule of planning—we did not include the whole array of participants." Instead, the steering committee consisted of Israeli urban professionals employing technical methodologies and representatives of Israeli ministries linked to political agendas and arguments. In efforts to achieve fairness, E. Barzacchi (interview) states:

> We tried to play devil's advocate and say "what would be good for the Arab people" according to our criteria. We used humanistic criteria, such as that the population growth rate would be

maintained on both sides. But if Palestinians were part of the process, they may have wanted internal migration to figure in more, or desire different zones for development.

Efforts to be fair and objective within a partisan structure will likely produce spatial patterns that reflect the assumptions and biases of the in-group. The 1994 metropolitan plan, although espousing objectivity and fairness, may thus have the same type of effects on intergroup relations as the partisan boundary drawing and planmaking undertaken since the Israeli conquest of Jerusalem and the West Bank in 1967. To Palestinians, metropolitan planning that is functionally based and unattached to political solutions will be seen as undermining Arab sovereignty claims to the city, no matter how "objective" the planning methodology used (H. Siniora, publisher, *Biladi-The Jerusalem Times*, interview). An alternative to the partisan structure of the metropolitan plan team structure would be a joint team of Israelis and Palestinians developing a plan that seeks to accommodate the needs and aspirations of both sides. Or, as Palestinian A. Aghazarian (lecturer, Birzeit University interview) declares in referring to plan- and boundary making, "We have to get into the room with the coloring pens." Unlike the current metropolitan planning structure, a joint Arab-Jewish planmaking process would have the chance of enabling genuine opportunities for peaceful coexistence.

Planning Outputs amidst Political Contest. There is an uncertain relationship between Jerusalem metropolitan planning and Israeli-Palestinian political negotiations over Jerusalem's status. How are these planning outputs and recommendations to be used amidst political contest? Metropolitan planners were told after completion of the June 1994 draft plan, "We are not allowed to publish it. You are not turning this draft into a final report" (A. Mazor, interview). Several participants[13] suggested that policymakers were hesitant to publish it because the plan would be viewed as attempting to change the "status quo" of Jerusalem before "final status" negotiations began (which is contrary to the September 1993 Declaration of Principles). A. Mazor mentions another reason—that the plan, because it seeks to be neutral and objective, would be a bad starting point for negotiations. He asserts that, "This is a professionally balanced solution, which is exactly what you do not start with in political negotiations." The visibility of such a long-term strategic plan might obstruct Israel's short-term negotiation tactics; in other words, one starts negotiations from strength, not from reasoned analysis. Another possibility is that the metropolitan plan will be ignored in the decisionmaking process. A. Mazor (interview) speaks of the positive atmosphere in planning sessions, where professional planners from the Israeli Ministries were willing to accept a common set of planning rules. At the same time, however, these Ministry professionals were detached from government decisionmakers, those politically appointed leaders of the ministries who make decisions with the prime minister. In the end, Mazor states, "The detachment from decisionmaking allowed Ministry representatives on our team to be professional, but probably at the expense of having an impact on the decisionmaking process."

To the extent that it has meaningful impacts on political negotiations, it appears that metropolitan planning assessments and recommendations will likely provide Israelis with covert baseline checks during political negotiations. As such, the metropolitan plan will be a supporting reference rather than a starting point. The greatest potential role of planning—enabling the conditions for freedom and mutual coexistence through the presentation of alternatives—would then be corrupted into a role serving political negotiators which will constrain opportunities for peaceful mutual coexistence.

Jerusalem and the West Bank

> How can Israeli and Palestinian interests go together territorially in the Jerusalem metropolitan area and the West Bank so that a viable Palestinian state can be created?
>
> —Jan de Jong,
> St. Ives Legal Resource and Development Center,
> in an interview

A study of a politically contested region is prone to consistently shifting ground in efforts to delimit appropriate scales of analysis. The transcendence of the Israeli-defined municipal borders of Jerusalem to the greater region demonstrated the false simplicity of examining the politically constructed "city." Now, the metropolitan scale must be linked to its larger political-geographic context to gain perspective

on how metropolitan dynamics are related to the gradual empowerment of Palestinian autonomy in the West Bank at large.

As discussed earlier, the *Declaration of Principles on Interim
Self-Government Arrangements* ("The Oslo I agreement") was signed
by Israel and the PLO on September 13, 1993, and contains a set of
mutually agreed-upon general principles and phases regarding a
five-year "interim" period of self-rule. The agreement states, in Article V (3), that the status of Jerusalem was not to be discussed in
the negotiations for the interim arrangements but would be one of
the subjects (along with borders, refugees, security, and settlements) left for the later negotiations on the permanent settlement.
The "Oslo II agreement," signed September 1995 by Israel and the
PLO, detailed the self-government arrangements in the West Bank;
it also specified the structure and powers, and election modalities,
regarding an elected Palestinian Council. The agreement map demarcated three areas of the West Bank: Area A (seven of the major
Palestinian cities where Arabs will enjoy full territorial and security
control); Area B (village areas where Palestinians would have territorial control, but security control would be shared); and Area C
(areas whose status had not yet been determined; includes areas Israel deems to be of strategic security value).[14] The agreement specified that the Israeli army would redeploy away from Areas A and B
in phases prior to "final status" negotiations over Area C.

Approximately 150,000 Jewish settlers in 1996 lived in about 140
settlements in the West Bank outside Israeli-defined Jerusalem,
comprising about 10 percent of the total West Bank population outside Jerusalem. The location of many of the Jewish settlements are
shown in Figure 6.2. Virtually no non-Israeli sovereign power offi-
cially recognizes the legality of these settlements in the occupied
West Bank (Alpher 1994). Jewish settlement contradicts international law, which states that "the occupying power shall not deport or
transfer parts of its own civilian population into the territory it occupies."[15] For the first ten years of Israeli occupation of the West Bank,
Jewish settlement was minimal and tied to security rationales. When
the Likud party came to power in 1977, there were only about five
thousand Jews living in thirty-four locations in the West Bank outside Israeli-defined Jerusalem (Alpher 1994). Over the next fifteen
years, the Gush Enumin ("Block of the Faithful") movement sought
settlements in the Arab-populated heartland of the West Bank in
order to prevent future separation of the West Bank from Israel. In

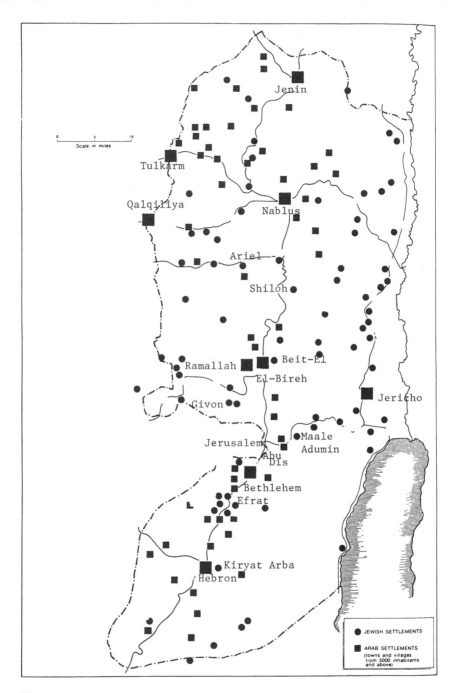

Figure 6.2 Jewish and Arab Settlements in the West Bank (Outside Israeli-Defined Jerusalem)

Source: Baruch Kimmerling. 1983. *Zionism and Territory: The Socio-Territorial Dimensions of Zionist Politics.* Berkeley: Institute of International Studies, University of California.

addition, minister Ariel Sharon was instrumental in placing Jewish settlements in locations that would sever and fragment the contiguity of Arab settlement (Alpher 1994). By the time Likud stepped down from power in 1984, there were 38,000 Jewish settlers (Benvenisti 1984). By early 1987, there were approximately 65,000 Jews living in more than 140 separate settlements throughout the West Bank (Benvenisti 1987b). With Likud's electoral victory in 1988, construction began again which significantly expanded the size of these settlements. Under the Labor government from 1992 to 1996, a "freeze" on settlements was instituted but applied to new settlements, not the expansion of existing ones.[16] Thus, Jewish settler population increased about 40 percent during the "freeze," facilitating in particular the consolidated encirclement of Jerusalem by Jewish spatial counterweights in the West Bank (Daniszewski 1996). In August 1996, this "freeze" on Jewish settlements in the West Bank was ended by the Israeli cabinet of Prime Minister Benyamin Netanyahu.

In order to construct these settlements in the West Bank, the Israeli government has used various means of land seizure.[17] The primary method is to declare areas that were Jordanian government land or whose ownership was not formally registered to be "state land" transferable to ownership by the Israeli government (Coon 1992; Shehadeh 1993). Other methods include the seizing of "abandoned" land of refugees and others who have left the West Bank, and the closure of land for military purposes. All told, by 1984, 41 percent of the West Bank had been seized by Israel, and an additional 11 percent controlled through use and access restrictions (Benvenisti 1985). It is estimated that by mid-1991, about 60 percent of the West Bank had been seized by Israel, with substantial other areas subject to restrictions on use and access (Coon 1992).

Separate planning processes in the West Bank—one for Israeli settlements and the other for Palestinians—have been established through military orders (Benvenisti 1987b). Israeli regional councils, established in 1979, dominate the planning of land-use zones, roads, and nature reserves, and have been used by Israeli authorities to channel services and benefits to Jewish settlers. Development outside of existing Arab village cores, meanwhile, is controlled by a centralized Israeli Higher Planning Council. Physical planning in the West Bank has been employed as a "tool in the scramble for control over space" (Benvenisti 1987b). Land-use classifications, dictated more by political than physical planning considerations, have been used to take control of lands remaining in Palestinian hands and as a prelude to further Israeli settlements (Benvenisti 1986b; Abdulhadi 1990). Israeli town planning schemes applied to the West Bank constrain outward growth of Palestinian villages. One plan, covering the metropolitan fringe of the Jerusalem area, is *Partial Regional Plan No. 1/82* (Figure 6.3). The Plan divided 110,000 acres proximate to Jerusalem proper into six major zones, projected a Palestinian population in year 2002 less than 1982 population, and placed close to 90 percent of the lands remaining in Palestinian hands off-limits to Arab construction (Abdulhadi 1990). Designated "Arab development" zones establish tight borders around already densely populated Arab villages beyond which no construction is permitted without explicit approval by the Higher Planning Council (Shehadeh 1993). Even though Arab growth in the West Bank outside Jerusalem is controlled, the presence of even greater Israeli restrictions within the city has resulted in significant Arab population increases outside the city.

Jewish settlers in the West Bank (outside Israeli-defined Jerusalem) are of two types—"heritage" settlers of the Gush Enumim settlements are there to establish a national-political presence in places of religious-historic significance; "economic" settlers are there for quality of life reasons, the generous subsidies provided by the Israeli government for West Bank habitation over the years,[18] and the ability to live inexpensively while still within the commuting zones of Jerusalem or Tel Aviv. It has been estimated that about 60 percent of settlers are "economic" and 40 percent are "heritage" (Alpher 1994). Most of the former live on the fringes of the territories proximate to urban employment—in the Jerusalem area and the Jerusalem corridor, and in western Samaria near the former green line. Most of the latter, in contrast, live in the mountain ridge heartland of the West Bank. As of 1995, almost 80 percent of Jews in the West Bank outside Israeli-defined Jerusalem are in "high-demand" areas within commuting range of either Jerusalem or Tel Aviv (J. de Jong and B. Hyman, interviews). The greatest population is in the Jerusalem metropolitan "spatial counterweights" of Givat Zeev, Maale Adumin (the largest Jewish settlement in the West Bank), and Efrat. The strong majority of Jews in these high-demand areas are likely "economic" settlers, there more for affordable housing than religious significance.[19]

The location of these settlements will have profound effects on both the interim and permanent peace settlements between Israel and the PLO pursuant to the September 1993 Declaration of Princi-

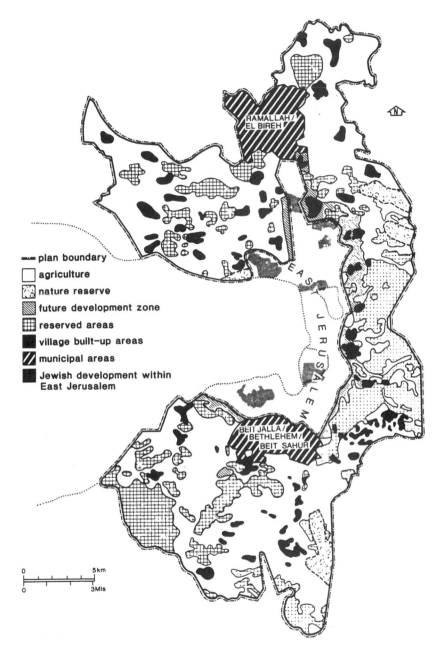

Figure 6.3 Israeli Regional Plan for Palestinian West Bank-Jerusalem Metropolitan Fringe

Source: Anthony Coon. 1992. *Town Planning under Military Occupation: An Examination of the Law and Practice of Town Planning in the West Bank.* Aldershot, U.K.: Dartmouth.

ples. The political significance underlying the Jewish "thickening" of Jerusalem through spatial counterweights is illuminated by the preliminary Israeli proposals for a final territorial arrangement of the occupied territories. The Jaffee Center for Strategic Studies recommends in their "moderate territorial compromise" (see Figure 6.4) that 89 percent of the non-Jerusalem West Bank be restored to the Palestinians and 11 percent of the West Bank—mainly the "high-demand" areas—be annexed by Israel, taking in about 70 percent of Jewish settlers in the West Bank (Alpher 1994). Significantly, Israeli control over east Jerusalem is treated as a fait accompli and is not counted in the 11 percent Israeli annexation figure. The report concludes that the greatest difficulty in implementing this "moderate territorial compromise" will be that the Palestinians'

> process of political rationalization must pass through one more phase—recognizing the impossibility of recovering all of the pre-1967 West Bank and East Jerusalem. (45)

The September 1995 Oslo II agreement, in designating zones of Palestinian empowerment in the West Bank, did little to constrain Israeli pursuit of the abovementioned strategy. The cities of Ramallah and Bethlehem were transferred to full Palestinian control; in addition, a few Area B "dents" of Palestinian territorial control will occur southeast of Jerusalem (a swath running from Beit Sahor to e-Azariya) and near the Jerusalem corridor. Yet Israel's options remain open regarding the West Bank areas inhabited largely by Jews. How these options will be exercised in future negotiations is indicated by the late Prime Minister Yitzhak Rabin's speech to the Knesset October 13, 1995, before that body's 61–59 approval of Oslo II. Rabin spoke of the changes to Israel's borders that he would have pursued as part of the permanent settlement:

> First and foremost, united Jerusalem, which will include both Maale Adumin and Givat Zeev, will be the capital of Israel, under Israeli sovereignty. . . . Other changes will include the addition of Gush Etzion, Efrat, Betar, and other communities, most of which are in the area east of what was the Green Line prior to the Six Day War.

The Palestinian view is that UN Security Council Resolution 242,[20] upon which the negotiating framework rests, requires total

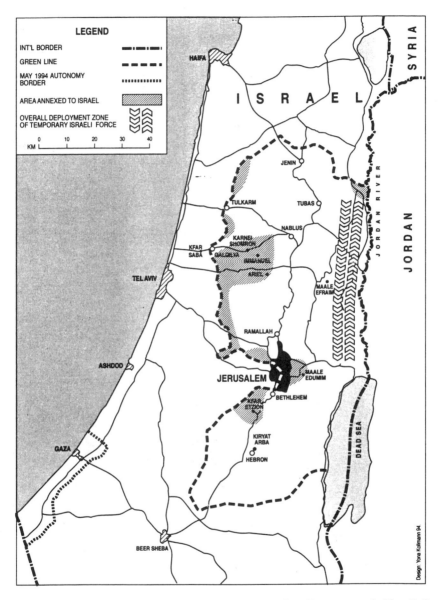

Figure 6.4 "Moderate Territorial Compromise" as Recommended by Jaffee Center

Source: Joseph Alpher. 1994. *Settlements and Borders.* Study No. 3. Final Status Issues: Israel-Palestinians. Tel Aviv: Jaffee Center for Strategic Studies.

withdrawal of the Israeli presence from the West Bank, *including* east Jerusalem. They point out that the international community has not recognized the annexation of east Jerusalem to the State of Israel.[21] Thus, the set of Israeli actions regarding east Jerusalem, the spatial counterweights, and the thickening of the Jerusalem corridor, among others, are all threats to a just and lasting peace that must be reversed as part of the permanent peace settlement. The Israeli view is that Resolution 242 allows for border modifications and recognizes Israel's right to have secure borders. One observer notes that "A new eastern border for Israel is in the process of being formed, but the precise location remains unclear" (*Jerusalem Post International Edition*, October 7, 1995).[22]

The 11 percent strategy of the Jaffee Center—creating a "Greater Jerusalem"—will likely be the most accommodating Israeli position (J. de Jong, interview). More aggressive Israeli positions would entail greater fragmentation of the West Bank (see Figure 6.5). One strategy would call for the breaking up of the West Bank into three Palestinian enclaves, the annexation of major Jewish settlement blocs to Israel, and the protection of "corridors" linking them to the

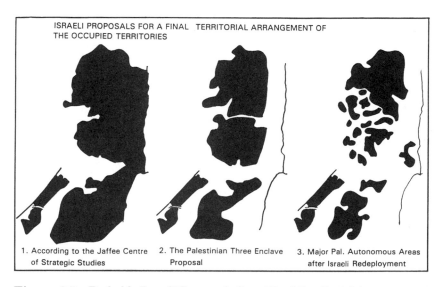

Figure 6.5 Probable Israeli Proposals for a Final Territorial Arrangement of the Occupied Territories

Source: Jan de Jong. 1994a. "What Remains? Palestine after Oslo." *News from Within* 10, 12: 3–14. Jerusalem: Alternative Information Center.

eastern settlement areas of the Jordan Valley. The most fragmentary strategy would be to seek to solidify the territorial arrangement resulting from interim-phase Israeli redeployment away from major centers of Palestinian population and cantons of villages. Possible futile negotiations over Jerusalem in the future may bolster advocates of this "status quo" strategy. The large Area C zones of Oslo II allow Israel the discretion to delay wholesale territorially based Palestinian empowerment.

A complex relationship exists between the future political geographies of Jerusalem and the West Bank. For either side, negotiation strategies regarding the two are ultimately inseparable. Yet, the phased D.O.P. process has thus far disconnected issues of Palestinian empowerment in the West Bank from those of Jerusalem's political future. Even a "moderate" 11 percent annexation strategy by Israel during "final status" negotiations would significantly strengthen her claims to the eastern part of the Israeli-defined Jerusalem. Israel will likely be a tough negotiating partner and propose more aggressive geographic strategies as a means toward achieving the 11 percent goal ultimately. M. Warshawski (director, Alternative Information Center, interview) asserts that the goal of Israel is "to have the most possible cards at the negotiation table. Their strategy is do the maximum now and bargain for the maximum." To the extent that negotiations focus on the metropolitan fringe and what to do about the Jewish presence in the spatial counterweights, attention and energy is diverted away from the issue of sovereignty and political control in east Jerusalem. The Palestinians appear to be in danger again of being pushed backward, similar to 1967 when Arab claims to pre-1948 west Jerusalem land and property were displaced by debates over the political status and control of east Jerusalem. The process of "political rationalization" (Alpher 1994) under this scenario that might be required again of Palestinian society may be too much for the Palestinian National Authority's emerging system of governance to absorb while maintaining sufficient legitimacy in their people's eyes.

The logic of the September 1993 D.O.P. appeared initially to be that resolution of the West Bank problem would come through separation of Jewish and Arab populations into contiguous areas, rather than fragmentation of the West Bank into smaller cantons. This was supported by Y. Rabin's public statements in late 1994, such as: "We cannot keep having this mixture of Jews and Arabs";

and "We have to decide on separation as a philosophy. There has to be a clear border." Further support is gained in Article IV of the D.O.P., which states that the "two sides view the West Bank and the Gaza Strip as a *single territorial unit*, whose integrity will be preserved during the interim period" (italics by author). This logic would be disrupted by the creation of a "Greater" Jerusalem of Israeli-annexed spatial counterweights because such extension of Israeli sovereignty practically divides the Palestinian "single territorial unit" into two (Figure 6.5, proposal 1). A fuller refutation of the "single territorial unit" goal of the Oslo accord would be the creation of enclaves or cantons of Palestinian authority (Figure 6.5, proposals 2 and 3). Either of these two West Bank political geographies would be a model facilitating a "Greater" Jerusalem of primarily Israeli control with cantons of Palestinian autonomy.

Israeli development patterns in and around Jerusalem, together with municipal annexation proposals, are establishing important geographic precedents and parameters for "final status" negotiations. Although Article V of the D.O.P. expressly states that "The outcome of the permanent status negotiations should not be prejudiced or preempted by agreements reached for the interim period," it is hard not to conclude that the interim territorial arrangements concerning the West Bank are creating narrow ground for Palestinians in negotiations over the future status of Jerusalem.

*   *   *

The different future scenarios regarding Jerusalem and West Bank political geographies will influence the productive viability of each side, and thus their ability to coexist politically as neighbors. I now look at economic scenarios under four different territorial configurations of Israel and a potential state of Palestine: (1) eleven percent Israeli annexation of West Bank; (2) three-enclave Palestinian configuration with Israeli west-east corridors; (3) "interim phase" redeployment configuration consolidating Israeli control over Jewish settlements in the West Bank; and (4) the establishment of an international border using the pre-1967 green line.

The 11 percent annexation strategy (Figure 6.5, proposal 1) protects economically the substantial Israeli housing market in Givat Zeev, Maale Adumin, and Efrat and would likely stimulate industrial development in Mishor Adumin. Places of residence such as Maale Adumin would increase in attractiveness to Jews and start to compete with residential developments, such as Modiin, to the west. At the same time, the intrusion of a Jewish corridor to the east of Jerusalem would tend to functionally separate north from south West Bank and increasingly constrain Palestinian access north-south through Jerusalem. Through these efforts, Arab east Jerusalem may be increasingly disconnected from the rest of the West Bank. A counterinfluence here is that topographical conditions largely force all north-south travel to go through Jerusalem. Thus, no matter the Israeli and Palestinian territorial configurations, economic connections between Palestinian West Bank and Jerusalem will likely remain. Nonetheless, such Israeli annexation would assuredly interfere with Palestinian plans to develop the Al-Quds (Jerusalem) district of the West Bank into the focal point of a potential state of Palestine, where tourism, government, public institutions, and commercial and service establishments would predominate (Center for Engineering and Planning 1992).

The strategy aimed at creating three Palestinian enclaves in the West Bank (Figure 6.5, proposal 2) protects for Israel a corridor from it to Jordan that has great economic potential. The metropolitan Jerusalem plan (p. 162), itself, identifies the great importance in potentially developing the Jerusalem-Jericho-Amman axis. According to J. de Jong (interview), a planned road connecting Ashdod (Israel) with Amman (Jordan) could be the site of major high-technology and industrial activities benefiting from access to Jewish and Arab labor pools and consumer markets. Assuming future accommodation between Israel and the Arab world, this economic potential could transform Jerusalem from an economic backwater to a major hub. Formerly "cul-de-sac" Jerusalem would then be at the center of a Arab-Jewish overland axis of trade and industry. However, this scenario further fragments the economic viability of a potential Palestinian state. In particular, Israel would control a significant amount of land between the Dead Sea and Jericho, an area identified as capable of housing the projected future stream of Palestinian immigrants from outside the West Bank (K. Tufakji, Arab Studies Society, interview).

The most fragmentary strategy—solidification of Israeli redeployment locations established during the "interim phase" (Figure 6.5, proposal 3)—would decrease spatially the conflict zones by placing Israeli guns "high and dry"; consolidating Israeli control in areas away from Palestinian population nodes. This might increase the security of the Israeli real estate and housing markets in the Jerusalem region, possibly more than in the 11 percent strategy because of the increased buffer from Palestinian autonomous areas. On the other hand, this territorial scenario would create a severely handicapped Palestinian entity physically incapable of developing itself economically on a regional basis. Such economic underdevelopment would likely cause tremendous social tension, which would work against Israel's own self-interests regarding peace and stability. Such social tension would be lessened to the extent that Israel can promote Jordan as an economic magnet to current and potential West Bank/Palestine residents.[23]

The creation of a state of Palestine using the pre-1967 green line would impose significant actual and future economic costs upon Israel. Actual economic costs would be due to the probable vacating of their housing units by most of the approximately 166,000 Jews living in east Jerusalem and more than one-half of the 150,000 Jewish settlers beyond in the West Bank,[24] and would entail a substantial loss of capital assets (housing stock, infrastructure, community facilities). Future economic costs include the forgone benefits of a secure and expanding housing stock in the spatial counterweights in the region, and the economic and investment benefits of linking Jerusalem to a high-technology corridor east of the city.

On the other hand, the contiguous territorial shape of a Palestine produced by using pre-1967 borders would enable the PNA to more fully engage in long-term, comprehensive planning to meet the challenges of projected population growth, infrastructure rehabilitation and expansion, and refugee resettlement. Palestinian planners, in *Master Planning the State of Palestine: Suggested Guidelines for Comprehensive Development* (Center for Engineering and Planning [CEP] 1992), make this argument in support of the formalization of pre-1967 borders:

> There must be increased land area to improve land carrying and productive capacity and secure better access and control over adequate natural resources, which is essential for enhancing the viability of the state and its socio-economic development requirements.

The use of pre-1967 borders would create a Palestinian state with relatively free corridors and access to other Arab countries and the coast.[25] Even with these borders, however, planning policy in a new state of Palestine would still face tremendous challenges. The CEP planning report provides insight into these challenges:

1. Occupation has caused substantial distortion and destruction of Palestinian social and economic bases, as well as critical physical and ideological fragmentation of the Palestinian human resource base.

2. The Palestinian declaration of statehood in 1988, the economic and social conditions of the *intifada*, plus the increasing flow of funds done without a comprehensive Palestinian plan have put the "political cart ahead of the horses of development."

3. In light of increased but disparate sources of external funding, there are inefficiencies of project-by-project development occurring without spatial coordination.

Assuming Palestinian statehood using pre-1967 borders, the CEP report projects that the 1990 population of 2.2 million in "Palestine" (including east Jerusalem and the Gaza Strip) would increase to 4.8 million in 2000, including 1.5 million immigrants from outside. The region of Jerusalem (Al-Quds district), which extends to the Jordan River in the east, is expected to grow from 584,000 population in 1990 to 1.4 million in 2000; population density would increase from 277 to 658 persons/ square kilometer. A total of 122,500 dwelling units would be needed in the Jerusalem region between 1993 and 2000 to meet expected housing demand. The Palestinian city of east Jerusalem ("Al-Quds"), itself, is expected to grow from 136,000 Arabs in 1990 to 300,000 in 2000. An assumption used in the CEP report is that "All Jewish colonies [neighborhoods] within the boundaries of the state [of Palestine] will be vacated and housing units credited to the Palestinian housing stock." J. de Jong (interview) criticizes this aspect of the report; he states that "Using only one model—that of restored sovereignty to all the West Bank and east Jerusalem—stirs the imagination by presenting a rosy view, but it is unrealistic."

The CEP report states that a new state of Palestine, unlike other developing countries, would only experience natural city population increases, not super-natural. Instead, there would be a gradual transformation of some towns and villages to semiurban as they acquire urban functions while maintaining a dominant traditional lifestyle. K. Tufakji (interview) goes one step further to suggest that planning policy should attempt to establish new Arab towns in the area of unused and inexpensive land stretching from the Dead Sea to north of Jericho. This would avoid the expensive rehabilitation of infrastructure and the urban fabric in existing cities (such as Ramallah and Nablus), decrease the destruction of agricultural land surrounding these existing cities, and increase the security of the new state by creating a north-south buffer of Palestinian population.

* * *

In the end, negotiations over the territorial arrangements of Israel and a prospective state of Palestine will entail two main lines of arguments. First, and more visible, will be the ideologically based arguments linked to religious claims and political security issues. But alongside these emotive issues will be less passionate, but nonetheless important, considerations of each state's economic viability and sustainability with new political borders. Urban and regional planners have much to contribute to these sustainability arguments, because many are based on development and economic criteria. While an economically viable and self-sufficient state of Palestine can do much to further regional security, a handicapped Palestine that furthers short-term Israeli interests would likely lead to regional instability with long-term costs to all Middle Eastern states.

Has Israel Achieved Its Goals Pertaining to Jerusalem?

Israel appears on its way toward achieving through partisan planning its goal pertaining to the unification of Jerusalem. The two major means utilized—boundary drawing and demographic planning—have created a landscape conducive to Israeli sole political control. Yet, at the same time, this landscape is an urban fabric of vulnerable interfaces and interethnic instability. From the Israeli perspective, the buffering effect of its political unification may be overcome by the inflammatory effect of its interface geography. Political unification may be solidified at the expense of security; domination and subjugation achieved at the expense of urban and regional stability.

Israeli actions since 1967 have increased Israeli political control of the city. Growth strategies have sustained a solid Jewish majority within municipal borders drawn by Israel. At the same time, the location of new neighborhoods has created a continuous Jewish presence within the city and thus a functional and demographic unification. The result has been a "semi-rational structure" of the city not easily segmented or divided politically (A. Shachar, Hebrew University, interview). This is supported by Palestinian Z. al-Qaq (co-director, Israel/Palestine Center for Research and Information, interview):

> With Israeli annexation of the city and service integration, one starts to think that separation is not practical or feasible.

Outside the city borders, "thickening" strategies have achieved part of what Israel has wanted—it is hard to draw a geographic line dividing Arab from Jew. This requires that attempts to divide sovereignty outside the city focus on functional, rather than geographic, criteria. The existence of the spatial counterweight cities creates the necessary foundations for future Israeli annexation strategies. Yet the landscape of domination—both in and outside the city—appears to be one of internal frictions and vulnerability that increases, not decreases, interethnic instability. An urban setting that expresses daily the asymmetry of territorial claims and rights is likely not sustainable unless the subordinated group voluntarily forfeits its claims, an unlikely scenario. Domination and partisan planning become exposed as strategies within conditions of ethnopolitical contest, not as solutions to ethnic polarization.

Israeli policy since 1967 has likely weakened Israel's authentic hold on Jerusalem while it has strengthened its ability to control it politically. Such political control is built on false foundations. Genuine and moral authority in a multiethnic city honors the centrifugal tendencies of ethnicity within integrative institutions and processes of city building and administration capable of appealing to the cross-communal and social-psychological needs of each group. When political control of a multiethnic city occurs without such moral authority, there is likely the stimulation of those very characteristics of the out-group—built on appeals to exclusionist, national ideology—that formed the rationalization for such disputed political control in the first place. Y. Golani, Ministry of the Interior (interview), spoke of this paradox: "As we strengthen our hold on Jerusalem, there is increasing terror all around."

The Fallacy of Partisan Planning

> In this endless struggle, how can you gain control?
>
> —Michael Romann,
> Tel Aviv University,
> in an interview

The major internal friction produced by partisan planning is the spatial expression of Jewish penetration into the former Arab side of the green line. Such penetration was absolutely vital to Israel's goal of furthering its political control of the city. Yet it simultaneously brings the two antagonistic parties closer spatially in the urban system. M. Romann,[26] professor of geography, Tel Aviv University (interview), speaks of a "dialectics" of separation and control. Interactions between the two goals of ethnic separation and political control are multiple and complex to the point of being potentially contradictory. In cities such as Jerusalem, both parties may likely want to be separate from each other spatially. Indeed, historic neighborhood patterns in the city pre-1948 created a multicultural mosaic of distinct Arab and Jewish communities. Yet with political competition over disputed territory comes the need to penetrate your opponent's territory as a way to strengthen your sovereignty argument. Over time, the means toward achieving the political control goal—that of penetration—creates spatial conditions of instability that may militate against the penetrator's actual control over the urban environment. Subsequent rounds of penetration are needed to control an urban fabric of complex ethnic geographies and unstable interfaces. Yet such actions further manipulate ethnic geographies, creating new spatial axes of tension rather than eliminating the sociospatial causes of intergroup conflict.

In Jerusalem, political competition since 1967 has brought Jewish and Arab communities closer spatially. Demographically based planning in pursuit of political control meant that the *location* of new Jewish neighborhoods was just as important as the *pace and extent* of development. Thus, the new satellite neighborhoods after 1967 were built in "east" Jerusalem across the old green line. If Israel simply wanted to safeguard a Jewish majority in the city, west Jerusalem areas could accommodate extensive Jewish growth in relatively safe environs separate from east Jerusalem. With the goal of political control, however, penetration of the east became vital. The type of penetration of the Arab tissue was done at a community level. Israeli expansions finger into and fragment Arab urbanization but at the same time attempt to stay separate through the use of dedicated infrastructure systems and natural geological divides. In this way, Israel wanted to penetrate the larger Arab fabric while still remaining separate within their own communities (Romann, interview). Penetration at more micro scales—neighborhood or block-based—would have too abruptly abandoned Jewish goals pertaining to interethnic separation and community identity.

Israeli partisan policies aimed at penetrating east Jerusalem—even though pursued with "separation within penetration" objectives—increase Jewish vulnerability. This has produced a situation described by R. Twite (Leonard Davis Institute of International Relations, Hebrew University, interview): "Jews have Jerusalem but cannot use it in its entirety." Under this scenario, the dominating side in an urban system becomes as much a loser as the dominated as Israelis find that major portions of the city are off-limits to them because of fear and neglect. It seems that the greater the territory that one side seeks to control politically in a contested urban environment, the less genuine authority it will likely have over the out-group population. This, in turn, stimulates further unilateral actions (geographic or military) to maintain claimed political authority. The fallacy of partisan planning is that its goal—political control—is achievable in the short term, but only at the expense of an urban stability required for the exercise of genuine authority. Partisan planning's success creates urban conditions in the short term conducive to its defeat in the long term.

> There is a different reality when you live in an area of constant tension.
>
> —Avi Melamed,
> Arab Advisor,
> Municipality of Jerusalem

Planning decisions that physically and symbolically extend one group's territorial claims create a landscape likely to exacerbate actual intergroup tension and potential conflict. Israeli urban policy in the long run will be counterproductive to its goals of building and safeguarding a Jewish Jerusalem. Significant Israeli fingering into eastern Arab Jerusalem increases potential violent interfaces between Israeli and Palestinian communities. The extensive spatial reach of Jewish neighborhoods adjacent to ghettoized and fragmented Arab villages provides multiple and undefensible interface points where interpersonal and intergroup conflict can occur. These interfaces create conditions where the psychological imbalance of relative deprivation may spur increasing intergroup conflict and violence. Interviews with several discussants[27] focused on the nature and location of these geographic hot spots.

Potentially volatile interfaces are classifiable into three geographic locations: (1) along the old 1949–1967 green line/border; (2) along new interfaces created in annexed, "frontier" parts of Jerusalem; and (3) along the outer Israeli municipal border of today. These are areas of frequent tension due to the proximity of Arab and Jewish residence and/or because an ongoing set of ethnic incidents has created a negative atmosphere. Table 6.2 itemizes the most often mentioned potential hot spots.

The potentially antagonistic neighborhoods on the narrowest ground are those in the first category. The demarcation of the green

Table 6.2 Examples of Vulnerable Interfaces in Jerusalem

	NEIGHBORHOODS	
	JEWISH	ARAB
Near 1949–1967 green line	Abu Tor	Abu Tor
	Gilo	Beit Safafa
	East Talpiot	Jabel Mukabber
"Frontier" penetration lines	Neve Yaakov	Beit Hanina
	Pisgat Zeev	Shuafat
	Givat Shapira	Issawiya
Along contemporary outer Israeli municipal borders	Neve Yaakov/Pisgat Zeev	A-Ram
	Har Homa (planned)	Beit Sahor
	Gilo	Bethlehem

line dividing Jerusalem 1949–1967 often divided proximate neighborhoods, such as in the Abu Tor area. In other cases, Israeli building after 1967 just over the green line penetrated close to existing Arab villages. The contact points along these "frontier" penetration lines not adjacent to the green line represent Israeli efforts to fragment the north-south Arab axis (Givat Shapira and Issawiya) or otherwise compete for space (Neve Yaakov and Beit Hanina). The final set of interfaces represents contact points along the contemporary outer border of Israeli-defined Jerusalem. This type of interface is paradoxical because the Israeli-delineated border, meant to separate peoples, has actually drawn the two sides closer in space due to the land use competition over Jerusalem. Much of A-Ram's growth can be attributed to its location just over the municipal border and thus its ability to act as a safety net for Arabs unable to live in Israeli-defined Jerusalem due to housing restrictions. The contemporary border, far from separating and sealing, creates increased interaction and points of conflict between the antagonistic groups.

Buffer or Flashpoint?

Despite Jerusalem's geography of urban instability and vulnerable interfaces, it may be that Jerusalem can pacify West Bank nationalism and be a buffer against intergroup tension. If this is true, a certain amount of instability created by the city's spatial structure can be absorbed due to other moderating influences in the urban system. In some ways, Jerusalem does act as a buffer against interethnic conflict and violence. E. Felner (interview), of the Israeli B'Tselem human rights organization, states that the Israeli Army's use of force in east Jerusalem has been less than in other West Bank areas because "With world attention upon Jerusalem, Israel must show the facade of a unified city." Civil rights and the availability of material benefits may also have a moderating influence on interethnic tension. An increasing number of east Jerusalem Arabs are applying for Israeli citizenship to gain better access to social services.[28] In addition, cooperative and practical joint ventures between Arabs and Jews may better Arab living conditions and "lead, not to coexistence per se, but to an increased willingness to be tolerant" (A. Melamed, interview). Likewise, any spending increase in Arab neighborhoods by the Municipality and government in the future may satisfy some of the immediate Palestinian demands that their basic human needs be met.

There is also the influence of Israeli democracy on the proximate Palestinian population. A. Melamed (interview) speaks of the "slow ongoing diffusion" of democratic ideas such as individual rights to the Palestinian Jerusalemites. However, this nexus between Israeli democracy and Palestinian society is likely to be significantly more complex. M. Benvenisti (interview) explains:

> It is not Israeli democracy that is moderating the Palestinians, but the fact that the Palestinians think they can use Israeli democracy by playing right against left.

Benvenisti asserts that Palestinian advocacy of moderation (such as espoused by F. Husseini, Palestinian leader in Jerusalem) can exploit left-right cleavages within the Israeli polity and society and find ideological allies. A more confrontational Palestinian approach, in contrast, would create a "tribal effect" and consolidate Israeli opinion against them.[29] Thus, democracy's moderating influence on intergroup conflict may come more from its indirect "window into Israel" effect than any direct influence its material benefits may have on lessening political aspirations. A final consideration that may moderate intergroup conflict in Jerusalem is its very potentiality as a flashpoint or lighting rod for conflict. M. Benvenisti (interview) asserts that this "potentiality is a reality which guides peoples' actions and attitudes." With this explosive potential, both sides know there are practical limits within which they must operate and lines they should not cross. Under these extreme conditions, "Violence may not be chosen because there is more to lose through violence then through other acts." Importantly, Benvenisti points out that the "absence of violence does not mean the absence of conflict. Symbolic and nonviolent acts can be more effective."[30]

Despite these potentially moderating effects of Jerusalem on intergroup conflict (or at least the violent outward indicators of such conflict), the explosive potential of the city remains. In a circumstance where urban inequality is an expression of deep-rooted power disparities, influences that moderate division but leave unaddressed sovereignty-based conflict will be ultimately futile. The buffer effects thus are temporary at best and are unlikely safeguards against the city's acting as a flashpoint for violence and conflict in the future.

The vulnerable interfaces created through partisan planning leave a legacy to Palestinians much as apartheid cities have done to black South Africans. Spatial structure and the built environment reify social and political inequalities. As pointed out in Safdie (1986, 262), the "contrasting patterns of the clustered village and the Ministry of Housing super-block becomes signposts of territoriality and segregation" (see Figure 6.6). The psychological experience of relative deprivation can be stark along the vulnerable interfaces. Intensifying this effect further is the fact that the Palestinian population is more progressive and better educated then in other Arab countries. N. Friedland, professor of psychology, Tel Aviv University (interview), points out:

> It is not just a poor person in a shack living next to a rich person's villa; it could be a physician living in a shack next to a rich person's villa.

The presence of vulnerable urban interfaces presents those seeking peace in the region with significant obstacles. Y. Golani (Ministry of the Interior, interview) describes the Israeli peace strategy as seeking

Figure 6.6 A Jewish-Arab Interface (Jewish Ramot Allon is in the foreground, the Arab village of Bet Iksa in the background. The "municipal border" parallels the valley that separates Jew from Arab).

Source: Scott A. Bollens

to "decrease the ground for terror" by negotiating with the majority of the Arab population, extending rights to them and enhancing their position. The goal is to isolate and disconnect the extremists on both sides. In Jerusalem, however, the extensive spatial reach of Jewish neighborhoods adjacent to ghettoized and fragmented Arab villages provides multiple and undefensible interface points where violent actions can occur. Because of their concrete expressions of Israeli dominance, they will be likely foci of extremist actions in the Jerusalem area, thus broadening the ground for terrorist groups. Political strategies aimed at peace and moderation of intergroup tension may likely be unable to compensate for the significant and pervasive instability rooted in the city's spatial and social structure.

Should any gradual political empowerment of the local Palestinian community in Jerusalem take place as part of a permanent settlement, the city's spatial structure may in the short term encourage an increase in traumatic urban events. The neighborhood interface areas in the Jerusalem region will provide magnets for Arab activists who reject the terms, or the basic idea, of a Jerusalem settlement with Israel. This would repeat the cruel irony that in the first three years of the Oslo "peace process" more Jewish lives, not fewer, were lost due to political violence.[31] Palestinian empowerment would then in turn lead to calls for Israeli military action to solidify Jewish neighborhoods in annexed Jerusalem.[32] A critical question then is—can Israeli political leaders sustain peace efforts regarding Jerusalem sovereignty in the face of a short-term increase in violence in the urban region? The destabilized urban environment of Jerusalem created by partisan policymaking will argue strongly for its renewed implementation. Partisan policymaking in this way generates the need for itself. The internal and self-fulfilling logic of partisan policymaking will likely stand as a formidable impediment to urban and regional peace.

* * *

Whether performing the role of buffer against ethnic conflict or flashpoint for it, Jerusalem—and the question of its political status—will play the central role in making or breaking the peace settlement between Israel and the Palestinians. Peaceful relations between Israel and the Palestinian people without a mutually agreed-upon settlement of the Jerusalem issue paints an improbable picture. N. Friedland, psychology professor who has been involved in mediating terrorist crises, points us in an important direction in dealing with Jerusalem. He asserts that the creation and maintenance of communal identity is key to dealing with conflict situations. In Jerusalem, for there to be communal identity on both sides, there needs to be clarity—often expressed through symbolism—regarding the two parts of the city. I now investigate how conflict over Jerusalem's political status may be managed so as to move it toward mutual and peaceful coexistence.

The Future of Jerusalem: City and Sovereignty

When you negotiate Jerusalem, you negotiate not only the present and future, but you negotiate the past.

—Ehud Olmert,
Mayor of Jerusalem,
November 10, 1994

Israeli plans for and practices in Jerusalem are therefore the central challenge facing Palestinians.

—Edward Said,
Al-Hayat,
December 10, 1993

What Jerusalem are we talking about?

—Zakaria al Qaq,
IPCRI,
in an interview

Jerusalem may be like the West Bank and Gaza in the future, with compromise and partial pullout. The intensity of emotions argues instead for direct conflict.

—Shlomo Hasson,
Hebrew University,
in an interview

Jerusalem Negotiated: Toward Mutual Coexistence

City administration and urban planning can either obstruct or facilitate a solution to the political problem that is Jerusalem. For the past thirty years, it has restricted Palestinian communal and societal development to narrow ground. Alternatively, planning and development policies could broaden the ground upon which the Palestinian society and polity can mature. For example, it could redraw municipal borders to encompass more Arab communities, color most green areas on planning maps a different color, and create neighborhood councils with actual authority. Such actions would produce a completely different Jerusalem from the viewpoint of city management and planning. However, Jerusalem is and will remain, first and foremost, a nationalistic conflict. As such, it is not a municipal issue, but one of sovereignty. Not dealing with the root causes of urban turmoil—sovereignty and political empowerment— means that traumatic urban events undertaken by fringe groups threatened by exclusion will increase in magnitude and variety. The distorted urban landscape of vulnerable and sharply asymmetric Arab-Jewish interfaces would provide multiple points of attack for such groups. When the root causes of conflict are not addressed, the structural, deep-rooted, and historically based tension characteristic of Arab-Jewish relations will frequently express itself in a specific urban event (terrorist bombing of a municipal bus), or through the connecting of an everyday, practical issue (regulation of amplification of mosque prayers) to these unresolved societal issues. A traumatic urban event indicates or opens up latent unresolved societal tensions.[33] This politicization can lead to the magnification of the urban manifestation of national tension (an urban riot) or to a deep societal self-reflection (such as the Israeli public attempting to cope on a social-psychological basis with the peace process amid terrorist attacks). In contrast, when sovereignty is effectively addressed, the urban setting is able to express a symmetry of territorial claims, and such traumatic disruptions to the urban system will decrease over time. In this case, fringe and terrorist groups would be the ones on narrower ground because the majority of both urban populations would condemn violence as too costly to sustainable urban existence.

Acknowledgment of opposing claims of sovereignty, at urban and national levels, seems a necessary first step toward the effective management of polarized cities. In a contested city, each side must be provided with political recognition and adequate land and productive carrying capacity to sustain its identity and viability. The health of both urban communities will alleviate interethnic tension as urban issues, not national ones, become the object of political deliberations. Only through such coexistent viability of competing communities can a city be said to be truly unified socially and economically.

The traditional use of the concept of "sovereignty" has implied an absolute holding of power over specified territory and its people (Baskin and Twite 1993) and has been perceived as an "indivisible and all-embracing quality" (Lapidoth 1992). This meaning of the word holds little promise for resolving the political status of Jerusalem. Israel's definition of the territory over which it holds "sovereignty," supported by the oft-quoted claim that the city is the "eternal and undivided capital of Israel," excludes any possibility for desired Palestinian "sovereignty" in east Jerusalem. The solution set given these two political negotiating positions is null. As S. Hasson (interview) states emphatically, "Given the current rhetoric, there is no way to bridge the gap." Two key social-psychological reconceptualizations are required to move away from the trap of exclusivity above—a recognition on Israel's part that the contemporary boundaries of Jerusalem are not "holy" but "political"; and a redefining of sovereignty, on the part of both Israel and the Palestinian Authority, to encompass inclusive and shared approaches. When approaching the issue of political control of Jerusalem, "One must define the boundaries of Jerusalem. What Jerusalem are you talking about? And, who controls those boundaries?" (G. Baskin, Israel/Palestine Center for Research and Information, interview). One can delineate the holy boundaries of the Old City and contrast them to the political boundaries of 1948 (small Jerusalem) and 1967 (annexed Jerusalem). Further, these political boundaries today are submerged within the functional boundaries of the metropolitan system. Today, the land-use competition is about "Who is going to control the outer boundaries?" (B. Hyman, Ministry of the Interior, interview). Which Jerusalem one talks about, and the assumptions one brings to negotiations concerning the tractability of boundaries, will determine the size of the potential solution space in deliberations over Jerusalem's future political status.

An approach to negotiating political control in Jerusalem put forward by the Israel/Palestine Center for Research and Information (IPCRI) (Baskin and Twite 1993) would require compromise and increased flexibility regarding Jerusalem's boundaries on the part of both Israelis and Palestinians. This model of "scattered sovereignty" would establish geographic boundaries of Israeli and Palestinian sovereignty within the present boundaries of Jerusalem and possibly in the metropolitan fringe as well. Jewish communities (in both west and east Jerusalem) would be under the sovereignty of Israel, while Arab communities in annexed Jerusalem would be within Palestinian sovereignty. Sovereignty would be "scattered" because of the dispersed and complex mosaic patterns of Arab and Jewish communities.[34] As G. Baskin (interview) states,

> Since the city is segregated, one can still draw lines on a map that determine sovereignty. Because both communities are interested in one Jerusalem, however, these lines of sovereignty would be drawn on a map, not on the ground.

A reconceptualization of boundaries and of "Jerusalem" itself would be required for "scattered" sovereignty to have a political chance. Palestinians would need to grant concessions concerning claims to pre-1948 west Jerusalem; G. Baskin (interview) explains that: "The upcoming debate over Jerusalem will likely begin in 1967, not 1948." In addition, Palestinians would need to recognize post-1967 Jewish neighborhoods in annexed Jerusalem through the recognition of Israeli sovereignty over these communities. In this way, Palestinians would need to make a distinction between post-1967 Jewish neighborhoods in "Jerusalem" and Jewish settlements in the "West Bank." In return for these Palestinian concessions, Israel would need to recognize the boundaries of today's Jerusalem as a political, not holy, creation. In particular, Israel would need to recognize Palestinian sovereignty over existing Arab communities and their likely areas of expansion. This would include recognition of Palestinian sovereignty over the inner east Jerusalem core and the likely establishment of their political capital and administrative buildings there.

An expansion of Jerusalem's borders to encompass the entire metropolitan area would include within the new city approximately equal Arab and Jewish populations, thus likely increasing the parity of sovereignty solutions. For example, there could be two ethnically based municipalities under a joint umbrella metropolitan council (H. Siniori, interview). K. Tufakji (interview) states that the chances that Jerusalem can be solved geographically increase with a metropolitan federalism of two sovereignties. Significantly, however, metropolitan governance must be used as a supplement, not replacement, for a sovereignty strategy *within* today's municipal borders. Allowing Palestinians sovereignty outside of Israeli city borders, but not inside, would be consistent with earlier patterns of partisan planning and would not address effectively the root causes of ethnic conflict. Metropolitan governance approaches can be misused. Regional governance lacking federalism, or without split sovereignty within Jerusalem's pre-1967 area, would amount more to occupation than responsible governance.

In addition to the reconceptualization of boundaries, the idea of sovereignty must be redefined. Establishing geographically scattered sovereignty where Israeli and Palestinian authorities would exercise absolute control would be crippling to the urban system, producing administrative fragmentation, psychological separation, and service delivery disabilities. Sovereignty would need to move from exclusive and absolute power to control exercised within an inclusive and shared framework. In the IPCRI proposal, the two ethnically based municipalities would have the right to make decisions in their sovereign areas, guided by the provisions of a Jerusalem Charter, which would serve as the primary source of joint authority and legitimacy for the governmental structures and policies in all parts of Jerusalem. This charter, or constitution, would stipulate certain fundamental rights of individuals, basic planning regulations that would guarantee that the essential character of the city be maintained, and establish consensual solutions regarding sensitive citywide issues, such as policing and the extent and distribution of immigration. In addition, the charter would incorporate cooperative governance arrangements in areas such as economic development and infrastructure.

Such a joint Arab-Jewish city constitution would entail a voluntary limitation of each side's sovereignty that was mutually recognized and mutually implemented on both sides. This notion of sovereignty is distant from the traditional concept and is more closely aligned with more recent uses of the concept, such as in the European Union (EU). There, each of the sovereign countries voluntarily accepts limits on its own sovereignty in order to become part of a stronger and larger sovereign body. In such a case, sovereignty is shared, not used exclusively; it is diffused through multiple levels and relative, not all-encompassing and absolute. And, it is something that is given through sharing, not taken through unilateral action.

S. Hasson (Hebrew University, interview) recommends that "Sovereignty can be dispersed over different layers of the political system, thus mitigating conflict." He suggests a multilayered approach to handling Jerusalem, wherein the best way to organize its contentious political space is through the creation of new institutions at different geographic levels—national, metropolitan, municipal, and submunicipal. Each level would have different functional areas pertaining to Jerusalem—national (tourism and holy places); metropolitan (regional cooperation over population and borders issues, and service delivery); municipal (city-scale decisions by a unified city council); and submunicipal (devolution of authority over cultural and neighborhood issues to community groups). This institution building would not come all at once, but through an "ongoing process that proceeds through several stages, involves mutual learning and leads to social, institutional and political transformations" (Hasson and Kouba 1994, 27). Such an incremental, pragmatic approach to Jerusalem parallels the basic approach of the September 1993 Declaration of Principles, which signalled the "plausibility and resonance of a process-oriented and cautious approach, based upon trust building, functional cooperation and pragmatic-concrete action" (Hasson and Kouba 1994, 27).

A significant advantage of this incrementally built and multilayered conception of sovereignty is its allowance for social and mutual learning. By starting with critical and pragmatic issues and proceeding carefully, psychological barriers to the reconceptualization of sovereignty can be addressed and hopefully overcome. For there to be a sharing of Jerusalem, Israeli policymakers must feel that there are cracks in the so-called national consensus that Jerusalem is Israel's "eternal and undivided capital." N. Friedland (interview) speaks of the difficulty many Israelis have in emotionally accepting a politically divided city. The question of Jerusalem's status, in isolation, produces such a consensus. However, if Jerusalem's status is perceived as part of a larger set of processes and relationships, the Israeli public might respond differently. At this stage, G. Baskin (interview) suggests that "Political realities may become stronger than ideological myths." These realities include the ability to have a genuinely accommodating Israeli-Palestinian relationship, increased personal and group security, and the opportunity to have Jerusalem recognized as Israel's capital by the international community. Cooperative Arab-Jewish ventures across several levels of authority pertaining to Jerusalem will also appeal to the charitable and humanitarian traditions of Jewish faith. Over time, dual Israeli-Palestinian sovereignty in Jerusalem might be increasingly perceived as sharing the city rather than dividing it; as creating something more than there is now, rather than cutting it in two. This is an exercise, it is true, of vocabulary and perceptions. But it would be more than simple rhetoric. Jerusalem will never be a unified and great city unless it can be shared.

Reconceptualizing Urban Planning and Policy

> There will always be two communities; two groups. The city will be one. There is not much that architecture or urban planning can do about that.
>
> —Shadi Ghadban,
> Chair, Architecture Department of
> Birzeit University,
> Ramallah, West Bank,
> in an interview

> If you didn't have political gains to be realized, you wouldn't have planning.
>
> —Hubert Law-Yone,
> Professor of Urban Planning at
> Technion Institute, Haifa, Israel,
> in an interview

Urban planners and administrators affect through their daily decisions the important spatial elements and community dynamics of a politicized urban geography. They cannot, nor should they, plead innocence by claiming impotency in the face of larger sovereignty conflict. H. Law-Yone (interview) claims that Israeli planners practice the self-delusion that planning is separate from politics, even though planning is one of the biggest tools of political struggle and many have come from a background where politics and planning are intertwined. If urban professionals separate from the political world by positioning themselves as technicians, they are deluding themselves and allowing the political winds to carry them. There is no surprise then that political realities rather than planning considerations have significantly shaped Israeli planning decisions since 1967 in Jerusalem and the West Bank.

Jerusalem and other cities of intense conflict offer urban planning and policymaking the opportunity to transform itself—from a profession capable of implementing partisan policies based upon technical reasoning to a morally articulate profession dedicated to the accommodation of deep differences. H. Law-Yone (interview) speaks of the "reflective practitioner" who is politically aware and thus in charge of her decisions. Conflict in polarized cities is ultimately about sovereignty and not urban service distribution. Thus, urban policymakers should contribute to larger sovereignty debates their ideas concerning each side's needs for territorial identity; land, urban services, and natural resources; and inclusive governance at neighborhood and municipal levels. Such urban planners would become valuable participants within the increasingly divided contexts of contemporary world cities. The main clients for these planners are the urban system and environment, which are the ultimate losers in a politically motivated land-use competition. In Jerusalem, urban infrastructure patterns have been strained, growth patterns distorted, and important physical environmental resources eroded in the face of political needs. One Palestinian interviewee (A. Aghazarian, Birzeit University) asserts, "I don't doubt the Jews' love for this city. But they are killing it because of their love for it."

Sovereignty is ultimately tied to land. This has been clearly portrayed by the important role and effects of Israeli land-use policy in creating geographical obstacles to the drawing of sovereignty lines. Thus exposed is urban planning's deep connection to political motivations and impacts. The key for planners is to make use in the future of such a connection to broaden, not restrict, opportunities for peaceful coexistence. It is unlikely that an urban profession such as planning can, by itself, create freedom and peace. But, it may likely be capable of creating urban conditions that are enabling of such human goals. Urban planning has two important roles to play in moving Jerusalem toward coexistent viability—as a community bridge builder; and as an articulator and educator concerning the land and community requisites for rebuilding Palestinian society.

As bridge builders between ethnic communities, urban planners are capable of increasing the willingness of each side to be tolerant. A. Melamed (interview) speaks of the dilemma often confronted by joint Arab-Jewish ventures in the city—the same people who are positive forces in community bridge building are susceptible to being captured by larger political obstructions. Urban planning's role at this time is critical—to effectuate a manageable balance between cooperative practical ventures and the more emotive political issues.

This connection of the practical with the political, often avoided by planners due to fear or intimidation, actually provides the urban professional with an important access point into the complex dynamics of a politically contested city. Melamed suggests that "once the line is crossed to the political, you gain something very important—you can reduce the explosive potential." The benefits of these practical joint ventures guided by planners would include the betterment of living conditions, an increase in the psychological readiness of both sides to participate in a political arena of shared sovereignty, and the enabling of a more natural evolution in intergroup relations, which can attenuate ethnic conflict. The bridge-builder role of planning amidst political contest should be nurtured within the profession not only by changing the goals of planning, but also by changing who is involved in doing the planning itself. Urban planning should encourage the introduction of diverse personal histories into its professional ranks. Whether working for a government or an NGO, Israeli and Palestinian urban professionals would be well-positioned to articulate their respective community concerns while having knowledge of citywide public administration and fiscal realities.

Planners also have a critical role in addressing directly the need for parity of urban conditions, by being articulators and educators about the land and community requisites for rebuilding Palestinian society in the Jerusalem region. There are many planning- and development-related needs and tasks ahead to reconstitute an urban society depleted by disempowerment. Some of these are the:

- Need for a coherent land use and development strategy for Palestinian Jerusalem; the documentation of housing needs, deficiencies, and limitations under Israeli control; and the land and service needs required for a healthy and productive Palestinian sector;

- Need for a collective process of Palestinian community and economic development in the Jerusalem region, such as done by a public authority that would be empowered to expropriate, re-parcel, and develop in pursuit of housing and other public goals;

- Need for financial institutions to provide credit loans or subsidies for people who want to build in the Jerusalem area;

- Need to build and maintain a consortium of development-related nongovernmental organizations (NGOs) in Palestinian Jerusalem;

- Need to argue that coexistent viability is in the interests of the city at large and each of its antagonistic groups. Urban professionals can help Palestinians articulate what is good for them in Jerusalem, and help counter Israeli conceptualizations of the Palestinian "public good."

Coexistent viability and shared sovereignty would acknowledge and honor the centrifugal tendencies of ethnicity within the integrative institutions and processes of city building and administration. Both sides of the political contest would be provided with adequate land and productive carrying capacity to sustain their identity and viability. At the same time, the self-sufficiency of both urban communities would alleviate interethnic tension as urban issues of joint interest, not national ones of separate interest, become the object of local and metropolitan deliberations. A reconceptualized urban planning profession in Jerusalem could play an instrumental role in achieving such coexistent viability. No other profession is more suited for this task than is urban planning, with its education in land-based issues and its experience of working with a multiplicity of interests and claims.

P ART III

Belfast— Greyness Where Color Matters

O the Bricks they will bleed and the rain it will weep,
  And the damp Lagan fog lull the city to sleep;
  It's to hell with the future and live on the past;
  May the Lord in His mercy be kind to Belfast.

—Maurice James Craig,
  "Ballad to a Traditional Refrain" (excerpt)

Figure 7.1 Newtownards Road, East Belfast

Source: Scott A. Bollens

7

Territoriality and Governance

Background

Belfast is an urban setting pervaded by an overlapping nationalist (Irish/British) and religious (Catholic/Protestant)
conflict. It has been since 1969 a violent city of sectarian
warfare.[1] From 1969 through 1994, the "Troubles" in Northern Ireland resulted in 3,169 dead, 38,680 injured, and 10,001 bombings
(*The Guardian* September 1, 1994). Belfast has borne the brunt of
this violence. More than one thousand of the 1,810 fatal incidents
from 1969 to July 1983 occurred in the Belfast urban area (Poole
1990).[2] Forty-one percent of all explosions during the Troubles have
occurred in the Belfast urban area, with almost 70 percent of bombings aimed at housing occurring in the urban area (Boal 1995). Attacks on shops, offices, industrial premises, pubs and clubs, and
commercial premises have been disproportionately concentrated in
Belfast. Violence in Belfast has been inextricably linked to the
maintenance of ethnic territory and identity. It has been the main
means used to colonize the outer margins of urban ethnic community space and to repair fractured and threatened ethnic identity
(Feldman 1991; Bell 1987). Unlike the Jerusalem case where that
city contributes an additional layer of difficulty to the resolution of
national sovereignty conflict, there is no Belfast problem that exists
independently of the Northern Ireland problem (Gutmann and
Klein 1980). Nevertheless, it is critical to examine Belfast, because
it is by far the most populated city in the state[3] and is the capital of
contested Northern Ireland; it is an important stage upon which the
broader nationalist conflict is performed.

Although religion is a basic component of personal and group loyalty, the conflict is exacerbated by the fact that religious identities coincide strongly with political and national loyalties.[4] The allegiances of Protestant "unionists" and "loyalists" are with Britain, which since 1972 has exercised direct rule over Northern Ireland. Catholic "nationalists" and "republicans," in contrast, consider themselves Irish and commit their personal and political loyalties more to the Republic of Ireland to the south. The border between Northern Ireland and the Republic of Ireland, established in 1920, created a secure unionist majority in the north through the inclusion of six of the nine counties of the historic province of Ulster (see Figure 7.2). Without such a border, Protestants would have been substantially outnumbered in a unified Ireland.[5] Political boundaries on the island thus create a "double minority syndrome" (Benvenisti 1986a); Protestants are an island-wide minority threatened by possible unification, and Catholics are a minority in Northern Ireland threatened by Protestant and external British rule.

Physical and Demographic Setting

The city of Belfast, like Northern Ireland as a whole, has a majority Protestant population. According to the Northern Ireland Housing Executive (NIHE), the 1991 city population of 279,000 was comprised of an estimated 57 percent Protestant/other and 43 percent Catholic (see Figure 7.3).[6] The Catholic percentage has been increasing over the last few decades due to higher Catholic birth rates and Protestant out-migration to adjoining towns (see Figure 7.4). In 1981, the city of Belfast was about 62 percent Protestant/other and 38 percent Catholic (NIHE figures). In particular parts of the city, Protestant decline and Catholic growth are starkly portrayed by population trends. In north Belfast and Protestant west Belfast together, the Protestant population of 116,000 in 1971 declined to 51,750 in 1991, with expectations of a further drop to 39,000 in 2001 (Department of the Environment for Northern Ireland [DOENI] 1992a). The religious composition of the subarea was 79–21 percent Protestant-Catholic in 1971; 57–43 percent in 1991; with forecasts for a 48–52 percent Catholic majority in this subarea in 2001 (DOENI 1992a).[7] The larger region—the Belfast Urban Area

Figure 7.2   Northern Ireland and Belfast

Source: Ronald Weitzer. 1990. *Transforming Settler States: Communal Conflict and Internal Security in Northern Ireland and Zimbabwe.* Copyright © 1990 The Regents of the University of California. Berkeley: University of California Press.

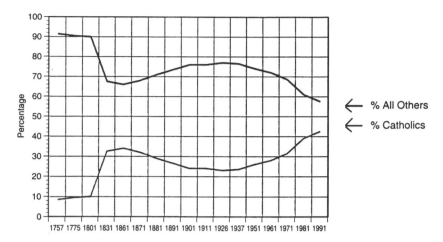

Figure 7.3 Religious Composition of Belfast City Population 1757–1991: Catholics and All Others as Percentage of Total City Population

Source: Frederick Boal. 1995. *Shaping a City: Belfast in the Late Twentieth Century*. Belfast: Institute of Irish Studies, Queen's University.

(BUA)—is composed of the city of Belfast, plus the surrounding towns of Lisburn, Newtownabbey, Castlereagh, North Down, and Carrickfergus. These suburbs have lesser Catholic populations (on average, about 20 percent) than Belfast city. As such, the 1991 BUA population of 476,000 is more Protestant than in the city alone—approximately 65 percent Protestant/other and 35 percent Catholic (NIHE figures).

Both Belfast city and the larger urban region have faced significant population declines since 1971. Core city declines started before this, with population peaking at 443,000 in 1951. Since then, the core city has decreased in population size by 37 percent. Growth in the urban area but outside the city continued between 1951 and 1971, with development spreading on to the lower slopes of the surrounding hills. Belfast urban area population peaked at 582,000 in 1971; since then, urban area population has declined to today's 476,000, a 19 percent decrease. It is only the outer reaches of the Belfast area—a ring of towns within commuting distance of the downtown core—that have shown population growth in the last two decades. The greater Belfast area inclusive of these exurban areas is home to about 727,000 residents, about one-half of the approximately 1.5 million residents of Northern Ireland. The combination

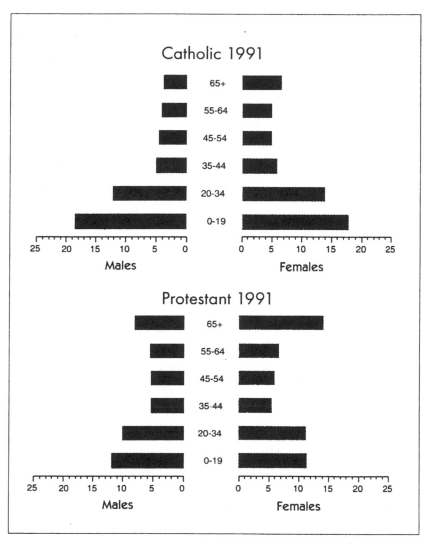

Figure 7.4 Age Distribution of Catholic and Protestant Populations in Belfast City 1991

Note: Percentages of female and male populations within different age intervals. Note the younger age of the Catholic population and the greater proportion currently in, or approaching, child-bearing ages.
Source: Frederick Boal. 1995. *Shaping a City: Belfast in the Late Twentieth Century*. Belfast: Institute of Irish Studies, Queen's University.

of Belfast core city decay, suburban stagnation, and exurban fringe growth has been described by Boal (1994) as a "radical spatial transformation . . . within the urban region that, overall, displays a static population size."

Although the city of Belfast is part of a larger urban region, I focus for most of this analysis on issues pertaining to the city of Belfast proper. I do this because demographic proportions have greater parity, ethnic issues have greater salience, and land-use and development problems are more complex and potentially inflammatory in the city than they are elsewhere in the Belfast Urban Area. Regional dynamics involving growth, migration, and housing assuredly add to or decrease ethnic pressure in the city, as will be discussed. Still, the city proper contains a set of root issues and conflicts that in all likelihood will need to be addressed at the level of the city, not the larger region.

The city of Belfast's political geography is one of multisector segregation that both reflects and intensifies conflict (Budge and O'Leary 1973; Schmitt 1988). There has been a stubborn persistence of Protestant-Catholic segregation through the decades, with the greatest increases in sectarian separation associated with periods of communal instability (Boal 1996). Protestant-Catholic employment segregation has resulted over the last one hundred years in residential patterns of clearly identifiable communities (Feldman 1991). Even before interethnic violence ("the Troubles") began in 1969, segregation was widespread, with 64 percent of Belfast households living on segregated streets that contained less than 10 percent of the other ethnicity (Keane 1990). Intense sectarian hostility and violence, erupting in the summer of 1969, led to widespread intimidation, sudden and large-scale population movement, and the burning of whole streets of dwellings. Between 1969 and 1973, in the face of rioting, general disturbances, then terrorist bomb and gun attacks, an estimated 60,000 Belfast residents were forced to leave their homes, moving from vulnerable and destabilizing interface areas to neighborhoods where their ethnic group was dominate (NIHE 1991; Boal 1982 and 1994). This accentuated the degree of Protestant-Catholic segregation; by 1977, 78 percent of households lived on segregated streets where the minority was less than 10 percent (Keane 1990).[8]

The severity of ethnic segregation is displayed when a wider geographic scale—that of the ward—is used (see Figure 7.5). Of Belfast city's fifty-one electoral wards, thirty-five contain one reli-

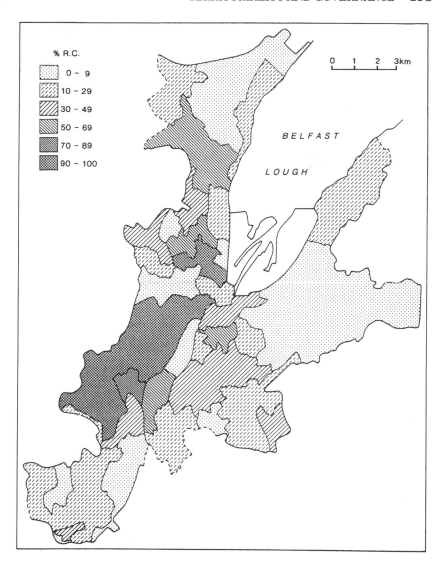

Figure 7.5 Distribution of Roman Catholics in Belfast Urban Area

Source: Frederick Boal. 1994. "Belfast: A City on Edge." In Clout, Hugh (ed.) *Europe's Cities in the Late Twentieth Century*. Amsterdam: Royal Dutch Geographical Society.

gion that dominates 90 percent or more of the population (*The Independent on Sunday*, March 21, 1993). The Catholic neighborhoods of The Falls, Andersonstown, Ardoyne, and Short Strand are easily identifiable; as are the Protestant areas of Shankill, Sandy Row, and Newtownards Road (Whyte 1985). The Catholic "heartland" is composed of greater west Belfast, centered on the Falls neighborhood; the primary Protestant "heartland" has traditionally been the Shankill neighborhood. Residential segregation is reinforced through exceedingly low levels of Protestant-Catholic interaction in terms of such activities as movement to bus stop, grocery store, and to visitors or family; and readership of newspaper and football team loyalties (Boal 1969). Catholics make up 55 percent of the city's population west of the Lagan River; compared to only 12 percent east of the river. Thus, the "terms 'East' and 'West' Belfast carry considerably greater symbolic baggage than their directional qualities alone would suggest" (Boal 1994, 147). Economic deprivation, although characteristic of numerous neighborhoods—both Protestant and Catholic—is most acute in the predominantly Catholic ghetto of west Belfast, where the unemployment rate among economically active males in 1985 was 47 percent (Gaffikin and Morrissey 1990). South Belfast, more middle-class and with greater owner-occupied housing stock, exhibits greater ethnic mixing than west or east as this once largely Protestant area now contains a substantial Catholic minority. North Belfast, meanwhile, is in a difficult state of flux of Protestant decline and Catholic growth, with multiple interfaces and isolated pockets of ethnic concentrations (DOENI 1992a). Because of this territorial instability, ethnic violence and terror have been intense. The Duncairn Gardens interface in north Belfast that separates Catholic New Lodge from Protestant Tiger's Bay was described as a "sectarian murder-ground" (B. Morrison, Town and Country Planning Service, Belfast Divisional Office, interview), having been the site of 20 percent of all sectarian violence in the city (K. Sterrett, Town and Country Planning Service, interview).

Political Control

From 1972 to early 1999, legislative power for Northern Ireland has been held by the British House of Commons in Westminster, of which only seventeen members come from Northern Ireland.[9] The unionist-majority Northern Ireland Parliament, the governing body for the province up until 1972 and linked to the formulation of discriminatory and unjust laws, was held to be incapable of fair and capable governance, and the British enacted "direct rule" in the midst of sectarian conflict in 1972. Executive power for Northern Ireland under direct rule has been possessed by the Secretary of State for Northern Ireland, who is chosen from the party ruling at Westminster. The result of direct rule has been "an almost complete absence of representative participation and accountability" (Hadfield 1992). The thinking behind direct rule was that the removal of policy formulation and implementation from the bitter sectarian conflict would make it more efficient and effective (Loughlin, 1992). Ministers in charge of Northern Ireland governance take their political cues from Westminster, and have tended toward an inherently conservative, non-risk-taking approach to the province's controversial issues (P. Sweeney, Department of the Environment for Northern Ireland, interview).

The authority of local governance in Belfast and elsewhere in Northern Ireland was significantly eroded by "direct rule." It was at the local level of government that sectarian bias was most evident, especially in the fields of public employment, service delivery, and housing (Loughlin 1992). Thus, today the locally elected fifty-one-member Belfast City Council has severely constrained policymaking power in planning, urban service delivery, and housing; it is predominantly an advisory body (Hadfield 1992). Instead, most power in these policy areas has been located in appointed boards—such as the Northern Ireland Housing Executive—or in central executive agencies—such as the Department of the Environment for Northern Ireland—which are responsible to British ministers rather than to local politicians (Hadfield 1992; Loughlin 1992). Civil servants in Northern Ireland government charged with Belfast urban policy have thus seen themselves within the political framework determined by Westminster. This centralized policymaking structure is viewed as capable of depoliticizing local planning issues and holding in abeyance the larger community power struggles (Douglas 1982; Blackman 1991). Administrators of urban policies for Belfast have viewed themselves as above local conflicts and often take pride in their technocratic approach (Loughlin 1992).

There are five major political parties in Northern Ireland. Protestant-aligned parties are the Ulster Unionist Party (also called the Official Unionists) and the Democratic Unionist Party. While both favor continued links with Great Britain, the UUP is often more moderate than the DUP (Whyte 1990). Catholic-aligned parties are the Social Democratic and Labor Party (SDLP), expressive of moderate constitutional nationalism, and Sinn Fein, the political wing of the provisional Irish Republican Army (IRA), which advocates physical force as an appropriate means toward separation from the union. The centrist party is the Alliance Party, which favors continued union with Great Britain but advocates the establishment of accommodating structures in Northern Ireland to reduce Unionist hegemony. Whyte (1986) has observed that Protestants are socially fragmented in terms of denomination[10] and class but politically unified in support of unionism. In contrast, Catholics are socially cohesive, but face internal political disagreement. Whereas all political parties supported by Protestants favor continued links with Great Britain, Catholics experience internal disagreements over how such links might be severed—nationalists of the SDLP favoring constitutional means; republican followers of Sinn Fein advocating physical force—and tend to favor more than Protestants the centrist Alliance Party. Generally, there has also been greater antagonism between SDLP and Sinn Fein supporters than between UUP and DUP followers, with many SDLP supporters giving their secondary preference votes in proportional representation elections to the Alliance Party rather than to Sinn Fein (Whyte 1990). Nevertheless, splits within the unionist camp can be intense, especially during recent negotiations with Catholic-aligned parties over a possible political settlement.

Despite the limitations on the authority of Belfast City Council, local elections do illuminate Belfast residents' political allegiances and the direction of future policy under possible devolution of

Table 7.1   Percentage of Local Council Seats Won in 1993—Belfast and Northern Ireland

	BELFAST CITY	NORTHERN IRELAND
Ulster Unionist Party	31.4	29.0
Sinn Fein	19.6	12.5
Social Democratic and Labor Party	17.6	21.9
Democratic Unionist Party	17.6	17.2
Alliance Party of Northern Ireland	9.8	7.7
Other	3.9	11.7

Source: Boyle, K. and T. Hadden. *Northern Ireland: The Choice* (London: Penguin), p. 55.

power to local government. Protestant-aligned parties have traditionally controlled the city council. Table 7.1 displays the relative sizes of the major political parties' constituencies in the 1993 local elections, both city-specific and Northern Ireland–wide. Of particular note in the local list is that unionists held close to 50 percent of the Belfast seats (facilitating a working majority on most occasions), compared to 37 percent for Catholic-aligned parties.[11] Also, the republican Sinn Fein showed greater strength in Belfast than provincewide.

In 1997, a significant change occurred when Belfast local elections resulted in the loss of the long-held majority control by Protestant-aligned political parties. Combined, nationalist, republican, and middle-of-the-road Alliance Party representatives now held twenty-six of the fifty-one seats on Belfast City Council. This working majority resulted in the selection of the first nationalist mayor in the city's history. Table 7.2 displays the political configuration of the current Belfast City Council, as well as the provincewide distribution. Political support for the republican Sinn Fein increased both locally and nationally since 1993, with its greater support remaining in Belfast.

A significant alteration of Northern Ireland governing institutions and constitutional status is specified in the April 1998 *Agreement Reached in the Multi-Party Negotiations* ("Good Friday Agreement"). This agreement, approved by more than 70 percent of Northern Ireland voters May 1998, outlines a process which would transfer day-to-day rule of the province from Britain to a new

Table 7.2   Percentage of Local Council Seats Won in 1997—Belfast and Northern Ireland

	BELFAST CITY	NORTHERN IRELAND
Ulster Unionist Party	25.5	27.8
Sinn Fein	25.5	16.9
Social Democratic and Labor Party	13.7	20.7
Democratic Unionist Party	13.7	15.6
Alliance Party of Northern Ireland	11.8	7.0
Other	9.8	12.0

Sources: Tonge, Jonathan. 1998. *Northern Ireland: Conflict and Change.* London: Prentice Hall Europe, p. 53; Belfast city council webpage (www.belfastcity.gov.uk).

directly elected Northern Ireland Assembly, in which Protestants and Catholics will have shared power. The accord states that Northern Ireland will remain within the United Kingdom as long as a majority in the province wants to remain there.[12] In response to nationalist desires, the new assembly and the Irish Parliament are to form a North-South Council to coordinate and encourage cross-border cooperation. To reassure unionists, a Council of the Isles will be created to link the governments in Northern Ireland and Ireland with the British government and with new legislative assemblies being set up in Scotland and Wales.

As specified in the agreement, a 108-member Northern Ireland Assembly was elected in June 1998 based on proportional representation.[13] As Table 7.3 indicates, this polling resulted in an Assembly of dispersed power. The two more moderate parties in the middle—the Protestant-aligned Ulster Unionist Party and the Catholic-aligned Social Democratic and Labor Party—have more seats than the more hardline loyalist Democratic Unionist Party and republican Sinn Fein, although these differences are not great. Splits within the Protestant camp between the pro-agreement UUP and the anti-agreement DUP could jeopardize the workability of the Assembly and other new governing institutions. As in 1997 local elections, the balance of power between Protestant-aligned parties and Catholic-aligned parties showed greater

Table 7.3   Percentage of 1998 Northern Ireland Assembly Seats Won

	NORTHERN IRELAND (108 seats)	FROM BELFAST CITY CONSTITUENCIES (24 seats)
Ulster Unionist Party	25.9	25.0
Social Democratic and Labor Party	22.2	20.8
Democratic Unionist Party	18.5	16.7
Sinn Fein	16.7	20.8
Alliance Party of Northern Ireland	5.6	4.2
Other	11.1	12.5

Sources: BBC News, Assembly Elections, State of the Parties (www.news.bbc.co.uk); *Belfast Telegraph* web page (www.belfasttelegraph.co.uk).

parity from Belfast city constituencies than from throughout Northern Ireland.

A twelve-member multiparty executive is to be constituted on the basis of proportional vote. If this cabinet is successfully appointed, the Assembly would then have authority to pass legislation in devolved areas, which are those currently within the responsibility of the Northern Ireland Departments of Finance and Personnel, Economic Development, Environment (which includes most urban policy functions), Education, Health and Social Services, and Agriculture. No Assembly decision would be approved unless there are parallel majorities in both Protestant and Catholic camps or if it is acceptable to 60 percent of those voting, including at least 40 percent from each camp. The Secretary of State for Northern Ireland retains executive responsibility, and the Westminister Parliament legislative authority, for those matters not devolved to the Assembly.

The challenges of governance and policymaking discussed in this book under third-party direct rule remain highly salient under a possible alternative governance arrangement. This is not to underestimate the extraordinary opportunities related to the negotiated transformation of Northern Ireland's governance. Rather, it is to assert the importance attached to the capacity of any political arrangement, no matter how constituted, to implement programs and produce outcomes that make a meaningful difference in a divided society. Under either direct rule or local rule, some effective policymaking must occur that moves the society toward mutual accommodation and away from rigidity and status quo. Seen in this light, the political negotiations successfully culminated in April 1998 represent a first, but by no means sufficient, step toward normalizing Northern Ireland. The new governing arrangement specified in the 1998 agreement also leaves open the question of urban government and policymaking, the main topic of this inquiry. I discuss ways that urban policy can contribute to reinforcing a possible move toward peace initiated by the April accord and historic May vote. Even with possible advances at regional and international levels, the urban part of the puzzle remains as problematic today under potential forms of local control as it did under British direct rule.

Without effective and progressive policymaking, a conceivable new governance for Northern Ireland will produce gridlock. That both sides must concurrently gain from public policy is made clear by two facts. First, the 1998 agreement allows that significant op-position from either Protestants or Catholics to a policy proposal is sufficient to defeat it. This ability of either ethnic grouping to de-rail policymaking means that proposals will likely search for com-mon ground. Second, the May 1998 vote itself was not equally supported across sects; one exit poll on election day showed that Protestant support for it barely passed 50 percent while Catholic voter support surpassed 95 percent. The new set of governing in-stitutions in Northern Ireland and the United Kingdom anticipated in the 1998 Agreement will likely blossom or flounder depending upon how well new policies coming from these bodies deliver on both Protestant and Catholic hopes for a different society. "On-the-ground" policies pertaining to housing, economic development, human services, social inclusion, growth, and development[14] will help determine the quality and sustainability of Northern Ireland's governing institutions.

Economic Aspects

> The political and constitutional issues of course are important, but are not overwhelmingly the main frame of reference in which peo-ple locate the conflict.
>
> —Smith, D. J. (1987)

Part of the challenge facing any new set of governing institutions in Northern Ireland is an economic one. In a 1987 survey of more than 1,650 people in Northern Ireland, as many respondents thought of the causes of sectarian conflict in terms of social and economic con-ditions and the rights of citizens (33 percent) as in terms of politi-cal/constitutional issues (33 percent) (Smith, D. J. 1987). This feeling held for Catholics as well as Protestants. It becomes signifi-cant then to examine the economic conditions of Belfast and North-ern Ireland that existed both before and during the years of interethnic violence and which will pose an obstacle to future peace building in the city.

Although the city dates to 1603, growth of the textile, shipbuild-ing, and engineering industries in the late 1800s was what stimu-lated Belfast's rapid expansion (NIHE 1991). By the late 1800s, Belfast resembled many of Britain's industrial cities—row upon row of "two up two down" kitchen houses in the shadow of textile mills and engineering works. Since 1971, the Belfast region and its economic base have faced significant economic decay and transformation. In 1991, 20.3 percent of the city's economically active residents were unemployed (Northern Ireland Council for Voluntary Action 1993). Over a twenty year period, more than 42,000 jobs were lost to Belfast city residents. Manufacturing employment declined from 30 percent of the city workforce to 15 percent (Boal 1994). The ethnic civil war has contributed to this manufacturing decline, but there were more structural influences too. Whyte (1990) points out the vulnerability of the export-oriented Belfast economy to slumps in the world economy and to sluggish growth in Britain, a major buyer of Belfast exports. Only the service sector has stemmed the tide of economic decay in Belfast since 1971, growing from 23 to 33 percent of the city economy. However, this service growth has until recently not been in retail trade, but in government and security-related jobs. Since 1971, these jobs have increased from 6 percent to 16 percent of the local economy. Today, a substantial one out of six city residents are employed in either public administration or security-related expenses. Since the mid-1990s, there has been some economic recovery amidst periodic cessation of hostilities. City center revitalization, supported by government subsidies, has improved the retail service sector there and enhanced the city's ability to attract regional customers (A. Cebulla, Northern Ireland Economic Research Centre, interview). Still, the Belfast city economy remains skewed toward jobs not linked to production of added value, but to the maintenance and stability of a conflicted society.

The size of the public sector reflects both the high levels of need in Belfast as well as the substantial expenditures on law and order. The artificiality of the Northern Ireland economy is linked to the fact that it is substantially subsidized by Britain financially (Gorecki 1995). In 1991–1992, almost 40 percent of total public spending in Northern Ireland came in the form of a direct subsidy, or "subvention,"[15] from the British central government (Livingstone and Morison 1995). In 1992–1993, Boyle and Hadden (1994) report that the subvention was up to 3.5 billion pounds sterling, representing almost 50 percent of total Northern Ireland public expenditure of 7.5 billion pounds. The Belfast economy's shift from manufacturing to public administration and security is traceable in part to the Troubles. Cebulla (1994) observes that the Troubles gave the propensity toward economic de-concentration found in many industrial cities "an added impetus exaggerating the trend." He adds that "total employment in the city may thus not have looked much different in the absence of the Troubles; yet, Belfast's economy has been structurally altered, and its private sector in particular, weakened." In a similar vein, economists F. Gaffikin and M. Morrissey (University of Ulster, Jordanstown; interviews) point out that "Long-term economic trends are in many ways global. However, the manifestations of them in relation to particular groups and particular spaces produce complex patterns of disadvantage in Belfast." It is thus worthwhile to explore the economic impacts on both individuals and spatially defined subareas of Belfast.

Catholics traditionally have borne the burden of economic disadvantage in Northern Ireland. Catholic males by 1971 were 2.62 times more likely to be unemployed than Protestant males (Whyte 1990). Ten years later, the Northern Ireland male unemployment rate for Catholics was 30 percent; for Protestants 12 percent (Rowthorn and Wayne 1985). This Catholic-Protestant differential remains today, with the most recent figures in 1991 showing a 28 percent Catholic male unemployment rate and a 12 percent Protestant rate (1991 Census).[16] Such an economic gap sharpens and embitters the sectarian divide. In a report to the Standing Advisory Commission on Human Rights (D. Smith 1987), factors that could contribute to these Protestant-Catholic differentials—such as class, location, education, and age—were statistically controlled. Yet there remained a large extent of unemployment differential unexplained. Smith concluded that no adequate explanation for this remaining difference has emerged "apart from discrimination and unequal opportunities." In the sectarian geography of Belfast, an additional problem facing residents seeking employment is the "chill factor" caused by intercommunity hostility and fear. A. Cebulla (interview) points to real and perceived violence as a major inhibitor of access to employment. Such inhibition falls more on Belfast Catholics because employment has traditionally been less spatially proximate to them. Eversley (1989) states that a major cause of Catholic economic disadvantage has been "the reluctance of Catholics to take jobs which are located in, or which entail travelling through, what to them are unsafe areas." In a recent Belfast Residents Survey (Department of the Environment for Northern Ireland 1994a), this effect of sectarian geography is profoundly illustrated. When Catholics in inner west Belfast who were out of work were asked where they would be prepared to work, twice as many indicated "elsewhere in the European Community (outside Great Britain and the Republic of Ireland)" than in traditionally Protestant "East Belfast."

Workplaces are commonly segregated environments in Northern Ireland. Employer reports to the Fair Employment Commission (1993) showed in 1992 that more than 70 percent of firms with between twenty-six and fifty employees, and more than 40 percent of firms with between fifty-one and one hundred employees, had fewer than ten Catholics (or Protestants) in their workforce. Although total employment figures show a religious breakdown (62 percent Protestant; 37 percent Catholic) that is roughly proportionate to the size of each ethnic group's economically active population, this is masking substantial workplace segregation.[17]

A second method of gauging the differential impacts of economic influences is not on individuals per se, but across neighborhoods of Belfast. Robson, Bradford, and Deas (1994) calculated a "relative deprivation" measure for all electoral wards in Northern Ireland based on a set of social and economic factors.[18] Nine of the ten most deprived wards in Northern Ireland were in Belfast city. Table 7.4 lists the ten most deprived wards in Belfast.

Table 7.4   The Ten Most Deprived Wards in Belfast

WARD NAME	RELIGION	
Falls	Catholic	(> 90%)
New Lodge	Catholic	(> 80%)
St. Annes	Protestant	(> 80%)
Clonard	Catholic	(> 90%)
Shaftesbury	Protestant	(> 70%)
Woodvale	Protestant	(> 90%)
The Mount	Protestant	(> 90%)
Island	Protestant	(> 90%)
Shankill	Protestant	(> 90%)
Duncairn	Protestant	(> 90%)

Source: Robson, Bradford, and Deas 1994. *Relative Deprivation in Northern Ireland.*

This spatial distribution illuminates several attributes of economic deprivation in Belfast. Catholic disadvantage is apparent in their ward ratings at the top of the Robson deprivation list. If only unemployment rate is examined, six of the seven wards in 1991 were Catholic where the percentage of economically active residents that were unemployed was above 40 percent. However, Table 7.4 indicates that spatial deprivation of Protestant areas is also common, with seven of the ten worst wards in Protestant neighborhoods (using the 14 criteria Robson index). This illustrates the depth of economic and social decay across both communities. Within a traditional and still present circumstance of Catholic-Protestant differentials, both of the antagonistic communities are being hard hit by economic restructuring. A major antideprivation program, Making Belfast Work (MBW), has used the Robson index to target thirty-two wards in the Belfast urban area that experience deprivation relative to the Northern Ireland average. In these wards, 49 percent of Catholic males and 37 percent of Protestant males were unemployed (Breen and Miller 1993; DOENI 1995). Such unemployment levels are not only high, but unemployment tends to be long in duration. Both ethnic groups combined, 64 percent of unemployment benefit claimants in one survey had been out of work for longer than one year; 36 percent for longer than three years (DOENI 1995).

Urban economic policy must then address not only Catholic deprivation and lingering Catholic-Protestant disparities, but also Protestant deprivation, which is likely contributing to that community's perception of threat and isolation. The level of economic pain felt by the residents and communities of Belfast is severe and debilitating. What makes the addressing by government of this economic dislocation more difficult is that it will need to take place in a contested city of traditionally warring communities. As F. Gaffikin and M. Morrissey (interviews) assess, "Even normal industrial cities are segmented and polarized through deep economic and social restructuring over the last three decades. In Belfast, this has been superimposed over sectarian interfaces."

Sectarian Geographies and the "Peacelines"

Patrick Corry, aged 61, Catholic civilian. Killed August 2, 1969, by the Royal Ulster Constabulary. Hit on the head with batons during altercation between local people and RUC. Unity Flats off Upper Library Street.

—First death in Belfast attributable to the Troubles
Source: Sutton (1994)

August 31, 1994:   IRA announces ceasefire.
September 11, 1994: Loyalist paramilitaries announce ceasefire.
February 9, 1996:   IRA declares end of ceasefire. Office building in the Docklands (London) bombed.

Violence and intimidation have created in the city of Belfast rigid sectarian boundaries that have severely fragmented and distorted the urban fabric. During the early years of the Troubles, many public housing estates quickly self-segregated. In the first eight years of urban civil war, the percentage of households in public housing that resided in streets of complete or near-complete segregation rose from 59 to 89 percent (Boal 1995). The Catholic "heartland" of the Falls areas consolidated. Many Protestants, meanwhile, had a greater ability to out-migrate, due to both higher income status and fewer sectarian obstacles; and many of them chose this option. In the subsequent decades, Protestant out-migration coupled with higher Catholic birth rates has created a landscape of densely populated and active Catholic neighborhoods, on the one hand, and lower-density, socially depleted, and physically deteriorated Protestant communities, on the other.

One is struck in the city of Belfast with the ever-present sectarian content and symbolism of the built environment.[19] With the exception of mixed south Belfast, many areas in the city are easily identifiable as "green" (Catholic) or "orange" (Protestant). Potent and emotion-laden symbols identify whose area one is in—the presence of a Catholic or Protestant church; curbstones painted either green, yellow, and white (Catholic) or red, white, and blue (Protestant); the presence of an Ancient Order of the Hibernians meeting place (Catholic) or "Orange Order" lodge (Protestant); street names and the presence or absence of Irish language translations; and the names of shop proprietors along commercial corridors. The most politically expressive identifiers of sectarian space are the murals painted on the sides of buildings and walls. Republican murals commemorate politically potent historical events such as the Easter Uprising of 1916 or the Hunger Strikes of the early 1980s; celebrate resistance to repressions ("Brits out now"); focus on IRA victories and martyrs; make connections to other international human rights movements (such as in South Africa and Palestine); and commonly portray the Irish Tricolor flag. Loyalist murals, meantime, emphasize historical events such as the lifting of the Siege of Derry in 1689 and King William's successful Battle of the Boyne in 1690 or provide connections to the historic Ulster Volunteer Force; identify contemporary loyalist paramilitaries; and commonly use identifiers such as the "Red Hand of Ulster" and the Union Jack.[20] In addition to these physical symbols, marches by Protestant "Orangemen" commemorating historic days (in particular, the annual Twelfth of July celebration of the Battle of the Boyne) implant in the landscape potent sectarian meaning and inflame tensions in Catholic neighborhoods adjacent to parade routes.

The city is one of physical barriers that symbolically separate proximate Catholic and Protestant residential neighborhoods. Although Belfast is an example of multisector segregation rather than two-sided partition,[21] the extent and severity of intercommunity hostilities since the late 1960s has necessitated the building of physical partitions, so-called "peacelines," between neighborhoods at sixteen locations (see Figure 7.6 and Table 7.5). These have been constructed in interface areas where rival and proximate communities have engaged in territorial conflict (Northern Ireland Housing Executive 1988; O'Connor 1988). The locations of these physical partitions can mirror spatial patterns of violence and territoriality first established a century ago (Feldman 1991). Most of the peacelines are located in west and north Belfast, where population shifts following the outbreak of violence in 1969 were greatest. The physical dividers are built of varied materials—ranging from corrugated iron fences and steel palisade structures, to permanent steel or brick walls, to more aesthetically pleasing "environmental" barriers of landscaped railings and multicolored walls, to "buffer" zones of vacant space or alternative nonresidential development. Police stations of the Royal Ulster Constabulary (RUC) are often located on or near these peaceline interfaces (see Figure 7.7). The most infamous peaceline—at Cupar Street—separates the Catholic Falls and Protestant Shankill neighborhoods of inner west Belfast (see Figure 7.8).

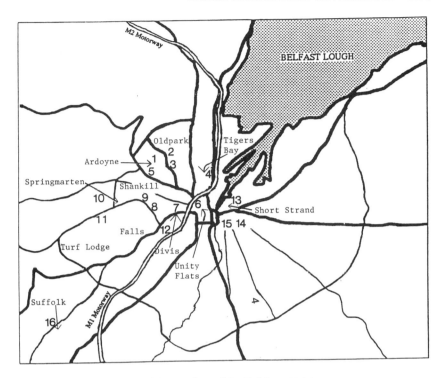

Figure 7.6 Location of "Peacelines" in Belfast 1994

Source: Frederick Boal. 1995. *Shaping a City: Belfast in the Late Twentieth Century*. Belfast: Institute of Irish Studies, Queen's University.

The hyper-segregated sectarian and peaceline geography of Belfast has performed vital roles in maintaining community perceptions of security in the context of an urban civil war.[22] B. Murtagh (University of Ulster, Magee College, interview) claims that segregation has been instrumental in furthering community feelings of security in the face of extremely abnormal living conditions. Peacelines provide a certain psychological security by demarcating a well-defined defensive boundary to a particular community's territory (Murtagh 1994a). In addition, it should be emphasized that such community partitions and peacelines are not the cause of the problem, per se, but rather reflections of the underlying political and religious conflict (M. Graham, Northern Ireland Housing Executive, interview). Yet, these physical manifestations of the Troubles in

Table 7.5 Peacelines of Belfast

PEACELINE	ADJACENT NEIGHBORHOODS	
	CATHOLIC	PROTESTANT
North Belfast		
1. Alliance/Glenbryn	Ardoyne	Alliance
2. Elimgrove Street	Oldpark Avenue	Torrens
3. Manor/Roe Street	Roseleigh	Groomsport Court
4. Duncairn Gardens	New Lodge	Tiger's Bay
5. Crumlin Road	Ardoyne	Shankill
West Belfast		
6. Unity Flats	Unity Flats	Lower Shankill
7. Northumberland/Ardmoulin	Divis Flats	Shankill
8. Cupar Way	Falls	Shankill
9. Ainsworth Avenue	Springfield	Woodvale
10. Springmartin Road	New Barnsley	Springmartin
11. Springhill Avenue	Ballymurphy	Springmartin
12. Roden Street	Falls	Shaftesbury
16. Stewartstown Road	Lenadoon	Suffolk
East Belfast		
13. Lower Newtownards Road	Short Strand	Island
14. Bryson Street	Short Strand	Ballymacarett
15. Cluan Place	Short Strand	Cluan Place

Note: Numbers correspond to Figure 7.6.
Sources: Environmental Design Consultants 1991; and Boal 1995

Belfast create a set of significant problems both to urban policy-makers and the adjacent neighborhoods. First, uncompromising ethnic territoriality obstructs efforts to strategically plan for the needs of city residents in terms of housing and community facilities. Second, sectarian interfaces and peacelines create intimidating and inhumane environments debilitative of healthy community functioning. I now explore these adverse consequences.

The problems created by territoriality that are encountered by policymakers are numerous. All cities, by their nature, are dynamic

Figure 7.7 Antennas of Oldpark Royal Ulster Constabulary Station near Elimgrove Peaceline, North Belfast

Source: Scott A. Bollens

Figure 7.8 Cupar Way Peaceline Wall Separating Catholic Falls (left) and Protestant Shankill Neighborhoods (not shown). This is the largest of the physical dividers in Belfast.

Source: Scott A. Bollens

organisms where changing economic and demographic processes occur that involve intricate interrelationships between activities. In the city of Belfast, however, static sectarian boundaries have been overlaid upon these dynamic urban processes so as to create two cities—one Catholic and growing in population; the other Protestant and declining in size. Peacelines and sectarian geography obstruct the natural expansion or evolution of urban space across these boundaries. W. McGivern of NIHE (interview) poignantly states that

> Belfast is not a normal city, where neighborhood evolution would be a natural progression . . . where neighborhoods change without revolutions and open warfare developing.

The distorting effects of sectarian geography on urban policy are most pronounced in the provision of housing, where "Differential demand for housing between Catholics and Protestants interact with static sectarian boundaries" (D. Murphy, Northern Ireland Housing Executive, interview). The conflicting political imperatives impacting upon policymaking are illustrated by these interview comments from two Belfast councilpersons:

> The status quo stands. I'm against anything that alters the status quo because I think it creates fear. Anything that breaks the balance destabilizes and I'm against. (N. McCausland, Ulster Unionist Party)

> I understand, and fully accept, the fears of Protestants concerning an invasion of Catholics into former and current loyalist areas. In the long term, though, Catholic movement to areas that are derelict will occur sooner or later. (J. Austin, Sinn Fein Party)

The Northern Ireland Housing Executive (NIHE) "simply cannot say there is to be a Catholic housing estate in an area that is traditionally Protestant" (J. Hendry, Queen's University of Belfast, interview). Thus, the increasing Catholic needs for housing (due to greater population growth) cannot be met by building new dwelling units in Protestant areas or by locating Catholic residents in existing units there. This is so even though many Protestant areas have experienced depopulation and have vacant land or high vacancy (void) rates. In this way, "Peacelines have created a housing demand/supply equation of imbalance" (M. Graham, NIHE, interview). V. Blease, also of NIHE[23] expresses it this way:

> If we didn't have a Catholic-Protestant problem, we wouldn't have a housing problem. The land for housing is there, just not in the right locations.

To avoid inflaming local tensions in this ethnically circumscribed world facing housing policymakers, two options remain—there is either Catholic overcrowding and the building of Catholic units closer to peacelines than security would otherwise suggest; or urban policymakers must look outside the core city to build new housing instead of using vacant housing stock in core city neighborhoods.[24]

Another planning problem produced by sectarianism is that it creates obstacles to policy aimed at improving the housing stock and quality of life. Such housing policies seek to demolish high-density housing and build lower density units with more livable open space.[25] But, the high-rise apartment complexes found in some Catholic areas are seen as symbols of territoriality, and the maintenance of these often decrepit high-rise apartments becomes viewed as a way to protect sectarian turf. One famous demolition involved a substantial part of the Divis Flats complex in the Falls neighborhood. Despite being done for solid planning reasons and to improve Catholic quality of life, it was seen by many in the nationalist community as an attempt to dilute Catholic voting power in the city. Efforts to demolish the remaining Divis building and redevelop the Unity Flats high-rise areas in inner north Belfast have similarly faced stern protests and calls to adequately house all Catholics who would be displaced, a hard task given the limited "green" land in Belfast. In this way, attempts to improve housing stock amidst sectarian territoriality may actually exacerbate ethnic conflict.

Sectarian geography also distorts transportation and economic development efforts. One potent example is the construction of Lanark Way in the 1980s, meant to link the Falls and Shankill neighborhoods to a proximate industrial park. In reality, this economic development strategy produced, instead, a connection between the two sectarian heartlands that became an oft-used escape route for terrorists. A gated barrier then had to be created to cut off one of the few intercommunity road connections in west Belfast, leaving a troubling legacy. Ethnic circumscription of Belfast space also disrupts the normal use of community facilities such as parks and leisure centers, social service offices, shopping centers, baby clinics, and community meeting places. In an urban environment where perceived "neutral venues" are few and far between, individuals from one ethnic group will often not use the nearest community facility because of the perception that it is trapped in the other group's territory. In a Protestant enclave in west Belfast, for example, only 8 percent of residents used the nearest shopping center because it was perceived to be in Catholic territory (Murtagh 1994a).

Finally, in a city where territoriality is paramount, urban policymakers by necessity are put in the political hot seat when discussing what to do with declining and underutilized, frequently Protestant, communities. Referring to the Protestant Donegall Pass area of predominately elderly and dependent residents, R. Strang (formerly with Northern Ireland Housing Executive, interview) speaks of the "drastically depleted and grossly distorted nature of the indigenous population" and asks who is to be planned for there. The government faces a critical choice in responding to this problem of Protestant community decline. In normal circumstances, such areas would experience transformation from one land use to another or from one ethnic group to another. But, in Belfast, the maintenance of community viability is intimately connected to the protection of political territoriality.

To avoid inflammatory territorial changes and incursions, policymakers become linked at great public expense with efforts to maintain ethnic territory. Two examples—Suffolk Estate and Cluan Place—exhibit how government has responded to the political complexities presented by declining Protestant neighborhoods. The Suffolk Estate in west Belfast is a small Protestant housing estate surrounded by mainly Catholic housing. Under threat (both physical and symbolic) from growing proximate Catholic areas, its population has declined from 1,500 to 800 today.[26] Housing stock deteriorated as voids and rent arrears increased in the 1970s and early 1980s (see Figure 7.9). Sectarian conflict has required the building of the Stewartstown Road peaceline separating Protestant units from the busy

Figure 7.9   Dilapidated and Voided Structures in Protestant Neighborhood of Suffolk, West Belfast

Source: Scott A. Bollens

arterial road. In addition, the NIHE has put more than five million pounds into the rehabilitation of residential dwellings in order to maintain community viability for its remaining eight hundred residents. This huge expense in physical infrastructure and housing rehabilitation achieved some stability; yet the Protestant population continues to decline in the face of sectarian tension. Meanwhile, pressure for new housing for Catholics in nearby Lenadoon continues to mount. A housing planner (interview)[27] involved with Suffolk presents the dilemma faced by urban policymakers: "What do you do with Suffolk? Who is to say to Protestants there that there is no future?" The second example, Cluan Place, is in predominately Protestant east Belfast but is adjacent to the Catholic enclave of Short Strand and feels under threat from it. Here, similar to Suffolk, per-unit public expenses to maintain this twenty-unit residential subdivision as Protestant have been substantial. A peace wall has been constructed separating the backyards of Cluan Place and Short Strand residences. In addition, infrastructure had to be moved to accommodate the new partition (R. Strang, interview). Such investment does not make sense from a citywide perspective, but rather is derived from goals pertaining to the maintenance of social-psychological well-being amidst ethnic war.

Besides their adverse impacts on urban policymaking, sectarian interfaces and peacelines create intimidating and inhumane environments that debilitate healthy adjacent community functioning. "Peacelines," asserts D. MacBride (Community Development Center—North Belfast, interview), "tear the heart out of a community." Although they were constructed to provide psychological security, living along a peaceline presents a direct threat, imposes restriction on movement, and creates and reinforces a deteriorated quality of environment. The NIHE admits in a published 1988 report on violence and urban renewal that:

> The so-called "peace-lines" are in fact a contradiction in terms. They are in many instances characterized not by peace and harmony between neighbors, but by conflict, tension, damage to property and continuing instability.

Councilperson J. Austin (Sinn Fein, interview) claims that the "peacelines should never have been put up in the first place," because they reinforce psychological barriers. Communities along the peacelines experience multiple deprivations (Murtagh 1994a,b), including poverty, poor access to services, an image problem, and limited community cohesiveness. The walls have direct adverse effects on adjacent estates, such as deterioration and housing voids (especially on the Protestant side), and cause indirect psychological problems as they present daily reminders of ethnic strife (D. Murphy, NIHE, interview). Peacelines can be important destabilizing influences on communities already suffering from socioeconomic deprivation.

Peacelines are not the causes of ethnic conflict in Belfast, but rather are ugly reflections of the emotion-laden urban geography of fear and territoriality. Physical partitions actually perform a functional role in a conflict environment by providing some sense of community and individual security. In the end, however, they contribute problems of rigidity and citywide dysfunctionality to the Belfast ethnic puzzle that policymakers involved in the land use and spatial development of the city must somehow address. P. Sweeney (interview) sums up the problem: "Belfast will never function as a city with these walls of hate and division."

Urban Engagement: Participants and Principles

The test of a policy designed to create public order in the midst of internal war is not whether it conforms to conventional liberal assumptions, but whether it produces order.

—Richard Rose,
Northern Ireland: A Time of Choice

This section examines the approach that Belfast urban policymakers have taken toward the realities and challenges of sectarianism. It first outlines the major governmental participants in the formulation and implementation of urban policy in Belfast, and the role community activism has played in urban policy. It next assesses the general philosophical stance of these policymakers toward the sectarian divide. It then examines the specific interaction between policy and sectarianism in two important areas of governance: town planning and housing policy.

Participants in Belfast Urban Policy

The public sector—both administrative and security-related—plays a disproportionate role in both Belfast and Northern Ireland. General expenditure per capita in Northern Ireland ($6,800 U.S). was 35 percent higher in 1992–1993 than the United Kingdom average ($5,100 U.S.).[28] Public expenditures for housing in Northern Ireland are more than 50 percent higher per capita than in Britain (HM Treasury 1994). Security expenditures per capita are 250 times more than in Britain; industrial and employment expenditures per capita are over 300 times greater. Thus, although government has been removed from local control since 1972, its role is much more significant than in other parts of the U.K. and Europe. In many ways, the social and physical fabric of Northern Ireland and Belfast has stayed as intact as it has during the ethnic war due to the inordinately large public sector and its provision of services such as housing and employment schemes (P. Sweeney, DOENI, interview).

Under the Northern Ireland Act of 1974, the dominant policymaker concerning urban development and planning is the Department of the Environment for Northern Ireland (hereafter DOENI).[29]

The size and reach of the department is such that P. Sweeney (DOENI advisor, interview) labels it the "department of everything" and describes it as a confederation of often disparate services created after direct rule. DOENI goals are set by the Secretary of State and are: (1) to strengthen the economy; (2) to target social need; and (3) to combat terrorism (G. Mulligan, DOENI, interview). Within or connected to the DOENI are five major entities involved in Belfast urban policy—Town and Country Planning Service, Belfast Development Office, Northern Ireland Housing Executive, Belfast Action Teams, and Making Belfast Work.

The Town and Country Planning Service is responsible for creating the framework within which development takes place and for regulating development. Belfast Urban Area plans are statutory (they have the force of law) and establish a broad policy framework for future growth over the next fifteen or so years. Physical development policies within an area plan seek to clarify the extent and location of future development. In contrast to general plans or zoning schemes in the United States, Belfast area plans (like their British counterparts) are more flexible and less specific (G. Worthington, head of Belfast Divisional Office, Planning Services, interview). A second type of plan, local or subject plans, are done for more specific subareas requiring more detailed investigation. They are to be consistent with the broad policy framework of the area plan, although they do not necessarily have the force of law (DOENI 1994b). Recent local plans in Belfast have included those for the Harbor area, the city center (including the major Laganside waterfront project), and the Lagan Valley Regional Park.[30] Most planning and project applications, both private and public, are reviewed by the Planning Service for consistency with the area plan.[31] The Belfast City Council (District Council) is to be consulted during the review process by DOENI's planning service divisional office. In cases where there is a difference of opinion between a district council and the divisional planning office, the decision is referred to a planning service directorate. This local consultation provides one of the few access points for local government into the planning and development process in Northern Ireland. However, this access appears to be more procedural than substantive. In the 1992–1993 period, the directorate decided in favor of the divisional planning service more than 85 percent of the time (DOENI 1994b).

Town planning in Northern Ireland has an erratic history. In 1921, upon Northern Ireland's creation, the province broke away from the British system of planning[32] because it was viewed as too complicated, and as addressing problems—such as the spread of suburbs and ribbon development—that were not relevant in Northern Ireland. Importantly, the Northern Ireland populace had not gotten used to the idea of planning. As J. Hendry (Queen's University, interview) states, the "Irish did not want to be told what to do, especially by the British." After World War II, Northern Ireland copied the British system in a piecemeal fashion. By the time of the first regional plan in Northern Ireland (the *Matthew Plan*), planning was viewed as a way to create a stable context that would stimulate outside investment into the state (J. Hendry, interview). Thus, the Matthew Plan recommended the creation of new towns as a method to stimulate economic growth away from the burgeoning Belfast area, the imposition of a stopline to spatially curtail Belfast growth, and the development of motorways to improve access to hinterlands.[33] Since direct rule in 1972 and the removal of town planning from local authorities, area plans are done by the centralized DOENI, and are occurring without a strong regional strategic framework such as proposed by the Matthew Plan (J. Hendry, interview).

The second policymaking unit, the *Belfast Development Office* (BDO), has a more active orientation toward changing and regenerating the urban system. Whereas town planning guides and regulates development, the BDO actively seeks to put things on the ground, promoting and coordinating the physical regeneration of Belfast. It focuses on the physical regeneration of neglected or abused urban areas as a means toward their economic and social revitalization. The BDO is composed of administrators and civil servants, not town planners. Through Comprehensive Development Schemes (CDS), Environmental Improvement Schemes (EIS), and Urban Development Grants (UDG), the BDO seeks to facilitate the rebuilding of Belfast through partnerships between government and private investment. In the 1980s, these three programs expended about 86 million pounds sterling (1991–1992 prices) (Cebulla 1994). During the Thatcher years of deregulation, the BDO was instrumental in cutting through red tape in Belfast. Oriented toward single project marketing and development, R. Strang (interview) suggests that BDO was a way to short-circuit the statutory planning process in order to more quickly revitalize dying and damaged parts of Belfast.

The BDO has focused primarily on the redevelopment of the city center as a means of regenerating the city at large. In a period of employment decline and population loss, few institutional investors were operating in the central city in the 1970s. Moreover, property development decline was experienced as commercial property became targets of paramilitary bombing campaigns, which left the city center deserted and surrounded by a security cordon and manned security gates (S. Brown 1985; Cebulla 1994). The BDO has sought to spatially concentrate public investment incentives to bring both multilocational retail franchises and office developments into the central core of Belfast, one of the few areas of the city deemed to be "neutral" in terms of sectarian geography. It has heavily subsidized land purchase and assemblage by government through its CDS program, private investment through its UDG program, the improvement of capital infrastructure (such as roads) and the general upgrading of the urban environment through its EIS programs, and entered into agreements with private investors to buy back properties after fifty years (K. Sterrett, DOENI, interview). A prominent central project has been the development of Castle Court, a major retail complex one block from City Hall. In addition, the DOENI created its own development company to develop and leverage private investment for a planned major mixed-use complex—Laganside—along the Lagan River. Outside the city center, the BDO has worked on community regeneration schemes through its decentralized Belfast Action Team (BAT) offices.[34] However, significantly more public expenditures have gone into the city center through CDS, EIS, and UDG subsidies than they have into the surrounding neighborhoods through BAT projects. The main benefits from BDO actions are seen as coming from access to new jobs in the "neutral" city center, not from new jobs locating in sectarian neighborhoods (Cebulla 1994; DOENI 1987).

A third major urban policymaking unit is the *Northern Ireland Housing Executive* (NIHE). It is the comprehensive housing authority for Northern Ireland, charged with the provision of new public housing, the rehabilitation and maintenance of existing units, and the allocation of public housing units to needy households and individuals. It is the largest public housing landlord in the United Kingdom, with direct responsibility for one-third of Northern Ireland's housing stock. The NIHE controls about 36,000 properties in Belfast city alone (J. McPeake, NIHE, interview). Housing provision and allocation in Northern Ireland and Belfast have long been contested. Before direct rule, housing policy by Belfast city showed a strong pattern of political influence and sectarian bias (Singleton 1983). The British government identified housing provision as one of the major areas of grievance in the state (Cameron Report 1969). Indeed, one of the "ignition points" for the Troubles was the Caledon Affair, in which an unmarried Protestant girl had been allocated a house in County Tyrone while several large Catholic families remained unhoused (Singleton 1983). In response, the NIHE was created in 1971 to centralize housing policy and insulate it from local political biases. From its first day, NIHE's credibility has been closely connected to its use of objective allocation and new-build criteria. Between 1971 and 1995, the NIHE built 18,500 public housing units in Belfast city, with another 10,000 in the BUA outside the city (J. McPeake, NIHE, interview). The middle of the 1980s, in particular, was a time of extensive public housing building, about 1,500 units per year. The quality of NIHE housing has been praised, with housing and landscaping standards higher here than in Great Britain. R. Strang (interview) explains that "We realized that in order to survive, we had to build to the highest possible standards." By 1991, the level of housing unfitness had been reduced from 24 percent in the early 1970s to 8 percent (NIHE 1995). A quasi-nongovernmental organization (quango), the NIHE is funded through the DOENI.

Belfast Action Teams (BAT) are one of two means urban policymakers have used to direct regeneration efforts to disadvantaged residential communities. Headed by senior civil servants, these units liaise with local communities through decentralized offices for the purposes of encouraging social and economic regenerative measures. A. Cebulla (interview) claims that while the top level of urban policy emphasizes city center revitalization, BATs (along with Making Belfast Work, discussed below) represent a different track aimed at community deprivation. The BAT program, originally under the auspices of the BDO, established in 1987 and 1988 nine decentralized, community-based government offices charged with connecting community needs to government programs and resources.[35] Each BAT leader was allocated between 700,000 and one million British pounds per year to direct to community needs. Although there have been some positive impacts on the ground, no strategic policy drove BAT coordination in the early years. Thus, there were widely disparate BAT approaches and experiences (R. Davison, Shankill BAT leader, interview). In addition, BAT projects at times were inconsistent with the policies and budget priorities of statutory agencies (V. McKevitt, Ardoyne/Oldpark BAT leader, interview). This independent discretion by BAT leaders led to images of them as "freelance cash dispensers" (R. Davison, interview) and "cowboys with no responsibility who have gone native" (V. McKevitt, interview). Because of these problems, the BAT program was institutionally connected in 1994 to the more strategic Making Belfast Work antideprivation program.

Making Belfast Work (MBW) seeks to target resources to the thirty-two deprived electoral wards in the city. Established in 1988 in the midst of horrendous sectarian tension and violence, it was created as an emergency and tactical response during a time when government authorities thought that they might lose control over Catholic west Belfast (P. Sweeney, interview).[36] MBW established a pot of money that government departments could access if they showed they were redirecting part of their normal budgets into areas of high unemployment and economic deprivation. It was a bidding mechanism that would provide incentives for skewing government expenditures toward deprived areas (Cebulla 1994). It traditionally has funded physical revitalization efforts through the channeling of money to groups (such as churches) not allied with republican and loyalist paramilitaries. A major revision of MBW occurred in 1994 and 1995 that has reoriented the program toward joint community-government partnerships inclusive of all community groups, and toward a broader definition of regeneration beyond solely bricks-and-mortar (DOENI 1994c and 1995).[37]

Community Activism amidst Strife

There exist in Belfast complex webs of interaction between community-based, political party, and governmental interests. In a contested city, political party interests that focus on issues of sovereignty and political control intersect on the ground with neighborhood interests that focus on issues of urban need such as employment, housing, and physical conditions. This intersection can be a tangled web of seeming compatibility but internal friction. The nature and results of this interplay produce the "public" that seeks to influence urban policy, and which urban policymakers, in turn, must somehow address. Since 1972, communities[38] in Belfast have had no immediate electoral input into local policy. With this "democratic deficit," Belfast neighborhood activism has often been reactive, obstructive, and reflective of sectarian division. Extremists and hardliners, often backed by paramilitaries, have often been able to control community-based processes of involvement with government (D. MacBride, interview; Murtagh 1994a). Such control can obstruct the amount of independent action exercised by moderate community leaders and liberals, and can magnify public perceptions of government as biased, uncaring, or even conspiratorial.

In the midst of horrific violence in the 1970s, there existed an "energetic and enthusiastic community development 'movement' which did succeed in crossing the sectarian divide" (Lovett, Gunn, and Robson 1994). In many cases, neighborhood-based opposition to the redevelopment and road building schemes of government had stimulated interethnic collective action and a sense of solidarity among working-class communities in the face of a perceived uncaring bureaucracy. For example, Protestant and Catholic community groups united in the 1970s to oppose the proposed Belfast Urban Motorway because of its adverse cross-ethnic effects on working-class inner city neighborhoods (Blackman 1991). Government has also assisted community-based efforts. A Community Relations Commission, established in 1969, sought "confidence-building" within each ethnic group—through the stimulation of community development projects and the nurturing of local organizations—as a means toward betterment of cross-community relations. Influenced by radical, nondirective approaches to community development, different forms of community organizing sprung up in the 1970s, including neighborhood-based groups, single-issue organizations focused on such issues as crime, and larger volunteer organizations having full-time staff. Underneath the surface of commonality across community actions, however, was a conflict within the movement about the nature and purpose of community development—was it to support the state or to challenge it (T. Lovett, University of Ulster, Jordanstown, interview)? An additional difficulty was that the devolved power-sharing government of 1974, viewing the community movement as too radical and likely to usurp the function of elected representatives, disbanded the Community Relations Commission.

In the 1980s, community-based activities became increasingly fragmented and coopted by government through the attachment of strings to the receipt of funding (Lovett, Gunn, and Robson 1994). The Action for Community Employment (ACE) scheme, in particular, has been the subject of much criticism for its "make-work" orientation and its channeling of funds to church-based groups (T. Lovett, interview; C. Bradley, Northern Ireland Council for Voluntary Action, interview). Community groups that were able to buy into ACE schemes "found their concerns narrowed as they had to fit a particular mold set by the funder" (T. Lovett, interview). Similarly, community projects funded by the International Fund for Ireland tended to be top-down, focused on enterprise development rather than community development, and run by clergy and businessmen (T. Lovett, interview). The involvement of Sinn Fein in politics subsequent to the IRA hunger strikes of 1981 had raised fear in government of paramilitary control of community groups in Catholic areas. Government responded to Sinn Fein's emergence in the form of "political vetting,"[39] whereby community groups that "have the effect of improving the standing or furthering the aims of a paramilitary organization, whether directly or indirectly" are excluded from government funding. During this time, the voluntary sector grew and started to fill the void created by the fragmenting and politically vetted neighborhood-based community sector.[40] Tension developed between these two sectors, as the voluntary sector at times usurped functions of the neighborhood organizations (T. Lovett, interview). One positive linkage between government and community was established in 1987, with the establishment of Belfast Action Teams as decentralized liaison offices.

In an increasingly difficult environment where broader political and local community issues interacted, cross-community work by neighborhood-based groups decreased in the 1980s. Since the early 1980s, the prevalent pattern has been that community-based activism has reflected or even exacerbated social divisions. For instance, debates concerning urban and housing renewal and new road locations focused on the maintenance of an ethnic group's neighborhood population and thus its territorial defense (Northern Ireland Housing Executive 1988; Blackman 1991). Osborne and Singleton (1982), in a case study of a new west Belfast housing project, viewed the community planning process as a "microcosm of the wider political battle for territory." In other cases, community activism created splits even within ethnic groups, as is evident in the separate Catholic constituencies—church and Sinn Fein—of west Belfast community employment groups (Gaffikin and Morrissey 1990). One exception to this rule of division has been an interethnic coalition of community organizations—Community Technical Aid—that sought to develop cross-community responses to urban plans and projects (O'Connor 1988; Blackman 1991).

Efforts to improve Protestant-Catholic community relations in the 1980s and 1990s have been difficult at best. Programs such as holiday schemes were viewed as having temporary effects: "People went back into their communities with no change in attitudes" (B. Hutchinson, community activist, interview). Community relations schemes were also viewed by Protestants as "Catholic relations" ploys set up to impress international observers; and by Catholics as counterinsurgency efforts by government (B. Hutchinson, interview). In 1990, a new quasi-governmental body, the Community Relations Council, was established "to increase understanding and co-operation between political, cultural and religious communities in Northern Ireland" (Northern Ireland Community Relations Council 1994a). Its major challenge is to move community relations work beyond crisis management to more proactive and long-term bridge building between Protestants and Catholics (M. Fitzduff, Community Relations Council director, interview). Difficult debates concern the role of government in promoting community welfare, especially the appropriate relationship between community development (CD), a term denoting programs aimed at enhancing life *within* communities, and community relations (CR) programs, aimed at improving life *across* communities.[41] Urban policymakers and community members must find ways to improve and enrich the self-confidence and identity of deprived communities without solidifying ghettoization, community separation, and interethnic competition over government funds.

A potential sea-change in government's treatment of communities is represented by the 1995 Strategy of the antideprivation Making Belfast Work program. Community interests are now to be included with those of statutory government agencies and the private sector in "area partnerships," which may undertake an advocacy role, directly undertake local projects or act as a vehicle to channel public funding to local projects (DOENI 1995, 13). The inclusion of community in policymaking represents an awareness that locally perceived needs may be different than government's, and that community input may improve urban policy. It seeks to address the problem that the priorities of many government bodies that interact with Belfast communities are tied to aggregate measures incapable of tapping into the unique conditions and needs of a particular community (P. Sweeney, interview). However, important issues remain to be addressed in this more inclusive style of government: (1) to what extent will partnerships be *representative* of the nongovernmental and government sectors?; (2) to what extent will they be genuinely *inclusive* of local interests?; and (3) will government be *receptive* to these new sources of community input?

*   *   *

Although intraethnic differences in community dynamics can be at times as great as interethnic ones,[42] Catholic-Protestant differences in the dynamics and coherence of their community organization are nonetheless evident. The out-migration of upwardly mobile Protestants from inner city neighborhoods has left their former communities fragmented, depleted of professional skills, and commonly absorbed by feelings of threat. In contrast, upwardly mobile residents on the Catholic side for many years could not or did not want to move spatially. Ironically, then, "Catholic communities tend to be more developed organizationally at the same time as they are geographically more constrained" (D. McCoy, Central Community Relations Unit, interview).

> We learned that to survive the struggle, we would need an insurance policy around us . . . that insurance policy had to be the community.
>
> —Joe Austin,
> Belfast City Councillor and
> member of Sinn Fein Party,
> in an interview

> The problem of Catholic church-led community development is that it is not necessarily a very democratic one.
>
> —Vincent McKevitt,
> BAT leader,
> Ardoyne/Oldpark,
> in an interview

The stereotype of Catholic community organizing in Belfast is that it is confident, articulate, well connected to outside parties, and internally cohesive. There appears to be an element of truth to this stereotype. However, there are important qualifications that should be made to this image of Catholic community dynamics.[43] Primary among them is that significant internal divisions exist between church supporters and moderate nationalists, on the one hand, and republicans, on the other. The introduction of Sinn Fein into politics in 1981 reinforced a growing division between nationalists and republicans. The former group advocates a moderate and constitution-based solution to the Northern Ireland problem and aligns itself politically with the SDLP. It tends to draw from the Catholic middle and professional class, which British-based education, welfare, and fair employment legislation helped create (W. Glendinning, Community Relations Council, interview). Links between this group and the conservative and middle-class followers of the Catholic church have thus been natural (B. Murphy, interview). Republicans, in contrast, are more accepting of physical force as an appropriate means toward separation from the United Kingdom and are more likely to align themselves tactically with the Irish Republican Army campaign and politically with Sinn Fein.[44] They tend to draw more from the working class and the dispirited unemployed of the Catholic community. A common feeling is present among republicans that the Catholic Church was too conservative during the Troubles, not supporting them in their time of need and distress (B. Murphy, interview). During the Troubles, Sinn Fein was able to capitalize on this void by articulating the fears of the working-class Catholic community and saying, "We will look after you and protect you in a physical sense" (B. Murphy, interview).

Commonality of opposition to Sinn Fein by the SDLP, Catholic Church, and government created partners in practice. Government funding of community regeneration projects was most commonly directed to the "safe hands" of church-based organizations and SDLP-affiliated groups of businesspeople. Community groups with social and economic views similar to Sinn Fein's, but not aligned with them, found themselves cut off from government funding. Political vetting made some community-based organizations circumscribe their interests and contacts. Community groups sympathetic to Sinn Fein that have survived under political vetting have developed "a certain level of sophistication in using community-based, self-help structures rather than politicians."[45]

> It's easy for Protestants to sit back and say "no"; it's harder to say, "This is how we are going to help change events."
>
> —Billy Hutchinson,
> Springfield Inter-Community Development Project,
> in an interview

> While the Protestant population was tapped into government for fifty years, Catholics created their alternative structures and have done it well. Since 1972, we have been left with no structures.
>
> —Nelson McCausland,
> Belfast City Councillor and
> member of Ulster Unionist Party,
> in an interview

Protestant communities are better off, on average, than Catholic communities in terms of social and economic indicators. In many respects, however, it is the Protestants who are "in retreat, having lost so much territorially, culturally, and politically" (J. Redpath, Shankill community leader, interview).[46] Generally, Protestant community organizing has been less developed and active than Catholic, although that gap may be beginning to narrow. The Protestant community feels threatened by change, both at the city level due to demographic and neighborhood decline and at the national level due to a perceived dissolution of constitutional unionism over the last decade. They often have a lack of confidence in their abilities and their elected councillors, and in many areas are unorganized and lack adequate neighborhood-based leaders.[47]

Much of the depletion of Protestant community coherence is traceable to the out-migration of middle-class Protestants from the city of Belfast to adjacent cities. As S. Corbett (Central Community Relations Unit, Northern Ireland Office, interview) explains, "What is valued by Protestant individuals—to be upwardly mobile and move away to better oneself—is damaging from a community development perspective." Often, Protestant leaders today must address a sectarian community that has experienced a traumatic and profound sense of loss since the removal in 1972 of the Northern Irish government, a power structure that benefited and protected Protestants. Profound differences between Ulster Unionist Party advocates and more hardline Democratic Unionist Party backers are evident in the face of peacemaking efforts. The "veto" mentality and resistance to change prevalent among many Belfast Protestants is not conducive to community organization and development, which is ultimately about bringing forth change. Or, as Redpath states in Weiner (1976) in reflecting upon a Save the Shankill Campaign, "Its strength as a veto body is its weakness as an achieving body."

*   *   *

"Community relations" in many ways is the antithesis of politics.

—Mari Fitzduff, Director of
Northern Ireland Community
Relations Council,
in an interview

Among the greatest obstacles to effective urban policymaking in Belfast are local city councillors, whose relative lack of power frees them to be extreme in their interactions with government. They often have little to lose from being scaremongers who emphasize division, conflict, and single ethnic identity. Government units become easy targets for local councillors who rant and rave at consultation meetings as a way to show their communities that they care (J. Hendry, interview). Indeed, the confrontational and divisive rhetoric is often key to their being elected. Local politicians increase their "leadership" role most easily by tapping into separate constituencies, not by seeking to span them (M. Fitzduff, interview). In their ability to thwart efforts by government to move communities forward, local politicians in Belfast "lead from the back" (D. MacBride, interview).

Local politicians are particular obstacles to the establishment of cross-community bridges. To the extent that better interethnic relations may facilitate demographic shifts with the breakdown of territoriality, community relations is inconsistent with the maintenance of a politician's ethnic constituency. For these reasons, constituents are frequently more advanced and imaginative than their politicians on issues such as cross-community relations (M. Fitzduff and K. Sterrett, interviews). At times, community groups are seen as challengers to local councillors; in response, elected officials will curtail distribution of public information to these segments of the public.[48] There are often significant misfits between community beliefs and actions and a local politician's motivations, belief system, and behavior tied to electoral rewards (M. Fitzduff, interview). In the local politics of contested Belfast, urban issues become subordinated to arguments over nationalism, constitutionalism, and symbolism. One interviewee[49] described the "tragedy of the masquerade" represented by monthly city council meetings that resemble juveniles on a playground more than locally elected officials in a forum.[50] Local issues become lost. For example, the city council provided minimal input into the 1987 Belfast Urban Area Plan as unionist councillors became preoccupied with the signing of the Anglo-Irish Agreement.[51] The subordination of city welfare is represented by a city council that is "more obsessed with Sinn Fein showing up at a public inquiry than in the development issues of the Shankill" (K. Sterrett, DOENI, interview).

Greyness Where Color Matters

> Grey—neutrality, autonomy, indecision
> Orange—King William III, Ulster, Unionism
> Green—shamrock, Ireland, Irish Nationalism
> —Buckley, A. D., and R. Paisley, *Symbols*

The operative principles for Belfast urban policymakers and administrators during "direct rule" have been to: (1) maintain neutrality of government's role and image in Belfast not biased toward either "orange" or "green"; and (2) assure ethnic stability through policy that manages ethnic space in a way that reacts to and reflects residents' wishes.[52] Policymakers face a recurring dilemma in dealing with the inflammatory geography of Belfast. There is tension within government between proactive strategies aimed at comprehensive urban betterment and reactive, pragmatic responses aimed at urban stability and security. Since these two objectives are often in contradiction—the first assumes a certain urban normality that the second dismisses—policymakers have often had to choose. Commonly, their selection of public actions has been aligned with the second objective of maintenance and stability. Since 1972, policy has been based on rational, objective, and dispassionate measures, often responding to documented need. This policy of ethnic-neutrality, or "color-blindness," has served organizational goals well, enabling government units to largely overcome the discriminatory legacy of their predecessors. Operating within the most contentious policy arena of housing, the Northern Ireland Housing Executive, in particular, has maintained much integrity as a fair allocator of public housing units through difficult times. W. McGivern, former Belfast regional director of NIHE (interview), states that "the main reason we exist is because we have the credibility." According to the Permanent Secretary of DOENI (R. Spence, interview), "although there are realities out there you cannot ignore, the department seeks in planning and housing to be neutral." Another portrayal of government policy is that DOENI "is practicing the art of the possible, in a circumstance where they are in a sectarian trap and they know it" (J. Hendry, interview).

Urban policymakers feel the best way to create stability is to respect the needs and desires of communities and residents. G. Mulligan of DOENI (interview), for instance, while acknowledging the inefficiencies of ethnic segmentation, states that "planning does not want to say how the society or economy should change." Instead, government's proper role is to reflect in its policies the needs and demands of residents and neighborhoods. The principle underlying government involvement here has been to "follow the wishes of the people" (D. McCoy, Central Community Relations Unit, Northern Ireland Office, interview) and to "go with the flow" (W. Neill, Queen's University; P. Sweeney, DOENI; interviews). Government policy has accepted that there is a certain inevitability to the conflict, and has "accepted divisions like planners elsewhere assume people prefer cars" (W. Neill, interview). Divisions in society are viewed as based on deep-rooted feelings and reinforced through terror; thus, "Changes have to come from within people; government cannot change people's minds" (R. Spence, interview). Policymakers and administrators amidst ethnic polarization do not want to be perceived as "social engineers," viewing such a role as producing more harm than good. D. McCoy (interview) states that in Belfast's sectarian complexity, "Government should not impose a top-down macro view of how the city should work; rather, it should be responsive and sensitive to the needs and abilities of local communities." G. Worthington, Belfast Planning Service (interview), claims that:

> We must recognize the realities of the situation. If we shifted color (of a neighborhood), the end result would clearly not

work. We're not about making social engineering decisions, or ones that would be perceived as such.

R. Spence, permanent secretary of DOENI (interview), states that an overall strategy toward managing such a divided city would be extremely difficult to devise and, indeed, would likely be counterproductive in bringing about conflict. Thus, the DOENI accepts peacelines as performing an important security-enhancing function for neighbors (Murtagh 1994a). In a city where "The real border in Northern Ireland is in men's minds," government policy must respect these divides or face adverse consequences (R. Spence, interview). The problem to DOENI, then, becomes not the peacelines per se, but how to strategically meet housing and other community needs given their presence (Murtagh 1994a).

Policymaking in Belfast, even when aimed at mutually beneficial effects across ethnic groups, is not easy. Government sticks close to objective standards and must watch the meanings behind their language in public documents because "words can cause alot of trouble here" (W. McGivern, NIHE, interview). The pressured bureaucratic environment of urban policymaking is described by D. McCoy (interview):

There are too many opportunities for mistakes. We are under the microscope of time. We take no large steps too quickly, lest we close the door behind them and shut out opportunities.

Planners and administrators feel that they are in a "no-win" situation in dealing with sectarianism. D. Murphy of NIHE (interview) states that new public housing construction can do little to solve the deep divisions within society, but could have disastrous effects if it infringes upon territorial claims. M. Graham of NIHE (interview) sees his role primarily as "one of damage control in a circumstance where criticism from one or both communities will always be there." He thus finds himself constantly "under the gun and unable to promote the organization proactively." In such circumstances, the proper role of government policy amidst polarization is to pragmatically respond to conflict conditions rather than create a comprehensive approach to dealing with them. The role is that of "societal reflector" rather than as "social engineer." This means that government policy should not be a lever to force change, but should facilitate and help communities in meeting their desires (D. McCoy, interview). In the contentious issue of housing, then, government should facilitate ethnic integration only if and when communities are prepared for it and want it. Until that time, community needs and desires for segregation must be accommodated.

The description of Belfast urban policymaking as "color-blind" is useful in portraying the general philosophical stance of government. Yet the label goes too far in its implication that officials are unaware of sectarian realities. In actuality, internal policy discussions within government units—usually not for public consumption—clearly recognize the sectarian realities and constraints of Belfast. R. Spence (interview) asserts that "Government strives to be impartial, but it is impossible to ignore the sectarianism." Thus, the label "color-blind" is more accurate in describing the intended effects of policy—as not favoring one ethnicity over another—than in characterizing the government's level of awareness of sectarian constraints. B. Morrison, DOENI planner (interview), suggests that through the mid-1970s, sectarianism was truly a "non-subject" within policy discussions. By the late 1970s, however, the sectarian landscape was more explicitly recognized and acknowledged by government officials: "It was as if we were carrying out a plan for two cities that happened to overlap each other." In dealing with specific projects and policies, "You had to know—orange or green—which area you were dealing with." This is then not color-blind planning in its fullest meaning, but a type of "plural planning" that acknowledges the limiting effects of static territorial claims on dynamic urban processes and interrelationships.

While this plural planning framework is sensitive to sectarian realities, government remains dedicated to color-blind (or neutral) impacts so as not to disturb the volatile territoriality of the city. Government officials do not blind themselves to, or ignore, sectarianism, but rather accept it as a characteristic of the urban setting that requires close study in the consideration of policy strategies aimed at improving urban life in Belfast. Indeed, sectarianism must be handled with great caution by paying close attention to the sensitivities of the two communities (W. McGivern, interview). R. Spence (interview) concedes the importance of this color-sensitivity:

> Traditionally, we said, "We're blind." This is an honorable position. However, to carry out our responsibilities further, we

must have an understanding of the two sides and their different needs.

I now explore the public stance that government has taken in regard to sectarianism in two policy arenas. They are town planning, which puts forth physical development policies to guide the extent and location of future development; and housing policy, dealing with the allocation of public housing units to Belfast residents. I find in both cases a consistent neutrality, and a public posture of color-blindness, in government's approach toward ethnic divisions.

Town Planning and Ethnic Divisions

Planning efforts since the 1960s for the Belfast urban area have emphasized physical and spatial concerns, and separated them from issues of localized ethnic conflict (Boal 1990). The *Belfast Regional Survey and Plan of 1962* (Matthew 1964) proposed a development "stop line" around the metropolitan area to spatially limit future growth, and it planned for the development of new towns outside the stop line to absorb spillover population growth. There was no mention whatsoever in the plan of the ethnically divided nature of Belfast. An ensuing detailed plan for the area within the "stop line" took note of ethnic divisions, but asserted that planning cannot be expected to influence them. It stated,

> It would be presumptuous, however, to imagine that the Urban Area Plan could be expected to influence religious . . . factors. Our proposals are designed specifically to facilitate individual and community choice, so that the social pattern desired by the individual and the community may readily be built up. (Building Design Partnership 1969, 5)

In contrast to plans in the 1960s concerned with growth limitation and dispersal, the 1977 regional plan, *Northern Ireland: Regional Physical Development Strategy 1975–1995*, took note of urban and economic decline brought on by demographic, economic, and ethnic factors. First, due to out-migration encouraged by the 1962 Plan, accelerated out-migration due to violent ethnic conflict, and a significant fall in the birth rate, Belfast city had lost 150,000 residents—one-third of its 1961 population—between the early 1960s and middle 1970s. Second, economic shocks in the mid-1970s were leading to lack of economic opportunities and civil unrest. And third, the plan recognized the segregative forces and intercommunal territorial identification within Belfast:

> A situation now exists where generally people are prepared to be housed only in what they regard as "their own areas." Whilst every effort will be made to break down these barriers, it will inevitably take many years to remove them completely. In the meantime the position as it now exists must be recognized and taken into account in the development of new housing areas. (Department of Environment for Northern Ireland 1977)

Both the 1969 and 1977 plans thus took note of the growing sectarian territoriality and supported a government role that would be accepting and accommodating of such ethnic demarcations. The DOENI's role would be to assure that the physical fabric of Belfast accommodated as much as possible the ethnic segmentation of its population.

The most recent urban area plan is the *Belfast Urban Area (BUA) Plan 2001* (Department of the Environment for Northern Ireland 1990a). Cebulla (1994) gleans from this plan three main policy objectives and priorities: (1) maintain and enhance Belfast's position in the region; (2) improve access to employment for residents from disadvantaged areas in the city centre; and (3) enhance the quality of urban living. The BUA plan neglects issues of sectarianism by defining them as outside the scope of planning. DOENI, in its plan adoption statement (1989, 2) "notes the views expressed on wider political, ecological, social or economic matters." However, it states that:

> It is not the purpose of a strategic land use plan to deal with the social, economic, and other aspects involved.

The department had earlier expressed this view at a public inquiry when it stated that the contentious "non-planning" issues of housing and social service delivery are outside the agency's specific domain (DOENI 1988). Not one of the strategic objectives of the plan involve explicitly an ethnic or sectarian issue (DOENI 1990a, 16). G. Worthington (interview) explains that "We can only take decisions within certain well-defined land-use parameters, although our customers don't always appreciate that this is the situation." Echoing earlier plans, the plan largely accepts sectarian divides in stating that "This strategy acknowledges the wishes of residents to continue living within their own areas." Even the bread and butter of land-use planning work—the forecasting of total and subgroup populations—is excluded from the plan, likely due to its ethnic and political sensitivity. I queried G. Worthington, head of the Belfast Divisional Office of the Town Planning Service, about this compartmentalization of the planning function in Belfast:

> **Author**: What is the appropriate role of town planning relative to sectarian issues?
>
> **Worthington**: Those issues don't intrude into our considerations. We don't particularly plan for one color or the other— orange or green. We do land-use planning, that's it.
>
> **Author**: Yet isn't sectarianism rooted in land, and thus land-use planning touches very closely?
>
> **Worthington**: We're aware there are two communities. But in the BUA plan, we are not down to that level of planning. In Belfast, we do not produce land-use plans for one territory or the other. We look at the whole area of Belfast in a broad, conceptual, and strategic way. We are not specifically planning for some type of ghetto system.
>
> **Author**: There is no mention of demographics in the BUA Plan.
>
> **Worthington**: This was a deliberate policy decision because inquiries into plans tend to get bogged down over demographic projection methods.
>
> **Author**: Is DOENI assuming there will be a Catholic majority in Belfast city in fifteen years?
>
> **Worthington**: Probably nobody has "overtly" made such an assumption. What difference would that make in land use

planning terms in any event? Catholics need all the housing, schools, churches, shops, all the facilities, just like Protestants do.

The last comment illuminates government's public stance. In more consensual cities, town planning of future development and service delivery would likely not be contingent on the forecasted ethnic makeup of the population, as Worthington declares. In Belfast, however, due to the strict territorial borders of sectarian populations in Belfast—and the lack of Catholic space and under-utilization of Protestant space—the relative growth rates of the two populations will have great effects on the size and locations of areas planners designate for housing and other needed land uses. Growth in the Catholic population requires challenging methods such as increasing the density of housing, "fudging" territorial boundaries to allow "green" housing in areas that might be perceived as "orange," or locating housing beyond the city borders of Belfast. Growth in the Protestant population, in contrast, could be met largely through housing in underutilized and vacant Protestant areas in the city. As D. Murphy (interview) asserts, "There are more opportunities in the broader planning sphere on the Protestant side than on the Catholic side." In the end, the needs for basic services and facilities may be the same between a Catholic and Protestant individual, as Worthington implies, but the means that government must use to meet those individual needs differ depending upon which side of the sectarian fence those needs appear.

What the BUA plan for 2001 does focus on are land-use issues involved in the revitalization of the city center and the commercial development along the city's Lagan River. The Department views this central city emphasis as beneficial to both ethnic communities because it is "neutral territory" (O'Connor 1988). This city center emphasis in the midst of sectarian warfare in the neighborhoods has been described as an attempt to "re-image" the city as a nonsectarian center that can be marketed to potential investors internationally (B. Murtagh, interview). In the end, the effort is to "create a city no one can recognize" while the difficult areas and hard issues are largely ignored. J. Hendry (interview) describes it as a "feel-good approach that stresses the city center as normal and good for people and investors." He exclaims that "It doesn't mention Catholic or Protestant. It can't. That is the political correctness of the thing."[53]

Public Housing and Segregation

Urban policy in Belfast regarding the allocation of public housing units to households necessarily becomes influenced by group territorial claims.[54] Since 1971, the official housing policy of the Northern Ireland Housing Executive (NIHE) has been based on (1) fairness and equality of allocations based on need, and (2) impartiality and nonsectarianism. Its public housing application guidelines (NIHE 1990a) declare that "The Executive is dedicated to the principle that priority must be given to those in greatest need." The NIHE has sought to create social order and subsequent social assimilation and not to allow for ethnically separate submarkets (Keane 1990). Significantly, at no time in more than twenty-five years has the NIHE been found guilty of political or religious discrimination in its allocation procedures.

The rules followed by the NIHE in allocation are color-blind. The waiting list for public sector housing units is a unitary one containing all individuals or households—both Catholic and Protestant—in need. The list is prioritized so that those in greatest need are highest on the list. Those in emergency circumstances (including housing disruption due to civil disturbances or sectarian intimidation) or those with special health and social needs are rated highest. Thereafter, applicants are ranked based on their present housing circumstances, such as degree of overcrowding and lack of amenities or disrepair. There is no identification on the waiting list of the religious affiliation of the applicant, nor does the NIHE classify their estates by religion. Each applicant is required to indicate one or, preferably, two locations at which he or she would be prepared to live, if offered accommodation. An offer of housing considered to be a "reasonable offer" by the NIHE is one in a "general allocation area" that contains the applicant's selected estate plus those estates nearby that NIHE considers similar (M. Graham, NIHE, interview). If two "reasonable offers" of accommodation are turned down, the applicant is moved down in the priority list.

This seemingly color-blind set of procedures becomes, in practice, a process that: (1) is shaped significantly by ethnic parameters, and (2) reproduces Belfast's sectarian geography. First, in the NIHE's geographic delineation of general allocation areas (within which "reasonable offers" can occur), sectarian territoriality is figured in so that an allocation area does not encompass mixed ethnicity (M. Graham, interview). Second, although NIHE does not classify its estates by religion, Belfast's residents and NIHE applicants most assuredly do—individual or household preferences are almost always for estates of like ethnicity. Despite NIHE's color-blind intent, then, public sector households show even higher rates of Catholic-Protestant segregation than private sector households (J. McPeake, interview; Keane 1990). In 1977, 89 percent of public sector households resided on streets that were completely or almost completely segregated, compared to 73 percent of private sector households (Boal 1995). A 1987 survey indicated that 55 percent of Executive tenants lived in Protestant estates, 27 percent in Catholic estates, and 18 percent in "mixed" estates (Smith and Chambers 1989).[55] This sorting is due not to deliberately segregative policies on the part of government, but rather to the allocation policy's dependence on self-selection, which has reinforced ethnic segregation. Allocation procedures, in their focus on public safety, also overtly accept differential housing markets. Allocation procedures require that displaced public sector households be re-housed in "safe and acceptable" locations, and guidelines note as unreasonable "an offer of accommodation in an area where few of the applicant's religion reside" (Keane 1990). Because of the strict territoriality of housing space in Belfast and NIHE's reliance on individual preference, the intended unitary waiting list becomes, in effect, two waiting lists (J. McPeake, interview; W. McGivern, interview; Singleton 1986). These realities frequently obstruct the executive's primary goal of housing those in greatest need first (Singleton 1986). Catholics with great housing need, compared to Protestants similarly situated, are more likely to experience the restrictive effect of the city's sectarian geography on the availability of a "reasonable offer."

* * *

In summary, the principles of urban policy engagement in Belfast have crystallized around government objectives to produce color-neutral impacts on city residents as a means toward stabilizing a volatile city. Government is not unaware of sectarian realities, but seeks policies and programs that are not viewed as disproportionately favoring one side over the other. In this way, government seeks neutrality, or "greyness," in policy impact in a situation where sectarian color matters. Town planning has largely assigned sectarian issues to policy domains that are outside its responsibility, leaving the city with no comprehensive or strategic approach to dealing with sectarian divisions. At the same time, housing allocation administrators have rationally designed a color-neutral set of criteria that have made them immune to discrimination claims, yet do not appear to be sufficient to effectively address the complexities presented by ethnic compartmentalization.

The two government activities examined—town planning and the housing allocation policy—are similar in that neither directly changes the city landscape in terms of newly built structures or urban activities. Town planning sets down a guide for future development, but does not engage in actual development projects. The housing policy discussed deals with the allocation of public housing units to Belfast residents, but applies primarily to units that already exist in the city. In most cases, the allocation scheme is implemented only after the difficult questions of where to construct new units have been answered. Such indirect effects on the urban landscape provide designers of planning and housing allocation policy with the opportunity to seclude themselves behind "neutral" demeanors and procedures. The case is much different, however, when government units are involved in project-based physical changes to the urban system, whether these be new public housing units or new economic activities. In these cases, the direct impacts of government actions on the inflammatory sectarian urban fabric bring the implementing agencies face to face with sectarian realities known to but avoided by town planning and housing allocation administrators.

8

Lost Opportunities, Unequal Outcomes

At the Sharp Edge

I examine in this section those government units that are involved in project-based changes to the urban landscape and explore the tactics they employ in dealing with sectarian complexities. I then document the absence of a strategic policy framework within which these actions could take place, and discuss the lost opportunities this presents in urban policy's ability to contribute to larger peacemaking efforts.

Government Tactics amidst Polarization

The Northern Ireland Housing Executive has had the most significant physical impact on Belfast neighborhoods through their building and redevelopment program. A second important unit is the Belfast Development Office, which has the physical tools and financing to remake the city's geography. These two units do not have the luxury of distance afforded the Town Planning Service and NIHE allocation managers—their actions have direct, physical, and visible effects on Belfast's inflammatory territoriality.

The NIHE has had to deal with sectarian realities in their redevelopment program, their justification for new public housing construction, the location of housing estates vis-à-vis peacelines and ethnic space, and in how they address integration and segregation of public housing. I now turn to each of these issues.

241

The construction and redevelopment of public sector housing by the NIHE in Belfast is ultimately linked to sectarian territory—its maintenance, decimation, or enhancement. Upon its creation in 1971, the NIHE had to deal with an appalling housing legacy in Belfast city. The city's Victorian-age housing stock was literally crumbling to the ground by the 1960s. Belfast City Council had been both slow and reluctant to provide public housing for renting, partially due to the weighing of local voting power toward business property owners rather than householders (J. Hendry, interview). In 1974, the NIHE revealed that 29,750 units of a total stock of 123,120 dwelling units (24 percent) were unfit for human habitation (NIHE 1991). Large areas of housing were derelict, and in the city's inner areas, 50 percent of city housing was unfit (NIHE 1991). Since 1971, the NIHE has built 18,500 public housing units in the city of Belfast city (J. McPeake, NIHE, interview), reducing unfitness levels from 24 to 8 percent during an urban ethnic war.[1] In the peak years of public housing construction in the 1980s, the NIHE was spending about 100 million pounds sterling per year on Belfast housing. Today, the Northern Ireland Housing Executive operates up to forty separate redevelopment areas of ongoing renewal activity (NIHE 1988). The NIHE construction program, inherited from its predecessor housing agency, was based at first on wholesale redevelopment, involving the large-scale clearing of old row housing and subsequent rebuilding at lower densities. K. Sterrett (DOENI, interview) asserts that many of today's physical manifestations of sectarian problems can be traced not to the Troubles themselves, but to the massive clearing and redevelopment of residential areas started in the 1970s. Subsequent programs, encapsulated in the 1982 Belfast Housing Renewal Strategy, have sought to moderate the severe disruption of communities caused by large-scale clearance through the phasing and sequencing of redevelopment, repair, and rehabilitation of existing units for a thirty-year life (Housing Action Areas), closer consultation with intended communities and, more recently, the encouragement of private investment in the renewal of housing areas.

NIHE's construction and rehabilitation program is predicated upon the extent of "urgent need" applicants on the public housing waiting list relative to existing housing opportunities of adequate quality (NIHE 1994b).[2] This is a viable and objective measure to justify new construction. Yet NIHE's housing programs become intertwined with each side's effort to maintain and solidify their own territory. Housing renewal plans are closely scrutinized by residents and political representatives for their effects on the maintenance of territorial claims. In particular, Protestants advocate new housing construction as a way to revitalize inner city communities and criticize NIHE for low putback rates and displacement. Catholics, meanwhile, call for new housing to meet the needs of their growing population and criticize NIHE for not expanding into unused "orange" areas. A complicating factor facing the NIHE here is that the calculation of housing supply and demand becomes convoluted. As earlier noted, the NIHE's waiting list, unitary in intent, becomes a dual waiting list in practice. Accordingly, the NIHE must actually calculate two urgent need measures—one for Catholics; one for Protestants. As M. Graham (interview) states, "NIHE responds to the indirect effect of peacelines in creating differential supply and demand." Similarly, D. Murphy (interview) asserts, "We don't build peacelines; but we do have to deal in our house building with the indirect consequences of them in terms of demography." The fact that "urgent need" applicants are estimated to be about 54 percent Catholic and 46 percent Protestant (W. McGivern, interview), together with the presence of a more constricted public housing supply on the Catholic side, means that a great majority of new public housing construction over the past twenty years has been in Catholic areas (J. McPeake, interview). Such actions, magnified by the city's territorial constraints on policy,[3] in turn fan the fires of those who claim that the NIHE has been engaged in a program of "de-Protestantization."

In its plans regarding the location of new or rehabilitated housing, the NIHE commonly comes face to face with sectarian realities. It acknowledges interfaces and peacelines as "locations where conflict can quite frequently occur and where the Housing Executive is seeking to manage and maintain homes on an impartial basis" (NIHE 1988). The NIHE does not identify a strategic approach to building housing near these areas. Instead, it seeks pragmatic tactics on a case-by-case basis within the limits set by sectarian geographies. In looking where increased Catholic need for housing can be met, W. McGivern (NIHE Belfast Office director, interview) explains that "It is not for us to try to define where a peaceline should be breached, that is a community decision." Similarly, any attempt to turn unused Protestant land into a Catholic transition zone would be tantamount to social engineering (J. McPeake, NIHE, interview). NIHE feels that it is not the proper government entity to push for such sensitive changes to sectarian geography. In proposing redevelopment plans in either community, the Housing Executive feels its role regarding security issues should be limited because "it is not their role to assess risk" (NIHE 1987). Rather, the NIHE is advised by three national agencies on security issues likely to arise from the housing plans. If these agencies, in order to reduce potential intercommunity conflict, require that walls or other physical barriers be constructed, the Executive then builds physical barriers as part of the housing development (NIHE 1988). However, because it is not deemed consistent with housing policy that housing resources be spent on the artifacts of community division, barrier costs are borne by other national agencies. Nevertheless, the Housing Executive admits that "By building barriers between communities, it is unwittingly accentuating the division in local society" (NIHE 1988). Peacelines that separate communities are built for valid short-term stabilization goals and can avert the full-scale evacuation of housing stock under threat. Yet such government-reinforced segregation goes against nonemergency public objectives. An NIHE (1994a) report recognizes the ill effects of hyper-segregation on the housing interests of the Executive. It states that:

> Segregation interferes with the flexibility of the housing market; it requires duplication in terms of the provision of new housing; it creates voids in peace-line and flash-point areas; and it causes otherwise suitable land to become sterile for housing purposes.

The development of the Catholic Poleglass estate in the mid-1970s is a striking example of housing policymakers and planners dealing in a pragmatic way with the city's static sectarian geography. A shortage of land for housing in the west Belfast Catholic ghetto necessitated one of three responses: (1) breaching of the peacelines in the city amidst an ethnic war to allow Catholic housing on Protestant territory; (2) increased densities and unlivable overcrowding on the Catholic side; or (3) the relaxation of the anti-sprawl "stop line" around Belfast to allow Catholic housing on agricultural land beyond the city's western borders (and within the administrative boundaries of the unionist city of Lisburn). In deciding on the third alternative, housing needs and the realities of ethnicity-based territorial constraints on the ghetto's expansion within the city overshadowed the spatial goals of discouraging urban sprawl and the de facto suburban expansion of Belfast (O'Connor 1988; Blackman 1991; Boal 1991). Still, significant and hostile majority opposition to the expansion of the minority community had to be overcome, from both Belfast and Lisburn local governments. For the Poleglass estate to be acceptable, major commitments were made by ministers and top civil servants to assure that it would be different. B. Morrison (Town Planning Service, interview) recounts a minister's comment to a top civil servant under questioning by the Lisburn council: "This is going to have to be the best bloody housing estate built ever anywhere." Because of a fear that the first houses available would be taken over by the IRA paramilitary, top civil servants, army personnel, and planners facilitated the movement of the first families using a midnight operation. At the same time, housing selection scheme rules were broken in order to accept families on the basis of their community leadership potential. Today, Poleglass is the site of some 2,000 Catholic families—an estate of good-quality medium density homes with adequate green space and community facilities. It has also avoided much of the violence of the Troubles (B. Morrison, interview).

An additional issue of sectarian salience facing NIHE is how the agency addresses public housing segregation. The existing policy is that the Executive believes people should have freedom of choice, that NIHE prefers mixed or integrated estates, but that it does not believe in forced integration (NIHE 1994a). In the face of intimidation and violence, people "voted with their feet to move into segregated camps" (W. Glendinning, Northern Ireland Community Relations Council, interview). It became impossible for NIHE to hold some estates as mixed. After three hundred homes were burned or severely damaged in the mixed estate of Glenard, for instance, it became impossible to recreate this area in today's Catholic Ardoyne as a mixed estate after rebuilding. Early 1970s violence, similarly, turned the Lenadoon estate from mixed to Catholic. On other occasions, the NIHE had planned the location of new estates in the hope of encouraging integration, but without explicitly promoting the concept (NIHE 1994a).

The NIHE has felt that there was little it could do to promote integration or prevent segregation amidst such tensions. Hence, there is no formal policy of promoting integration. In its First Annual Report, NIHE stated that it "does not believe that forced integration is any more desirable than a policy of deliberate segregation." After twenty years' experience, the NIHE (1991, 50) concluded that, "The prospect of integrated housing in interface areas is remote. Suspicion and a defensiveness towards existing boundaries and territory remains strong in both communities." More recently, the NIHE has engaged in an tentative discussion about the possibility of ethnic mixing should interethnic hostilities recede. A report by a NIHE advisory group (1994a) discusses the housing costs imposed by territorial segregation and the resulting supply-demand distortions. Significantly, it highlights the larger social costs of segregation, asserting that "Integrated estates are likely to be more stable and peaceable than segregated estates" (NIHE 1994a, 10–11). In any evolution of NIHE formal policy on integration, however, government must come to terms with the recent legacy of Manor Street housing in north Belfast. This area was redeveloped in 1987 and 1988 as mixed housing, resulting in new dwellings occupied by Catholic families at a location that was allegedly Protestant territory. A serious outbreak of violence occurred, with fifteen new dwellings burnt out and vandalized, and subsequently demolished by the Executive. Subsequently, a new peaceline barrier was erected. The government lost its substantial investment virtually overnight and a new physical partition was created.

The NIHE today views Manor Street as an "expensive experiment" that failed and whose time is not yet right to try again (M. Graham, NIHE, interview). It represents the limitations of a partial approach to the problem; an "example of trying to address conflict with housing while not addressing everything else" (D. MacBride, community leader, interview). Indeed, NIHE cannot be expected to promote integration apart from a comprehensive strategy that addresses ethnic compartmentalization on multiple fronts. J. McPeake (NIHE, interview) asserts that "It is hard to generate notions of integration in the housing front when many aspects of life are segregated. There is more to producing integrated housing than producing the bricks and mortar housing product." He points, in particular, to needed changes in employment and education. Absent a multifaceted approach to sectarian divisions and living with the legacy of integration failure on Manor Street, the NIHE will likely move in a rationally incremental way on the issue of integration. As D. Murphy (NIHE, interview) states, "We are dealing with a considerable amount of public money, so our choices have to be fairly realistic."

Similar to the NIHE, the Belfast Development Office (BDO) seeks physical changes to Belfast's landscape. It is a development facilitation unit that seeks to physically regenerate parts of Belfast and to integrate housing, economic, and planning initiatives (V. Allister, BDO, interview). It controls large sums of urban financial assistance programs—the Urban Development Grants aimed at the stimulation of private investment; Environmental Improvement Schemes aimed at upgrading the urban physical environment; and Comprehensive Development Schemes, which allow for the acquisition and redevelopment of derelict areas. Although most of this funding has been directed at the city center, the development office has also carried out projects amidst the strict territoriality of Belfast's neighborhoods, experiences to which I now turn. I focus on the physical changes that BDO has deemed appropriate when seeking to regenerate an urban fabric laden with sectarianism. Two main physical tactics have been used in non–city center regeneration: creation of neutral land uses between antagonistic sides; and the justification of physical alterations in interface areas based on the forecasted economic benefits of BDO-sponsored projects. Murtagh (1994a) calls these tactics "wedge planning" and "facilitating growth," respectively. Both of these techniques are environmental or physical methods aimed at diffusing sectarian interfaces, and both seek to build mutually beneficial uses along potential lines of conflict.[4] The main difference is in potential effects. Whereas the first method distances opposing sides through neutral infrastructure, the second method seeks economic gains for both sides and could facilitate nontrivial alterations to sectarian territoriality.

Wedge planning introduces a neutral land use as a means of separating rival neighborhoods. For example, redevelopment in east Belfast, using CDS and EIS programs, included the creation of a wide new road—with medians and a major landscaping embankment—that acts as a de facto peaceline. Adding to the separation of antagonistic sides, an elderly housing unit was constructed on the Protestant side. Through these methods, the "physical and psychological distance between the two communities was increased in a needed way" without recourse to the scarring effect of permanent walls (G. Mulligan, interview).[5] J. Hendry (interview) suggests that the use of roads in this way is a likely scenario in the future for underutilized areas in formerly Protestant territory. Yet, road building itself produces scars and distance, and goes against other city policies endeavoring to deemphasize car transportation in order to alleviate congestion. In the second type of physical tactic—facilitating growth—there is the introduction not of infrastructure, but a new development project whose cross-community economic benefits are used to justify physical alterations to the interface area. The Northgate development in the Duncairn Gardens area of north Belfast presents an informative illustration of this approach and is now examined. The local problems in this area are multiple and intense. This part of Belfast has been the location for terrible political violence, accounting for 20 percent of all sectarian killings during the Troubles (DOENI 1990b). A permanent wall peaceline was constructed dividing Catholic New Lodge from Protestant Tiger's Bay for almost the entire length of the Duncairn Gardens street (see Figure 8.1). There was "galloping dereliction" along the dividing street (B. Morrison, interview)—27 percent of interface frontage had been demolished; and 32 percent of all properties, and 43 percent of commercial properties, were vacant (DOENI 1990b). Catholic housing stock, already unable to meet demand, was endangered further by violence. Much of the Catholic housing fronting the peaceline has front sides grated to prevent damage from petrol bombs, and back doors are used instead for access. Tiger's Bay was fast becoming a ghost town due to Protestant out-migration. Forty percent of Tiger's Bay housing was vacant, and about 3.5 acres of derelict land lay adjacent to the interface frontage (DOENI 1990b). Psychologically, the remaining Protestant population felt frightened, embattled, and insecure (B. Murtagh, interview).

The BDO and the NIHE coordinated their efforts in the Duncairn Gardens area in order to "manage the evolution of the area." NIHE had a vested interest in rescuing the area because it contained a large and vulnerable housing stock. Twenty percent of a recently rehabilitated "housing action area" in Tiger's Bay was already vacant, while unmet Catholic housing needs intensified. Yet NIHE was unable or unwilling to lead the effort and turned to the BDO for leadership. The result of this was the Northgate proposal, facilitated by BDO in concert with the NIHE, planning services, and the local BAT. This project will acquire land for an integrated land use scheme, the core of which is to be an economic development district of industrial workshops and enterprises on the Protestant side that aspires to create neutral and mutually beneficial territory between Protestant and Catholic communities. In Protestant Tiger's Bay, 380 houses will be demolished; about 125 will be built anew in dif-

Figure 8.1 Part of the Duncairn Gardens Peaceline, Looking into the Catholic Neighborhood of New Lodge (Gate Open During 1995 Ceasefires)

Source: Scott A. Bollens

ferent Tiger's Bay locations behind the new industrial activities. Environmental improvements elsewhere in Tiger's Bay will involve "improvements to pedestrian routes, planted areas, and to gardens" in housing estates which have "poor or vulnerable boundaries" (Northgate site plan). In this way, the plan seeks to consolidate and upgrade Protestant housing stock in an otherwise declining area.

The combination of redevelopment and rehabilitation, and the sequencing of these programs, will likely be able to retain more Protestants in Tiger's Bay than if the whole area was redeveloped at once (D. Murphy, NIHE, interview). Protestants, in effect, would bear witness to the pushing back of the sectarian divide (or at least the thickening of the divide). As one government participant stated,[6] this represented a "novel approach for effectively fudging the peaceline." Yet, in return, Protestants would receive an upgraded and more coherent residential community with access to new employment opportunities. On the Catholic New Lodge side, the thickening of the buffer zone would allow the existing and endangered housing units to be maintained. Catholic residents would also have access to jobs across the street. However, new Catholic housing would still not be able to cross the street, and thus overall supply would not increase. One idea discussed would have rerouted Duncairn Gardens toward Tiger's Bay, thus opening up opportunities for Catholic housing on formerly Protestant land. Although "we tried to think of a planning reason for doing so" (B. Morrison, Planning Service, interview), this de facto redrawing of the sectarian interface to accommodate Catholic housing needs succumbed due to its potential inflammatory effects. Instead, the NIHE is seeking to engage in the sensitive process of identifying potential new housing areas elsewhere in north Belfast to meet expected Catholic demand.[7] The NIHE is attempting to identify these sites based on considerations of land use, access, convenience, territoriality, and the presence of symbols and icons. Such an assessment asks, "Will it be perceived by the other side that you are encroaching on their space?" Such is a risky business.

Marginalization of Planning and Strategy

Urban policy regarding the built environment of Belfast is engaged in by many government entities, including: NIHE (housing construction); BDO (economic regeneration); Belfast Action Teams (community development); Making Belfast Work (economic and human resource development); and the Planning Service (land use). The first four units are development entities capable of physically altering Belfast's built landscape and thus forced to deal pragmatically with sectarian land issues. Only the last unit—Planning Service—is composed of urban professionals capable of designing a comprehensive, systems-based, and strategic approach to sectarian land issues. Such a strategy would be more proactive and broader than, and thus help guide, the project-based tactics of the development entities. Unfortunately, town planning in Belfast—through its public stand of color-blindness—has done little to contribute to meaningful government policy aimed at addressing sectarianism in a productive and sustainable way. Despite the land use and territorially based implications of much of sectarianism, the town planning function, whose professional foundation is land use, has played a minor role in addressing ethnicity. K. Sterrett (DOENI, interview) critically observes, "Here and in Britain we seek to contain planning. We teach the rational-comprehensive approach, yet planning all around us is determined by politics." The impact of this is more than simply occupational marginalization. Rather, the lack of an explicit ethnic management strategy sets well-intentioned public actions adrift on the sectarian sea, with awareness only of what can be seen on the horizon, not of its broader sweep or wider dynamics. Lacking a strategic framework aimed at effective management of ethnic space, public actions by government units such as NIHE and BDO have primarily been ad hoc tactics rather than strategic acts; project-based rather than area-based; reactive rather than proactive; and have emphasized vertical rather than lateral government approaches. Planning in the strategic and comprehensive sense has been marginalized.

Town planning is responsible for creating the framework within which development is to take place in Belfast. It could play a central role in providing a reality check and frame of reference that development agencies can use when interacting with contested territoriality. Yet there has been "no coherent and strategic planning response to the troubles" (K. Sterrett, interview). Town planning has avoided dealing with ethnic conflict directly, leaving it to development agencies to deal with sectarianism on their own terms. Ethnicity becomes perceived not as a "planning" problem. Rather, sectarianism becomes a "security," "housing," or "community relations" problem separated from a larger strategic perspective (K. Sterrett, interview). Sectarian interface areas received no serious mention in the most recent Belfast Urban Area (BUA) Plan for 2001. When I asked G. Worthington (Head, Belfast Divisional Office, Town Planning Service) about the greatest role that town planning could play in bettering ethnic relations, he claimed that "I'm not sure there is necessarily a role." Belfast town planning "tends to take a five-mile high view and stands back" from the development process (G. Mulligan, DOENI, interview). Instead of providing a guide for managing sectarian space, Belfast town planning "has entrenched itself behind the wall of physical planning, where social, economic, and sectarian issues are pushed outside the wall" (J. Hendry, interview). This compartmentalization owes to the 1972 Planning Act of Northern Ireland, which provides town planning with a distinctive identification with land use and excludes issues dealing with the broader interactions between social and physical space (B. Murtagh, interview). It is revealing that the 1972 Act takes its lead from a British town planning system that, itself, has been found to be insensitive to issues of ethnicity. The administration of British town planning has "tended to focus on legal and technical aspects of land use and development and has not involved persistent and wide-ranging debates about the social purposes and goals of planning" (Thomas and Krishnarayan 1994). In addition, British planning practices a "color-blind" approach, in which planning authorities "promote a formal equality which, in practice, is insensitive to the systematically different needs and requirements of the population."[8]

Town planners in Belfast defend their profession's ideology of technical land use competence. Town planner B. Morrison (interview), an otherwise progressive practitioner, views the stance as beneficial. "Planning works quite well behind the scenes," he states; more deterministic actions by government are best left to others. In contested public discussions, "It can be useful for planners to adopt the technical and professional role because it allows them the ability to avoid confrontation" (K. Sterrett, Planning Services, interview). In the sectarian battleground of Belfast, "There is a sense of almost persecution where planners retreat into narrow technical roles" (W. Neill, interview). The town planning process becomes one viewed by planners as properly regulatory, not proactive and intervening. The comments of B. Morrison (interview) are illuminating:

Our regulatory role is our reason for being. To do this cleanly and properly, you would have nothing to do whatsoever with anything proactive. This posture as regulator influences us in terms of what we can outwardly do, or be perceived as doing.

Town planning becomes an arbitrator or referee, rather than a player, in the sectarian realities of Belfast. Although town planning provides professional advise and expertise to development agencies, they are constantly aware that they must be viewed as disinterested referees when deciding the fate of project applications.

In maintaining this narrow ground of responsibility, "Planners have marginalized themselves, and shut themselves off from urban realities through their shell-like existence" (B. Murtagh, interview). This marginalization and compartmentalization of town planning has meant that urban policy responsibilities "leak out" in ad hoc ways into the collection of development agencies such as NIHE, BDO, BAT, and MBW. The real cutting edge of public planning in Belfast becomes usurped by those policy professionals in the development agencies willing to work creatively to address sectarianism in ways that town planning has avoided. Yet tactical actions by government occurring outside an overall strategic framework produce problems. For example, the Duncairn Gardens project led by BDO may be capable over time of solving a localized interface problem. Yet, there is no urban strategy that addresses the fact that the general pattern of decreasing Protestant demand in the city has produced, and will produce, many more "Duncairn Gardens" in Belfast. Should BDO engage these tactics of interface diffusion at all localized sectarian divides associated with underutilized Protestant land? Or, should there be a concentration of public resources on a targeted set of interface areas? Such a strategy of interface intervention can only be developed based on knowledge of demographic dynamics that extend beyond proximate neighborhoods to include spatial relationships occurring at subarea, citywide, and regional levels. The project-based orientation of much developmental work cannot get to this level of sophisticated analysis. In addition, the engagement in tactical actions separated from strategy puts inordinate burdens on development agencies. The NIHE, for instance, has a vested interest in the effective management of sectarian space. They oftentimes, then, find themselves out front in government discussions regarding sectarianism and the proper role of government policy. Yet this extends the NIHE into policy domains outside their housing responsibility. After all, the NIHE is involved in only one facet of city building and should not be expected to design a comprehensive, multi-issue strategy. Rightfully, NIHE "says they want to enable but not to lead" (W. McGivern and R. Spence, interviews).

In the end, developmental interventions by units such as BDO or NIHE into the sectarian complexities of Belfast are not guided by a coherent, citywide strategic approach or by a set of guidelines directed at desired physical, social, and economic outcomes across the city. It is in the design of such integrated principles that town planning could make its most important contribution. No other participant in Belfast urban policy is capable of such a comprehensive and systematic approach to city building. Instead, town planning removes itself by emphasizing static land-use allocation and regulatory caution. Tactical actions amidst sectarianism, unsupported by a strategic framework, then run the risk of introducing additional sharp edges to an already barbed city.

The lack of a comprehensive strategy to guide urban decisions in Belfast has also meant that government approaches have been vertical and single-function, rather than lateral and coordinated across functions. Examples are numerous. There is a lack of coordination between the town planning service and the development office (J. Hendry, interview). The NIHE looks for another government unit to take the lead in designing the nonhousing part of community regeneration (W. McGivern, NIHE, interview). Funding from community-based Belfast Action Teams duplicates and counters other agency's efforts at times (V. McKevitt, BAT, interview). And project funding from the Making Belfast Work program becomes absorbed into different government units, rather than connected to a cross-departmental antideprivation strategy (B. Murphy, MBW, interview). With a lack of strategic integration across city-building decisions in Belfast, vertical policies and actions are incapable of effectively addressing a sectarian geography that is a complex system of physical and psychological relationships. For example, the closing of a public school by the Department of Education based solely on student population can have symbolic and destabilizing effects on an ethnic community's identity and can exacerbate population declines and housing stock erosion. Such single-issue or single-agency approaches will likely be ineffective in enhancing quality of life, and may even intensify ethnic tension. P. Sweeney (DOENI advisor, interview) states that each unit "is technically excellent, but it's the things that fall within the gaps that really make the difference."

In summary, government's approach to urban policy in Belfast has contained a set of self-limiting features. There is both separation of the town planning function from ethnic management responsibilities and fragmentation of policy along division and department lines. Combined, these factors decrease government's ability to mount an ethnically sensitive strategy that would be both multidimensional (physical, social-psychological, economic, and human development) and interdivisional (integrating planning, housing, and development units). Urban policies have sought orderly changes in the physical development of the city, but actions have been largely reactive to sectarian and societal realities. P. Sweeney, DOENI advisor (interview), reflects upon the deterioration of the Protestant Shankill neighborhood and suggests that it was not government policy that hurt the area, but a combination of major economic shifts and inner city neighborhood dynamics. Still, policymakers are not off the hook. Rather:

Planners could have been a lot more progressive in dealing with structural change. All this could have been anticipated. As such, planners stand accused and guilty. They needed to manage the environment rather than simply reacting.

He asks a disturbing question: "in a deeply fractured society, is there not a need for government to be more proactive, to be more progressive?"

Outcomes of Belfast Urban Policies

Despite the intended neutrality of government policy in Belfast city, there are uneven outcomes at individual and neighborhood levels. Meanwhile, community perceptions of urban policy can be quite different than the intended color-neutral outputs would suggest. This section examines the effects of urban policy on the: (1) distribution of resources between ethnic groups; (2) perceptions of community residents; and (3) distribution of benefits between central city and neighborhoods.

Neutral Means, Unequal Outcomes

In a city with segmented housing and employment markets, a government approach that emphasizes neutrality and equality of opportunity will likely not increase the equity of urban outcomes. Rather, it will tend to neutrally reflect the societal inequalities present. Thus, a neutral policy in an unequal society of dualities and separation will result in unequal opportunities through the replication of those dualities. Where sectarian territoriality constrains much of urban living, neutrality does not necessarily increase equity.

An excellent example of this effect is the NIHE allocation scheme. It epitomizes a neutral, fair, "color-blind" approach to allocating public housing units to those in need. No religious identification is ever part of an applicant's material. And it is an approach favored by residents battered by sectarianism. An analysis commissioned by the Standing Advisory Commission on Human Rights (STACHR) (Smith and Chambers 1989) found that the executive "has had striking success in creating confidence in the fairness of the system." This is much to the credit of the NIHE. However, this fair system is not producing fair outcomes. The STACHR study of public housing in Northern Ireland found that "In 1987, the public housing system did not succeed in delivering equal opportunities to Protestant and Catholic applicants." This is not due to direct discrimination (of which the study found none), but to the lesser access by Catholics to public housing due to the constraints of sectarian territoriality. The study found clear differences in average time on waiting list (Catholics wait longer compared to Protestants having similar, or even lesser, housing needs). The study found that for 1987, 23 percent of those requesting Catholic estates in Northern Ireland were housed; compared with 42 percent of those requesting Protestant estates.[9] For the Belfast urban area specifically, there is simply less public housing stock in the city available to a Catholic housing applicant. The study classified about 55 percent of NIHE units in Protestant estates and 27 percent in Catholic estates.[10] At the same time, the waiting list in categories classified as urgent need in Belfast was approximately 54 percent Catholic and 46 percent Protestant in 1995 (W. McGivern, Belfast housing director, NIHE, interview). Thus, Catholics face a disproportionately smaller available housing stock in Belfast at the same time as they experience disproportionately greater housing need. A color-blind policy template premised on applicant choice that is put atop this unequal base of conditions restricts Catholic "choice" to a housing market about one-half the size faced by Protestants. In the rigid territoriality of Belfast, province-wide discrepancies between Catholics and Protestants in their ability to access public housing become even more pronounced (Smith and Chambers 1989).

This combination of neutrality and inequality has led some to argue that NIHE and other government units should monitor more explicitly their impacts across the ethnic divide. D. McCoy of the Central Community Relations Unit of the Central Secretariat (interview) asserts that the "assumption underlying color-blindness is wrong—that an organization that says, 'We don't want to know what religion our clients are,' cannot discriminate."[11] Rather, religious monitoring of clients and outcomes is needed to see whether a policy is producing unequal outcomes, and to help design corrective policy where inequality is present. J. McPeake (NIHE, interview) similarly suggests that with color-blind policy, there are possible negative byproducts of normal operations that you do not know about and thus would not seek to correct. The STACHR report (Smith and Chambers 1989), itself, states the main implication of its findings is that the NIHE

> should now move towards explicitly and openly monitoring the results of its policies in light of the need to achieve equal opportunities for the Protestant and Catholic communities.

This policy recommendation has two important parts. First, its call for religious monitoring points Belfast urban policy in a direction away from its reliance on color-blindness and its public non-discussion of sectarian issues. Second, its aim to achieve equal opportunities directs Belfast policymakers away from their traditional emphasis on impartiality and neutrality. This is so because Smith and Chambers (1989 and 1991) use a broader definition of equal opportunity that goes beyond the absence of discrimination (as fulfilled by the NIHE) to include a fairer distribution of outcomes. In contrast to a narrow definition of equality of opportunity stressing the absence of obstacles to entry so that all reach the starting blocks, a broader definition calls for the consideration of structural conditions that promote inequality of outcome so that all not only get to the starting blocks, but also can compete fairly in the race. In the NIHE example, all applicants get to the starting blocks, but structural conditions tilt the race toward Protestant applicants.

Smith and Chambers (1991) summarize their investigations of housing and employment outcomes in Northern Ireland in this way:

> The view that equality of opportunity has been nearly achieved, and that remaining inequality is a reflection of historic discrimination which will gradually disappear, is emphatically contradicted by the weight of the evidence.

"Color-blind" equality of treatment by government does not translate directly into equality of opportunity, in the broader sense of this concept. Indeed, neutral government schemes may reflect and reproduce the societal inequalities and dichotomous conditions within Belfast.

The policies and practices of the planning service in Belfast display a similar pattern as NIHE's allocation program—a procedurally neutral program applied to a structurally unequal sectarian landscape. Procedurally, the planning service engages in a fair and neutral methodology regarding the review of project applications. Indeed, there does not appear to be any bias in project approvals based on the religious composition of the proposed location or the applicant's ethnicity (J. Hendry, interview). Still, the planning service does not address sectarian geography in a strategic way in its area and subject plans. Thus, the inequalities associated with sectarian territoriality will likely remain, and cause the procedurally fair planning approval process to result in unequal outcomes. A lesser number of projects can be proposed to meet Catholic needs because of the lack of land availability in ethnically circumscribed space. At the same time, those projects proposed for "Catholic" areas may face spatial and physical infrastructure constraints that financially jeopardize their success. In contrast, NIHE's policy regarding the construction of new public housing does seek to decrease Catholic-Protestant disparities by justifying most new construction on the basis of magnitude of "urgent need" on the waiting list, which is disproportionately Catholic. In the long term, then, this building program, by increasing the number of units available to Catholics, could create a situation where a "neutral" allocation scheme could produce equal outcomes. However, given the current uneven distribution of "Protestant" and "Catholic" estates and the likelihood that territoriality will remain strong in the foreseeable future, it will take decades for this building program to achieve a Catholic housing availability/need ratio similar to that of Protestants today.

A problematic feature of NIHE's new-build program is that it plays an instrumental role in facilitating or perpetuating the ethnic apartheid of the city. Belfast housing planners are faced with a dilemma in the planning of public sector housing. In their allowance for Belfast's polarized geography in allocation and construction decisions, and in their building of peacelines when deemed necessary, housing planners in the short term minimize and contain intergroup conflict or at least introduce no new sources of conflict.[12] NIHE (1991) states, "The prospect of integrated housing in interface areas is remote. Suspicion and a defensiveness towards existing boundaries and territory remains strong in both communities." In the long term, however, publicly condoned intergroup separation can more firmly reinforce and perpetuate divisions (Keane 1990; NIHE 1994a). To the extent that residential mixing is one prerequisite to addressing deep ethnic conflict, politically sensitive housing policy does little to alleviate, and may even intensify, urban polarization. Again, NIHE (1991) concludes, "Sadly, while the peacelines provide a physical barrier between both communities, in reality they represent barriers to a permanent solution." The sectarian geography of Belfast was created by the larger problem of ethnic conflict and the intimidation and violence associated with it. However, government policy has facilitated and furthered segregation through its policies. The STACHR report (Smith and Chambers 1989) on housing policy, concluded that NIHE actions "may reinforce segregation, although it is unintended." In the midst of urban civil war, this was probably a rational response by public authorities. Yet, B. Morrison (Planning Services, interview) worries that in planning Belfast, "We may be in danger of institutionalizing what are artificial boundaries." Territorial hardening initially associated with expression of community identity, once formalized and rigidified, becomes regulative of community experience as neighborhoods are held hostage to ossified boundaries. As Feldman (1991) points out, territorial hardening can play an instrumental role in the "reproduction of antagonism."

Government's condoning of sectarian segregation seeks short-term stability at the expense of longer-term individual and societal costs. There are severe "costs of self-segregation and separation" (M. Fitzduff, Northern Ireland Community Relations Council, interview). NIHE (1994a), for instance, states that segregation perpetuates and exacerbates societal divisions, facilitates control over housing estates by paramilitaries, and fosters a climate that stunts the social development of children. With segregation, learning about the other side comes not through mutual interaction and understanding, but through ugly portrayals and stereotypes. Public authorities will be compelled to deal with these social psychological costs because they can debilitate a city as much as war in its streets. Government's acceptance of sectarian segregation also increases the costs and difficulties of service delivery and urban administration. For instance, the siting of local service delivery offices (social security, for example) based on color-blind, technical methods of activity allocation can produce unequal opportunities if the site is perceived as off-limits to one ethnic group. In this way, a policy may be fair, but the way it is implemented or administered causes inequality (D. McCoy, CCRU, interview). Another example is that a resource center aimed at assisting both communities has to constantly fight against perceptions that it is in one or the other group's territory, and thus not in reality a "neutral venue" (D. MacBride, interview). On the other hand, the incorporation of sectarian realities in siting decisions causes a different set of problems that are fiscal in nature. In this case, normal planning methodology for siting facilities based on general population distribution and densities becomes transformed into siting often identical community facilities on both sides of the sectarian interface. This duplication of facilities—parks and leisure centers, social service offices, shopping centers, baby clinics, and community meeting places—taxes public expenditures and consumes land needed for other uses (J. Hendry, interview; B. Murtagh, interview). In the case of public education—segregated into two systems—the underutilization and scattered locations of Protestant schools in north Belfast mean that per-pupil costs there are twice those for Catholic schools.[13]

In a city where territorial changes and incursions can be causes for terrorist violence, policymakers have become linked with efforts to maintain each side's territorial claims. This is especially true for traditional Protestant areas that today are underutilized and that, in a normal city, would have evolved into Catholic areas. Such "Darwinian survival" of neighborhoods is not allowable where maintenance of community viability is closely linked to protection of sectarian territoriality. In an effort to contain civil disorder, government must rescue depleted communities—such as Suffolk and

Tiger's Bay—from imminent collapse. Instead of helping these "hospice" neighborhoods through the terminal stage, policy resuscitates these corpses at great public expense. In other cases, policy seeks to sustain a neighborhood "community" that years ago left for peripheral estates. These represent reactive tactics by government that solidify territoriality and promote urban sclerosis, not a strategic approach to addressing on a citywide basis problems facing the Protestant and Catholic populations. R. Strang, formerly with the NIHE (interview), points to the public costs of this approach:

> Where is the sustainability of maintaining a sterile territoriality? At some point, we will not be able to afford Belfast.

In the end, the short-term containment and abeyance of conflict has been attempted by Belfast policymakers through color-neutral policies. But, it has been at the expense of long-term social, psychological, and fiscal costs. In this way, the role of policy has been neutral, but its effects have not been benign. B. Neill (Queen's University, interview) questions whether urban policies are "neutral and in the public interest." He suggests that policy has not been neutral in its outcomes, and that it is debatable whether policies that decrease the future social, psychological, and fiscal livelihood of its residents are in the public interest. The long-term consequences resulting from the formalization of ethnic separation through housing, planning, and peaceline policies may paralyze the city for decades after the signing of the 1998 Multi-Party Agreement.

Public Perceptions

> We have been ignored.

> —Nelson McCausland,
> Belfast City Councillor and member of
> Ulster Unionist Party, in an interview

> Belfast was a city divided along sectarian lines by the planners, not necessarily by the inhabitants.

> —Joe Austin,
> Belfast City Councillor and member of
> Sinn Fein, in an interview

Redevelopment here was like South Africa's policy of clearing out black towns and moving them to the hinterlands. This is what it felt like.

—Jackie Redpath,
Greater Shankill Regeneration Strategy,
in an interview

What you do may be "scientific" but it will be viewed through orange or green spectacles.

—Will Glendinning,
Northern Ireland Community Relations Council,
in an interview

Government policy in the midst of urban civil war is bound to be viewed negatively and with suspicion, and Belfast urban policy does not escape such criticism. Nevertheless, there are aspects of urban policy viewed favorably by community leaders and residents. As mentioned before, the NIHE housing selection scheme has earned the agency high marks for fairness and impartiality. This is a tremendous feat because housing was probably the most contentious issue in Belfast before direct rule in 1972. The NIHE is rightfully proud of their achievements in this aspect of housing policy. Another part of government that has been rated positively is the Belfast Action Teams (BATs), decentralized and community-based liaisons between neighborhoods and government. BATs have had a measurable impact on people's attitudes toward government, helping communities feel they have some role and thus helping overcome feelings of alienation (V. McKevitt, Ardoyne/Oldpark BAT leader, interview). They have also helped improve government's image overall (G. Mulligan, interview).

A 1992 survey of 4,500 Belfast city residents (DOENI 1994a) assessed the impact of government urban regeneration policy. It found that overall satisfaction with the areas where people live was extraordinarily high (about 80 percent). However, this may be due, says co-author G. Mulligan (DOENI, interview), to a heightened sense of community loyalty in a conflict environment rather than to government policy. Positive changes were viewed in the areas of availability of shopping and entertainment facilities, housing, and health facilities. Negative changes were felt in employment, crime, and traffic. Job accessibility remained problematic. Ninety-one percent of respondents felt that "Young people in this area find it hard to get a job"; 33 percent felt that the only jobs available were in areas too dangerous to work. Consistent with DOENI's approach to sectarianism, the "focus of the report was the impact of policy on areas, not on religious groups per se" (G. Mulligan, interview). In only four of the eight statistical sectors used in the study can the spatial area be used as a proxy for religion. Using these four proxies only, overall satisfaction with neighborhood is lowest in the inner west sector of Catholic Falls and Clonard. At the same time, though, G. Mulligan suggests that there was no clear Catholic rejection of public authority in the survey. Residents of the heavily Protestant sector of inner east Belfast showed the greatest propensity to move from their current house, likely exhibiting the higher feeling of threat felt by Belfast Protestants.

Interviewees and secondary material present a different and more critical view of public policy than found in the 1992 DOENI survey. In the least, policy is portrayed as a remote mechanism that avoids the real issues of the city. M. Fitzduff (interview) takes the NIHE to task for construction decisions that "facilitate apartheid." D. MacBride, who works for a North Belfast community resource center (interview), characterizes government agencies as ignoring the difficulties and having their heads in the sand. She asserts that public entities are unaware of how their rigidly designed programs and definitions adversely impact Belfast's neighborhoods. Under direct rule, government is remote and distant, information is hard to get, and it is difficult for NGOs like MacBride's to identify the key personnel in government. G. Worthington, DOENI planner (interview), is aware of these perceptions: "Planners have a poor image in Northern Ireland. That's probably our fault. On the other hand, we can't be right all the time."

More than this characterization of government as aloof, there is the underlying current that urban policy has intentionally harmed one ethnic group or the other. G. Worthington (interview) knows that there is "certainly a perception out there that there is a hidden agenda; always the perception that 'everything is done on the other side of the peaceline.'" D. MacBride (interview) feels there is a sense that government "plays the 'sectarian card,' playing one community off against the other." And, J. Austin (Belfast councillor, Sinn Fein, interview), asserts that political events have made it expedient for town planners to divide the city along sectarian lines. Urban policymakers experience strong criticism from both ethnic communities, usually for different reasons (M. Graham, NIHE, interview). Catholic criticism targets government's inability to expand housing to meet their growing needs. Linked to the Catholic perceptions is the larger political issue of sovereignty. J. Austin (interview) summarizes the nationalists' view as having been abandoned and punished by the Northern Ireland state. In terms of livelihood, Austin says, there is a "case-hardened acceptance that nationalists don't get employment unless they are cheaper or low-skill; that employment has been the unionist reward for supporting the state." Protestant perceptions center on public actions' effects on community displacement and the feeling that policy is biased toward Catholics. N. McCausland (Belfast councillor, Ulster Unionist, interview) asserts that "DOENI bureaucratic bungling has destroyed Protestant neighborhoods in North Belfast," by replacing demolished housing too slowly to retain his constituencies there. He also states that the "government approach has been too reactive to the political shouting," pumping money into moderate nationalist enterprises in efforts to counter Sinn Fein's extremism. Many Protestants feel that the government is moving too quickly and closely to what they perceive as nationalist initiatives (S. Corbett, Central Community Relations Unit, interview).

A common claim among unionists has been that policy has had the intent of "de-Protestantizing" certain parts of Belfast city. Central to this perception is the history of the Protestant Shankill neighborhood. The Shankill area has severely declined, from 76,000 population in the 1960s to 26,000 in the mid-1990s. According to a local resident survey, the most important factor contributing to this decline was not the sectarian Troubles or economic decline, but government housing redevelopment programs.[14] J. Redpath (Shankill community leader, interview) describes the community as being "mugged by redevelopment and then left lying there."[15] A statement in the local newspaper (*Shankill People*, February 1995) sums up resident attitudes toward past housing policy:

> Redevelopment has torn the community of the Old Shankill apart and has never put it together again. The planner built flats and soul-less housing estates; they moved thousands of people to outside Belfast; they bulldozed the shops and wrecked the Road.

The reality of 1970s urban redevelopment in areas such as the Shankill is that both sides—government and community—are partially correct. First, government was acting in response to an existing and forecasted decline in the Shankill population (an area seriously eroded through economic shifts). As such, the community is wrong, in part, to view redevelopment programs as a cause of population change, rather than a reaction to change. On the other hand, the way government proceeded with redevelopment—large-scale clearing that outpaced rebuilding—was devastating to the community, in terms of both physical stock and community coherency and leadership. The pace of clearing dispersed the population from Shankill Road to peripheral estates, left behind a depleted population, and took apart the local community as an organic whole.

In its most extreme "conspiratorial" form, public perceptions exist that claim that security and military reasons underlie planning policy. These claims fall into three categories (Murtagh 1993). First, there is the claim that the Northern Ireland Office engineers population movements in a way that leads to more homogeneous and thus policeable ethnic space. Second, there is the perception that the police and British Army are involved in the design and layout of housing developments to secure them more effectively (Hillyard 1983; Cowan 1982). Third, there is the accusation that key planning decisions—such as housing demolitions and the building of the Catholic suburban Poleglass development—are dictated by wider political considerations. Murtagh (1993) and this author find no conclusive evidence of these conspiracies, political agendas, or the presence of "hidden planners."[16] Rather, what appears to be happening is that conspiracy perceptions are a consequence of government's not having an explicit planning framework for dealing with the realities of ethnic space. W. McGivern of NIHE (interview) proposes that the downside of government's neutral approach is that people fill in this void with conspiracy stories. And W. Glendinning (Community Relations Council, interview) forecasts that the "avoidance by government of the real schisms in the city will continue to fuel fears and distrust." The negative public perceptions of government as uncaring, biased, or conspiratorial confirm that intended policy neutrality is a difficult mission in a contested environment. Government must calculate in the future whether such negative perceptions are outweighed by real achievements on the ground. A government approach that is more open and strategic about sectarian realities may provide significant benefits to future Belfast governance.

Twenty Years of Deprivation[17]

The neutral stance of urban policymaking in Belfast has also tended to sidestep ethnic neighborhoods in important ways, favoring safer and less sectarian areas of focus. Much attention of urban policy and financial assistance has been directed at the city center, and these efforts have stimulated a renewal of the city core. Yet social and economic deprivation in the city's neighborhoods remain sadly intense and there is little improvement. There is a nagging impression that city center benefits are not reaching the downtrodden in the neighborhoods, and may even be gained at their expense. City center revitalization, supported through financial tools, has improved the position of the service sector there and has enhanced the city's position in the region (A. Cebulla, interview). The benefits of this attention were expected to be increased job opportunities for the residents of Belfast's ethnic neighborhoods. This would be consistent with one of the goals of the BUA plan 2001: "to improve access to employment by concentrating investment in areas which can be safely entered by both communities in the city" (Cebulla 1994, 15). The city center would provide a "neutral venue" for ethnic workplace mixing, combating the inhibition of labor mobility by real and perceived violence that had been documented as early as 1977. And the city center job emphasis could help break the segregative effects of neighborhood-based employment.

Survey results of employed Belfast residents (Cebulla 1994) displayed in Table 8.1 indicate that city center revitalization is not providing meaningful work benefits to Belfast residents. It appears that residents outside Belfast city have been the major beneficiaries of new city center jobs. Since, on average, they have more disposable income than city residents, they would also disproportionately benefit from new shopping opportunities. Within the city, the survey showed that residents in Protestant east Belfast were most likely to access the city center job market (Cebulla 1994, 93). The study concludes that for city residents, the position of the city center as an employment focal point was marginal (Cebulla 1994, 92). As A. Cebulla (interview) states, "The working class residents have a hard time fitting into the 'image' of the city center as plush and for middle-class consumption."

In one sense, this constitutes unfair criticism of DOENI's city center policies since policymakers do not have control over the re-

Table 8.1   Percentage of Belfast Residents Benefiting from City Center Employment

	% OF SERVICE JOBS CITYWIDE IN:	% BELFAST RESIDENTS WORKING RETAIL JOBS IN:
City center	21.8	4.9
Wider city center	44.1	7.9

Source: Cebulla, A. 1994. *Urban Policy in Belfast*, p. 92.

cruitment and employment policies of new retailers. In addition, low access to center jobs is probably due to low skill and education attainment levels, again outside DOENI's domain (R. Spence, permanent secretary of DOENI, interview). In this spirit, A. Cebulla (interview) states that it can be said that the DOENI has done their job, but that these programs are not going to solve the city's problems. Yet, since employment access to the city center was a key aspect of DOENI's BUA plan, some way must be found to link the city center strategy in a proactive way to the improvement of conditions in the city's disadvantaged communities. Absent this, socioeconomic deprivation will persist in city neighborhoods and community leaders will feel abandoned by policy. A recent public report (Sweeney and Gaffikin 1995, 9) presented the view of many in the nongovernmental sector that the city center development orientation has been "at the expense" of neighborhood renewal. Thus, not only is the city center focus not substantially helping the job prospects of neighborhood residents, but at least perceptually, it is interfering with them.[18]

There are few signs of change in the level or pattern of social and economic disadvantage in Belfast's neighborhoods over the last twenty-five years (Northern Ireland Council for Voluntary Action [NICVA] 1993; Cebulla 1994; J. Harrison, Making Belfast Work [MBW], interview). The main antideprivation program, MBW, spent 120 million pounds sterling in its first six years in efforts to stem economic disadvantage. Still, according to economic researchers F. Gaffikin and M. Morrissey (interview), all indicators of deprivation indicate insignificant changes. In a study of area deprivation from 1971 to 1991, NICVA (1993, 12) found that "Unemployment levels have progressively and disproportionately increased in the wards ranked highest in each analysis." Although the citywide unemployment rate stayed constant from 1981 to 1991, there is "a greater inequality in the distribution of unemployment now than in the 1980s" (NICVA 1993, 11). In fifteen of the city's fifty-one wards, the percentage of the economically active who were unemployed in 1991 was 30 percent or higher (citywide figure is 20.3 percent). The MBW claims that three thousand new jobs have been created directly or indirectly through MBW spending in its first six years (Making Belfast Work 1994, 7). However, program output measures are not linked to ward residents (J. Harrison, interview; Gaffikin and Morrissey, interview). Without this data, and in light of little improvement in area deprivation levels, it must be concluded that MBW was not reaching its intended goals of stemming economic disadvantage in Belfast's deprived neighborhoods.[19]

* * *

In terms of Belfast urban policy outcomes, this evaluation finds that neutral policies often reflect social and economic inequalities and are incapable of addressing two sectarian communities having different objective and perceived needs. In this way, neutrality is a means toward an end, not an end in itself that guarantees certain outcomes. In addition, government in contested Belfast, despite hard-earned praise in certain policy areas, is seen as uncaring, biased, or conspiratorial. Both Protestants and Catholics feel their community needs are not being addressed in an effective and responsive manner. Most dispiriting of policy outcomes, however, is its insignificant effect on lifting residents and their neighborhoods above levels of social and economic deprivation. Urban policy has provided to neighborhoods physical benefits through improved public housing and amenities rather than personal upliftment through job opportunities and human development programs. With this imbalance, the NIHE will increasingly play the role of landlord of a robust housing stock for the long-term unemployed (R. Strang, interview).

9

The Demands of Peace

Cities, by definition, are about conflict and contested space. It's how you manage conflict that is the issue.

—Paul Sweeney,
Advisor, Department of the Environment,
in an interview

Nobody is neutral in such circumstances. Everyone is partial. The key is to make positive use of this partiality.

—Mari Fitzduff, Director of
Northern Ireland Community Relations Council,
in an interview

The reactive and neutral posture of urban policy in Belfast has sought containment and abeyance of conflict. Yet the intended neutrality and community-reflective nature of urban policy appears insufficient to effectively address the complexities presented by ethnic compartmentalization. The ability to restructure the city in a normative and positive sense is foreclosed as government works only within the territorial blinders of its sectarian communities.[1] Belfast's urban policy approach has relied on single-dimensional responses by individual government units to complex urban phenomena having physical, social, and psychological aspects. A strategy which would coordinate public interventions has been sacrificed to often ad hoc project-based tactics by different government units at different times. This has decreased government's ability to mount an ethnically sensitive strategy that can constructively advance the welfare of the city's neighborhoods and residents. The policy-neutral posture suffers from unequal outcomes, poor public acceptance, and ineffectiveness in addressing deprivation in Belfast's ethnic neighborhoods.

This chapter examines the elements of an alternative approach to Belfast's urban policy—one more progressive, proactive, and openly cognizant of the city's potent ethnicity. Such a policy approach will be criticized by some as being too risky to implement during the early stages of Northern Ireland's political restructuring. I argue, however, that it is essential to consider these policy options so that more constructive urban actions could be taken as part of, and contribute to, larger peacemaking efforts in the future. Urban actions may help anchor and reinforce advances in larger political negotiations, bringing tangible benefits of peacemaking to city, neighborhood, and resident. Such a different urban policy approach will challenge policymakers to move beyond the feeling that any approach by government other than passive reflection amounts to intrusive and potentially damaging "social engineering." In the housing field, for example, alternatives to a color-neutral approach were commonly equated by interviewees with an integrationist agenda that might force ethnic groups to live side by side despite their preferences for segregation. Despite these concerns, many of those polled recognized the need for some movement by government toward more progressive and proactive management of ethnic problems and issues. B. Murtagh (interview) states, for example, "Planning and policy should go beyond the passive reflection of urban needs and demands and take on the social responsibility to affect change." This chapter seeks to outline, through the use of emerging, more progressive strands of urban policy, a proactive role for future Northern Irish governments in dealing with ethnic issues that would lie between passive reflection of need, on the one hand, and social engineering, on the other.

Managing Differential Community Needs

Who in this room can say that sectarianism has had no role to play in where we live, work, go to school, have as partners. If this is false, why is there no mention of sectarianism in government plans and documents?

—Will Glendinning,
Development Staff of NI Community Relations Council,
in an interview

We're not ignoring sectarianism, but addressing it in a subtle way.

—Housing Planner,[2]
NIHE-Belfast Division,
in an interview

Progressive Ethnic Management

A progressive ethnic strategy would acknowledge that single issue–based interventions into city building (whether it be land-use planning, economic development, or housing) ignore the complex reality of sectarian geographies. Its goal would not be the integration of antagonistic groups per se, but the coexistent viability of those sides within the urban system, whatever spatial forms and living patterns that might entail.[3] Murtagh (1994a) states that such coexistent viability will not come through color-neutral procedures, but through a more explicit accounting of ethnic factors in planning and development decisions. For example, he suggests that government engage in ethnic audits or impact statements that would forecast the impacts of proposed actions on ethnic community identity and stability. Qualitative, perceptual analysis would complement traditional projection tools of land-use planning, and community relations objectives—aimed at the improvement of interethnic tolerance and understanding—would be a central part of area plans and strategies. An ethnic management strategy would seek to bring sectarian considerations and issues more publicly into the planning and policy process. W. Glendinning (interview) recommends that planning and service delivery agencies consider locational, social-psychological, and community identification and maintenance factors in their plans and actions. He equates civil servants under the current approach with the family of an alcoholic. Like such a family confronting the disease, Belfast urban policymakers often have dealt with sectarian issues out of shock and in emergency situations. He suggests that there is power in more openly talking about sectarianism and policy before the shock comes. In the end, government officials come to terms with sectarianism in one way or another—either on a proactive and engaged level or a reactive and disjointed one.

The challenge to government officials is to talk honestly among themselves and with their citizenry about something that they have denied they do. In some ways, such as ethnic audits or impact statements, these new planning roles would only make more explicit what happens in government anyway (B. Neill, interview).[4] J. Hendry (interview) points to the high awareness by the planning service of the sectarian implications of proposed projects that come through their offices, and the author often found within the walls of government a sophisticated appreciation of the complexities of sectarianism. Nevertheless, this call for explicitness asks much of government officials—to come to terms with their own fears and feelings along the path of a more candid incorporation of sectarian issues into public policy processes (M. Fitzduff, interview). "By asking people to discuss these things," states W. Glendinning (interview), "you're asking them to expose their roles, to get beyond their professional demeanor." What would change under a more explicit strategy is that policy discussions of ethnic content would be shared with other government units and with community groups. Gained from more explicit accounting of sectarian realities would be an enhanced ability to design a multidimensional urban strategy, and the feeling by communities and citizens that they have some ownership of the public programs and a stake in assuring their successful outcomes. This would decrease suspicion of government and the propensity of residents to attribute ill and conspiratorial motives to government. As C. Bradley (NICVA, interview) asserts, "If government had been more explicit and honest up front with its explanations, conspiracies would not have filled the void in the past."[5]

An ethnic management strategy would challenge public officials to redefine the town planning function beyond its traditional role in Northern Ireland as land-use arbitrator. The planning profession, with its training in urban comprehensiveness and interrelatedness, is best qualified to prepare a multidimensional approach to ethnic management. B. Neill (interview) suggests that the "symbolic appropriation of urban space—through murals and other territorial claims—is very much a planning issue." To engage effectively with Belfast's potent sectarianism, however, town planning must be forced to break out of its entrenchment behind the wall of technical land-use allocation. Murtagh (interview) asserts, "Cultural specificity is a legitimate planning concern; instead, planning's goal is to be a technical and rational process." Because sectarian conflict has many urban dimensions—one of which is spatial—planning in Belfast should broaden in both its substantive reach—to encompass social-psychological and ethnic community identity issues—and its professional skills—to include community relations and conflict negotiation. Town planning could move from its current technical and land-use orientation to incorporate consideration of the social, economic, and psychological dynamics and requisites for the coexistent viability of Protestants and Catholics.

A progressive ethnic strategy would not view the two ethnic groups only in terms of their spatial and population requirements or in terms of only objective need. Instead, it would analyze ethnic communities as complex urban subsystems that contain interrelationships, dynamics related to viability or decay, and different lines of feedback (W. Glendinning, Community Relations Council, interview). This represents a more holistic view of ethnic community functioning that includes social-psychological issues of community identity. Interventions into these urban subsystems based only on land-use considerations is naive and potentially dangerous (R. Strang, interview). Focused solely on the criteria of population density and range, for example, planners would likely argue for the closing of a local State (Protestant) primary school in a declining area. Yet the closure can send emotional and practical signs to the Protestant community and increase their feeling of threat. Murtagh (1994b) suggests, instead, that social-psychological effects on the viability and sustainability of ethnic neighborhoods be injected as a decision criterion in the investment programs and capital and revenue decisions of public sector organizations. The key to assure the coexistent stability of competing spatial groupings is to maintain or develop differential local institutions such as community centers, health centers, youth clubs, schools, and churches.[6]

A progressive ethnic strategy would by necessity also have to engage multiple government units laterally, rather than the current circumstance of nonintegrated vertical responses. "For too long," says D. Murphy (NIHE, interview), "different departments have gone their own way, resulting in no comprehensive housing-social-economic approach to renewal." V. Blease, chief executive of the NIHE, suggests that explicitness of sectarianism is occurring in individual government units, but not across unit boundaries.[7] These vertical governmental responses and actions are incapable of addressing urban ethnic subsystems in a holistic way. The coordination of interdepartmental activities that has occurred has been the result more of innovative, lateral-thinking individuals within government, rather than a normal and structured practice (P. Sweeney, DOENI, interview). A report (DOENI 1993a) written by planners within the

NIHE and planning service argued for the routinization of such co-ordination through the development of an integrated regeneration strategy composed of housing, social, economic, and environmental/physical components. It appears most important that the developmental and regulatory functions of government, currently separated institutionally, be brought closer together.[8] Town planning can provide an urban system–based frame of reference and strategy able to guide developmental agencies in their interventions into contested territoriality. At the same time, the project-based experiences of development agencies such as the NIHE and BDO can provide models that town planners can use in the development of a citywide strategy of ethnic management. In addition, the NIHE report asserted that government actions be set within the wider demographic and economic changes of the region, and that they not address urban issues on a neighborhood-by-neighborhood basis.

The possible move toward a progressive ethnic strategy by government is on the minds of people both within and outside government. Whether it is a local politician stating that "It is difficult to see change coming and participate in it" (N. McCausland, interview), or a civil servant claiming that "We have learned and will continue to learn" (V. Allister, BDO, interview), the perception is that there is something better than the existing model of urban policy. More innovative, lateral thinkers are in high positions within the DOENI. For example, the former director of the Northern Ireland Voluntary Trust has been special advisor to the permanent secretary of DOENI, bringing with him a progressive community perspective. The permanent secretary himself was the designer of a community relations unit within the central secretariat, described below, and a principal architect of the cross-community Education for Mutual Understanding (EMU) compulsory component of all Protestant and Catholic public school curricula. In addition, institutional reorganization has placed the major social/economic policy, Making Belfast Work, within the heretofore physically oriented DOENI, thus increasing opportunities for needed policy integration. And, importantly, the 1989 Fair Employment Act provides the Northern Ireland government with a valuable precedent in modifying government policy amidst political controversy to more fully acknowledge ethnicity and more strongly pursue fair outcomes.[9]

Peace building in Northern Ireland aimed at energizing and reinforcing the 1998 multiparty accord will demand that the traditional protective approach by urban policymakers developed in the midst of urban civil war be reevaluated. It is incumbent upon urban policy professionals to help guide Belfast urban residents and neighborhoods, and policymakers themselves, away from their comfortable blinders. P. Sweeney (DOENI advisor, interview) asserts that "DOENI must be part of the overall change process in Northern Ireland. We have the responsibility to push back barriers, to open up, and to ask fundamental questions." B. Murtagh (interview) states that:

> Planners cannot change the broader societal context, but they can affect people's quality of urban life and ease tension. Peace will only hold if there is accommodation of differences; and planners can help here.

Emerging but isolated examples of new urban policy approaches exist in the city which consider sectarian realities more progressively. I turn to four notable examples—Northgate, Springvale, the Central Community Relations Unit, and Making Belfast Work. These experiences inform policy officials about both the rigorous requirements and fresh opportunities of an ethnic strategy premised on coexistent viability of competing ethnicities.

Emerging Innovative Policy Approaches

Acknowledging Ethnic Community Dynamics. The Northgate development in the Duncairn Gardens area of north Belfast was discussed previously in terms of how it seeks to physically restructure the sectarian divide and diffuse the interface. It seeks to create a more consolidated, coherent Protestant residential area, through demolition and subsequent partial rebuilding, which would be buffeted from the old interface by an industrial/economic project. Meanwhile, the effective moving back of the interface allows breathing room for Catholic housing units previously susceptible to destabilization. I focus now on two additional important aspects of this project: (1) the interagency cooperation used; and (2) the incorporation into the replanning of the area of a sophisticated analysis of the multiple facets of sectarian geographies. In 1990, the Under-Secretary (Planning and Urban Affairs) in the DOENI created a working group chaired by the head of the Belfast Development Office that included personnel from the planning service and the local Belfast Action Teams. The NIHE, at the same time, was a key stakeholder in the area, with about 30 million pounds sterling invested in the community area since 1976 (DOENI 1990b), and had lobbied for public sector attention to the stabilization of the Duncairn area. There were three objectives of the interdivisional work group (DOENI 1990b).[10] The first was to propose environmental ways of diffusing the interface, which had led to downturns in commercial activity, increased security barriers, and a declining and retreating Protestant community in Tiger's Bay. A second objective was to deal with housing problems "where contrasting features of the two communities combine with territorial and land constraints to produce a major housing problem". And, thirdly, the group sought ways to improve economic opportunity in the area (1991 unemployment rates were 48 percent in Catholic New Lodge and 30 percent in Protestant Tiger's Bay). The interface problem was deemed central and determining; and proposals sought to achieve long-term stability for the area.

The Northgate strategy is not derived from color-blind and banal discussions of land-use allocation, but employs a finely tuned sensitivity to sectarianism and its social, spatial, and psychological correlates. Sectarian geography is mapped in detail. For example, the study reports (DOENI 1990b) that "Catholic territory continues to extend north along the Antrim Road and westwards along the Cliftonville Road. This trend represents an erosion of formerly 'mixed' areas." Elsewhere, it states that "There is a collective perception in the Protestant Tiger's Bay community of being gradually outflanked by Catholic territory." Most revealing of government's awareness is the section examining the possible community responses—from local residents, local politicians, local church authorities, and local commercial interests—to DOENI's economic and housing actions. The area is characterized as one of mutual fear and suspicion, home to strong paramilitary organizations on both sides, and where Protestants are afraid of the Catholic spread across Duncairn Gardens street into Tiger's Bay. The report continues that, "The lack of NIHE activity in Tiger's Bay is interpreted as part of a government plan to allow the housing stock there to deteriorate to the stage where most of the Protestant population will leave." This Protestant fear is described by the working group as "extremely deep-rooted." In the Catholic New Lodge, meanwhile, there is resentment over being "fenced in"; and there is a fear of loyalist paramilitary strikes.

Because of the feeling of threat by the Protestant population in Tiger's Bay, the report anticipates possible adverse reaction to the development of an industrial/commercial project in perceived Protestant residential fabric. The report candidly states that "There is a real possibility of adverse reaction if the support of the community cannot be engineered by careful preparation of the ground." A net increase in residential units is considered as a means of trying to reestablish the Protestant neighborhood; however, the NIHE view "is that present demand does not justify the building of any new homes in the area." At the same time, NIHE was viewed by the working group as more likely supportive of a plan that would demolish most of its vacant rehabilitated housing and create a new physical barrier that would improve the security of remaining and rebuilt NIHE housing investments. NIHE would obtain a solution to the housing decline in the area and a more secure environment for its investment. The fact that the plan would demolish about twice as many Protestant houses as would be rebuilt "could become something of a political or sectarian issue." Thus, it was viewed as important that new houses be under construction before demolition of the older housing begins, to reassure Protestant residents that there is a commitment to the area.[11] Still, however, local political reaction is expected to be negative, especially from unionist councillors who perceive that the proposals "could lead to a further reduction in their votes." Such negative political reactions—"Local councillors have the potential to stir up local opinion against the proposals"—are viewed as jeopardizing the investment potential of the industrial/commercial district and its ability to play a central role in the diffusing of the ethnic interface. A further complicating factor is that redevelopment would require the demolition of an under-used Church of Ireland (Protestant). The report anticipates "vociferous protest from the congregation." The demolition of twenty-one commercial establishments is also expected to generate some negative reaction from traders, although this would be mitigated by their successful relocation.

The major problem, cites the DOENI report, is that the project "might be opposed on sectarian grounds, as taking away too much of the former Tiger's Bay area." While local residents should be delighted with the proposals, "The only potential difficulty therefore is that local politicians, or some local residents with very strong views, might swing opinion against the proposals." The working group worries that "Major irrational opposition could create significant obstacles; and that many of the local residents could be easily persuaded by individual politicians or others claiming to represent the community." To diffuse such possible negative reaction from within the local Protestant community, the government task team suggests that an existing Tiger's Bay community group with views sympathetic to the project's overall goals be nurtured and supported. In this way, local politicians and extremist residents could be outflanked. The current work of the community group "might usefully be built on, and the study proposals could even be presented as a response to the view of local residents." In this way, "The community is prepared, and indeed should come forward with some of the ideas itself." It is expected that the community group's views "can be influenced towards ideas closer to the study proposal and local support obtained before any of the proposals are made public."

The Northgate development strategy illustrates how government might pursue multiple objectives amidst a complex territoriality. It does this by using an interdivisional approach to policy development, utilizing land-use planning, economic development, and housing expertise along with input from the ground by decentralized BAT liaison offices. BDO brings to bear its expertise and financial tools regarding economic and commercial regeneration. The NIHE has knowledge of local housing markets and the practicality of rebuilding the residential stock. The planning office analyzes the various links between the proposed land uses and activities in the study zone. And BAT participants are able to tap into community and sectarian perspectives on proposed governmental actions. Through such integration, the planning problems arising from sectarianism are addressed in an imaginative and comprehensive way. Northgate shows that government is capable of analyzing the potential social, spatial, political, and psychological impacts of their actions on ethnic community identity. The analysis takes stock of each of the major participant groups in the urban subsystem, how negative public reaction may be mitigated, and endeavors to work with moderate community representatives. One problematic feature of the strategy is that its approach to community participation resembles more manipulation than consultation and runs the risk of antagonizing needed allies. In the end, the Northgate proposal is to be commended more for its innovative conceptualization than for its methods of community consultation.

Bridging the Ethnic Divide. The Springvale development scheme is an economic regeneration initiative begun April 1990 by the Belfast Development Office. Its innovativeness lies in how the proposed development project and major public investments have been configured to geographically and functionally span sectarian communities. The study area covers almost seven hundred acres of a two mile river valley in west Belfast that bridges both Protestant and Catholic territories. The area is characterized by high unemployment, housing pressures on the Catholic side, a poor physical environment, and inadequate service facilities (DOENI 1992b). The regeneration opportunity presented itself when a long-established engineering company downsized and relocated, leaving a prime vacant area perceived to be in Catholic territory next to the arterial Springfield Road. DOENI subsequently purchased the abandoned site and other land that transcended the Springfield Road, a known demarcation between Catholic and Protestant areas. In addition, the BDO extended the regeneration area beyond these purchased sites to include most the river valley stretching north and west. This further brought the Protestant community into the planning area and connected the two ethnic communities conceptually. The development opportunity thus links the two sectarian territories and is an abrupt change from DOENI's commonly used tactics emphasizing compartmentalization and segregation of ethnicities.

The plan, adopted October 1992, includes to the south of Springfield Road (in perceived Catholic territory) new housing to meet Catholic demand, a job training center, an Industrial Development Board advanced factory, and a new Springvale Business Park. Road access to and from the business park was a matter of much public discussion because of the territoriality of the area. In the end, a second access road was incorporated into the site design to assure both ethnic communities of their personal security (V. Allister, Springvale Development Team, BDO, interview). Internally, roads will have security barriers and gates and be clearly identified as private roads because of "the fear that gunmen would run up and down the road" (V. Allister, interview). In Protestant areas north of Springfield Road, there are to be major improvements and expansions of public recreation facilities, a new children's park, and a new industrial park. The Springvale initiative thus attempts to address both the differential and common needs of the two ethnic groups within its project area. It aims to address the housing needs of Catholics at the same time as remedying the underprovision of outdoor recreational facilities proximate to Protestant areas. Meanwhile, the project responds to the cross-community need for jobs by creating economic activities in the southern portion that are physically and psychologically accessible to both communities. Although private investment was not forthcoming into the development area in the first three years, there was by early 1995 a significant amount of public infrastructure and investment in place that could act as a catalyst in the future.

The potential for bridging the ethnic divide increased when the University of Ulster expressed interest in the possibility of having a campus in west Belfast. DOENI, in its preliminary evaluation of the Springvale area for the campus (DOENI 1993b), states, "In selecting the site for the proposed campus, it was felt desirable to span the Springfield Road to counter pressures of territorial identity which might be expected to mount in relation to an institutional proposal sited firmly on one side of the road or the other." Of critical importance in the evaluation was the question of access and the "front door" to the proposed campus (DOENI 1993b). Although the campus would be primarily within Protestant territory, the access to the campus would be much easier from Catholic territory via Springfield Road than from the Protestant Shankill area. But this would further the belief by Protestants that the campus would be a University of West Belfast for Catholics (B. Morrison, Planning Services, interview). Accordingly, the DOENI (1993b) evaluation of a Springvale campus draws attention to the need to link the campus by an accessway to either a major motorway or to ethnically mixed south Belfast. Through these means, the proposed campus would have ease of access to and from the rest of the urban region and province, and would not be seen as captured within the Catholic confines of west Belfast. As DOENI (1993b) states, "The perception which potential students and their parents have of the area is therefore of vital importance. Investment, and for many this may include investment in children's higher education, favors areas which are perceived to be safe and readily accessed."

A potential campus in Springvale challenges development planners to move away from their traditional approach of ethnic compartmentalization and segregation. If Springfield Road remains as the main accessway, the route could be "sanitized" through widening and the creation of security walls; or, new traffic caused by the campus could be integrated within the existing street fabric. V. Allister (interview) suggests that the latter approach is desirable, because a sanitized route "doesn't send the right message to a community such as this one." In addition, the police force, the Royal Ulster Constabulary (RUC), advised in a 1994 feasibility study by Touche Ross that the access road and the site itself be walled. This resembles traditional urban policy in Belfast and would likely create a prison for students and staff designed to keep the locals at bay (*The Guardian*, February 28, 1995). V. Allister (interview) again takes this approach to task: "If the university is to be a success, it's only because it doesn't have walls around it and it has programs in place that link it to the communities." In total, the Springvale initiative represents the potential for establishing links and bridges within a contested environment, rather than the building of breaks and walls. Physical decisions such as those regarding a potential campus will send emotive symbols to future generations about what Belfast either aspires to in hope or accepts in resignation.

Pursuing Fair Treatment by Government. The Central Community Relations Unit (CCRU) was established in 1987 within the Central Secretariat to advise the Secretary of State for Northern Ireland on all aspects of the relationship between ethnic communities. The Unit has three broad roles—to help formulate new ideas and strategies to improve interethnic relations; to challenge policymakers throughout government to take into account the effects of proposed policies on interethnic relations; and to review periodically policies and programs as to their effects on community relations. Government community relations policy is based on three prime objectives (CCRU 1995): (1) to ensure that everyone enjoys full equality of opportunity and equity of treatment; (2) to increase the level of cross-community contact and cooperation; and (3) to encourage greater mutual understanding and respect for different cultures and traditions. One of the creators of the CCRU, Ronnie Spence (interview), asserts that social and economic divisions will always be associated with instability, whether there is "peace" or not. As he points out, "It is a destabilizing influence if you feel worse off than someone else." Thus, it is critical that government be acutely aware and tackle the divisions created by differentials of social and economic justice and in parity of esteem. In other words, it is not enough for government to stand back in a neutral stance and leave unaddressed these destabilizing inequalities.

The CCRU represents an important point of change within government. With its review and challenge role, there is the formalization at a high level of authority of ethnic impact analysis within the policy process. P. Sweeney, DOENI advisor (interview), claims that it is the "most important move in government in the last twenty years." Policy Appraisal and Fair Treatment (PAFT) requirements mandate that government units turn in annual reports to CCRU describing the projected impacts on intergroup relations of their policies. The presence of CCRU will undoubtedly advance the extent of ethnic impact analysis within government. Critical to its future role, however, will be its breadth of review and challenge powers, its ability to affect meaningful policy change, and whether its definition of equality of opportunity and fair treatment is construed narrowly to mean removal of barriers or more broadly to require active remedying of inequalities.

* * *

Northgate, Springvale, and the CCRU are cases of innovative urban policy that consider more progressively and holistically the sectarian realities of Belfast. They are, however, policy strands that have not been knitted together into a strategic urban program. Still lacking is a citywide strategy to inform policymakers as to when and where to invest public money for the purposes of rebuilding city neighborhoods and normalizing Belfast's urban fabric. In other words, when should the Northgate or Springvale approaches be repeated and in what locations? Are there areas where progressive approaches are not appropriate and may even be harmful? Significant issues are now examined pertinent to the formulation of a comprehensive ethnic strategy aimed at the coexistent viability of competing ethnicities.

Spatial Targeting

> One cannot in some neat abstract academic way disaggregate the interplay of political forces from the cooler abstract understandings of need.
>
> —Mike Morrissey,
> University of Ulster, Jordanstown,
> in an interview

Protestants will always lose the argument about deprivation.

—Billy Hutchinson,
Springfield Inter-Community
Development Project,
in an interview

What if six Sinn Fein projects get turned down and the "hard men" of Ardoyne feel excluded?

—Frank Gaffikin,
University of Ulster,
in an interview

In targeting public resources, how are we to address Catholic objective needs and Protestant grievances related to alienation?

—Paul Sweeney,
DOENI advisor,
in an interview

An urban strategy aimed at coexistent community viability would call for government to target—spatially focus—resources in those areas in need where investment can make the most meaningful contributions to Protestant and Catholic community prosperity. The main experience that Belfast has had with spatial targeting of neighborhoods has been the Making Belfast Work (MBW) program initiated in 1988. The difficulties and evolution of this program thus inform a consideration of government's capacity for channeling investment in an strategic way. First, although intended as a need-based program in its first years, MBW became in practice more a politically determined program. This illustrates the dangers of not having an investment strategy. Second, the reframing of the MBW program in 1995 to link it to a community regeneration strategy gives government an important first lesson in formulating a city-wide framework of investment.

Making Belfast Work is a spatial targeting program begun in 1988; today it is the government's main method of "targeting social need" (TSN) in Belfast. TSN is one of three main priorities that guide government spending in Northern Ireland (D. McCoy, CCRU, interview; Northern Ireland Council for Voluntary Action 1994; F. Gaffikin, interview).[12] It is a government initiative and set of spending principles announced in 1991 which address areas of social and economic differences by targeting government policies and programs.

The thinking behind TSN is that community differentials contribute to divisions in the population by sustaining feelings of disadvantage and discrimination which in turn influence sectarian attitudes to broader political and security issues (Knox and Hughes 1994). Targeting to overcome disadvantage in a polarized city is problematic. In that disadvantage disproportionately affects Catholics, a TSN-based program by implication would have to positively discriminate (M. Morrissey, interview). One of the most detailed government statements on TSN speaks delicately about this issue:

> I must stress that the programme is about targeting resources and policies to address disadvantage and is not about positive discrimination which would be unlawful under existing law. However, since the Catholic section of the community generally suffers more extensively from the effects of social and economic disadvantage, the targeting of need will have the effect of reducing existing differentials. (Secretary of State to Standing Advisory Committee on Human Rights, 10 March 1992)

This statement illustrates the controversy that exists over the means deemed appropriate for addressing differentials, owing to the difference between narrow and broad interpretations of the concept of *equality of opportunity* (Smith and Chambers 1991). In the first case, obstacles and discrimination are lifted so that all can play on a level playing field. In the second case, in addition to removal of barriers, affirmative action is utilized to compensate for inequalities and the legacies of past discrimination so that all have an equivalent chance on that level playing field. Such a difference is highlighted by the contrast between the Fair Employment (NI) Act of 1976, which relied on narrow removal of discriminatory barriers and voluntary compliance, and the 1989 Fair Employment Act, which requires the use of broader affirmative action goals and timetables to remedy underrepresentation of Catholics in the workforce (Department of Economic Development 1989; Knox and Hughes 1994).[13]

For many years, Belfast urban policy was devoid of spatial targeting of community deprivation. This was not due to lack of knowledge. As early as 1977, a Belfast Areas of Special Social Needs (BAN) report documented two major need syndromes in the city's neighborhoods—one characterized by unemployment and low incomes; the other by poor physical and shelter environments.[14] Nevertheless, the three main public investment tools (UDG, EIS, and CDS) were directed into the city center. Urban development grants (UDGs) were seen as incapable of stimulating private investment in neighborhoods and, indeed, efforts to increase the UDG subsidy amount in deprived neighborhoods had shown limited effect (Cebulla 1994). In its efforts to balance economic opportunity in the city center and the addressing of social needs in the wider city, the MBW program was thus introduced as a way to combat neighborhood-based disadvantage.

The MBW program directs spending to twenty-six of the fifty-one wards in the city deemed most deprived based on a fourteen-criteria measure of social, economic, and physical factors. These "core" wards take in one-third of the city's population.[15] The total religious composition of MBW wards is about 55 percent Catholic and 45 percent Protestant (J. Harrison, Research Officer, MBW, interview). This propensity for disadvantage to be a Catholic phenomenon gained the program in its early years the label of "targeting Catholic need." In actuality, the number of eligible wards currently is roughly equal for each community (DOENI 1994c; DOENI 1995). MBW is a program that spatially targets neighborhoods rather than directly targeting individuals (Gaffikin and Morrissey 1990; Birrell and Wilson 1993). The expectation is that the benefits of job creation, physical improvements, and job training to deprived neighborhoods will flow to the people who live there. MBW was initially housed at the top of the governmental hierarchy in the Central Secretariat and was provided with about twenty million pounds sterling per year to spend. The intent of MBW was that resources would be distributed based on need to community groups in order to address the lack of economic opportunities and poor quality of life. Another important role that MBW was to play, through its Belfast Special Action Group (BSAG) of top civil servants, was to challenge and encourage mainstream departments, through MBW funding incentives, to redirect budgetary priorities toward addressing disadvantage.

The experience of MBW from 1988 through 1994 had not met expectations (DOENI 1994c; Sweeney and Gaffikin 1995). Although intended as a need-based program, there is a "messy negotiation with the real world when you try to intervene in an abstract level on the basis of need" (F. Gaffikin, interview). The program sacrificed its program goals to political expediency, both in terms of who received funding and the types of projects funded. On the Catholic side, money was channeled to the "safe hands" of church-based organizations and those related to the moderate nationalist SDLP party, bypassing groups associated with Sinn Fein (interviews: C. Bradley; J. Austin; V. McKevitt; R. Davison). At the same time, new capital investment and enterprise centers became favorite symbols to MBW officials because of their visible political payoffs in legitimizing the program; human resource development and training were deemphasized. In these first six years, MBW tried to walk a tightrope between responding to objective need (its intent) and political demands and imperatives. This resulted in an ad hoc allocation of resources, a lack of transparency in funding decisions, and, ultimately, a program driven by clientalism. MBW funding responded in tactical and piecemeal ways to the short-term demands of different forces rather than seeking strategically to balance them within a long-term framework (F. Gaffikin and M. Morrissey, interviews).

In 1994–1995, MBW engaged in a major revision endeavoring to address these sources of ineffectiveness. Its spending was now to "address need and not merely respond to demand" (DOENI 1994c), meaning that a strategic approach would now anchor the program from the strong political winds. The "need" driving program funding would in part be defined by "area partnerships" which are to be representative and inclusive of community, public, and private sectors. In this way, need is not to be statistically measured by government bureaucrats, but defined in a consensual fashion by collaborative government-community entities.[16] MBW funding will also likely direct its attention more than in the past to long-term capacity building through education and training, especially of youth. In this approach, there is a shift toward empowering people to look for and access jobs rather than focusing solely on job creation and new capital investment (J. Harrison, MBW, interview). People, as well as physical areas, are to be regenerated through education, and training in community organization and leadership (P. Sweeney, interview).

This reorientation of MBW toward a more rationalistic approach based on need presents both opportunities and potential new problems. The process of self-evaluation it undertook showed innovative leadership and a government unit open and willing to learn.[17] In many ways, MBW is a test-bed for government in redefining its role amidst the complex sectarianism of Belfast. The MBW shift is a move away from a culture of responding to those political demands that are articulated most clearly toward a partnership approach emphasizing agreement on the needs of an area (B. Murphy, MBW deputy director, interview). An important observation here is that MBW is not seeking to move all the way from political demands to objective need, but to some consensual development by public, private, and community sectors about what "need" entails and requires in each specific neighborhood. Indeed, community-defined need can differ significantly from objective need in the political terrain of Belfast. The new reliance on community partnerships was, in fact, predicated on the fact that "What people on the ground want and what government's perception of the needs of an area are don't necessarily match" (J. Harrison, interview). Inclusive community involvement is a positive step forward. The main difference between old and new MBW might be that a more inclusive community organization may now be making demands on government rather than politically skewed ones. The formulation of community-defined needs is also important for government in its efforts to sensitively respond to the qualitatively and quantitatively different needs of its Catholic and Protestant populations. This is something government has a hard time doing when it applies its own universal criteria of allocation.

Despite these positive aspects, a newly designed MBW program implemented without sufficient anchoring in citywide strategy may be blown around by the winds of community-defined need. This would be to the detriment of cost-effective targeting and would reinforce an entrenched and sclerotic territoriality. What is needed is a strategy of community investment that can be used to review whether bottom-up, community-expressed "needs" are compatible with citywide objectives. In this way, community needs are matched up against a strategic framework that provides an important reality check. Such a community investment strategy could have a well-defined neighborhood prioritization scheme to assure that MBW public investment does not simply respond to the "area partnership" board that can shout the loudest politically, is best organized, or has the greatest capacity to develop successful MBW proposals.

Sectarian segmentation and competition make it extremely difficult to target government resources to deprived areas and individuals in Belfast. In particular, disaggregating political needs from socioeconomic needs is problematic. Nevertheless, targeting is absolutely essential in a historically unequal society where inequality contributes to political division. The MBW experience points to the dangers of a government targeting policy when it operates outside a strategic framework. Although eligibility for MBW funding is premised on need, actual allocation to groups and projects through 1994 has been ad hoc and political demand–driven within these defined wards of deprivation. Under its revised format, MBW seeks to respond to the qualitatively different needs of its Catholic and Protestant populations through community-inclusive partnerships. The move toward consensus-based definitions of need through area partnerships, however, requires that government formulate a city-wide strategy of investment that can guide its responses to community-perceived needs and desires.

Strategic Investments for Community Viability

> Unless you deal in the setting of policy with the fact that these two communities are moving in different directions, you're in trouble. You don't want to hold Catholics back, but you must move Protestants ahead.
>
> —Jackie Redpath,
> Greater Shankill Regeneration Strategy,
> in an interview

Many strands of Belfast urban policy are driven by need criteria that are quantifiable. The foremost examples are the justification of new public housing construction on the basis of "urgent need" on the waiting list; the linking of public housing redevelopment to the magnitude of housing "unfitness" as defined in provincial statute; and the eligibility for MBW funding premised on a statistical measure of deprivation. The use of these objective and often quantifiable need criteria increases the defensibility of government actions amidst contested terrain. Such criteria help buffet government from the strong political and sectarian winds. The allocation of MBW funding shows the strength of these winds and how political imperatives and clientalism can overshadow efforts to target public resources effectively.

The concept of "need," however, takes on added complexity in a city of social-psychological territoriality. Catholic objective needs of housing and associated urban amenities contrast commonly with

Protestant needs for community maintenance and identity, which are less tangible and harder to quantify. Objective need-driven "neutral" policy, although rational from a government view, is not sensitive to these differential needs of Belfast's ethnic communities. From a purely quantifiable need viewpoint, many Protestant neighborhoods, due to out-migration and thus lack of demand for new housing, are not viable for government investment in housing and social services. To put money there would be inefficient and ineffective and in normal cities it would not occur. Yet, in Belfast's sectarian landscape, such areas cannot always be avoided by policymakers because territory is equated with political claims. For these reasons, some Belfast urban programs are making initial and tentative steps toward criteria other than quantifiable need. DOENI now "recognizes the community needs of an area that might require us to go beyond the strict standards of the Housing Executive that might say we shouldn't do it" (R. Spence, permanent secretary, interview). And, two of DOENI's member units—MBW and NIHE—display shifts. The need criteria that guide the revised MBW are not necessarily quantifiable need as defined by government but need as defined by community-government partnerships. And the NIHE has taken initial steps away from strictly need-driven housing construction in its 1995 *Belfast Housing Strategy Review*:

> The Executive remains open to the evaluation of new building in areas of low demand taking account of community views, financial risks, and future viability where wider regeneration goals are being pursued.

The NIHE, at times, has adroitly bent its need-based rules to achieve wider community regeneration goals. In areas where the NIHE is incapable of declaring a redevelopment program because the housing is not statutorily unfit (but nonetheless facing substantial vacancies and in poor shape) or housing demand is not present, the NIHE has had the DOENI take the lead through its declaration of the area as a Comprehensive Development Scheme (CDS). A CDS allows the clearing of substantial areas that can include housing and a subsequent alteration in land use. The NIHE contributes housing as part of the picture (often at levels much lower than that cleared), but there are also commonly commercial, industrial, or environmental improvements as part of the scheme. The NIHE in this way is able to consolidate and improve its housing stock for those people who want to stay. W. McGivern (NIHE, interview) contends that "We have effectively created housing need by taking out significant numbers of housing units." Without the CDS process, it would have been more difficult for the NIHE to justify their expenditures in an area of high vacancies and low demand. Still however, as W. McGivern (interview) asserts, "Housing alone does not solve the problems faced by the Protestant community. With only new houses built, there will be simple leapfrogging and voiding of other houses in the city." What is needed, then, are fuller regeneration efforts that do not simply move Protestants around, but attract some back into Belfast's neighborhoods. Thus, the hope is that the nonresidential part of these community regeneration efforts will lead to increased housing demand and an upward spiral toward fuller community viability and functionality. One housing planner[18] stated, "Housing can not be in a vacuum. At the end of the day, we are only landlords. You generate a community and we'll house them."

Besides the Duncairn/ Northgate example already discussed, an illustration of how community viability can be factored into policy decisions took place regarding the Alliance neighborhood of north Belfast. This Protestant neighborhood is on a peaceline and suffers from terrible physical dilapidation and low housing demand. On Protestant need criteria only, this would be an unlikely place for public investment. An NIHE report (1990b) states that the area "appears to have entered into terminal decline." Of the 445 houses in Alliance existing in 1984, 127 had been demolished and a further 147 were vacant by 1991. The 171 occupied houses in 1991 represented 37 percent of the total 1984 housing stock (DOENI 1992a). Household and population figures were forecasted to decline further; the waiting list for housing there was not significant. The NIHE concluded (1990b, 4) that "Expenditure to bring dwellings up to required standards is simply not value for money even if the Executive had such funds available." Need-based policy would allow this neighborhood to die. However, if you tell Protestants that there is no need in Alliance, "People will laugh" (D. MacBride, interview). Local residents and their politicians argued that if investment into Alliance was not forthcoming, the whole neighborhood would deteriorate, with decay spreading subsequently to the neighboring Glencairn community. At that point, stated the argument, pressure would mount for the peaceline separating Protestant Alliance from

Catholic Ardoyne to be moved into Protestant territory to accommodate new Catholic housing on heretofore Protestant land. Escalation of tension and violence would accompany such territorial incursions. Failure of the NIHE to respond to calls to regenerate Alliance would be viewed as conspiracy (DOENI 1992a). The NIHE, as part of a DOENI comprehensive development scheme that will clear substantial areas and build workshop places, approved a plan where it will rebuild more houses than objective need may dictate but at a level less than full put-back. Of the four hundred houses originally in Alliance, one hundred houses will be rebuilt after clearing, in phases of twenty-five to test whether demand may justify it. The Alliance neighborhood will not be physically recreated as it was, nor will it be left to die due to its sectarian importance. The hope is that a rebuilt Alliance, although smaller in housing units, will be more vital.

Notwithstanding their positive impacts on community viability, these and any further shifts in government policy away from quantifiable need-based policy in order to address areas of demographic decline and physical decay are, and will be, problematic. First, this shift toward a broader definition of "need" would severely stress the urban development budget and lessen the ability of policy to target objective need. At some point, policymakers would not be able to afford the continued maintenance of Belfast's neighborhoods. Second, it is doubtful that the strategy would be effective in achieving its goals if money is spread around the multiple Protestant neighborhoods of decline. R. Strang (interview) claims that:

> Further injections of capital hardware (housing, buildings, and cosmetic environmental works) are essentially empty gestures if in "Protestant" locations the socioeconomic structure is so malformed and damaged as to preclude any realistic prospect of natural community regeneration.

He lambastes the "scenario that by building houses in declining areas, busloads of cherry-cheeked children will fill out all the houses." He argues that public housing and investment in areas where need exists more in a political than an objective sense will likely exacerbate the problem of nonviability. This is so because investment where objective need is not present will produce a supply of housing that the community cannot support. The result will be housing voids, disuse and dilapidation that will over time erode even the more stable parts of the neighborhood.[19] Thus, an investment program aimed at sustaining Protestant community viability must be targeted at certain areas to avoid a wholesale maintenance of ethnic territories which is self-defeating and corrosive. A third problem related to moving away from a strictly need-based urban policy is that it exposes government to the strong sectarian winds of Belfast. As W. McGivern (NIHE, interview) says, "Criterion other than the statutory 'unfitness' definition may be appropriate. But, we are then moving out of the comfort zone." Catholics would make a legitimate argument that any lessening of the government's commitment to addressing objective need would be a retreat from social justice and responsible governance.

We are left with two inadequate policy choices. The current need-based formulae are not sufficiently sensitive to the quantitatively different types of need across the ethnic divide. On the other hand, a broadening of the definition of need to include community viability would address the "Protestant" problem in Belfast but, in the end, would probably do more harm than good to Catholics and Protestants alike. Urban policy does require greater proactive management of the ethnic map than under current need-driven criteria, able to pursue viability of antagonistic communities. At the same time, if policymakers try on too wide a scale to assure Protestant community viability they will spend a significant amount of money in a holding pattern directed at maintaining Belfast's sterile mosaic of ethnic territories. R. Strang (interview) exclaims, "Government can stick their fingers in dikes and holes all over the place, but it may not make sense."

What is needed is a citywide strategy that identifies and prioritizes community need so that wider regeneration initiatives (as in Duncairn Gardens and Alliance) can be appropriately targeted to areas capable of recovery. At the same time, areas not worthy of investment should be abandoned, with residents encouraged to relocate, through transfers, to areas targeted for public investment. This strategy would utilize criteria supplemental to objective need, but they would be sufficiently defensible to anchor the strategy against strong political winds. It would be necessary to its success that multiple government participants play roles in the formulation and implementation of the citywide investment strategy. A broadened and imaginative town planning profession could contribute meaningfully by assessing the developmental, spatial, and socioeconomic aspects of neighborhoods and prioritizing their potential for community viability. It is only town planning that is capable of having a citywide view of the relationships between and within Belfast's sectarian neighborhoods. Making Belfast Work, already designed as a targeting program, would likely constitute the primary vehicle for skewing spending toward those neighborhoods most worthy of public investment. The number of MBW-eligible wards might be reduced or prioritized to achieve citywide objectives more effectively. Belfast Action Teams "are an ideal mechanism for taking the temperature out there on the ground" (J. Harrison, interview); as such, they would be key mediators between community-articulated needs and citywide strategic objectives. The host DOENI would be instrumental in integrating its units' activities related to community investment, continuing to shift from its historic emphasis on physical and land-use development to include the social and economic dimensions of community-based regeneration.

Toward Coexistence. A citywide strategy of community investment needs to meet the differential needs of Protestant and Catholic communities on an equitable basis. Since needs are different, however, equity does not imply replication of policy for the two groups, nor even numerical balance in government outputs. Rather, equity means that policy should be sensitive to the unique needs of each community while keeping in mind the overall good of the city. Decline in the Protestant population must be managed, not neglected, in order to produce a vital but geographically consolidated Protestant population. Investment in Protestant areas could be based on a triage model.[20] This means that investment should be targeted to certain areas with the best chances for community viability. These areas should be close to employment opportunities (actual and potential), be capable of building upon growth's economies of scale, and have the potential for active community participation.[21] They would be the focus of government support, in terms of housing (including speculative housing not tied to documented need), social services such as education, environmental improvements, and job training. But this is only one-half of the picture for the Protestant community. In other areas characterized by poor living conditions, voids, and blight, there should be transfers of public housing tenants to targeted areas of community investment and subsequent clearance of these decayed communities. This is the hard part of the strategy politically. As one housing planner states (interview),[22]

> This model presupposes nonviability in certain situations. How do we get to that stage and who develops the message? Who is to say there is no future for Protestants in Suffolk?

Despite inevitable Protestant outcry and political resistance, this policy and message is not only socially responsible, but absolutely essential for effective governance and the betterment of Protestant living conditions citywide. The current government strategy of color-neutrality, in fact, does more harm than good to the Protestant community and to the public fisc. Consolidation under a triage planning model, in contrast, has a better chance at truly regenerating the Protestant communities of Belfast. This strategy would not simply be a reallocation of local population across Protestant neighborhoods. Rather, integration of government efforts and interagency community regeneration would provide the chance to expand the Protestant population base in the city through renewal of targeted neighborhoods. For Protestants, the choice is between a Belfast of marginal estates and neighborhoods that perpetuate a static territoriality and a Belfast that enhances viability and identity for a set of "heartland" Protestant neighborhoods. For government, the choice is between public expenditures that protect a geographic holding pattern derived from urban civil war and spending that creates more focused and vital parts of Protestant Belfast. Opposition to this shift in government policy would come not only from Protestants, but from the Catholic community too. According to D. MacBride (interview), "There is more awareness by Protestants of Catholic housing needs than recognition by Catholics of Protestant needs for community maintenance." Catholics would have to accept that housing policy, in addition to building houses in response to need, has an legitimate role in maintaining and enhancing viability of selected Protestant areas. Under a new government approach, Catholics would gain from a more viable Protestant community that would be less burdened by the sense of threat and able to develop confidence in itself. Such a Protestant population could be able to engage as more willing and productive partners with Catholics in seeking urban reconciliation.

A citywide strategy of coexistent community viability must also be capable of meeting the objective needs of the Catholic community. In the circumstances of rigid territoriality sustained by current policy and with a threatened Protestant population, these needs are hard to meet. To the extent that a community viability strategy is able to spawn greater Protestant urban confidence amidst a larger peace, the sectarian territorial limits on Catholic expansion may be attenuated in certain places. Such loosening of Belfast's ethnic geography through engaged Protestant-Catholic negotiation would benefit Catholics. A strategy of coexistent viability could also open up opportunities for community relations not now possible under government's color-neutral approach. B. Murtagh (interview) suggests that place-based negotiations in the forms of covenants or contracts could be possible between specific Catholic and Protestant neighborhoods. For example, an agreement could stipulate that some Catholic housing could be built in Protestant territory in return for a guarantee of increased community facilities or speculative housing for Protestants. These agreements would move perceptions away from a win-lose situation and formalize interethnic cooperation.

Any loosening of territoriality due to a shift in government policy toward coexistent viability may open up opportunities for integrated housing. Yet, government strategy must be sufficiently sensitive to the fact that neighborhood interfaces present different challenges across the city in terms of the potential for community tension. Urban policy should not force integration upon city residents, but facilitate it in more stable areas for households who are motivated. In cases of volatile and threatening neighborhood instability, on the other hand, urban strategy's enhancement of the coexistent viability of communities may well entail the continuance of spatially segregated neighborhoods for decades to come.

Integrated housing would disproportionately benefit Catholics because such housing, by necessity, would be built in orange areas heretofore foreclosed to Catholics. If peace were to advance in Northern Ireland, the NIHE (1994a) indicates that the development of integrated housing in a few trial areas may be desirable. An interesting characteristic of such an integrated housing strategy is that the NIHE, in actuality, would have to allocate to Protestant households a greater share of the estate than their need figures would otherwise elicit (J. McPeake, NIHE, interview). Otherwise,

Catholics would tend to overwhelm the intended mixed estate due to their disproportionate magnitude on housing waiting lists.[23] For Catholics, it is a tradeoff but a beneficial one. They may not get as many placements in the estate as objective need would dictate, but they would have greater housing availability overall because such integrated estates would open up "Protestant" land. From a public interest view, integrated housing is also important because it directly counters the hyper-segregation of the city's neighborhoods.[24]

* * *

These are the components of a Belfast urban strategy that is not color-neutral, but sensitive to the differential needs of its two communities. It responds to both the social and psychological needs of the Protestant population for community viability and identity, and the objective needs of the Catholic population for housing and room to grow. The strategy is based on "color where color matters." This shift in government approach will place the public sector in the middle of the overall change process in Northern Ireland and Belfast, not relegate it to the color-neutral sidelines. The public investment strategy responds to the fact that change and difficult decisions must be part of urban policy if it is to play a role in advancing peace in Belfast and Northern Ireland. It will not be easy for government to depart from objective need criteria that have been moderately successful in legitimating its authority over a contested city.

In a new Belfast, government must be more explicit with its citizens about the goals and objectives that it is pursuing. Development agencies such as NIHE and BDO must be more up front and provide the reasons behind proposed actions. As we have seen, there are some steps being taken by government toward a more imaginative and holistic approach toward community need. However, doubts remain as to its desired publicity. One planner comments, "If we go explicit with some of the things we are doing, we could inflame the situation." In the end, however, as one housing planner asserts, "We must come up front and stop hiding behind the euphemisms." A case in point illustrates the pitfalls of euphemisms and opaque steps. In consultations with communities regarding the Belfast Housing Strategic Review, the NIHE language concerning the possibility of building units in areas of "low demand" is most assuredly code for Protestant community regeneration.[25] Sinn Fein representatives saw clearly through this code and severely criticized the movement away from objective need criteria. On the other hand, Protestant politicians were not strongly supportive because the wording was buried in bureaucratic language and did not illuminate an overall strategy toward bettering Belfast's Protestant communities. The step toward a new approach then faltered. Instead, the NIHE and other government units should pursue fuller and more explicit strategies and enunciate the advantages to both Protestants and Catholics from an urban strategy of coexistent viability.

The Future of Belfast: City and Sectarianism

The resolution of the broader Northern Ireland conflict will depend on whether Alliance and Ardoyne or Tiger's Bay and New Lodge can get along.

—Brenden Murtagh,
University of Ulster—Magee College,
in an interview

We need to create a notion of how, without violence, things can move forward.

—Billy Hutchinson,
Community leader
(elected to Northern Ireland Assembly June 1998),
in an interview

In the midst of potentially momentous political change, Belfast resembles in many ways a war zone with both sides losers. It is a place of physical dereliction, sadness, and introspection. In many ways, the change that was upon the city during the mid-1990s period of on-again, off-again ceasefires and negotiations resembled an alcoholic who had stopped drinking but was doing little to change those habits linked to drinking. Peace was at hand, but it was a tenuous one lacking progress toward a political settlement that would solidify it. Indeed, the condition approximated more the absence of war than the presence of peace. The reemergence of republican hostilities in February 1996 substantially retarded any normalization and improvement in community relations that may have occurred in Belfast during the preceding one and one-half years of ceasefires. Although elections in Northern Ireland in June 1998 to create a

108-member Northern Ireland Assembly could be a catalyst for peace, the hard issues of arms decommissioning, prisoner release, and policing remain after generations of ethnic bloodshed. It is not hard to be pessimistic about Belfast's future.

Belfast is the central stage upon which this seemingly intractable political conflict is being performed, and is thus connected intimately to any larger peace. In Belfast, urban circumstances dealing with jobs, housing, social services, and community identity can modify—for better or worse—the influence of political tensions on city residents. In a future where possible new governing institutions in Northern Ireland face monumental challenges, urban-based, on-the-ground strategies could make the difference in Belfast between peaceful coexistence and the reemergence of armed urban conflict. Whether Belfast urban policy is able to effectively address the differential needs of its two communities may determine the future quality of life in this city more than the institutional and constitutional changes emergent in 1998.

In the least, it seems that urban policy should do all that is necessary not to create obstacles to peace building. More than that, however, those involved in the formulation and implementation of urban policy have a responsibility to more proactively facilitate and enable the coexistent viability of both urban communities in Belfast. Amidst the uncertainty of political change, urban strategies of intergroup accommodation may offer one of the few potential authentic sources of ethnic centripetalism and tolerance. They can contribute to larger peace-building efforts practical principles that foster the coexistent viability of antagonistic sides in terms of territorial control, urban resources, and preservation of ethnic identity. Peace-building efforts at the level of daily urban interaction between ethnic groups and between individuals are indispensable not only to urban stability, but because they can provide breathing spaces of hope amidst the daunting challenges of societal change.

We have seen in Belfast how urban policy and planning have attempted to neutrally address the sectarianism that has fundamentally shaped the city's social geography. The policymakers of Belfast, in contrast to the partisan approach of Jerusalem planners, attempt to deal pragmatically on a neutral basis with the day-to-day, local-level symptoms of sovereignty conflict. This neutrality on the part of town planning in Belfast, however, is a retreat from its potential to contribute to ethnic management. Despite the land-use and territorially based implications of much of sectarianism, the town planning function has played a minor role in addressing ethnicity. Centralization of the planning function to an extralocal level has removed territorial questions from the local level in an effort to depoliticize planning. Generally, attempts by Belfast policymakers to separate development goals from ethnic realities may be politically expedient, but they appear to be neither realistic nor effectual. This centralized technocratic approach, according to Douglas (1982), might hold temporarily in abeyance community power struggles, but it will contribute little toward solving them. There is also a difference in Belfast planning between a national perspective focusing on specific interventions and a local perspective more encompassing of, and sensitive to, daily urban living (Blackman 1991). Because it emphasizes piecemeal rather than comprehensive planning, the centralization of local policymaking in Northern Ireland has produced fracturing of urban policymaking among numerous extralocal bodies, and the substantive separation of spatial planning concerns from the broader social concerns of housing, social services, and ethnic relations.

We have witnessed how policies regarding land use planning and housing allocation that are neutral in intent can reinforce sectarian disparities. The exclusion of distributional issues from metropolitan plans and the use of neutral public housing allotment formulas likely reproduce rather than moderate ethnic segregative patterns. Although this approach contains intergroup conflict in the short term, it likely hardens territorial identities and further discourages a climate for intergroup negotiations in the long term. In an unequal society of dualities and separation, color-neutral policies will result in unequal opportunities through the replication of those dualities. Where sectarian territoriality constrains much of urban living, neutrality does not increase equity.

There have been public actions by government units that, out of necessity, address sectarianism on the sharp edge. The direct impacts of these government actions on changing the sectarian fabric bring the implementing agencies face to face with the sectarian realities known to, but avoided, by town planning and housing allocation administrators. New building and redevelopment of public housing becomes intimately connected to issues of territorial maintenance, while economic development schemes such as in Northgate can disturb existing sectarian dynamics. Yet those urban policies that address sectarianism do so without the aid of a strategic framework aimed at effective management of ethnic space. Thus, government actions have primarily been ad hoc tactics rather than strategic acts; have been project-based rather than area-based; have been reactive rather than proactive; and have emphasized vertical rather than lateral government approaches.

The urban policy framework used for the past twenty-five years aimed at neutrality, maintenance, and stability may no longer be appropriate in Belfast. Its reactive protection of the status quo defends a rigid and sterile territoriality, and reinforces the physical and psychological correlates of urban civil war. As Belfast and Northern Ireland shift uneasily along the continuum from civil war to peace, urban policymakers confront the question of whether, and when, urban policy should shift direction so it is a progressive part of the peacemaking process and not a burden to it. For urban policy to meaningfully contribute to peacemaking, the process and practice of city building in Belfast would need to be reconceptualized. Urban policy requires greater proactive management of the ethnic map than under current color-neutral criteria. Such progressive ethnic management by government would be more strategic than its past "societal reflection" role, but less remote and mechanistic than a "social engineer" role. In transcending color-neutrality, public policy needs to be: (1) proactive; (2) ethnically aware (and explicitly so); (3) able to strategically address the different needs of Catholic and Protestant communities; (4) integrated across government functions; and (5) conducive to diverse community input. Acknowledgment of the different needs in a divided city presents government with significant obstacles. The end that government should strive for in such a circumstance is the *viability* of the two communities. This is because community viability and identity are keys to peaceful urban living amidst political contest. The goal of progressive ethnic management would be the coexistent viability of antagonistic groups within the urban system, whatever spatial forms and living patterns that might entail.

A citywide strategy of community investment would need to be developed to meet the differential primary needs of Protestant and Catholic communities on an equitable basis. Since needs are different, however, equity does not imply replication of policy for the two groups nor even numerical balance in government outputs. Rather, equity means that policy should be sensitive to the unique primary needs of each community while keeping in mind the overall good of the city. Both Protestant and Catholic communities have significant objective and psychological needs related to social and economic deprivation and group identity. Yet primary needs contrast across ethnic groups—objective ones in the case of the Catholic population for new housing and community services versus social-psychological needs of the Protestant population for community viability and identity. Effective governance should address both these community needs because, in a deeply divided city, one community's needs are not more important than the other's.

A key consideration in future policymaking will be how government addresses the less tangible social-psychological needs of Belfast Protestants. We have seen that a blanket approach to maintaining Protestant territory in the city of Belfast will likely fail, leading actually to worsened conditions of currently fit housing stock. In this sense, unanchored tactics aimed at maintaining all Protestant neighborhoods would be worse than government taking a hands-off approach entirely. As an alternative, decline in the city's Protestant population could be more strategically managed in order to produce a vital but geographically consolidated Protestant population. The goal here is not maintenance of Protestant territory, but viability of the city's Protestant community. All participants— Protestants, Catholics, government—would likely agree that it is the vitality of people and community that is important, not the protection of a lifeless and dysfunctional geography of hate. Community viability would thus be developed as a criterion that supplements, not replaces, objective need-based measures for allocating public resources and activities in Belfast. Significantly, both the rationales and operational forms of new supplemental criteria would need to be clear and defensible. If not, public policy, heretofore supported primarily on need-based foundations, will find itself driven by the strong sectarian pressures of Northern Ireland.

Viability objectives connote not the diffusion but the concentration and targeting of public resources across Protestant Belfast. A citywide strategy could be developed that identifies and prioritizes Protestant neighborhoods in terms of their potential for regeneration. Public initiatives such as Duncairn Gardens and Alliance could then be appropriately targeted to those areas most able to recover; for instance, those with potential private sector interest and where communities can be rebuilt around existing and new community

facilities and infrastructure. At the same time, this strategy requires that difficult decisions be made concerning which neighborhoods be cut off from publicly funded life support. Similar to a
medical doctor's utilizing a triage approach to an emergency, public
resources would be concentrated on those ill neighborhoods that
would most benefit from treatment. A consolidated, more viable
Belfast Protestant population may over time feel less threat, and
could assume a greater willingness to allow some normalization of
Belfast's geography to meet a portion of Catholic objective needs.

Multiple government and community participants would play
roles in the formulation and implementation of an integrative vision
and policy for community regeneration that addresses effectively the
differential needs of Belfast's ethnic communities. These include
town planning, Making Belfast Work, Belfast Action Teams, the Department of the Environment generally, and community-based "area
partnerships." Town planning has a moral and professional responsibility to shift out of its technical and land-use blinders to incorporate consideration of the social, economic, and psychological
dynamics and requisites for coexistent viability of Protestant and
Catholic populations. Training and education of professional planners through professional organizations, such as the Royal Town
Planning Institute, and local universities, such as Queen's University of Belfast, should prepare planners to deal with the complex issues of planning amidst ethnic difference. This calls for studio-based
workshops that involve students in the multidimensional analysis
and planning of ethnic neighborhoods. Students and practitioners
should be exposed to the rudiments of ethnic impact analysis, qualitative surveying, conflict resolution, and community relations techniques. In the end, ethnic content in courses will inculcate in
students the ability to empathize with "the other." After all, planners
must come to terms with their own views of ethnicity and race before
they can be expected to plan for peaceful coexistence.

Participants other than town planning will also play key roles in
a new Belfast urban strategy. The antideprivation Making Belfast
Work program, already designed as a targeting program, would be
a primary vehicle for skewing spending toward those neighborhoods most worthy of public investment. Belfast Action Teams
would be key mediators between community-articulated needs and
citywide strategic objectives. And the host DOENI would be instrumental in integrating its multiple activities related to community

investment and planning. One of the more important roles of a new urban strategy would be that it would guide government in its increased interactions with communities. Community involvement through proposed "area partnerships" must not occur in a strategy vacuum but rather needs to be anchored by a public strategy of community viability and investment. To maintain connections to community groups and leaders, the new urban strategy within government should not be structured hierarchically. Rather, it should penetrate multiple units and agencies and provide numerous points of access for community input. In this way, numerous government units are capable of social learning and adaptation within a guiding framework of community viability. Collaborative structures within government would also help institutionalize those innovative city-building approaches that currently depend upon the support of lateral-thinking individuals in key governmental positions.

This would be a Belfast urban strategy not color-neutral, but sensitive to the differential needs of its two sectarian communities. It responds to both the psychological needs of Protestants for community viability and identity and the objective needs of the Catholic population for housing and room to grow. The strategy is based on color where color matters. This shift in government approach would create an urban policy able to contribute to, and reinforce, larger peacemaking efforts. Peace demands this type of responsible governance.

PART IV

Conclusions

10

Urban Policy on Narrow Ground

The studies of Jerusalem and Belfast have illustrated how urban policymakers and planners cope with rival urban communities that interact daily across ethnic divides. Municipal policies regarding these places become intertwined with territorial and sovereignty disputes reflecting religious, cultural, and nationalist conflict. Concurrently, the city introduces a set of characteristics—proximate ethnic neighborhoods, territoriality, economic interdependency, symbolism, and centrality—that can bend or distort the relationship between ideological imperatives and the manifestations of ethnic conflict. Urban policymakers endeavor to translate fundamental governing ideologies into on-the-ground outcomes in urban arenas. The self-contradictory and unintended effects of urban policy that commonly result are due not to its impotence in the face of ideological dictates, but rather to the complexities of urbanity through which such ideologies are filtered and upon which urban policy operates. City policies make a difference—intensifying urban instability in Jerusalem, and hardening ethnic compartmentalization and urban sclerosis in Belfast.

Urban Policy amidst Polarization

The Jerusalem case bears witness to the fallacy of partisan planning. Since 1967, political unification of Jerusalem and Jewish security have been pursued by Israeli policy through boundary drawing, demographic planning, and public spending imbalances. Demographic planning has facilitated the pace, extent, and location of Jewish development, simultaneously restricting and fragmenting Palestinian growth. City spending disparities have consolidated advantages for the city's Jewish neighborhoods and residents. Restrictions on Palestinian political expression and their de facto exclusion from city decisionmaking debilitate group identity and autonomy. Yet the urban landscape of domination produced by Israel is one of internal frictions and vulnerable interfaces that increases, not decreases, interethnic instability.

The fallacy of Israeli partisan planning in Jerusalem is that its very success—in creating urban conditions of domination and subjugation—leads to urban and regional instability, which erodes Israel's genuine control over the city. Described by Dumper (1997) as the "central paradox" of Israeli urban policy, the fate of Jerusalem today remains undetermined and contested despite thirty years of unilateral actions. The urban policies selected to operationalize Israeli goals of political control and security are begetting a landscape conducive to antithetical outcomes—heightened political contestability and increased Jewish personal vulnerability. Territorial policies that exude dominance create an urban spatial structure of vulnerable interfaces and provocative disparities. Urban distributive inequalities meant to harden Jewish control of the city weakens Israeli moral and political claims to be the city's sole guardian. And, in a context where Palestinian institution building in and near Jerusalem encounters both Israeli roadblocks and tension between Palestinian local initiative and national leadership, unilateral Israeli actions are in danger of creating an authoritarian and radicalized Palestinian presence in Jerusalem.

The methods that strengthen in the short term Israeli unification of the city create arguments over the longer term that directly challenge such political claims. Partisanship is exposed as a strategy, not a solution, to the polarized city. It creates not urban control, but strong reactions that destabilize the urban system and any larger political agreements linked to it. Traumatic disruptions to the urban system will continue in the presence of partisan urban policies, with the city a flashpoint and target ever capable of exploding. The emotive power of Jerusalem as a holy city and as the urban center of a potential Palestinian state will likely constitute a significant mobilizing tool for Palestinian leader Arafat and successors in both overcoming internal divisions and negotiating with Israel. Simultaneously, it will likely continue to be a magnet for violence perpetuated by Arabs living in the deprived cities and villages of the West Bank and Gaza.

The Belfast encapsulation of nationalistic conflict demonstrates the insufficiency of neutral policy intervention in a city of strict territoriality and shifting demographics. Antagonistic groups are both proximate and separate, creating a set of physical ethnic interfaces with both psychological and tangible benefits and costs to city residents and policymakers. An inordinately large public sector has been needed in response to a fraying society. Policy neutrality amidst ethnic strife, or "greyness where color matters," may be successful in not adding new sources of ethnic tension. Management of ethnic space in this way is viewed by the government as reacting to, and reflecting, residents' wishes, and as the best way to avoid exacerbation of sectarian tension. Yet it appears incapable of creating co-existent viability of antagonistic ethnic communities because these two communities experience different primary needs and face contrasting future trajectories. Neutrality is associated with unequal outcomes, poor public perception, and ineffective upliftment of Belfast's economically deprived. In addition, when development agencies necessarily engage in tactics of engagement that deviate from color-neutral principles, they often occur on an ad hoc and project-specific basis in the absence of a strategic framework of progressive ethnic management that could guide them. Because the urban arena is intimately connected to the prospective larger peace, the urban policy framework used for more than twenty-five years aimed at maintenance and stability may no longer be appropriate. Urban policy should meet the demands of peace by redirecting its energies toward the vitality of people and community, not the protection of a lifeless and dysfunctional geography of hate.

The two cities share a common sorrow, but they also provide insight into the role and effects of government intervention in societies that are at different points along a continuum from disruptive strife to sustainable peace. The partisan planning of Jerusalem represents the most assertive, least accommodative model. The professional demeanor and neutral intentions associated with Belfast urban policymaking have sought to suspend war and take some hesitant steps toward peace. Similar to alcoholic drinkers who differ widely in the extent to which they confront their basic problems and defects, the two cities show disparate approaches to the root issues underlying urban ethnic conflict and tension. The Jerusalem policymaker would be characterized an active drinker engaged in actions detrimental to his own health, while the Belfast policymaker has been for more than twenty-five years an abstainer who stopped drinking but was doing little to change basic behaviors associated with imbibing. Neither policymaker has addressed the basic underlying causes of urban conflict, as was done in the transition away from apartheid in South Africa, and thus neither can be said to be in productive recovery. Northern Ireland's 1998 "Good Friday" accord and Israel's Oslo peace process constitute efforts to address such root causes, but neither process has been extended to the urban policymaking arenas of these two cities.

Three tables of comparative information are presented to highlight differences and similarities across the two cities. Table 10.1 describes the differing contexts of conflict. Table 10.2 emphasizes the diverging urban policy goals and strategies. And Table 10.3 highlights the public sector and community participants and relationships involved in the implementation of each city's urban policies.

The cultural, psychological, and political aspects of ethnonational conflict differed across the case studies, as well as the spatial and economic characteristics of the urban arena. These considerations establish contexts that inform the more specific explorations of urban policy. In terms of the cultural nature of the conflict (Table 10.1, number 1), the Middle East conflict encompasses a clash between fundamental values and cultural meanings; specifically, between occidentalism and orientalism. In contrast, both sides of the Protestant-Catholic clash in Northern Ireland use European terms of reference and encompass more an intracultural split. Paradoxically, however, there is a greater sense of intimacy shared by the combatants in the Middle East conflict than in the Northern Ireland one. The psychology of the conflict (10.1.2) in the Middle East is as between warring intimate brothers, while the Northern Ireland conflict is experienced as one between distant strangers with a considerable degree of callousness.

Conflict is experienced differently in the two cities (10.1.3). Jerusalem's conflict is felt as a focal point or lightening rod for the expression of three of the world's major religions and the nationalistic fervor attached to two of them. Northern Ireland's conflict is experienced as parochial and peripheral. In terms of who holds power in the societies to affect change (10.1.4), Jerusalem's stage is primarily occupied by two internal parties—the Israelis and Palestinians—but it is a rostrum behind which lie many international

Table 10.1   Contexts of Conflict

---

1. CULTURAL NATURE OF CONFLICT

Jerusalem   Clash between cultures, between "universal systems of values"; abyss of world views. West meets east.

Belfast   Intraculture split. No abyss of cultures. North-south/ east-west components but both within European context.

2. PSYCHOLOGY OF CONFLICT

Jerusalem   Conflict amidst knowing about the other. "Brothers" in a long family battle.

Belfast   Conflict out of ignorance; learning about/ through stereotypes. "Strangers."

3. FELT SIGNIFICANCE OF CONFLICT

Jerusalem   Centrality and internationalization of conflict.

Belfast   Parochial, peripheral.

4. POWER

Jerusalem   Two parties from within; connected to international supporters.

Belfast   A third party from outside.

5. SECURITY AND THREAT

Jerusalem   Political, group-based security through Jewish majority, no political division, and geographic dispersal of Jews throughout city.

Belfast   Interpersonal security through segregation and partition of ethnic groups.

6. URBAN SCALE

Jerusalem   Physical space and buffers between communities.

Belfast   Proximity and tight quarters.

7. URBAN SEGREGATION

Jerusalem   Segregation/ ethnic geography strict.

Belfast   Segregation/ ethnic geography strict.

8. USE AND MEANING OF LAND

Jerusalem   Israeli-Arab divergent views of land utilization, land ownership, and the development process.

Belfast   Different demands on land due to Protestant-Catholic divergent demographic profiles.

9. URBAN GROWTH PROSPECTS

Jerusalem   Politically motivated growth amidst land competition.

Belfast   Stagnancy and limited growth. A city of the economic past.

---

participants. Power in Belfast has been held for more than twenty-five years by a third party from the outside—the British government—although argument over this characterization is part of the conflict itself.

The nature of security in the urban arenas is characterized differently in the two cities, as well as the means toward achieving this sense of safety (10.1.5). Jerusalem's security for the Jewish population as a whole is to be ensured through the maintenance of a Jewish demographic majority, political unification of the city, and the presence of Jewish residents throughout the city's geographic area. This is a political security that is established through barring of physical or political divisions in the city. Jewish control of the entire city is seen as essential to the political security of Israel and its people. That the means toward achieving city control and political security might endanger individual Jewish lives through the creation of vulnerable interfaces is seen as an unfortunate cost of achieving these larger political goals linked to group protection and identity. In Belfast, interpersonal security from political and targeted violence is emphasized, which encourages segregation and physical partition of competing ethnic groups. In contrast to Jerusalem where territorial expansions and incursions are pursued as a means toward Jewish security, Belfast ethnic groups have retreated—under governmental oversight—into their respective territories amidst the hell of urban civil war.

The geographic scale of an urban arena of conflict (10.1.6) presents different sets of obstacles and opportunities to policymakers interested in peaceful urban coexistence. The scale of Jerusalem's urban system is large, characterized by sprawling suburbs that encircle the core, physical buffer zones, and a metropolitan mosaic of Israeli and Palestinian growth nodes and corridors. Belfast's scale is one of tight quarters and proximity, with limited opportunities for spatial distance between antagonistic sides. Middle-class migration to suburbs outside the city does enlarge the scale of the urban system, but not necessarily the scale of conflict because interethnic accommodation more commonly occurs in Belfast's suburbs. Related to geographic scale is the degree of segregation between ethnic groups (10.1.7). Both Jerusalem and Belfast have strict ethnic segregation in the sense that warring sides do not live next to each other on the same street. However, the texture of this segregation differs, with Jerusalem's segregation more coarsely grained than Belfast's.

The use and meaning of the land resource in contested cities commonly have underlying political and cultural meanings (10.1.8). In Jerusalem, the meaning behind land use at first bears commonality across Jewish and Arab societies. Both equate the use of land with furthering political claims of ownership. In the Jewish case, however, there is an assertive re-creation of the land in terms of "creating facts on the ground" that were not there before. In the urban arena, this has commonly meant turning agricultural and open space into residential compounds. For Arabs, in contrast, political claims on the land are strengthened by a "staying on the land," or steadfastness (*sumud*), whereby land is viewed as life giving and worthy of long-term stewardship. Ownership of land is also strikingly different in the two cultures. In contrast to Israeli individualized ownership and commodification of land, Palestinian land is commonly held communally, often by large and extended families. Finally, in terms of development of the land, Israel has traditionally utilized government sponsorship and funding to create large residential complexes over relatively short periods. In contrast, Palestinian society, like many of its Arab country counterparts, has had limited experience in mass housing schemes by collective public or private entities. In Belfast, different demands put upon the land resource are not caused by cultural differences over the meaning of land, but rather by different demographic profiles. A faster-growing Catholic population puts pressure on government to find underutilized "orange" land for housing and community facilities. The declining Protestant population, meanwhile, fights adamantly to maintain existing ethnic territory and pushes for government programs that might bring suburbanized Protestants back into the city.

The prospects for urban economic growth (10.1.9) provide a context that can disrupt or stabilize ethnic conditions in a city. Economic development of the Jerusalem region is an important ingredient of the political competition over land in the area. To the extent that it is facilitated by either side in order to strengthen political claims in the region, politically motivated economic growth that disproportionately favors members of a single ethnic group will likely intensify conflict. On the other hand, regional economic development as part of an interdependent "new Middle East" is viewed by some as potentially ameliorative of overall political discord in the region. Belfast has been in the unfortunate position over most of the last three decades of dealing with sectarian strife

amidst a context of economic stagnancy and socioeconomic deprivation. The zero-sum character of ethnic conflict becomes highlighted
in such a circumstance of scarce economic resources.

I compare in Table 10.2 the specific urban policy goals, strategies,
and techniques used in the two cities. These contrasts constitute the
core part of the research project, investigating the characteristics of
urban policymaking amidst ideological imperatives and city polarization. Government goals (Table 10.2, number 1) assert the ends
toward which public actions are to be guided in a society of conflicting ethnic groups. These government goals may or may not be
aligned with one specific ethnic group. In the case of Jerusalem,
they are; in the case of Northern Ireland, government goals transcend group-based loyalties. In the Northern Ireland case, this is because public authority has been held by a third party overseer.
Israeli urban policy seeks to control the urban system politically
through "unification" in order to assure security to its people and
country. The British government, in its urban policymaking in
Belfast, emphasizes violence prevention and urban ethnic stability
as its overriding goal.

Urban operationalization (10.2.2) in a contested city seeks to de-
rive from often abstract political goals—be they security and control, stability, or reconciliation—a set of practical objectives that
direct day-to-day urban policy decisions. In Jerusalem, political control and security is to be achieved by the spatial and demographic
entrenchment of the Israeli presence in and around the urban system through strategic, politically motivated planning. Israeli security and control is sought through methods that counter any
potential physical redivision of the urban area and the development
of even nominal Palestinian political autonomy within the city. In
Belfast, violence prevention and urban stability is to be achieved
through a neutral stance by government that seeks noninflamma-
tory treatment of each ethnic group but otherwise suffers from a
limited strategic view toward solving practical urban problems. It is
illuminating of the ambiguities of urban policy that both the Israeli
government in Jerusalem and the British government in Belfast
speak a similar language of stability and security. Yet the means
they advance toward achieving it—indivisibility, in the first case;
and partitioning, in the second—are diametric opposites. In its pursuit of urban stability, the British government in Belfast condones
exactly what Israel refuses to countenance—strict ethnic territoriality reinforced by physical partitions. The difference in urban

Table 10.2 Urban Policy Goals, Strategies, and Techniques

1. GOVERNMENTAL GOAL (IDEOLOGY)

Jerusalem   Political control ("unification") and security.
Belfast   Violence prevention and stability.

2. URBAN OPERATIONALIZATION

Jerusalem   *Entrench*   use strategic planning to embed Israeli presence spatially and demographically and assure that urban system is indivisible with no physical barriers.

Belfast   *Neutralize* manage ethnic territoriality in a way that accepts physical barriers, but otherwise sacrifices strategic policymaking.

3. URBAN POLICY STRATEGY

Jerusalem   Partisan.
Belfast   Neutral.

4. POLICY AND ETHNIC IDENTIFICATION

Jerusalem   Advocacy of Israeli interests. Institutionalized unfairness toward, and/or neglect of, Palestinian interests.

Belfast   "Color-neutrality" in order not to disturb volatile territoriality.

5. SPATIAL TECHNIQUES

Jerusalem   Domination, penetration, exclusion.
Belfast   City divisions as increasing manageability; viewed as necessary. Environmental methods of diffusing interface tensions.

6. POLICY "LENS"

Jerusalem   Territoriality (coarse-grained). Macro-scale (communities, blocks, region).

Belfast   Territoriality (fine-grained). Micro-scale (neighborhoods, housing estates).

7. SPENDING ALLOCATION

Jerusalem   Spending/urban service imbalance.
Belfast   Spending allocation influenced by combination of objective needs and political demands.

8. PLANNING POTENCY

Jerusalem   Planning active. Creation of facts. Facilitate change and development. Moral and spiritual responsibility upon planners.

Belfast   Planning passive, reacting to perceived demands (for separation and security). Hesitant to facilitate change toward a different urban future. Shy away from moral responsibility.

(continues)

Table 10.2 (*continued*)

---

9. PLANNING AND BIAS

Jerusalem   Bias—both through implementation of planning and its intentional absence.

Belfast   Perception of bias; presence of conspiracy theories. Alternative explanations subordinate to perceptions. Perception of policy tied to larger feelings of isolation and community threat.

---

application lies in the fact that it is Israel's self-interested definition of security that dominates Jerusalem policy, whereas in Belfast security is defined in terms of its effects on both groups. In addition, Israel's notion of political security for the group emphasizes geographic aggrandizement to the detriment, at times, of interpersonal or individual security. In contrast, the British government's focus on security at the individual level lends itself to urban segregation and containment strategies.

Two of the urban policy strategies (10.2.3) elucidated in chapter 2—partisan and neutral—are represented in the case study cities. In Jerusalem, the utilization of land-use planning and regulation as territorial tools and the wide intergroup disparities in public spending constitute a *partisan* approach to urban planning and administration. Ethnic criteria overshadow functional factors in the distribution of urban benefits such as housing and building approvals, roads, and community facilities. Planners and administrators legitimize and institutionalize a dual, unequal system of public authority. Israeli planners commonly seek to mask this partisan approach as technical and noncontroversial. For example, Israeli neighborhoods are constructed in contested areas in the Jerusalem region to respond to "natural city growth." Metropolitanization of Israel's authority in the region is proposed on the basis of its functional and service efficiency benefits. And the city's spending imbalances are concealed behind a benign policy of encouraging neighborhood mosaic patterns.[1] In Belfast, the British government's strategy to deal pragmatically on a neutral basis with the day-to-day, local-level symptoms of sovereignty conflict constitutes the *neutral* approach. Removal of the urban policymaking function to an extralocal level sought to remove territorial questions from the local level and to depoliticize planning. Belfast metropolitan plans commonly downplayed or disregarded the role played by ethnic conflict in fundamentally shaping the city's social geography. Intergroup equity issues are excluded from metropolitan plans, public housing allotment formulae utilize color-blind procedures, and town planning marginalizes itself by separating its spatial planning concerns from the broader social concerns of housing, social services, and ethnic relations.

The identification and treatment of ethnicity by urban policy-making (10.2.4) are derived from government goals and strategies. Jerusalem's urban policy advocates and furthers Israeli interests in the region; it is fully conscious of ethnic affiliation and disproportionately favors its own group. There is institutionalized dominance by Israelis in the city, providing monopoly or preferential access to policymaking for members of the dominant group. In Belfast, one of the primary aims of government policy has been to establish and maintain itself as a color-neutral participant not biased toward either "orange" (Protestant) or "green" (Catholic). The difference in approaches toward ethnic identity in the two cities is highlighted by the clearly defined population ratio objectives of Israeli planners in Jerusalem compared to the hands-off approach to ethnic demographic profiles by Belfast policymakers. Ironically, however, this intentional disengagement in Belfast from the demographic question puts policymakers in a consistently reactive position vis-à-vis differential neighborhood dynamics that threaten government's goal of violence prevention and urban stability.

In order for urban policy strategies to physically shape the city, specific spatial techniques (10.2.5) must be applied to the urban arena. These techniques are viewed through a policy "lens" (10.2.6) based on larger spatial or societal contexts. In Jerusalem, urban policies, equating land occupation with political control, spur territorial extensions that penetrate and diminish minority land control. Such activities, in combination with selective extension of the municipal border since 1967, have increased both Jewish spatial and demographic domination of disputed territory. The "lens" through which these spatial techniques are applied is a coarse-grained territorial one. In order to decrease the risk of vulnerability of Jewish settlers, Israeli policy has sought macro-scale penetration at the level of community or subarea, not a micro-scale and more inflammatory integration at the level of neighborhood or street. Thus,

Israel has sought the difficult mix of both territorial control of Palestinians while keeping some spatial distance from them.[2] In Belfast, urban policy attempts to diffuse intergroup tensions along interfaces by sustaining each group's territories. The "lens" is a much more fine-grained territorial one than in Jerusalem, with segregation occurring at a micro-scale between proximate neighborhoods and even single housing estates. The tight territoriality of Belfast increases the likelihood that relatively minor government actions involving development or service provision will set off local unrest, and can explain much of the hesitancy of government planners to engage in actions that might be construed as disruptive of the territorial status quo.

In addition to policies that affect the spatial distribution of growth in the urban region, city governments also allocate urban services and spending across ethnic neighborhoods (10.2.7). There are wide intergroup disparities in city spending and community facilities across Jewish and Palestinian neighborhoods in Jerusalem. Estimates provide a range of between 4 and 17 percent of city spending directed at Palestinian areas, whose residents constitute about 30 percent of the Israeli-defined city's population. In Belfast, objective needs and political demands have commonly become entangled in determining urban spending decisions. This is so because strictly needs-based allocations (such as public housing construction) that commonly favor Catholics are seen as threats by Protestants to their community viability and may thus stimulate intergroup tension. In areas such as employment, major questions remain regarding whether equality of opportunity requires removal of discriminatory barriers only, or necessitates affirmative action that compensates for past disparity in treatment or current structural obstacles.

The strength of the planning and policymaking function (10.2.8) is partly determined by the degree of partisanship of policy. Unilateral policies (in Jerusalem) require forceful regulation and development actions that create change and reinforce domination. There is a moral and spiritual responsibility upon urban policymakers to structure the Jerusalem urban region to Israel's advantage. In contrast, Belfast policymaking has been passive, seeking to suspend sectarian tensions by managing ethnic space in a way that reacts to, and reflects, residents' wishes. In both cities, urban policymaking has been, or currently is, associated with bias (10.2.9). Jerusalem planning is genuinely biased toward Israeli interests, both in its active implementation (creation of new Israeli neighborhoods) and its intentional absence (lack of outline plans in Palestinian neighborhoods). It also produces biased outcomes in circumstances where uniform requirements—such as the registration of land—are applied to the differing developmental contexts of Israeli and Palestinian society. The bias in Belfast's policymaking is more perceived than actual. Conspiracy theories by both communities claim that urban policy has sought ends that intentionally harm one ethnic group or the other. Whether it is claims of "de-Protestantizing" neighborhoods, or the punishment of republican Catholic ones, feelings of community isolation and threat drive perceptions more than actual policy outcomes.

Table 10.3 next explores the significant policymaking participants and relationships in the two polarized cities. The formulation and implementation of urban policy amidst ethnic polarization can generate internal tension within the implementing government. This includes conflicts in purpose between agencies at a common level of government, or between two or more levels of government. Policy implementation can also substantially influence an out-group's sense of community, the development of its own nongovernmental set of institutions, and its propensity for political mobilization.

Two foci of urban policymaking exist—a regulatory capacity that seeks to manage future development through planmaking and ordinances; and a developmental capacity that seeks to promote and otherwise facilitate urban growth (Table 10.3, number 1). Whereas the former creates a vision and framework for city growth, the latter is more involved in project-specific changes to the urban landscape. In an ethnically polarized city, these policy foci are commonly at odds within the implementing government. In Jerusalem, active development-oriented institutions and organizations exerting pragmatic, proactive, and dynamic strategies have dominated a passive and reactive regulatory control system. The Israeli regulatory system has largely failed to contain politically motivated development in and around Jerusalem, sacrificing the fiscal and environmental sustainability of the urban system. The regulatory system, at other times, has been utilized for partisan objectives—suspending Palestinian growth in certain sectors until such time as Israeli development organs can "create facts" in those contested areas. In Belfast, the regulatory part of town planning has absolved itself from issues

Table 10.3 Participants and Relationships

---

1. PLANNING: DEVELOPMENTAL VERSUS REGULATORY

Jerusalem   Development part of planning dominates regulatory part. Relationship between regulatory and development not constructive.

Belfast   Development part of planning dominates regulatory. Regulatory planning limited role and power. Development agencies more explicitly recognize ethnic issues. Relationship between regulatory and development arms not constructive.

2. LOCAL AND CENTRAL RELATIONS

Jerusalem   Local government subordinate to central policies of penetration and control.

Belfast   Local government impotent amidst central policies of neutrality and inattention.

3. LOCAL POLITICIANS

Jerusalem   Absence of cross-community deliberations amidst Palestinian boycott.

Belfast   Unionist councillors reinforce divisions amidst demographic decline of constituents. No Catholic boycott. Sinn Fein part of local politics since 1981.

4. COMMUNITY

Jerusalem   Goal of unification includes fragmenting of out-group's sense of community.

Belfast   Goal of community identity and self-sufficiency for each side.

5. CIVIL SOCIETY

Jerusalem   Palestinian civil institutions handicapped by Israeli policy and national leadership. Cross-ethnic advocacy entities play key connective role.

Belfast   Two civil societies or one? Problematic relationship between community development (single-identity work) and cross-community efforts.

6. URBAN DEPRIVATION AND MOBILIZATION

Jerusalem   Palestinian relative deprivation increasing; organizationally fractured.

Belfast   Catholics' relative deprivation decreasing; politically organized.

---

of ethnic tension and management, forfeiting its potential role in outlining urban principles of ethnic coexistence. Absent this ethnic planning framework, development agencies have stepped into the void and, out of necessity, undertaken project-specific actions that explicitly recognize the city's ethnic divide. The result is that ethnic planning is reduced to a set of ad hoc and tactical responses to ethnicity, rather than seeking its proactive and strategic management.

In addition to the intralevel relations above, there exist important interlevel (central-regional-local) aspects of urban policy formulation and implementation (10.3.2). The local planning function in both cities has been shaped or preempted by national planning objectives. Urban policy has required centralization in order both to embed government policy within the ethnic arena (Jerusalem) and remove it neutrally above the partisan fray (Belfast). In Jerusalem, Israeli urban policies based on issues of national security and immigrant absorption have overridden or contradicted municipal planning policies that emphasize local concerns regarding environmental protection, land-use compatibility, public and fiscal health, and aesthetic considerations. National development strategies and projects have been implemented, with or without Municipality agreement, through modification of local plans by a district commission composed of central government ministry personnel. In this way, local planning's goals pertaining to urban sustainability have largely been bypassed by national planners' pursuit of specific ideological ends. The Belfast case represents an extreme intergovernmental case, with direct rule having removed decisionmaking authority from local policymaking bodies. Because it emphasizes vertical and tactical policy rather than comprehensive, or lateral, planning, this centralization of urban policymaking in Northern Ireland has fragmented government initiatives among numerous extralocal bodies. Thus, land-use/spatial concerns become detrimentally separated (as in the 1990 Belfast Urban Area Plan) from related issues of housing, social services, and ethnic relations. Lacking an effective local political forum capable of making "trade-off" decisions across policy areas, urban policy becomes the net outcome of a set of uncoordinated, single-function centralized interventions.

The distorted nature of local government is evident in both polarized cities (10.3.3). Amidst the Palestinian boycott of municipal elections as illegitimate, the Jerusalem city council is absent of cross-community dialogue and left-wing Israeli politicians become the de facto "representatives" of the Arab Jerusalem community. The absence of Palestinians from the city council also provides a rationale to more hard-line politicians for continued underprovision of services to Arab neighborhoods. They point out that a refusal on the part of Arabs to play the local political game of interest representation and bartering necessarily translates into meager political benefits. The local political level in Belfast, partly owing to its impotent character, has been a platform for derisive nationalistic fervor. Unlike Palestinians in Jerusalem, there has been no Catholic boycott of local elections. The inclusion of the republican wing of Catholic politics—Sinn Fein—in local politics since 1981 has fuelled the confrontational and divisive quality of local politics. Faced with Sinn Fein's presence, and the erosion of its own constituent base through demographic decline, unionist local politicians have felt cornered and commonly reinforce and intensify city divisions through their rhetoric.

The sense of local community amidst ethnic polarization and contested government can take a beating (10.3.4). The goal of Israeli political unification in Jerusalem has meant the intentional spatial fragmentation of the Palestinian sense of community. Israeli penetration of the east isolates Palestinian neighborhoods from each other. In Belfast, community is intimately connected to territoriality. The symbols of identity—religious institutions, schools, language, murals—are of paramount importance to the maintenance of ethnic territoriality. A minority but demographically ascending Catholic population, together with a majority but declining Protestant population, creates a difficult condition whereby both communities feel under threat. In both cities, internal and natural divisions within minority populations have enabled urban governing regimes to manipulate political resistance through the intentional exploitation and intensification of these cleavages. In Jerusalem, differences between local and national Palestinian political communities exist which Israel seeks to widen through the extension of economic benefits and urban services to cooperative neighborhoods. In Belfast, political vetting of funds for community development has sought to enhance a split between nationalists and republicans that is in part driven by differing economic circumstances and an inherent disagreement over appropriate political strategy.

Civil society is that layer of nongovernmental organizations (NGOs) and community-based organizations that exists between community and government (10.3.5). In antagonistic settings, where normal channels of political expression are blocked by government, NGOs can play key roles in expressing opposition to government policy and legitimacy, enabling political opportunities at the urban level for an aggrieved party, and nurturing local organizing capacity on the part of an out-group. Palestinian civil institutions have been restricted from locating in Israeli-defined Jerusalem, handicapping their ability to provide basic services to the city's Arabs. The creation by Israel policy of a void in Palestinian service provision impedes the development of local organizing capacity on the part of moderate Arab Jerusalemites, and runs the risk of creating an authoritarian and radicalized Palestinian presence in Jerusalem. An additional constraint facing local Palestinian NGOs is the tension that exists between Palestinian local initiative and national leadership. Cross-ethnic advocacy groups play a key role in connecting the Palestinian cause to Israeli and Western media, and in supporting human rights against both Israeli and Palestinian violations. Belfast NGOs, in the absence of effective local government, are critical in bringing community needs and demands to the British government. It is a city, however, characterized by dual civil societies. This presents a dilemma to government as to whether it should assist the development of each community separately, or work to bridge NGO work through cross-community efforts.

Belfast Catholics and Jerusalem Palestinians face contrasting material and organizational conditions (10.3.6). In Jerusalem, grievances resulting from a partisan urban strategy that has constructed an unequal metropolis are strong, while the organizational difficulties of the Palestinian community (both inherent and imposed) dampen potential oppositional mobilization. In Belfast, Catholic grievances over material conditions may be attenuating due to needs-based, nonpartisan urban policy; yet the organizational attributes of the republican Catholic opposition have been resistant to governing regime efforts to dampen them. The future paths of political mobilization of the prejudicially treated, organizationally fractured Palestinian community in Jerusalem and the benignly treated, politically organized republican community in Belfast will help clarify whether it is primarily a sense of urban deprivation or the qualities of its political organization that drive an urban minority group toward communal resistance.

Politically, the Palestinian population in Jerusalem is a more moderate one than the Catholic population in Belfast. Support for militant rejectionists groups such as Hamas resides mostly in Gaza and West Bank areas, while support for Sinn Fein is greater in Belfast than elsewhere in Northern Ireland. Thus, Arab violence in the Holy City is disproportionately engaged in by people not from the city, whereas Belfast violence is more likely generated by those living in the city. This difference between Arab and Catholic local political communities is traceable, in part, to the generally better economic conditions in Jerusalem than in Belfast. Economic deprivation in Belfast's Catholic neighborhoods has reinforced political disempowerment while relatively better economic opportunities for Arabs in Jerusalem vis-à-vis the West Bank has moderated political opposition. Governing regime efforts in both cities to suppress radical local opposition appear more successful in Jerusalem than in Belfast. Still, such success may be short-lived as Israeli across-the-board restrictions on Palestinian political activity creates a hole that could be filled by the more radical Hamas. With its network of social service activities, Hamas could take root among east Jerusalem's Arab residents in a way similar to Sinn Fein among west Belfast's Catholic residents.

Ideology, Urban Policy, and Ethnic Conflict

Polarized cities, because they encapsulate larger conflicts, become transformed from urban organisms into symbols of wider, national sovereignty claims. Confronted with difficult mixtures of nationalist issues and local service disputes, urban policymakers have used different approaches—partisan (Jerusalem) and neutral (Belfast). Ethnonationalist conflicts shape basic urban parameters and constrain planning options regarding the use of space. Clearly cities do not exist independently of the larger ethnic conflict of their regions and countries. The twenty years of partitioned Jerusalem—the creation of Middle East war—affected the subsequent spatial development of west and east Jerusalem and separated rival communities physically from one another. Similarly, political imperatives rather than planning considerations have significantly shaped Israeli planning decisions since 1967 in east Jerusalem and the West Bank. Urban ethnonationalist conflict in Belfast has spawned aberrant peacelines throughout the urban tissue, and a government ideology of "color-neutrality" since direct rule has produced an equally anomalous dichotomized urban policy.

Cities and their policymakers are key agents in reifying political and moral ideologies. Urban policymakers seek to give concrete meaning to ideological goals such as political control, ethnic separation, security, and fairness. Urban policymaking endeavors to provide protective cover to these often controversial ideological goals through its provision of a language of seeming technical objectivity. For instance, the operationalization of a partisan ideology will likely seek to transform international, or macropolitical, issues of sovereignty and territorial conflict into more mundane, depoliticized micropolitical issues of urban management. International territorial disputes become deliberations over municipal boundary adjustments; contentious settlement patterns become municipal government actions responsive to "natural" city growth; and issues of political recognition on an international scale become matters of local consultation on a municipal level. In these and other ways, the main task of urban planning and policymaking in ethnically polarized cities is to legitimize and concretize ruling ideologies.

Beneath the surface of urban strategies lie the motivations and rationales of urban policymakers and planners who operate daily in ethnically polarized cities. Implementers of partisan Israeli policy in Jerusalem are cognizant of the partisan parameters within which they operate and their allegiance is first to the state, then to professional norms. In many interviews, urban policymakers shifted between political and technical terms of reference. Planners' relationship to the contentiousness of the political parameters within which they work is an ambiguous one. On the one hand, there is frustration and impotence; on the other, there is attraction to the important professional role they are asked to perform. Planners' emphasis on functionality and practicality provides them with a "safe space" within which they can address emotion-laden and contestable issues. In Belfast, policymakers' public stance of color-neutrality has separated urban policy from ethnic realities. The overly technocratic and compartmentalized character of town planning, specifically, is symptomatic of a profession that has retreated from contributing on a strategic or comprehensive basis to ethnic management. Despite the land-use and territorially based implications of much of sectarianism, town planning, whose professional foundation is land use, has played a minor role in addressing ethnicity. In contrast to government's public stance, ethnic sensitivity on the part of policymakers and bureaucrats in internal discussions is acute and can, at times, figure prominently in decisionmaking. There are also emerging urban policy approaches that consider more progressively the city's sectarian realities. Yet, policymakers remain hesitant to speak explicitly in public forums about ethnicity and urban policy, and the emerging strands of innovative ethnic policy remain isolated and disconnected from a broader vision of progressive ethnic management.

* * *

Despite the powerful ideological contexts within which urban policymaking occurs in contested societies, evidence from Jerusalem and Belfast indicates that cities do matter amidst conflict. Polarized cities are not simply mirrors of larger nationalistic ethnic conflict, but instead can be catalysts through which conflict is exacerbated or ameliorated. The manifestations of ethnic conflict in urban arenas are not readily predictable from the ideological and political parameters of the larger conflict. Rather, the city introduces a set of characteristics—proximate ethnic neighborhoods, territoriality, economic interdependency, symbolism, centrality—not present to such an extent on wider geographic scales. These urban features can bend or distort—for better or worse—the relationship between ideological disputes and the manifestations of interethnic conflict. Whether urban policy moderates, exacerbates, or passively reflects the broader historical conflict is dependent upon the implementation strategies chosen, the spatial, economic, and psychological conditions and contradictions they generate in the built landscape, and the organizational and mobilization qualities of the oppositional group. Policy and planning decisions regarding land use, housing, economic development, and service delivery can independently harden or widen intergroup cleavages. Because urban policymakers and planners affect through their daily decisions important spatial elements of the politicized urban geography, they are important mediating agents amidst larger nationalistic ethnic conflict.

Cities have independent effects on the relationship between ideological conflict and urban conflict, but in ways that are complex and not easily predicted. The urban organism frequently appears too complex to be fully molded by ethnonational or civic ideologies. This is due, in part, to the inherent difficulties of defining on a concrete level the operative forms of often abstract ideology. In the Jerusalem case, for example, the Israeli goals of political control and security have been operationalized as a strategy that seeks penetration of Palestinian settlement areas. Yet, it could be argued that an alternative strategy of assuring planning authority and development capacity for both ethnic groups could lead to greater political stability and security for Israel. In Belfast, the government goal of violence prevention and stability has been operationalized as a policy strategy that condones separation and containment of ethnic groups. Yet, one could argue that more genuine urban stability might be achieved through cross-community bridge building and an urban policy approach more responsive to the qualitatively different needs of the two sectarian populations. Fundamental ideologies do not articulate clear-cut urban methods and techniques needed to achieve them. Such ambiguity provides urban policymaking with its semi-autonomous space.

Urban policy, an important operational form of a governing ideology, is capable of refuting moral dictates on a practical level through the generation of unforeseen consequences and contradictions that endanger ideological policy goals. The narrow ground of urban realities can confront ruling ideologies with formidable challenges, creating pockets of unintentionality that can frustrate the governing regime and provide mobilization opportunities for a political opposition. The fact that Israel has chosen the territorially penetrating route toward political control means that security at the individual, if not group, level has been endangered. Partisanship aimed at dominance creates threats to individual security instead. In Belfast, significant practical problems are associated with a color-neutral policy approach amidst differing objective and perceptual community needs. And, significantly, such a "hands-off" approach toward ethnicity aimed at the containment of violence and the achievement of an urban equilibrium likely strengthens in the long term the urban conditions of sectarian compartmentalization conducive to intergroup instability. Seemingly successful in operationalizing fundamental ideology, Israeli and British urban policymakers may find themselves paradoxically creating the very conditions of urban volatility that government goals were formulated to avoid.

The urban implementation of ethnonationalist ideology (in the case of Jerusalem) or civic ideology (in the case of Belfast) necessarily confronts the issue of ethnic territoriality. This nexus between policy and territoriality provides insight into the tensions created when broad ideologies or goals are operationalized in the urban arena.

Territorial control sought by partisan policymaking can be elusive, subject to both self-created instabilities and shifting geographic delineations. One of the central means of operationalizing partisan ideology involves the penetration or dispersal of the out-group population in order to diminish its group coherence and ability to coalesce politically. The spatial distribution of competing ethnic groups and jurisdictional boundaries can be altered in pursuit of partisan goals of control and subordination. Yet these efforts at territorial penetration and control can create conditions of interpersonal insecurity, vulnerability, and urban instability. Control through penetration sacrifices the security of ethnic separation, and can start a governing regime down a path of ever-increasing and ever-destabilizing incursions into out-group population areas in pursuit of political control. Territorial control strategies tend not to have a clear end point. This is because effective territorial control achieved at one scale—for example, urban—can expose the partisan ethnic group to vulnerability at the next more expansive scale—in this case, regional or metropolitan. In this way, as Sack (1986) states, territoriality tends to engender territoriality. Israeli policy that has achieved a strong Jewish majority within "Jerusalem" confronts a metropolitan region that is more Arab than Israeli. At that point, metropolitanization becomes a logical extension of the Israeli partisan strategy.

Territoriality also permeates the urban implementation of more benign civic ideologies. Belfast's color-neutral approach to policymaking does not relieve planners from addressing sectarian territoriality. Indeed, neutrality obligates policymakers to monitor the distribution of policy benefits and costs across ethnic territory. Whereas the Jerusalem case illustrates the destabilizing effects of disrupting ethnic territories in an effort to dominate the landscape, the Belfast case shows that abundant respect for territoriality also has ill effects. Policymakers, in their acquiescence of strict territoriality, put themselves in the position of institutionalizing what are in reality artificial boundaries, protecting a lifeless and dysfunctional geography of hatred rather than directing their energies toward the vitality of people and community. As ethnic territories are solidified, the dynamic channels and flows of interaction needed for healthy urban functioning become sclerotic and degenerative. It appears that ethnic territory in a polarized city should not be disrupted to the point of threat and intergroup instability, but at the same time it must not be allowed to solidify and harden to the point of urban system dysfunctionality.

* * *

The importance and semiautonomy of urban policy found to exist amidst conditions of ethno-ideological polarization addresses the study's main research question, and leads to the consideration of whether the net effects of urban policy strategies exacerbate or ameliorate larger ethnic conflict. I now summarize the arguments put forth in this study regarding the effects of urban policy on ethnic relations and conflict.

Development decisions by the Israeli government that seek to physically and symbolically extend its territorial claims in and around Jerusalem create an urban landscape that exacerbates sovereignty-based ethnonationalist conflict. The urban policies selected to operationalize Israeli goals of political control and security are begetting a landscape conducive to antithetical outcomes—heightened political contestability and increased Jewish vulnerability. The significant Israeli spatial fingering into eastern Arab Jerusalem adjacent to ghettoized and fragmented Arab villages provides multiple vulnerable interfaces where violent actions can traumatically disrupt the urban system. The belief that partisan policy and domination can be a solution to the polarized city is exposed as a falsehood. Israeli territorial policies not only restrict Palestinian control over their own settlement patterns, but fragment Palestinian group identity and, ironically, the potential crystallization of a moderate Arab Jerusalem political community. Effects of Israeli territorial policies and de facto local political exclusion of the Palestinians combine to produce urban ethnic conditions of instability and conflict. Urban policy strategies have solidified and increased relative group deprivation on the part of Palestinians, contributing further to the preexisting tensions owing to contested political claims. Palestinians in Jerusalem, although better off socioeconomically than those in the West Bank and Gaza, experience more acutely the significant and growing degree of relative deprivation vis-à-vis their Israeli co-residents. In addition, unequal service provision across

Jewish and Arab communities weakens Israel's moral and political claim to be the guardian over all of the city. Despite obfuscation of partisan planning as a technical exercise, and whether the city-builder is fully aware of his role or not, partisan planning deepens polarization because the disenfranchised minority views the planner as a guardian and perpetuator of disputed political structures.

It should be noted that local moderating effects on conflict have existed in Jerusalem that might attenuate rather than stimulate ethnic conflict. In the past, conflict was moderated by the informal patronage system under the Kollek administration that rewarded compliant neighborhoods and co-opted Palestinian local elites. This source of conflict moderation has lessened with the breakdown of family-based leadership structures during the *intifada*. Currently, moderation is potentially caused by a generally lesser degree of force used by the Israeli government against Palestinians in Jerusalem than in the West Bank due to the city's position on the international stage, and by the proximity of the Palestinian population to an Israeli democracy that provides some civil rights and social service benefits to Jerusalem Palestinians. In addition, Israeli-Jordanian accommodation (regarding citizenship and control of the city's Muslim holy places, for instance) has compromised the emergence of a stronger local Palestinian resistance and has thus been consistent with Israeli goals. The fact that an increasing number of local Palestinians are applying today for Israeli citizenship indicates that this moderating influence may be increasing in effect.

Overall, however, it is unlikely that these local moderating influences can absorb, or compensate for, the significant instability created by the city's spatial and political structure. Partisan policymaking follows an internal and self-fulfilling logic that stands as a major impediment to urban peacemaking. The existence of vulnerable urban interfaces embedded within the city's spatial structure presents those seeking peace in the urban region with significant obstacles. If any empowerment of the Palestinian population occurs in or around Jerusalem as part of the peace process, there would likely be an increase in violence at these interfaces by Palestinians not prepared for, or in agreement with, the requirements of urban accommodation. This is so because these interfaces are both concrete expressions of Israeli dominance and the areas of greatest vulnerability. In the face of such increased urban and regional instability induced by the spatial structure of Jerusalem amidst the beginnings of interethnic accommodation, the question becomes whether political momentum toward peace can survive and reversion toward domination strategies be avoided. The destabilizing urban consequences and contradictions of urban partisan policy will argue strongly for its renewed implementation.

In Belfast, the containment and abeyance of conflict have been primary motivations behind the urban policy of the British government. The main means toward conflict containment—the condoning and formalization of ethnic separation through housing, planning, community development, and "peaceline" policies—likely provides short-term stability at the expense of longer-term opportunities for intergroup negotiation and reconciliation. A centralized technocratic approach that separates development goals from ethnic realities might suspend community power struggles, but it will contribute little toward solving them. Intergroup conflict may be contained in the short term, at the same time that Protestant-Catholic divisions are perpetuated by a hardening of territorial identities that may paralyze the city long after the political restructuring of Northern Ireland. The limitations of a distant, neutral planning approach in polarized cities are exposed in Belfast. Because urban institutions in a polarized city are often rejected by the minority group, such government intervention will, at worse, exacerbate conflict or, at best, be unsuccessful in ameliorating conflict. This is so because municipal planning concerned with how material resources are distributed sidesteps the root causes of sovereignty conflict. While the Belfast Protestant majority might view British rule during the past three decades as bearable, the Catholic minority has viewed it as a top-down reinforcement, if not imposition, of the Protestant majority's ideology. Despite hard-earned praise in specific policy areas (such as public housing allocation), it is ironic that a policy approach that seeks neutrality creates a gap in community connectiveness that is filled in by conspiratorial theories on both sides of the ethnic divide. Protestants focus on policymakers' apparent efforts to displace orange neighborhoods to make room for Catholics, while Catholics equate policymakers' inability to meet objective urban needs with their political allegiance to Britain.

Centralized policymaking as practiced in Belfast creates a local political atmosphere of reaction and dependency, one that obstructs the emergence of cross-community forums that might mediate ethnic tensions. Lacking local political forums, urban policy commonly puts local community groups in defensive postures that tend to solidify intergroup antagonisms. Similarly, community development efforts within an ethnic neighborhood aimed at supplying needed self-confidence and capacity to a threatened area also lead more often to ghettoization and inter-neighborhood competition than to Catholic-Protestant bridge building and cooperation. The legacies of community activism in the absence of local democracy, and in rejecting or criticizing urban authority, have created a multilayered terrain upon which constructive government-community partnerships must be built.

Unlike in Jerusalem, the neutral policymaking of Belfast has likely lessened relative group deprivation between Protestants and Catholics. Intergroup material conditions will not intensify differential political claims, as witnessed in Jerusalem. At the same time, however, the inability of urban policy to significantly affect the deep extent of socioeconomic deprivation across *both* Protestant and Catholic populations maintains an environment that punishes community confidence and debilitates efforts to improve sectarian relations. In addition, a symptomatic approach to the polarized city focused on material conditions is inherently incapable of effectively dealing with the political roots of urban ethnic territoriality and dysfunctionality. Postponement of political instability may be achieved, but with tremendous opportunity costs incurred along the way. The reactive protection of the status quo by a policy aimed at neutrality, maintenance, and stability defends a dysfunctional and sterile territoriality, and reinforces the physical and psychological correlates of urban civil war. If urban policy is to shift direction so that it is part of the change process toward peace, and not a burden to it, it must direct its energies toward the vitality of people and community, not the protection of a petrified territoriality that reifies mutually exclusive political positions.

*   *   *

In Jerusalem and Belfast, these future urban trajectories darkly portray vicious patterns and processes obstructive of urban ethnic coexistence. Partisan policymaking in Jerusalem creates an urban system of instability and conflict that produces in a self-fulfilling way the perceived need for greater subjugation. The insufficiency of policy-neutrality in Belfast solidifies ethnic mental and physical maps, making color-neutral policy both increasingly difficult to implement and irrelevant, if not damaging, to larger peacemaking. Actions taken in these cities by national and local policymakers will play critical roles in whether these somber trajectories are fulfilled, or whether alternative futures of sustainable mutual coexistence are pursued. These urban arenas hold key positions in operationalizing "ideologies of coexistence" as a means toward contributing to larger peace processes among peoples and nations. Future policy strategies in these urban arenas can potentially define in Jerusalem the terms of Israeli-Palestinian peaceful urban coexistence and thus the broader character of the Middle East peace process. In Belfast, they can potentially constitute a progressive approach to sectarian relations that can both respond to the differential objective and psychological needs of the two ethnic groups in an urban setting, and establish an urban laboratory of mutual coexistence which can support that society's steps toward peace. The narrow ground of these urban arenas does not have to constitute dire straits, but may provide the sense of shared crisis necessary for peace to be constructed out of a city's daily conflicts and complexities. There will be no Middle East peace without Jerusalem, and no Northern Irish peace absent Belfast.

The Challenge of Urban Coexistence

This study has illuminated the inherent limitations of two urban policy approaches in polarized cities. Partisan planning exacerbates conflict, and even more importantly, constructs through its outcomes an argument for its continued implementation. In contrast, neutral planning suspends antagonisms in the short term, but buys such abstinence from violence at the expense of reconciling competing visions of nationalism and sovereignty. One alternative urban policy approach—"equity" planning—may be problematic and unlikely until broader sovereignty issues are solved. Redistributive policies that would favor members of the materially disadvantaged ethnic groups—Jerusalem Arabs or Belfast Catholics—would likely be counterproductive if they occurred outside of broader negotiations over sovereignty and political control. Thus, for urban policy strategies to alleviate ethnic conflict, they must seek coexistent viability of antagonistic groups in the urban setting while at the same time connecting these policies to larger peace and reconstruction efforts. Urban strategies cannot address directly the root ideologically based causes of urban polarization. That is the domain of diplomatic national-level negotiations. But urban policymakers can contribute practical principles that foster the coexistent viability of antagonistic sides in terms of territoriality, public service availability, and preservation of ethnic identity. Urban policy can increase our social learning of how the root causes of ethnic polarization can be addressed and reconciled on the city scale.

The goal of a "resolver" urban strategy—the fourth type of policy approach—is to accommodate competing ethnic needs without sacrificing the soul of urban life and the city itself, and to contribute such urban policy principles to national-level negotiations dealing with overarching sovereignty claims, basic social structures, and power relationships. The narrow ground of urban life does not need to be one of boundedness and coercion, but can provide a challenge to policymakers in these settings to be more creative in designing urban arenas of coexistent viability. Rather than waiting indefinitely for the initiation or implementation of larger political settlements, urban policymaking can facilitate and reinforce larger peacemaking efforts. The benefits of urban peace and coexistence can be a spark to larger sovereignty deliberations, with the concrete principles of daily life supplementing and reinforcing the more abstract principles of internationally negotiated settlements. Cities are important microcosms of regional and international conflict, and thus can provide useful models of ethnic relations to national negotiators and diplomats. As the nation-state is decreasingly seen as the territorial answer to contemporary problems, the set of international-national-urban linkages revealed at the 1996 United Nations Conference on Human Settlements (Habitat II) may play increasingly important roles in building and sustaining ethnic peace.

Policies and principles of urban coexistence are not to be a substitute for larger political negotiations, and would indeed fail outside a framework of national peace and reconciliation. At the same time, though, urban strategies of accommodation will likely be an indispensable part of overarching political deals. Urban-based strategies that incorporate ethnic management criteria can supply useful lessons for broader interethnic negotiations and policymaking, and can furnish models for the distribution of international financial aid by governments and private organizations meant to solidify and deepen a negotiated peace. Tangible urban-level efforts and diplomatic national-level negotiations should be combined to create multifaceted peacemaking efforts. Urban accommodation without a national peace would leave the city vulnerable and unstable, while a national peace without urban accommodation would be one unrooted in the practical and explosive issues of intergroup and territorial relations.

*   *   *

Acknowledgment of opposing claims of sovereignty and territoriality, at urban and national levels, is an essential step toward the more effective management of polarized cities. To achieve this goal, there are three main political options concerning the structuring of local governance in contested cities—physical separation, two-tier federated governance, and consociational city government. Advocates of the more extreme physical partition approach to urban polarization point to Nicosia (Cyprus), where since 1974 a United Nations-maintained butter zone has physically separated the city into Greek (south) and Turkish (north) municipalities. This has created separate and self-contained municipalities of contested yet equal standing on either side of the barrier, and has resulted in each of the two urban regimes having a solid territorial base that has set the foundation for some bridge building in the past. The Greater Nicosia Master Plan 1981–2001 planned for two scenarios (with and without partition), incorporated elements of flexibility and openness, and has at times resulted in functional integration across the urban partition (Wolfe 1988). The applicability of this physical segmentation model to Jerusalem, Belfast or other polarized cities would create an urban setting that expresses a symmetry of territorial claims. With the penetration of daily urban policy decisions by sovereignty conflict lessened, the potential for constructive local leadership to address urban frictions on a cooperative basis could increase. However, physical segmentation presents numerous logistical problems, especially as, in the case of Jerusalem (and to a lesser extent, Belfast), competing ethnic groups, although segregated from each other, are not concentrated in particular sectors or directions. More specifically, former Arab east Jerusalem has a substantial Jewish population residing across from the old green line, and Belfast's sectarian geography of eastern Protestants and western Catholics is complicated by the Protestant heartland to the west and a segregated mosaic pattern to the north. A stronger argument against physical partition is its effect on city diversity and functionality. Indeed, an irony in applying this strategy of political resolution to troubled urban settings is that cities would need to physically break apart in order for there to be resolution of sovereignty claims and peacefulness of urban coexistence. When contemplating this urban future, one must consider whether the cost of physical separatism—the death of the old city— is a worthy sacrifice.

A second, more moderate approach to resolving basic sovereignty conflict in urban areas is to keep the metropolis physically connected but to establish a two-tier structure of local governance sensitive to territorial claims. Two-tier governance structures include the creation of a metropolitan government that manages the entire urban region, with ethnically homogeneous local governments expressing their own interests and needs.[3] Or, there might be a single city government supported by autonomous cantons or boroughs of ethnic homogeneity. A proposal for federated governance in Jerusalem—the Borough Plan debated from 1968 to 1977—envisaged a single municipal government under dual sovereignty, the representation of Palestinians in the running of the city, and the creation of separate boroughs such as existed in the Greater London Council.[4] Again, however, where urban ethnic geographies are intertwined, the creation of ethnic local governments (or boroughs) becomes logistically problematic. Either drastic relocation must occur to ethnically sort the urban region, or local boundaries must be drawn in disfigured, noncontiguous ways that dampen ethnic community cohesiveness. If two-tier delineation of local government is not possible or viable, the third approach to the political restructuring of contested cities is to create a local "consociational" democracy. Here, there is accommodation or agreement between political elites over a governance arrangement capable of managing ethnic differences. A local conflict-accommodative government is established that utilizes power sharing, ethnic proportionality within the public sector, community autonomy, and minority vetoes. Such a local authority for Belfast in the future would mimic the power sharing Northern Ireland Assembly created in 1998.

These three political options concerning local governance and sovereignty in contested cities—physical separation; two-tier federated governance; and consociational city government—run the gamut from least to most interethnic cooperation. In a physically partitioned city, sovereignty is divided and ethnic groups are isolated from one another. The creation of a two-tier system of local government shares the sovereignty of the urban areas between two ethnic-specific local authorities. There is unity or cooperation at the higher level of government (metropolitan or city) but functional and political division at the lower level (city or borough). A consociational or power-sharing city government is one of joint sovereignty wherein two nations or peoples exercise sovereignty. Political arrangements such as these that are responsive to contested sovereignty are likely required for resolution of the urban tensions that exist in Jerusalem and Belfast. However, on their own, these structural solutions may provide autonomy and sovereignty at the expense of ethnic separation and isolation and, ultimately, urban and regional dysfunctionality. Physical separation tears at the heart and soul of the urban region, hermetically sealing antagonistic sides behind walls of hatred. Political separation through a two-tier structuring of local government is more moderate; yet, without urban strategies aimed at coexistent viability of both sides, it also can lead to a functionally disconnected and economically stagnant urban area for one or both groups. Even joint, power-sharing political control of the city, without on-the-ground urban strategies that reify mutual tolerance and coexistence, can disintegrate into a condition of urban paralysis amidst policy vetoes.

Negotiated agreements over the restructuring of political power and control are essential, but not sufficient, for peace to advance. It is, instead, urban policymaking that is uniquely positioned to operationalize an ideology of ethnic coexistence in a city of historical contentiousness. Urban policy strategies that improve interethnic coexistence are a critical part in the advancement of peace, and should be part of, and contribute to, regional and international peace and reconstruction efforts. Local policies aimed at the basic needs and coexistent viability of competing ethnic groups constitute the sole authentic source of ethnic centripetalism and tolerance amidst a set of local and national political agreements that would otherwise be susceptible to ethnic hardening and fraying. National and international agreements over political power and control, while absolutely necessary, impose abstract and remote sets of rules and institutions upon the urban landscape. Political arrangements such as consociational democracy that might emerge from such national peace accords respond to the basic dual needs for sovereignty and political control, but represent agreements at the political level, not that of daily interaction between ethnic groups and individuals.

Progressive and ethnically sensitive urban strategies can anchor formal agreements concerning local political power. In the case of consociational democracy, properly designed urban strategies can provide a policy space of positive-sum outcomes that can obstruct the development of a mentality of policy gridlock and destructive ethnic vetoes. In the case of two-tier governance, they can foster interaction between semi-autonomous local ethnic governments and hinder a de facto separation that might otherwise develop with political separation.

For urban policy to perform a resolver role in making and building peace, the process and practice of city building will need to be reconceptualized in order that it may inspire or support two-tier, consociational, or other forms of accommodative forms of democracies. An urban strategy of "coexistent viability" is indicated for cities that are susceptible to, immersed in, or emerging from intense intercommunal conflict and violence. Urban policy will need to acknowledge and honor the centrifugal tendencies of ethnicity while maintaining the integrative institutions and processes of city building and administration. Specifically, urban policymaking must, in its methods of analysis and decisionmaking, explicitly account for the importance of ethnic community identity, territoriality, and symbolism embedded in the urban landscape. At the same time, it must be able to address constructively the city's ethnicity when it is obstructing the functionality of the urban region and the meeting of basic needs regarding public health, shelter, public services, and economic opportunities. In other words, city planners must both respect ethnic territoriality where it constitutes a healthy source of community cohesiveness, and break ethnic territorial boundaries where they impose chains that enervate and distort urban functionality and vitality. Often, territoriality is linked to political claims for sovereignty and control. Here, urban policymakers can contribute their expertise and analyses to political deliberations regarding the land and resource needs that would be required for the self-sustainability of a new semiautonomous unit in the urban region. In other cases, territoriality is linked to fear and threat of community decline on the part of a majority and/or empowered ethnic group. Here, urban planners can be instrumental in dealing with the social-psychological needs for community identity, viability, or security. A key here is to address the real concerns of communities and individuals and to de-link these concerns from the maintenance of a static or counterproductive territoriality. An accommodative urban strategy will likely require an engagement in equity policy that disproportionately targets territorial and material benefits to the objectively disadvantaged ethnic group (in the case study cities, Jerusalem Palestinians and Belfast Catholics) while tending to the psychological needs and well-being of the materially advantaged, in terms of their security, ethnic identity, and neighborhood vitality.

*   *   *

Prescriptions for peace-advancing urban policy strategies discussed in this book involve a fundamental shift in policy direction in the Jerusalem case, compared to the recommendation of a set of more specific, yet equally important, changes to policy strategy in Belfast. The neutrality of Northern Ireland's governance under "direct rule" has surely been a less regressive agent than the partisanship practiced by Israel since 1967. At the same time, recent political progress in Northern Ireland opens the opportunity for innovative reform of Belfast urban policy. Thus, in making policy recommendations, I have had the luxury in Belfast to offer more detailed and focused prescriptions than in Jerusalem, where a basic and radical overhaul of governing ideology, which is required for tension to be alleviated, must occur before more specific considerations of policy tactics.

In Jerusalem, the practice of urban policymaking would need to be restructured so that it broadens, not restricts, opportunities for peaceful coexistence. Urban policymaking and planning would need to be transformed from a profession capable of technically implementing partisan policies to a morally articulate profession dedicated to ethnic accommodation and the resolution of land-based political conflict. Urban policymakers would then be obligated to contribute to larger sovereignty debates their ideas concerning territorial identity and characteristics; communal requirements for land, urban services, and natural resources; and basic social organization at submunicipal and municipal levels. It is unlikely that an urban profession such as planning can, by itself, create freedom and peace. But it may be capable of creating urban conditions that are enabling of such human goals. Planner-resolvers must address directly the need for parity and security of urban conditions. This can occur through the articulation of the land and community requisites for rebuilding Palestinian society in the Jerusalem region, and through argumentation that "coexistent viability," not domination, is the path toward intergroup and interpersonal security. A reconceptualized urban planning profession in Jerusalem could play an instrumental role in achieving such coexistent viability. No other profession is better suited for this task than is urban planning, with its training in land-based issues, its link to political processes, and its awareness of the nexus between environment and individual behavior and perceptions.

In Belfast, urban policymaking would need to be reconceptualized so that it is part of the change process toward peace, not a burden to it. Government should facilitate those spatial forms and living patterns that are most conducive to community viability and identity for *both* ethnic groups. Equity does not imply replication of policy for the two groups, nor numerical balance in government outputs. Rather, it means that policy should be sensitive to the unique primary needs of each community while keeping in mind the overall good of the city. Both Protestant and Catholic communities have significant objective and psychological needs related to social and economic deprivation and group identity. In terms of urban policy formulation, however, there are different primary imperatives coming from the communities, which governance must effectively address: (1) objective needs of the Catholic population for new housing and community services; and (2) social-psychological needs of the Protestant population for community viability and identity. Decline in the Protestant population must be more strategically managed in order to produce a vital but geographically consolidated Protestant population. The goal would not be the maintenance of Protestant territories, but the viability of Protestant communities. A consolidated, more viable Belfast Protestant community may over time feel less threat, and a greater willingness to allow some normalization of Belfast's geography to meet some of the Catholic objective needs. Town planning has a moral and professional responsibility to shift out of its technical and land-use blinders to incorporate consideration of the social, economic, and psychological dynamics and requisites for coexistent viability of Protestant and Catholic groups.

* * *

The challenges of urban policymaking in the Middle East and Northern Ireland inform policymakers in other urban regions in the world split by ideological conflict. A focus on the urban planning function of government has revealed the intent, role, and limitations of public policy in its efforts to address the ethnic complexity that permeates inflammatory cities. Findings from this study of the interaction between public policy and ethnicity have generalizability far greater than the cases of polarized ethnic turmoil found elsewhere in the world. Lessons for the planning and policymaking communities will also likely be applicable to the growing number of multiethnic cities across the world that are not polarized, but reside close nonetheless to the ethnic breaking point. The ethnic fracturing of many of these nonpolarized urban populations creates a "public interest" that bears signs of fragility and cleavage similar to polarized situations. When governmental techniques of divided cities (whether in Britain, America, or elsewhere) adopt or condone territorial and physical means that increase security and segregate classes or races, they move toward the polarized circumstances studied here. Based on my research, the following principles of urban policymaking amidst ethnic conflict are put forth for consideration and debate.

Lacking effective resolution of root issues of ethnic conflict, explosiveness will be an integral part of the urban situation. The explosive potential will always be there—it is like a flame, sometimes bright, sometimes dim, but it will not vanish. Urban areas can be both receivers and activators of ethnic violence and instability. In the first case, larger tension penetrates the urban arena and manifests itself in traumatic disruptions and human tragedies. In the second case, urban incidents and events will supply proximate and concrete rationales for violence and unrest owing to unresolved deeper causes. Government and residents must be willing to accept this explosiveness on personal, group, and societal levels. Partisan planning exacerbates ethnic conflict and the potential for explosiveness, creates conditions of instability it was established to prevent, and constructs the need for its further implementation, irrespective of its adverse outcomes on peace.

Neutrality is not necessarily fair. Neutrality and color-blindness in policy, when applied in urban settings of structural inequality, do not produce equitable outcomes. Governments must avoid the comfort of acting as benign outsider to ethnic conflict. Neutrality in policy may be a means toward some agreed-upon goal, but it is not an end in itself. Equality of opportunity is not sufficient when life choices have been constrained by societal expectations and actions. In other cases, seemingly uniform requirements dealing with land ownership or development can have disparate effects across cultures having different values and customs.

Separation breeds contempt. Separation in urban settings breeds contempt. Learning of stereotypes is made easier if you do not know the other person. It is harder to demonize someone when you are interacting with them. Gates and boundaries (physical or psychological) in urban areas have two effects: (1) provision of safety; and (2) reinforcement of "the other" as threat. The goal of policy should not be integration per se, but a "porous" society where diversity can coexist and communities are free to interact, if they choose. The need to minimize the procreators of fear and stereotypes—ghettoization and separation—outweighs the short-term costs of urban porosity.

An ethnic group under perceived threat has psychological as well as objective needs. Conflict will be most evident when one ethnic group is seen as ascending; the other descending. For a threatened urban ethnic group, psychological needs pertaining to viability, group identity, and cultural symbolism can be as important as objective needs pertaining to land, housing, and economic opportunities. Urban policymaking must incorporate these nontechnical, subjective aspects of community identity into a planning profession that heretofore has been biased toward objective and rational methods. Because territoriality is a psychological as well as a spatial concept, policymakers must not unduly disrupt ethnic territorial patterns. Yet, because territoriality has distinct spatial consequences, neither should urban policy allow it to solidify to the point of urban sclerosis.

The goal of urban policy should be accommodation, not assimilation. Urban policymakers should take stock of color, not dismiss it, and seek to accommodate the unique needs of each ethnic group. This is not the traditional model of ethnic assimilation, but one that is accommodative of ethnic difference and focused on coexistent community viability.

Genuine political leadership seeks accommodation, but divisive political gamesmanship is easy and rewarded. True political leadership would accommodate difference, not exploit ethnic divisions as a way to keep in office. Cross-community relations is in many ways the antithesis of politics, which is based instead on the separation of constituencies and the pursuit of policies favorable to a frequently unrepresentative "voting public." Political leaders should be rewarded when they bridge, not reinforce, ethnic cleavages.

Majoritarian democracy does not fit with contested cities and states. Reliance on majority-minority democratic norms is problematic where cross-community coalition building is limited. This is exacerbated when minority groups are further disempowered by their lack of participation in the political process, or when the voting public is significantly different than the general public.

An essential step in effectively addressing ethnic divisions is a difficult and easily deniable one—that there exists a problem of which I am part. Genuine "peace" requires that a set of personal and group traumas be exposed. These are still submerged in the two study cities, in Jerusalem's case by unilateral policy; in Belfast's by the hands-off posture of policymaking. There exists a psychological tension between the comfort of ethnic identity and the unease of dealing with the "ethnic other." Dealing with "the other" takes a person away from feeling sure of his personal views of the world toward initial defensiveness, then confusion when perceived notions do not fit with reality. Out of this loss of self can come the beginnings of accommodating the other. Such interpersonal adaptation builds the foundation for the articulation of more progressive public policies aimed at ethnic accommodation, not domination or assimilation.

The common goal of urban management in both ethnically polarized and divided urban environments is to accommodate plural needs without sacrificing the soul or functionality of urban life. Policymakers and planners in both types of cities must address the complex spatial, social-psychological, and organizational attributes of potentially antagonistic urban communities. They must be sensitive to the multiethnic environments toward which their skills are applied, and to the ways that empowered groups legitimate and extend their power. The problems and principles of city building in polarized cities provide guidance to all those who cope with multiple publics and contrasting ethnic views of city life and function.

Appendix 1

Research Issues
(Expanded Outline)

Contextual Factors

Ethnicity and legal frameworks.	To what extent are deep ethnic cleavages acknowledged within the legal frameworks of urban policy and planning? Is differential treatment by ethnic group directly legislated?; indirectly facilitated?
Urban institutional differentiation.	Is there ethnic-based differentiation of city and neighborhood institutions and organizations, or efforts to institutionally integrate competing ethnic groups?
Basic values.	Within each ethnic group, to what extent are there shared (or conflicting) values concerning ethnic issues across the participants in the planning process (politicians, administrators, planners, residents)?

Policy Issues and Goals

Urban ethnic issues.	What are the major urban manifestations of ethnic conflict? Is it possible to classify different types of urban symptoms based on

their degree of conflict and/or potential for resolution?

Treatment of ethnic conflict.

Is amelioration of ethnic conflict acknowledged explicitly as an appropriate role for urban planning policy? If so, through what means is this amelioration to occur? Are issues of ethnicity depoliticized at the city level and through what means?

The city's interest: policy goals and objectives.

How is the public interest defined—overarching or differentiated by ethnicity? To what degree do development goals and objectives differ between ethnic/racial communities?

Citizen participation—processes.

What is the quality of citizen participation in the formulation of policy? Are intergroup collaborative policy processes used? What are the characteristics of community organizations within contested urban environments?

Urban Decisionmaking

Agenda setting.

How inclusive is the identification of alternative urban policies that might further city goals and objectives? In what ways do ethnic or ideological factors limit local policy and planning alternatives?

Decisionmaking rules.

What decisionmaking criteria are used to allocate urban services and policy benefits? (1) functional-technical; (2) partisan-ethnic; (3) proportionate-equity? Do these criteria differ by type of urban issue?

Planning/policy-making roles.

What is the practicality and effectiveness of the four planning models—neutral, partisan, equity, and resolver—in a polarized city? What combinations of strategies are used, and why? Are there alternative models of urban planning?

Territoriality and policy.

Do planners address ethnic territoriality? If so, through what means do they seek to acknowledge or transform it? Is there the identification of neutral, or bicommunal, geographic areas? If so, for what purposes?

Policy Outcomes

Implementation.

Are policies modified during implementation to accommodate or combat conflicting ethnic needs? What discretion do administering entities have to modify policy to address ethnic realities?

Results.

What is the geographic distribution of urban spending and services across ethnic subareas of the city? For overall urban spending patterns and within specific service categories—Land-use/plan allowances; building permit approvals; housing construction; economic activities; transportation projects; other infrastructure; noxious facilities.

National-local intergovernmental relations.

Degree of national-local intergovernmental friction. Are there compromises available to integrate national and municipal perspectives?

Conflict Outcomes and Mechanisms

Patterns of conflict intensification (amelioration).

To what extent do local policies intensify or lessen ethnic conflict? In what circumstances does urban policy lessen ethnic conflict? When does it intensify ethnic conflict or produce a breakdown in planning policy process?

Formal mechanisms for reducing conflict.	What formal governmental mechanisms are present to mediate interethnic differences over urban policy issues? Use of concessions or interethnic negotiated agreements?
Informal mechanisms for reducing conflict.	What informal channels/ modes of political contact exist to deal with minority grievances on practical urban matters? Are there channels available that allow minority to access government without having to recognize its legitimacy? Role of minority "notables"? Role of heads of minority institutions?
Intraethnic effects and cross-cutting cleavage patterns.	What are the effects of urban policy decisions on intraethnic relations? Mass versus elite differences? Differences between classes of like ethnicity? Between neighborhoods of like ethnicity? On what issues does support (or opposition) for urban policy cut across ethnic lines (Jew-Arab; Catholic-Protestant)?

Community Dynamics and Organization

Intersection of national and local interests.	Within a single ethnic group, in what ways do national issues and political leaders influence the organization and potential effectiveness of urban interests and initiatives? Conversely, is community activism in urban settings capable of influencing national-level discussions concerning sovereignty?
Community organization in a controlled environment.	What survival techniques are available to community groups suppressed by a controlling government? What are the more effective means of expression under conditions of subordination?
Restructuring community.	In times when greater autonomy is granted and/or a controlling regime is ended, how can communities and their leadership

transform themselves from protest organs into productive co-partners?

Change and Evolution

Changes in planning strategies.	What changes, if any, have occurred in how ethnic factors are addressed in the urban aspects above: (1) city planning goals; (2) legal and institutional relationships; (3) urban decisionmaking rules; (4) planning roles and strategies; (5) conflict management strategies?
Change—underlying factors.	Are changes in planning strategies due to economic, political, or ideological imperatives? Have changes been locally inspired or imposed on city from external governmental levels?
Change—effect on ethnic conflict.	How have changes in planning strategies, if any, affected the level and nature of ethnic conflict in the urban region? In the country at large?

Appendix 2

Interviews Conducted

Jerusalem (40)

October 14, 1994–January 13, 1995

Gershon Baskin	International Director. Israel/Palestine Center for Research and Information (IPRIC).
Zakaria al Qaq	International Director. IPRIC.
Israel Kimhi	Jerusalem Institute for Israel Studies. City planner—Municipality of Jerusalem (1963–1986).
Arie Shachar	Director, Institute of Urban and Regional Studies; Leon Safdie Professor of Geography. Hebrew University. Mt. Scopus.
Robin Twite	Joint Director. Project on Managing Political Disputes. Leonard Davis Institute of International Relations. Hebrew University.
Avi Melamed	Deputy Advisor on Arab Affairs. Municipality of Jerusalem.

Job affiliations/positions at time of interview.

Albert Aghazarian   Director, Public Relations, and Lecturer of Middle East History. Birzeit University. Ramallah, West Bank.

Shadi Ghadban   Professor and Chair, Architecture Department. Birzeit University. Ramallah, West Bank.

Michael Warshawski   Director. Alternative Information Center. Jerusalem.

Benjamin Hyman   Director. Department of Local Planning. Ministry of the Interior. Israel.

Ibrahim Dakkak   Member of Board of Directors; Coordinator of Occupied Territories—Palestinian Economic Council for Development and Reconstruction (PECDAR). West Bank.

Shlomo Hasson   Senior Lecturer. Department of Geography. Hebrew University.

Eitan Felner   Researcher. B'TSELEM: Israeli Information Center for Human Rights in the Occupied Territories. Jerusalem.

Sarah Kaminker   Chairperson. Jerusalem Information Center. Former urban planner with Municipality of Jerusalem.

Khalil Tufakji   Geographer. Arab Studies Society. Member. Palestinian-Israeli Security Committee.

Maher Doudi   Researcher/Project Officer. Society for Austro-Arab Relations. Jerusalem (Shuafat).

Meron Benvenisti   Author. Former city councilman and Deputy Mayor—Municipality of Jerusalem, Director—West Bank Data Project.

Jan Abu-Shakrah   Housing Rights Coalition. Formerly with Palestine Human Rights Information Center (PHRIC).

Nira Sidi	Director. Urban Planning Policy. Municipality of Jerusalem.
Ilan Cohen	City Manager (General Director). Municipality of Jerusalem.
Sarah Hershkovitz	Head, Strategic Planning Unit. Municipality of Jerusalem.
Elinoar Barzacchi	City Engineer—Municipality of Jerusalem (1989–1994). Co-director of Steering Committee—Metropolitan Jerusalem Plan. Professor of Architecture—Tel Aviv University.
Uri Ben-Asher	District Planner. Jerusalem District. Ministry of the Interior.
Miloon Kothari	Habitat International Coalition—United Nations Representative.
Rami Abdulhadi	Principal. Center for Engineering and Planning. Ramallah, West Bank.
Adam Mazor	Co-author of Metropolitan Jerusalem Master and Development Plan. Professor of Urban Planning at Technion Institute. Principal—Urban Institute Ltd. (Tel Aviv).
Naomi Carmon	Associate Professor of Urban Planning. Technion Institute. Contributor—Israel 2020 Master Plan.
Jan de Jong	Planning consultant. St. Yves Legal Resource and Development Center. Jerusalem.
Rachelle Alterman	Professor of Urban Planning. Technion Institute. Contributor—Israel 2020 Master Plan.
Hubert Law-Yone	Professor of Urban Planning. Technion Institute. Contributor—Israel 2020 Master Plan.
Nehemia Friedland	Professor of Psychology. Tel Aviv University.

Michael Romann	Senior Lecturer in Geography. Tel Aviv University.
Mahdi Abdul Hadi	President. Palestinian Academic Society for the Study of International Affairs (PASSIA).
Hanna Siniora	Publisher, *Biladi: The Jerusalem Times*. Chairman, European Palestinian Chamber of Commerce.
Amiram Gonen	Associate Professor of Geography. Hebrew University—Mt. Scopus.
Yehonathan Golani	Director. Planning Administration. Ministry of Interior.
Samir Abdallah	Director. Economic Policy and Project Selection. Palestinian Economic Council for Development and Reconstruction (PECDAR). A-Ram, West Bank.
Ziad Abu Zayyad	Co-Editor. *Palestine-Israel Journal*. Jerusalem. Member (1991–1993)—Palestinian negotiating team, Israeli-Palestinian negotiations.
Ibrahim Matar	Deputy Director. American Near East Refugee Aid. Jerusalem
Shlomo Moshkovitz	Director. Central Planning Department. Civil Administration for Judea and Samaria. Beit El, West Bank.

Other Individuals Consulted

Shaul Sapir	Rothberg School for Overseas Students. Hebrew University of Jerusalem (Mt. Scopus).
Nora Kort	Catholic Relief Services. Jerusalem.
Alexandra Odeh	Catholic Relief Services. Jerusalem.
Elan Kaive	Architect. City Hall Project.

| Kobi Ariel | Architect. The Jerusalem Center for Planning in Historic Cities. |

Kobi Ariel — Architect. The Jerusalem Center for Planning in Historic Cities.

Joseph Glass — Professor. Department of Geography and Institute of Contemporary Jewry. Hebrew University. Mt. Scopus.

Kerry Abbott — Agency for Relief and Development. East Jerusalem.

David Gorman — Research analyst. Project on Managing Political Disputes. Leonard Davis Institute of International Relations. Hebrew University.

Matti Evan — Division of Town Planning. Ministry of Construction and Housing. Jerusalem.

Nasser Arafat — Student. Architecture Department. Birzeit University. Ramallah, West Bank.

Zoughbi Zoughbi — Independent Conflict Mediator—Palestinian community. Bethlehem.

Ann Marie Kindrachuk — Palestine Human Rights Information Center (PHRIC). Jerusalem.

Belfast (34)

January 13–March 30, 1995

Frederick Boal — Professor of Geography, School of Geosciences. Queen's University of Belfast.

John Hendry — Professor of Town and Regional Planning. Department of Environmental Planning. Queen's University of Belfast.

Ken Sterrett — Town and Country Planning Service. Department of the Environment for Northern Ireland.

Gerry Mulligan — Central Statistics and Research Branch. Department of the Environment for Northern Ireland.

Mari Fitzduff	Director. Northern Ireland Community Relations Council.
John McPeake	Assistant Director for Strategy, Planning and Research. Northern Ireland Housing Executive.
Brendan Murtagh	University of Ulster, Magee College. London/Derry.
George Worthington	Head. Belfast Divisional Office. Town and Country Planning Service. Department of the Environment for Northern Ireland.
Dennis McCoy	Central Community Relations Unit. Central Secretariat. Northern Ireland Office.
Sam Corbett	Central Community Relations Unit. Central Secretariat. Northern Ireland Office.
Will Glendinning	Development Staff—Work and Community. Northern Ireland Community Relations Council.
Tom Lovett	Community Education, Research and Development Centre. University of Ulster, Jordanstown.
Frank Gaffikin	Lecturer. University of Ulster, Jordanstown.
Mike Morrissey	Lecturer. University of Ulster, Jordanstown.
Paul Sweeney	Advisor. Department of the Environment for Northern Ireland.
Michael Graham	Northern Ireland Housing Executive. Belfast Regional Office. Information Officer.
David Murphy	Northern Ireland Housing Executive. Belfast Regional Office. Client Technical Services.

Bill Morrison	Superintending Planning Officer. Belfast Divisional Office. Town and Country Planning Service. Department of the Environment for Northern Ireland.
Julie Harrison	Research Officer. Making Belfast Work. Department of the Environment for Northern Ireland.
Victor Allister	Springvale Development Team. Belfast Development Office. Department of the Environment.
Rowan Davison	Team Leader. Upper Shankill Action Team. Department of the Environment.
Jackie Redpath	Greater Shankill Development Agency/ Greater Shankill Regeneration Strategy.
Nelson McCausland	Councillor. Belfast District Council. Castle Electoral Area. Ulster Unionist Party.
Bill Neill	Professor of Town Planning. Department of Environmental Planning. Queen's University. Head of Royal Town Planning Institute—Northern Ireland.
Vincent McKevitt	Team Leader. Ardoyne/Oldpark Action Team. Department of the Environment.
Deirdre MacBride	Housing and Projects Officer. Community Development Centre, North Belfast.
Colm Bradley	Northern Ireland Council for Voluntary Action (NICVA). Belfast.
Robert Strang	Independent Consultant. Formerly Assistant Director of Development and Planning. Northern Ireland Housing Executive.
Andreas Cebulla	Northern Ireland Economic Research Centre. Belfast.
Ronnie Spence	Permanent Secretary. Department of the Environment for Northern Ireland.

William McGivern   Regional Director-Belfast. Northern Ireland Housing Executive.

Billy Hutchinson   Project Director. Springfield Inter-Community Development Project. Belfast.

Joe Austin   Councillor. Belfast District Council. Oldpark Electoral Area. Member: Sinn Fein.

Brian Murphy   Making Belfast Work—Central Office. Department of the Environment. Formerly Team Leader—Springfield Action Team.

Notes

Chapter 1. Urban Arenas of Ethnic Conflict

1. Another example of a contested city was pre-1989 Berlin. However, it presents a model of conflict different than the cases here in that the Wall did not divide ethnic or religious groups, but rather was built due to East-West geopolitical factors.

2. The Sarajevo urban region consists of a Muslim-majority city next to Serbian eastern suburbs and their Republika Srpska. Mostar is politically shared between Muslims and Croats as part of the new Muslim-Croat federation in Bosnia.

3. Ethnic groups are composed of people who share a distinctive and enduring collective identity based on shared experiences or cultural traits (Gurr and Harff 1994). Such group awareness can be crystallized through such factors as shared struggle, territorial identity, "ethnic chosenness," or religion (A. Smith 1993).

4. Nationalism is defined here as in Snyder (1993)—a doctrine wherein nationality is the most important line of cleavage for establishing membership in societal groups, and overrides or subsumes alternative criteria such as social class, economic class, or patronage networks.

5. Nationalism is not necessarily a fragmenting force. Civic nationalism can supply an overarching loyalty to pluralistic societies (Lijphart 1977). Even civic, inclusive nationalism (such as that by the African National Congress in South Africa), however, can be stimulative of conflict in opposing an ethnic regime.

6. Not all nationalistic ethnic conflict is contained within a single state. Ethnic groups can straddle state boundaries and thus require international attention. The Kurdish population resides in four countries—Turkey, Iran, Iraq, and Syria (Gurr and Harff 1994). Also, the Palestinian diaspora in the Middle East resides in the West Bank, Jordan, and Syria.

7. I borrow this helpful concept from historian A. T. Stewart's *The Narrow Ground: Aspects of Ulster 1609–1969*, which described the problems inherent when peoples having diametrically opposed political wills live together on the same land.

8. Peacemaking and reconstruction at the urban scale can at times be more difficult than at a regional scale. This was illustrated by the need to postpone municipal elections in postwar Bosnia and Herzegovina in August 1996, while national elections—although flawed—were carried out the following month.

9. The urgent need for accommodative policy models was the primary conclusion of a 1987 Salzburg (Austria) Seminar on "divided cities" consisting of more than fifty faculty and fellows from twenty countries (Benvenisti 1987a). The author was rapporteur for that seminar. Countries represented included Germany, Lebanon, Israel, Jordan, the West Bank, Egypt, Northern Ireland, Cyprus, the United States, the former Yugoslavia, Turkey, and Poland.

10. Even the nationalist wing of the African American civil rights movement espoused political participation as an appropriate means toward an effective share in the total power of the society (Carmichael and Hamilton 1967; Grant 1968).

11. Guinier's (1994) provocative argument against the fairness of American democracy takes her close to rejection of existing rules of governance as being inherently incapable of representing minority interests in a majoritarian democracy.

12. In the case of Montreal, the enactment of language policy accommodative of the Francophone population indicates that urban reform may not be able to attenuate nationalist calls for territorial separation and autonomy. Whether urban reform can obviate the success of separation efforts is an open question. See M. Levine (1990).

13. Belfast, Northern Ireland—a political flashpoint for political violence—has a very low violent crime rate. In contrast, Los Angeles' or Detroit's violent crime rates in the early 1990's were overwhelming but politically motivated crimes are minuscule.

14. Besides O'Leary and McGarry, inventories of different ethnic management techniques include M. Smith (1969)—modes of collective accommodation; Esman (1973)—regime objectives; Palley (1979)—constitutional devices; and Gladdish (1979).

15. Because these incentives attempt to point politicians and voters inward toward moderation, this approach has been called "centripetalism" by Sisk (1995).

16. Interview: Michael Romann, lecturer in geography, Tel Aviv University, at Jerusalem Institute for Israel Studies, December 16, 1994. Romann refers to this dynamic as the "dialectic between control and separation."

17. Interview: Dr. Nehemia Friedland, professor of psychology, specialist in terrorist negotiations, Tel Aviv University. December 15, 1994.

Chapter 2. Cities as Catalysts

1. Unfortunately, the relationship could be reversed. A national peace process may be held hostage by nonresolution of urban political and local territorial issues (for example, Sarajevo and Mostar in the former Yugoslavia).

2. I parallel Lijphart's (1977) discussion of nationalism here, in which he differentiates between an "ethnic" or exclusive nationalism and a "civic" or inclusive one.

3. For example, should policy seek equality of opportunity or equality of outcome? Should policy favor removal of discriminatory barriers only, or also take remedial action to compensate for past injustice?

4. The idea that there should be minimum standards dealing with basic human needs and rights was endorsed by the United Nations in 1966 in its *Covenant on Economic, Social and Cultural Rights* and *Covenant on Civil and Political Rights*, both of which are legally binding on those countries ratifying them. The International Labor Office (1977) has also proposed and defined a human-needs approach to economic development.

5. This predicted sequence of events is similar to Gurr's (1993) finding that the liberalization of a repressive regime may facilitate mobilization for violent out-group protest which, in turn, can result in the reimposition of coercive rule.

6. It is not my intention here to calculate the relative contributions to ethnic conflict of urban conditions, on the one hand, and aspects of an ethnic out-group's political organization and leadership, on the other (see Rule 1988 for an articulation of "relative deprivation" and "political mobilization" theoretical camps). Rather, I am interested in how urban policies may affect each of these antecedents of ethnic conflict.

Chapter 3. Investigating Urban Policy and Conflict

1. Urban polarization can also take the physical form of two-sided partition, wherein opposing sides are physically separated from each other by an impassable physical barrier (examples include pre-1989 Berlin, contemporary Nicosia, and 1949–1967 Jerusalem).

2. Jerusalem: October 1994–January 1995; Belfast: January–March 1995.

3. I used as a work base the Institute of Urban and Regional Studies, Hebrew University of Jerusalem; and the Department of Geography at Queen's University of Belfast.

4. It is thus far more inclusive than that defined by the city (town) and regional planning profession, specifically.

5. To some readers, urban policing will be noticeably absent from this list. It is a core issue in polarized societies that is outside the scope of this study. I focus on the planning-related and often land-based policies that structure opportunities and costs in contested cities, rather than the maintenance of societal order through police and military force. Policing in polarized societies is commonly systematically biased, politicized, lacking in accountability, and disproportionately representative of one ethnic group (Weitzer 1995). Depending on one's vantage point, policing in polarized cities is viewed either as a source of order or a cause of instability. The Israeli Police, Border Police, and Israeli Defense Force (IDF) control the environment in the Jerusalem region. In its effort to normalize Jerusalem as part of Israel, the police force is responsible for the city's security, in contrast to the Israeli Defense Force's control in the West Bank (Human Rights Watch 1993b; Benvenisti 1995). Pursuant to the Oslo agreement, the IDF has been redeployed away from major Palestinian cities, where a newly empowered Palestinian Police Force is present. In smaller West Bank villages, security responsibility is shared between the IDF and Palestinian Police. In Belfast, the local Royal Ulster Constabulary (RUC) has been the main police force, supported by the British Army. The RUC continues to be plagued by claims that it is biased against Catholics. As of 1992, only 7.4 percent of the RUC force was Catholic (Livingstone and Morison 1995; Weitzer 1995). Security forces in Northern Ireland have also been targets of political violence, with 287 police officers and 637 soldiers killed between 1969 and 1982 (Livingstone and Morison 1995). The Multi-Party Agreement of 1998 established an Independent Commission to make recommendations for future policing arrangements in Northern Ireland.

6. All interviews were conducted in English. In only one case—an Israeli interview—did this cause a hardship to the interviewee. I used a Hebrew-language research assistant as an intermediary in this one interview.

Chapter 4. Israel's "Jerusalem"

1. The "Arab" label connotes ethnicity; the "Palestinian" name connotes statehood and nationality. There is no way to disentangle these two terms in describing the primary non-Jewish population group within contested Jerusalem. Because the consistent use of one label or the other would be inadequate, I use the terms interchangeably in this book.

2. In 1992, the population of Tel Aviv was 357,000 (Jerusalem Municipality 1994a). The largest concentrations of Palestinians in areas currently or formerly occupied by Israel include Arab Jerusalem (about 180,000 population) and the cities of Gaza (200,000), Nablus (120,000), and Hebron (100,000) (Palestinian Academic Society for the Study of International Affairs 1993a).

3. In 1992, for example, the rate of natural increase in the city for Arabs was 3 percent; for Jews 2.1 percent (Jerusalem Municipality 1994a).

4. In 1990, orthodox Jews made up 28.5 percent of all the city's Jews. By 2010, this percentage is expected to be 38 percent. Growth of orthodox neighborhoods is also increasing conflict with nonorthodox Jewish residents, focusing on urban activities, such as car driving, viewed by the orthodox to be inappropriate occurrences on the Sabbath.

5. This geographical labelling is disputable. Palestinians make no contrast between West Bank and east Jerusalem, with the latter part of the former. International law supports this assertion, equating the Israeli "occupation" of east Jerusalem with that of the larger West Bank. My labelling is not meant to judge the issue, but rather I make the distinction for analytical purposes between the urban area and the larger West Bank region.

6. This functional region is bounded by Jericho to the east, Bet Shemesh forest and Modiin to the west, Shilo Valley and Male Lvona to the north, and Hebron to the south.

7. About 130,000 Palestinians from the occupied West Bank and Gaza Strip worked in Israel in 1993 (Krystall 1993).

8. Bahat (1990) states that the British administration preferred to employ Arabs rather than Jews 2 to 1.

9. This resolution (181 II—the Future Government of Palestine. 29 November 1947) called for the internationalization of Jerusalem within a context of a recommended partitioning of Mandatory Palestine into Jewish and Arab states. The resolution was approved by the national leadership of the Jewish community in Palestine, and rejected by the Arab Higher Committee.

10. Special arrangements between Israel and Jordan allowed the nominal continuation of Hebrew University operation.

11. U.N. General Assembly Resolution 303 (IV). Internationalization of Jerusalem and the protection of the Holy Places. 9 December 1949.

12. *Records of Knesset Proceedings* (Divrei Haknesset). Volume 4 (2nd Sess.), pp. 81–82. Statements on Jerusalem and the Holy Places made by Israel's Prime Minister, David Ben-Gurion. 5 December 1949.

13. Jordan's role in the Israeli-Palestinian conflict has been complex. It has been at times an unintentional partner, at other times a willing ally, to Israel because their actions have tended to compromise the possibilities for Palestinian resistance and empowerment. Besides Jordanian neglect of east Jerusalem 1949–1967, accommodation in the 1994 Israeli-Jordanian Agreement regarding citizenship and control of the city's Muslim holy places has obstructed the emergence of a stronger local Palestinian presence.

14. *Law and Administration Ordinance (Amendment No. 11) Law, 5727*, 27 June 1967. And, *Municipal Ordinance (Amendment No. 6) Law, 5727*, 27 June 1967.

15. Israeli annexation of east Jerusalem has been held invalid, and has been deplored, in a series of U.N. declarations from 1967 to 1971, including resolutions 2253 (ES-V), 2254 (ES-V), 252, 267, and 298. See Lapidoth and Hirsch 1994.

16. Jerusalem Arabs in the annexed city have a "dual and ambiguous" legal position of being Israeli "residents" but not "citizens" (Romann and Weingrod 1991). They were granted by the Israeli government the status of Israeli "residents" and thus pay taxes, and are eligible to receive social security benefits and vote in municipal elections. However, an overwhelming majority have Jordanian citizenship and are not able to vote in Israeli national elections.

17. Presentation before Global Peace and Conflict Studies unit, University of California, Irvine, May 1998.

18. In 1996, areas A, B, C comprised 3, 27, and 70 percent, respectively, of the land area of the West Bank exclusive of east Jerusalem.

19. According to Oslo II, additional withdrawals ("further redeployments") of Israeli troops were to occur in three subsequent phases during the interim period (thus increasing the size of Areas A and B). The first effort at subsequent withdrawal was stalled for nineteen months. Eventually, the Wye Agreement was signed in October 1998, anticipating full Palestinian control over 14 percent of the West Bank exclusive of east Jerusalem, joint control over 26 percent, and Israeli control over 60 percent.

20. Letters from Begin and Sadat accompanying the conclusion of the Camp David Agreements stating their position on the status of Jerusalem, 17 September 1978.

21. Romann (1989) calculates a 1986 dissimilarity index of 95.7, meaning that 95 percent of Arabs would need to move to achieve neighborhood level distributions of Arabs and Jews commensurate with citywide proportions.

22. Interview: N. Friedland, professor of psychology, Tel Aviv University.

23. The existence of this policy is affirmed in *Report of the Kubersky Committee of the Ministry of Interior of Investigating the Annexation of Territory East of Jerusalem* (1992).

24. It should be noted that a strong majority of the Israeli government officials I interviewed identified it as such. These individuals differed, however, in their evaluation of the appropriateness of such a strategy.

25. Expansion from 9,400 acres to 26,800 (Bahat 1990).

26. Twenty-six percent non-Jewish in annexed borders, compared to 19 percent non-Jewish if only Jordanian east Jerusalem had been absorbed.

27. Amirav explains that the Interior Ministry was empowered to enlarge the municipal borders of Jerusalem, and that the words "annexation" or "unification" were never explicitly mentioned by the Knesset or by the government.

28. The pace of growth in the new neighborhoods has been phenomenal. From 1972 to 1983, population in these areas increased from 8,200 (3.6 percent of total Jewish population in city) to 78,500 (24.6 percent of total Jewish population) (Hyman, Kimhi, and Savitzky 1985).

29. Article 49 (6) of the Fourth Geneva Convention.

30. The establishment of Jewish settlements just outside Jerusalem municipal borders has used a similar geographic logic. The "suburban" settlements of Maale Adumin, Givat Zeev, and Gush Etzion/ Efrat had a total population of about 32,000 in 1993 (*Ha'aretz* December 27, 1993). These will be discussed in a later section examining the political and geographic links between Jerusalem and the West Bank.

31. Owing to the combination of high natural increase and limits on Arab in-migration to the city, more than 95 percent of the non-Jewish population increase within the city in 1993 was due to natural increase.

32. Kaminker (1995), of the Jerusalem Information Center, cites an even more restrictive figure—13.5 percent of annexed Jerusalem where Palestinians can live or develop. The Palestine Human Rights Information Center reported the figure in 1994 as about 13 percent (de Jong 1994a). The 21 percent I cite in the text should thus be viewed as a conservative estimate of the effects of Israeli actions.

33. 64,870 apartments built for the Jewish population; 8,890 apartments for the Palestinians.

34. Prior to 1991, there was general permission for Palestinians to visit the city, but not to live there. Under these rules, "illegal" residence was not uncommon (Hutman 1992).

35. Regulation 11 of The Law of Entry to Israel states that a permanent resident loses that status if he "becomes a permanent resident of another country." The law regards east Jerusalem as part of Israel, and the West Bank and Gaza Strip as foreign territory.

36. Proportional spending (30 percent) plus an additional 7 percent compensatory increment to bring Arab services to adequate levels over time would result in 37 percent budgetary allocation, compared to estimates of actual spending of between 4 percent (Amirav) and 17 percent (Benvenisti).

37. NIS = new shekel (Israeli currency used throughout Jerusalem). In 1994, rate of exchange was approximately three shekels to one U.S. dollar. Source for monetary figures: *Background Material for Discussion by the Ministerial Committee for Jerusalem Affairs* (Jerusalem 1994c). Unpublished. Reported in *Jerusalem Post*, November 2, 1994. See also Jerusalem (1994d).

38. Seminar on Jerusalem: Political/Religious Perspectives. November 10, 1994. City Hall.

39. The *Urban Coping* report referred to earlier was prepared by Olmert's head of strategic planning, S. Hershkovitz.

Chapter 5. Partisanship and the Palestinians

1. A Jerusalem capital fund established by central government and the Jerusalem Foundation consisting of private donations has supported infrastructure development in a city that, by itself, could never have afforded its post-1967 development.

2. One case is illustrative. Kollek was livid about Jewish expulsion of Palestinians in the Arab village of Silwan (Jerusalem) beginning in 1991, and subsequent forceful occupation by Jews of those residences. Kollek's reaction was unequivocal and political, understanding the actions as the culmination of the Likud party's "harassment and intimidation of the Arab population" (Friedland and Hecht 1996, 440).

3. Urban planners also experienced this excitement of salience in implementing apartheid policies in South Africa (see Bollens 1998a,b).

4. Figures for the three semiurban villages supplied by K. Tufakji, geographer, Arab Studies Society (interview).

5. Harb (1994) observes that fragmentation of Palestinian identity is also occurring on a regional basis due to the phased empowerment of Palestinian authority (the *Gaza-Jericho first* plan) and the frequent closure of Jerusalem municipal borders, separating Jerusalem Palestinians from West Bank Palestinians.

6. This view is moderate in contrast to those who reject peace with Israel or support an Islamic state of Palestine.

7. *FATAH (Palestine National Liberation Movement)* is the biggest and most influential faction of the Palestine Liberation Organization (PLO). Competing factions include the Arab nationalist *Popular Front for the Liberation of Palestine*, the Marxist-Maoist *Democratic Front for the Liberation of Palestine*, the guerrilla *Palestine Liberation Front* organization, and the militant organizations of *Jihad Al-Islami* (Islamic Jihad) and *HAMAS— The Islamic Resistance Movement* (Palestinian Academic Society for the Study of International Affairs 1995). Adding to the complex internal faultlines within the Palestinian/Arab population are supporters of the older Muslim Brotherhood, Arab Christians, Hashemite supporters of Jordan, and secular rejectionists.

8. Source: Ziad Abu Zayyad. Co-Editor. *Palestine-Israel Journal*. Jerusalem. Interview.

9. Identity of interviewee withheld upon request.

10. The Arab turnout in 1983, although small, was instrumental in allowing moderate mayor T. Kollek's Jerusalem One Party to remain in control of city council, whereas its very low turnout in 1993 affected the defeat of Kollek and the victory of hardline mayor E. Olmert.

11. The Civil Administration has been the Israeli governing authority for the occupied "West Bank."

12. R. Twite (interview) suggests that the spate of Palestinian protests over Israeli developments in late 1994 and early 1995 was because local protests were being tied to the larger peace process, which is supplying a key or foothold. It is not clear whether direction for these local protests came from local or national leaders.

13. Identity of interview source withheld upon request.

14. Identity of interview source withheld upon request.

15. This was also a major challenge faced by the African National Congress upon assuming control of South Africa government April 1994. See Bollens 1999.

16. Identity of interview source withheld to protect confidentiality.

17. R. Abdulhadi (interview) describes these strategies as *master planning* and *institutional planning*.

18. Source of interview withheld to protect confidentiality.

19. The PECDAR offices themselves cannot be located within Israeli-defined Jerusalem. Instead, they are in A-Ram, a stone's throw away from the municipal border and military checkpoint.

20. No restrictions are placed on U.S. Agency for International Development (US AID) money or on private funding. Thus, these sources are used to fund, minimally, health and education services in Arab Jerusalem (I. Matar, American Near East Refugee Aid, interview).

21. In addition to external money channeled through PECDAR, restrictions have been imposed on money flowing through the World Bank.

22. The right to housing is recognized in international law, especially in the *International Covenant on Economic, Social and Cultural Rights*, which Israel itself ratified in the early 1990s (M. Kothari, interview).

Chapter 6. Jerusalem, the West Bank, and Peace

1. Interviews: A. Mazor, chief architect; E. Barzacchi and Yehonathan Golani, two of the four steering committee directors; and U. Ben-Asher, S. Moshkovitz, and N. Sidi, steering committee members.

2. The Jerusalem metropolitan area as defined by commuting/ transportation patterns. Outer borders are Bet Shemesh forest/Modiin (west); Jericho (east); Shilo Valley/Male Lvona (north) and Hebron (south).

3. There is also a 91 percent Jewish majority in the western Israeli portions of the region outside the city, but this population constitutes only 5 percent of regional population.

4. Jewish growth does dominate west of the city, but that is within the uncontested borders of pre-1967 Israel.

5. Abu Dis was apparently discussed in informal Israeli-Palestinian talks over Jerusalem in Fall 1995 (*Jerusalem Post*, August 10, 1996); the Hizma site was reported by Said (1993); and the Ramallah site was discussed by Mayor Kollek's private Jerusalem Committee in March 1989 (Friedland and Hecht 1996).

6. For the two areas fully over the green line (Maale Adumin and Givat Zeev), the population ratio would shift from 70-30 Palestinian to 55-45 Jewish.

7. This represents the anticipated housing shortage in the Central District of Israel that Modiin is intended to meet (Ministry of Construction and Housing 1992, p. 34).

8. Reported in *Ha'aretz*, December 27, 1993.

9. The economic work group did examine different scenarios of border openness; for example, possibly open for economic transactions, but closed for residential location.

10. The model measured the relative size of adjacent competing populations (the more equal they were, the more potential for conflict); and each side's desirableness and need for the unclaimed land based on a measure of centrality.

11. A. Mazor was not forthcoming concerning how the classification of identifiable ethnic territory in the metropolitan region broke down Jewish versus Arab.

12. Statewide planning for the whole of Israel also is exclusionary. In the recent *Israel 2020* planning process, there were twenty-four Jews and one Arab on the planning team. The Arab was an Israeli student at Technion University in Haifa and "was highly influenced by the way we think" (R. Alterman and N. Carmon, planning professors, Technion University, interviews).

13. Names withheld upon request.

14. In 1996, areas A, B, C comprised 3, 27, and 70 percent, respectively, of the land area of the West Bank exclusive of east Jerusalem. The Wye Agreement of 1998 would move these percentages to 14, 26, and 60, respectively.

15. Article 49 (6) of the Fourth Geneva Convention. The United Nations voted 141-1 (Israel) that this Convention should apply to the West Bank.

16. Former Prime Minister Rabin made the distinction between "political" and "security" settlements, choking off subsidies for the former but supporting the continued expansion of the latter (*Jerusalem Report*, July 30, 1992, p. 5).

17. At the start of the occupation in 1967, Jews owned about 1,215 acres of land in the West Bank, about 0.5 percent of the land (Benvenisti 1984).

18. Under Likud government policies, public subsidies of up to 28,000 U.S. dollars per apartment had been offered to Jewish settlers (Friedland and Hecht 1996).

19. Newly constructed 4.5 room cottages in Efrat (southwest of Jerusalem) were selling for 200,000 U.S. dollars in early 1996. Upon the construction of bypass roads connecting Jewish settlements and a change in central government policy by the new Likud administration in mid-1996, real estate agents were reporting increases in property prices in the West Bank (*The Jerusalem Post*, August 10, 1996).

20. Resolution 242, adopted November 1967, requires Israel armed forces to withdraw from territories occupied during the Six Day War and calls for acknowledgment of the sovereignty, territorial integrity, and political independence of every State in the area (Lapidoth and Hirsch 1994).

21. U.N. resolutions 2253, 2254, 252, 267, and 298, respectively, considers the application of Israeli law to east Jerusalem as invalid, calls for Israel to rescind such measures, deplores the failure of Israeli authorities to do so, considers activities such as land expropriation as invalid and incapable of changing the status of Jerusalem, and, again, deplores Israel's lack of corrective action.

22. The creation of such a de facto new eastern border was set in motion in June 1998 actions by the Israeli Cabinet, which set up a new umbrella municipality that will give Jerusalem administrative powers in planning and building over Maale Adumin to the east and Givat Zeev to the north (Trounson 1998). A development scheme approved by the Cabinet in March 1997 had earlier included infrastructure, institutions, and public facilities for the Jerusalem–Maale Adumin area. See also de Jong (1994b).

23. It should be noted that the *Peace Treaty Between Jordan and Israel* (26 October 1994) views "economic development and prosperity as pillars of peace, security, and harmonious relations between states, people, and individual human beings."

24. I assume here that "economic" settlers, about 60 percent of Jews in the West Bank, would be amenable to relocation if offered the right monetary incentives.

25. The disconnection of the West Bank from the Gaza Strip would remain, even in this scenario favorable to Palestinians. An extraterritorial land corridor or land bridge between Gaza Strip and southern West Bank, consisting of an elevated highway, has been discussed.

26. I use M. Romann's "dialectics" framework of intergroup relations liberally in this section, and am indebted to him for his insights.

27. In particular, with A. Melamed, M. Romann, J. de Jong, and R. Twite.

28. Another reason cited is, with the Jordan-Israel Peace Treaty of 1994, Jerusalem Arabs can now become Israeli citizens without losing their Jordanian passports.

29. Such has been the effect of violent actions by Palestinian rejectionist groups such as Hamas and Islamic Jihad.

30. The symbolic center of Palestinian "governance" in east Jerusalem (the Orient House) presents an example of such nonviolent conflict.

31. Jewish deaths in Israel and the occupied territories due to political violence were seventy-five in 1995–1996, eighty-three in 1994–1995, and sixty-six in 1993–1994; compared to fifty in 1992–1993, and thirty-six in 1991–1992 (Trounson 1996). The figures are from September to September; their original source is Jerusalem-based Peace Watch. Jewish deaths in Israel proper during the first three years of Oslo, in particular, rose dramatically. Comparable figures for Palestinian deaths before and after the Oslo peace process began are not available. Israeli deaths due to political violence in 1997 (29) and 1998 (8 through September) lessened considerably (Wilkinson 1998).

32. Or, less likely, Israeli public calls for the relocation of eastern Jerusalem Jewish residents to the west.

33. An American example is the acquittal of the three Los Angeles policemen in the beating arrest of Rodney King and its leading to severe riots in south-central Los Angeles in April 1992.

34. A simpler geographic demarcation of sovereignty would be to use the pre-1967 green line to delineate west from east ("Whitbeck plan" in Baskin and Twite 1993). This "simple solution" is made difficult by the substantial Jewish population in "annexed" Jerusalem. One response might be to reestablish an Arab majority in east Jerusalem by redrawing eastern Jerusalem borders to include Arab communities now just outside the Israeli-drawn border. H. Siniori (interview) proclaims, "We can do exactly like the Israelis have done." In this plan, Jewish neighborhoods in eastern Jerusalem would be under Palestinian control, although residents would remain Israeli citizens.

Chapter 7. Territoriality and Governance

1. *Sectarian* is commonly used to identify the ethnic conflict in Northern Ireland as that between religious denominations or sects. I will use the "sectarian" and "ethnic" labels interchangeably.

2. More generally, political deaths have been an urban phenomenon, claiming 1.45 lives per 1,000 people in urban areas, 0.74 per 1,000 in rural areas (Poole 1990). Two of the thirty urban areas Poole investigated had higher densities of fatal incidents than Belfast (2.12 deaths per 1,000 people)—Armagh (2.25) and London/Derry (2.14). However, absolute numbers of deaths in the Belfast area were thirty-five times the former and ten times the latter.

3. What to call Northern Ireland is politically potent and thus disputed. Livingstone and Morison (1995) use "state" to connote the exercise of governance.

4. The political meaning behind religious labels is brought out by the fact that the more blatantly sectarian neighborhoods of working-class populations, despite having the lowest rates of church attendance, identify most strongly with Catholic or Protestant labels (F. Boal, interview).

5. The Republic of Ireland is approximately 96 percent Catholic.

6. Northern Ireland Census figures of 1991 show a distribution of 48 percent Protestant/other, and 39 percent Catholic in Belfast city. Because more than 13 percent of respondents did not state a religious affiliation (many due to its political sensitivity), these are undercounts. For this same reason, the religious composition for Northern Ireland, overall, must be estimated; in 1981, the Catholic proportion was put at slightly below 40 percent (Compton and Power 1986; Eversley and Herr 1985). In 1991, it was likely greater than 40 percent (Boyle and Hadden 1994).

7. For the city as a whole, the author was not able to obtain through interviews or secondary material government forecasts pertaining to religious distribution. This absence is a good indicator of government's stance toward sectarianism, as I will explore.

8. Keane (1985) found nearly 50 percent of households in 1977 lived on totally segregated streets, where there was no minority presence.

9. Two attempts during this period at "devolving" legislative power to a Northern Ireland Assembly failed. In 1974, a power-sharing Assembly disbanded after five months. Between 1982–1986, a Northern Ireland Assembly was created but had no power other than the power to debate.

10. The denominations of Belfast Protestants are split between Presbyterian and Church of Ireland, with a lesser percentage Methodist (1991 Census).

11. Across Northern Ireland, seventeen of twenty-six councils were controlled by unionist parties in 1993. Power-sharing arrangements between nationalists and unionists, whereby key positions are rotated or committee positions are assigned on the basis of proportionality, occurred in twelve of the twenty-six councils. Belfast city council has engaged in such practices only minimally (Beirne 1993).

12. This provision changing the constitutional claim of the Republic of Ireland upon Northern Ireland was approved by nearly 95 percent of the Republic's voters.

13. The current effort to devolve legislative power to a Northern Ireland Assembly contains certain characteristics that distinguish it from earlier endeavors at devolution. These include approval by the Northern Ireland electorate, linkage with the Irish Republic's relinquishment of its unconditional constitutional claim on Northern Ireland, inclusion of safeguards to protect group rights, greater legislative power, and integration within a larger system of multilayered governance including all of the United Kingdom and Ireland.

14. Not to mention issues such as decommissioning of paramilitary arsenals, release of paramilitary prisoners, and police reform.

15. The direct subvention from British central government covers the excess of public expenditures over locally generated taxes in Northern Ireland.

16. Female unemployment rates were also ethnically differentiated in 1991—Catholic 14 percent and Protestant 7 percent.

17. Catholics are underrepresented at senior levels (public sector) and management and administration levels (private sector), although there are positive trends in both cases (British government web site—*www.britain-info.org*).

18. Fourteen criteria were used, including income and job status, health, shelter conditions, physical environment, and education level.

19. The author walked and photographed all of the sectarian interface areas in Belfast. Regarding symbolism, see Northern Ireland Community Relations Council (1994b).

20. See Rolston, Bill. 1992. *Drawing Support: Murals in the North of Ireland*.

21. Two-sided partition, where the two antagonistic parties are hermetically sealed from one another, occurs in modern-day Nicosia, Cyprus; and formerly in Berlin and Jerusalem (from 1949 to 1967).

22. Sectarian interfaces are characterized not solely by physical peacelines, but occur anytime ethnic communities abut each other. They can occur psychologically and behaviorally within streets and blocks, and within so-called "mixed" areas (W. Glendinning, Northern Ireland Community Relations Council, interview).

23. Comment during question-answer period following author's presentation of field research findings to planning professionals and academics. Queen's University of Belfast, March 22, 1995.

24. In that most suburbs outside the core city are Protestant, attempts to expand Catholic areas outward are also susceptible to sectarian resistance.

25. The "put-back" rate under redevelopment is estimated at about 40 percent (meaning that whereas 100 units would be existing before redevelopment, 40 would be built after clearance). This is due to more livable residential densities, internal space standards, and parking requirements (D. Murphy, NIHE, interview).

26. The Suffolk area has been a source of sectarian conflict since the early 1970s. The future religious complexion of the Lenadoon estate there became the subject of a pitched battle between republican and loyalist paramilitaries and was the stated reason for the ending of the IRA's 1972

ceasefire. Today, Lenadoon is an exclusively Catholic estate (NIHE 1994a).

27. Identity of source withheld upon request.

28. Source: British government web site—*www.britain-info.org.*

29. It is the intention of the 1998 Multi-Party Agreement for the Northern Ireland Assembly to assume legislative authority in those areas currently within the responsibility of DOENI, along with those within the Departments of Finance, Economic Development, Education, Health and Social Services, and Agriculture. How this will affect organizational changes in these executive agencies and substantive changes in policymaking is unknown at this time.

30. A third tier of planning, regional, is done for all of Northern Ireland. The last one completed was the 1977 Regional Physical Development Strategy.

31. Certain proposed land uses are taken out of mainstream review, such as those affecting the "immediate community" (such as police stations). These often require a public inquiry and may be decided by the DOENI Minister himself. Oversight of peaceline construction is by the security forces; DOENI does not have authority.

32. The first planning legislation in Britain was in 1909.

33. Northern Ireland is unbalanced in terms of population distribution. The Belfast urban area dominates, with little in the way of second-order or third-order cities. This is why decentralization of economic activities into consolidated new settlements in the 1960s was seen as a means toward overall economic growth.

34. Belfast Action Teams in 1994 were removed from the BDO and linked with the Making Belfast Work unit within DOENI.

35. Belfast Action Teams are built on the model of City Action Teams introduced in Britain in 1985.

36. On March 6, 1988, three IRA members were killed by the British Army in Gibraltar. At the funeral of one of the deceased on March 15 in Milltown cemetery, Belfast, three Catholics were killed by a loyalist gunman. On March 19, two British Army undercover agents were killed after being abducted at the funeral of one of the March 15 deceased (Sutton 1994).

37. In addition to the urban policymaking units in the DOENI above, the Department of Economic Development (DED) seeks to strengthen and expand the industrial base. Within DED, the Industrial Development Board encourages the international competitiveness of Belfast's economic base, and the Local Enterprise Development Unit stimulates the potential of small businesses, especially their competitiveness for export markets.

38. Note that the two antagonistic ethnic groups in Belfast are often described as "communities." I am also interested in this section about how po-

litical and nationalistic issues penetrate and interact with "community" organizations that are often neighborhood based. In this latter use of the term, Belfast has not two, but between fifty and seventy-five "communities."

39. "Political vetting" is a chiefly British expression meaning "to subject to expert appraisal or correction." It had its origin in a Parliamentary statement on June 27, 1985, by the then secretary of state, Douglas Hurd.

40. The *voluntary sector* consists of large, often province-wide, organizations with professional workers who work on issues such as crime, vandalism, drugs, and homelessness. The *community sector* is composed of neighborhood-based groups with unpaid, part-time workers addressing multiple neighborhood issues.

41. An example of CD is place-based physical regeneration, while CR is exemplified by the required "Education for Mutual Understanding" school curriculum (Fitzduff 1993).

42. A difference F. Gaffikin (interview) highlights is that between deprived Shankill Protestants and relatively better-off east Belfast Protestants.

43. This account of Catholic community organizing draws upon accounts of Colm Bradley, who worked for the Falls Community Council during its formative years; and Brian Murphy, who as Springfield BAT leader worked to develop an Upper Springfield Development Trust for Catholic neighborhoods in west Belfast.

44. Catholic electoral strength in Belfast is contested by the SDLP and Sinn Fein. Based on 1997 elections, the former has seven members and the latter thirteen members on the fifty-one-seat city council. In the 1998 election for the Northern Ireland Assembly, each garnered five seats from Belfast constituencies. Province-wide, SDLP won 20.7 percent of local council seats and Sinn Fein 16.9 percent in the 1997 national elections. In the new Northern Ireland Assembly, the SDLP has 22.2 percent of seats, Sinn Fein 16.7 percent.

45. Identity of interview source withheld upon request.

46. The sense of Protestant loss is illustrated by this not uncommon type of remembrance: "We used to walk down that street as a youth and we were picked up by all the people whose fathers were lecturers at Queen's University and middle-class professionals. Now, the street is ninety-eight percent Catholic" (N. McCausland, interview).

47. This account of Protestant community organizing is based on first-hand accounts and reflections by Jackie Redpath, Greater Shankill Regeneration Strategy; and Billy Hutchinson, former loyalist political prisoner and now director, Springfield Inter-Community Development Project.

48. Identity of source withheld upon request.

49. Identity of source withheld upon request.

50. It is interesting to note that councillors from both sides of the conflict admit that less-publicized committee meetings show much greater Protestant-Catholic cooperation than city council meetings.

51. The Council, with assistance by contracted planning consultants, sought in 1996 to engage more constructively with the DOENI regarding the Department's plans regarding transport, housing, and retailing (F. Boal, Queen's University, personal communication, July 29, 1996).

52. These conclusions are based on interviews with government officials in DOENI central office, DOENI Town and Country Planning Service (Belfast Division), NIHE Belfast Regional Office; the Central Community Relations Unit of Northern Ireland Office, Central Secretariat; and with academics who have been involved in Belfast urban policy formulation and evaluation.

53. There is a complete absence of the words "Catholic" or "Protestant" from the BUA Plan 2001 (DOENI 1990a).

54. I focus here on allocation of public housing units. Urban policy dealing with the redevelopment and construction of public housing units presents a different set of issues and is treated in the next chapter.

55. "Mixed" estates are where the minority comprises 5–30 percent of the population (NIHE 1994a).

Chapter 8. Lost Opportunities, Unequal Outcomes

1. In reality, the Troubles may have stimulated redevelopment. Singleton (1986) states that "Housing reform and comparatively large injections of public money have been used in an attempt to achieve wider objectives related to the acceptance of the Northern Ireland State by 'disaffected' citizens." Money for Northern Ireland public housing stayed high even through the Thatcher years of fiscal restraint and retrenchment.

2. "Urgent," or priority, need applicants include those who are homeless, or facing threat of homelessness, due to natural emergencies, familial breakdown, or civil disturbances; those suffering from special health and social conditions; those living in an unfit house to be closed or demolished; and "key workers" (NIHE 1990a).

3. Without sectarian territorial imperatives, the extent of new housing for Catholics would be attenuated because vacant existing units in today's orange areas could be used to meet some of the need.

4. Note the similarity in tactical approach to that of Metropolitan Jerusalem in chapter 6.

5. The West-Link motorway elsewhere conveniently separates Catholic west Belfast from Protestant inner south Belfast. Still, a peaceline had to be built that fronts onto the expressway.

6. Identity withheld upon request.

7. This is existing unmet demand plus need created by future New Lodge redevelopment that will rebuild at lower densities.

8. The narrow definition of town planning in Britain may be further channeled in Northern Ireland. W. Neill, planning academic (interview), hypothesizes that civil servants brought with them during the introduction of direct rule a certain ethos that they should address urban problems directly. Planning-related decisions were thus appropriated by civil servants working in development agencies separate from town planning.

9. The religion of the applicant was not recorded, while the ethnic composition of the estate was classified in the STACHR report. The assumption used was that only Catholics request "Catholic" estates; Protestants "Protestant" estates. Household type and need differences between ethnic groups were not behind the percentage disparity; indeed, when these were controlled statistically, the disparity increased rather than lessened.

10. Eighteen percent of units were classified as in a "mixed" estate. Although this supplies some additional housing for Catholic applicants, it does little to narrow the gap between Protestant and Catholic access to the public housing market.

11. Another interviewee (name withheld) asserts that color-blindness is a falsehood anyway in NIHE allocation because "one can often find out the religion of a client through various devious ways."

12. This assumes that mixed estates may increase the potential for violence. Incidents at Farrington Gardens (now Catholic Ardoyne), Lenadoon, and Manor/Roe support this assumption. Yet, the relationship between residential patterns and potential for violence is not that clear (J. McPeake, NIHE, interview). For instance, segregated estates, more vulnerable to control by paramilitaries, may be more stimulative of urban civil war.

13. The Belfast Education and Library Board is responsible for state (Protestant) schools; the Catholic Church controls Catholic education. The integrated school sector is small.

14. As reported in Report Back Evening, February 6, 1995. Greater Shankill Community Planning Weekend.

15. The most emotive expression is the "Rape and Plunder of the Shankill" from Wiener, R. (1976).

16. Murtagh and this author would agree with Dawson (1984) that redevelopment has been used in certain areas in efforts to minimize inter-

community contact along the interfaces. This is qualitatively different than the fuller-bodied conspiracies discussed here.

17. Northern Ireland Council for Voluntary Action. 1993. *Twenty Years of Deprivation*. Public Affairs Information Project. Belfast: NICVA.

18. A 1994 assessment of urban policy in Britain concludes that property-led renewal often occurs at the expense of community development, and argues that there should be more community-targeted assistance (Robson et al. 1994).

19. Beginning in 1995, monitoring was to link MBW project data with area and resident outcomes.

Chapter 9. The Demands of Peace

1. Livingstone and Morison (1995) make a parallel argument in evaluating the broader state of democracy in Northern Ireland. Where political initiatives will not be pursued unless they have the support of both communities, the capacity of democratic politics to restructure society is largely forsworn.

2. Name withheld due to confidentiality.

3. The alternative to current urban policy "isn't that people will have to live in integrated estates, but that they can have that choice" (W. Glendinning, N. Ireland Community Relations Council, interview).

4. For example, the NIHE seeks advice from the local BAT leader about whether house building for Catholics along a transitional zone may be perceived as intruding on Protestant territory. The BAT leader monitors neighborhood icons and symbols, and the ethnic affiliation of nonresidential activities.

5. Bradley recounts that when government started a Targeting Social Need program, it issued no explicit guidance. Local politicians filled this void with rhetoric ("targeting Catholic need"). With subsequent greater community involvement, program objectives have been clarified and both communities now feel ownership of it.

6. Because greater ethnic sensitivity would likely result in service duplication and decrease efficiencies of public investment, a beneficial supplement to such a policy approach, as described later, would be a citywide strategy that prioritizes neighborhoods on the basis of potential increase in viability per investment unit.

7. Comment made in question/answer period subsequent to author's presentation of research findings. March 22, 1995. Queen's University of Belfast.

8. The Planning Service and the Belfast Development Office, for example, report to different undersecretaries within the DOENI.

9. The 1989 Act significantly strengthened the 1976 Act, which had relied on voluntary action by employers not to discriminate. The 1989 Act requires all concerns with more than ten employees to take "affirmative action" (including the setting of goals and timetables) if fair participation across religious groups is not being provided. Absent formal quotas, the Act has been able to apply considerable pressure on employers to take action to secure a reasonable balance between Protestants and Catholics (Boyle and Hadden 1994).

10. This report by DOENI, *Northgate Enterprise Park: Interim Report*, was never published. Only thirty copies were printed for internal circulation only. This confidentiality is indicative of the perceived sensitivity of dealing with sectarianism in a candid way.

11. In a publicly disseminated glossy brochure on the project, the DOENI is disingenuous in stating that "The development of the Northgate Enterprise Park creates the opportunity to develop a number of sites for new housing."

12. The other two are combating terrorism and regenerating the economy.

13. The 1998 multiparty accord calls for the British government to create a statutory obligation on public authorities in Northern Ireland to carry out all their functions with due regard to equality of opportunity in relation to religion. A new statutory Equality Commission will monitor this statutory obligation. The British government is also to create a new, more focused Targeting Social Need initiative aimed at "progressively eliminating the differential in unemployment rates between the two communities by targeting objective need."

14. The precursor to this report was Boal, Frederick W., P. Doherty, and D. G. Pringle. 1974. *The Spatial Distribution of Some Social Problems in the Belfast Area*. Belfast: Northern Ireland Community Relations Commission.

15. Robson, Bradford, and Deas (1994) developed the deprivation measure. Six additional "core" wards lie outside Belfast city. MBW also identifies additional wards that have pockets of deprivation or specific problems of disadvantage. These may be eligible for MBW funding, upon meeting certain requirements.

16. The "need" described here is that which will guide specific government funding and project decisions. Objectively measured need (by the Robson index) determines ward eligibility for MBW funds.

17. Indicative of its openness to change, several former critics and community spokespeople were brought into the process of evaluation and redesign of MBW.

18. Anonymity requested.

19. As R. Strang (interview) colorfully comments, "Areas that are blocked up, have broken windows and dirt areas provide a great adventure playground for kids on bikes, but it is not rational housing policy."

20. R. Strang (interview; and DOENI 1992a) refers to this as a "clearance/ heartland" strategy.

21. The Shankill area appears a logical target of community investment under this triage model.

22. Identity withheld upon request.

23. The Standing Advisory Commission on Human Rights (1990) anticipates this circumstance in stating, "NIHE should be exempt from strict applications of anti-discrimination law in cases where the goal is maintaining integration" (CM 1107 para 4.53–54 and 6.19).

24. The increased selling of NIHE housing units to eligible tenants and the emergence of a stronger private housing market may also facilitate integration, or at least the breakdown of ethnic boundaries. New owner-occupied housing construction was up to 85 percent of all new construction in Northern Ireland in 1994, reversing the trend toward greater concentration of NIHE housing. The downside of such private housing growth to city planners is that it occurs primarily outside Belfast city borders.

25. This is a firsthand account of a housing planner who participated in the consultation exercise. Identity withheld upon request.

Chapter 10. Urban Policy on Narrow Ground

1. In September 1996, an archaeological tunnel along the western wall of the Temple Mount was opened, setting off four days of violence in the West Bank, Gaza, and Jerusalem. Israeli officials and planners defended the tunnel's opening based on its expected benefits to tourists.

2. At the same time, Israel must increasingly deal with the spatial manifestations arising from *intra*-Jewish differences in demographic trajectories. Growth in the orthodox Jewish population in the city is requiring outward expansions of orthodox living areas and increasing conflicts over urban behavior between orthodox and secular Jews.

3. Examples of two-tier systems of metropolitan (county)-local governance in North America include Toronto, Dade County/Miami, and Minneapolis-St. Paul. In Europe, examples include Rijnmond and The Hague (Netherlands), Copenhagen (Denmark), Stockholm (Sweden), Frankfurt (Germany), Barcelona and Madrid (Spain), and Paris (Norton 1983).

4. The Greater London Council was created as a central authority that worked with fifty-two separately-elected borough governments from throughout the urban region. The boroughs had primary authority over

local services, the GLC authority over regional issues, with some powers concurrent or shared. Johannesburg (and other South African cities) have emphasized the metropolitan level of politics both as the focal point for local government transition negotiations and as a necessary element of postapartheid redistributive and reconstruction policies. The South African approach used metropolitanism as a means to integrate and transcend old local authority boundaries in order to eliminate their monoracial basis (Bollens 1998b; 1999). The metropolitan solution to contested sovereignty, in contrast, would retain, even create, single ethnic-dominant local governments as essential to the territorial and political expression of each side.

References

Abdulhadi, Rami S. 1990. "Land Use Planning in the Occupied Palestinian Territories." *Journal of Palestine Studies* 19 (4): 46–63.

Aberdach, Joel D., Robert D. Putnam, and Bert A. Rockman. 1981. *Bureaucrats and Politicians in Western Democracies*. Cambridge, Mass.: Harvard University Press.

Agnew, John, John Mercer, and David Sopher (eds.) 1984. *The City in Cultural Context*. Winchester, Mass.: Allen & Unwin.

Alexander, Ernest, Rachelle Alterman, and Hubert Law-Yone. 1983. "Evaluating Plan Implementation: The National Statutory Planning System in Israel." *Progress in Planning* 20, 2: 99–172.

Allport, G. W. 1954. *The Nature of Prejudice*. Cambridge, Mass.: Addison-Wesley.

Alpher, Joseph. 1994. *Settlements and Borders*. Study No. 3. Final Status Issues: Israel-Palestinians. Tel Aviv: Jaffee Center for Strategic Studies.

Alterman, Rachelle. 1992. "A Transatlantic View of Planning Education and Professional Practice." *Journal of Planning Education and Research* 12, 1: 39–54.

Akenson, Donald Harman. 1992. *God's Peoples: Covenant and Land in South Africa, Israel, and Ulster*. Ithaca: Cornell University Press.

Amiran, David H. K., Arie Shachar, and Israel Kimhi. 1973. *Urban Geography of Jerusalem: A Companion Volume to the Atlas of Jerusalem*. Berlin: Walter De Gruyter.

Amirav, Moshe. 1992. *Israel's Policy in Jerusalem Since 1967*. Working Paper Series No. 102. Center on Conflict and Negotiation. Stanford University.

Ardoyne/Oldpark Belfast Action Team. 1994. *Strategy Document 1994–97*. Belfast: MBW/BAT.

Arnstein, Sherry R. 1969. "A Ladder of Citizen Participation." *Journal of the American Institute of Planners* 35 (July): 216–224.

Ashkenasi, Abraham. 1990. *Opinion Trends among Jerusalem Palestinians*. Jerusalem: Leonard Davis Institute of International Relations. Hebrew University.

Ashkenasi, Abraham. 1988a. "Communal Policy, Conflict Management, and International Relations." *Jerusalem Journal of International Relations* 10, 2: 109–127.

Ashkenasi, Abraham. 1988b. *Israeli Policies and Palestinan Fragmentation: Political and Social Impacts in Israel and Jerusalem.* Leonard Davis Institute.

Azar, Edward E. 1991. "The Analysis and Management of Protracted Conflict." Pp. 93–120 in Volkan, Vamik D. , Joseph V. Montville, and Demetrios A. Julius (eds.) *The Psychodynamics of International Relationships. Volume II: Unofficial Diplomacy at Work.* Lexington, Mass.: Lexington Books.

Bahat, Dan (with Chaim T. Rubinstein). 1990. *The Illustrated Atlas of Jerusalem.* New York: Simon & Schuster.

Bailey, F. G. 1969. *Stratagems and Spoils: A Social Anthropology of Politics.* New York: Schocken Books.

Baskin, Gershon (ed.) 1994. "New Thinking on the Future of Jerusalem—A Model for the Future of Jerusalem: Scattered Sovereignty." Jerusalem: Israel/Palestine Center for Research and Information.

Baskin, Gershon, and Robin Twite (eds.) 1993. *The Future of Jerusalem. Proceedings of the First Israeli-Palestinian International Academic Seminar on the Future of Jerusalem.* Jerusalem: Israel/Palestine Center for Research and Information.

Beirne, Maggie. 1993. "Out of the Bearpit." *Fortnight* 317.

Belfast Areas of Special Social Need. 1977. Belfast: HMSO.

Bell, Desmond. 1987. "Acts of Union: Youth Subculture and Ethnic Diversity amongst Protestants in Northern Ireland." *British Journal of Sociology* 34, 3: 158–183.

Benvenisti, Meron S. 1996. *City of Stone: The Hidden History of Jerusalem.* Berkeley: University of California Press.

Benvenisti, Meron S. 1995. *Intimate Enemies: Jews and Arabs in a Shared Land.* Berkeley: University of California Press.

Benvenisti, Meron S. 1987a. Presentation at Salzburg Seminar #257. "Divided Cities." February 11. Salzburg, Austria.

Benvenisti, Meron S. 1987b. *The West Bank Data Base Project: 1987 Report—Demographic, Economic, Legal, Social, and Political Developments in the West Bank.* Jerusalem: WBDBP.

Benvenisti, Meron S. 1986a. *Conflicts and Contradictions.* New York: Villard Books.

Benvenisti, Meron S., et al. 1986b. *The West Bank Handbook: A Political Lexicon.* Jerusalem: Jerusalem Post.

Benvenisti, Meron S. 1985. *Land Alienation in the West Bank: A Legal and Spatial Analysis.* Jerusalem: WBDBP.

Benvenisti, Meron. 1984. *West Bank Data Base Project: A Survey of Israel's Policies.* Washington: American Enterprise Institute.

Benvenisti, Meron S. 1976. *Jerusalem: The Torn City*. Minneapolis: University of Minnesota Press.

Ben-Zadok, Efraim. 1987. "Incompatible Planning Goals: Evaluation of Israel's New Community Development in the West Bank." *Journal of the American Planning Association* 53 (3): 337–347.

Berry, Brian. 1989. *Theories of Justice*. London: Harvester-Wheatsheaf.

Bilski, Raphaella, Itzhak Galnoor, Dan Inbar, Yohahan Manor, and Gabriel Sheffer. 1980. *Can Planning Replace Politics? The Israeli Experience*. The Hague: Martinus Nijhoff.

Bilski, Raphaella, and Itzhak Galnoor. 1980. "Ideologies and Values in National Planning." Pp. 77–98 in Bilski, Raphaella, Itzhak Galnoor, Dan Inbar, Yohahan Manor, and Gabriel Sheffer. 1980. *Can Planning Replace Politics? The Israeli Experience*. The Hague: Martinus Nijhoff.

Birrell, Derek, and Carol Wilson. 1993. "'Making Belfast Work': An Evaluation of an Urban Strategy." *Administration* 41, 1: 40–56.

Blackman, Tim. 1991. *Planning Belfast: A Case Study of Public Policy and Community Action*. Aldershot, U.K.: Avebury.

Boal, Frederick W. 1996. "Exclusion and Inclusion: Segregation and Deprivation in Belfast." In Musterd, Sako, and Herman van der Wusten (eds.) *Segregation and Exclusion in Western Metropolitan Areas*. London: Routledge.

Boal, Frederick W. 1995. *Shaping a City: Belfast in the Late Twentieth Century*. Belfast: Queen's University, Institute of Irish Studies.

Boal, Frederick W. 1994. "Belfast: A City on Edge." In Clout, Hugh (ed.) *Europe's Cities in the Late Twentieth Century*. Amsterdam: Royal Dutch Geographical Society.

Boal, Frederick W. 1990. "Belfast: Hindsight on Foresight-Planning in an Unstable Environment." Pp. 4–14 in Doherty, P. (ed.). *Geographical Perspectives on the Belfast Region*. Newtownabbey, NI: Geographical Society of Ireland.

Boal, Frederick W. 1982. "Segregating and Mixing: Space and Residence in Belfast." Pp. 249–280 in Boal, Frederick W., and J. Neville Douglas (eds.). *Integration and Division: Geographical Perspectives on the Northern Ireland Problem*. London: Academic Press.

Boal, Frederick W. 1971. "Territoriality and Class: A Study of Two Residential Areas in Belfast." *Irish Geography* 6, 3: 229–248.

Boal, Frederick W. 1969. "Territoriality on the Shankill-Falls Divide, Belfast." *Irish Geography* 6, 1: 30–50.

Boal, Frederick W., and J. Neville Douglas (eds.). 1982. *Integration and Division: Geographical Perspectives on the Northern Ireland Problem*. London: Academic Press.

Boal, Frederick W., P. Doherty, and D. G. Pringle. 1974. *The Spatial Distribution of Some Social Problems in the Belfast Urban Area*. Belfast: Northern Ireland Community Relations Commission.

Bollens, Scott. 1999. *Urban Peace-Building in Divided Societies: Belfast and Johannesburg*. Boulder and Oxford, U.K.: Westview Press.

Bollens, Scott. 1998a. "Urban Policy in Ethnically Polarized Societies." *International Political Science Review* 19, 2: 187–215.

Bollens, Scott. 1998b. "Urban Planning Amidst Ethnic Conflict: Jerusalem and Johannesburg." *Urban Studies* 35, 4: 729–750.

Bradley, Colm. 1993. *Resourcing Local Community Development*. Belfast: NICVA, NIVT, and Resource Centers.

Breen, R., and B. Miller. 1993. "A Socio-Economic Profile of the Making Belfast Work Area." Belfast: MBW.

Brogan, P. 1990. *The Fighting Never Stopped: A Comprehensive Guide to World Conflict Since 1945*. New York: Vintage.

Brown, Michael E. 1993. "Causes and Implications of Ethnic Conflict." Pp. 3–26 in Brown, Michael E. (ed.) *Ethnic Conflict and International Security*. Princeton: Princeton University Press.

Brown, S. 1985. "City Centre Commercial Revitalization: The Belfast Experience." *Planner* (June): 9–12.

Buckley, Anthony D., and Rhonda Paisley. 1994. *Symbols*. Belfast: Community Relations Council, Cultural Traditions Group.

B'Tselem. 1995. *A Policy of Discrimination: Land Expropriation, Planning, and Building in East Jerusalem*. Jerusalem: B'Tselem—The Israeli Information Center for Human Rights in the Occupied Territories.

Budge, Ian, and Cornelius O'Leary. 1973. *Belfast: Approach to Crisis, A Study of Belfast Politics 1613–1970*. London: Macmillan.

Building Design Partnership. 1969. *Belfast Urban Area Plan*. Belfast: BDP.

Burton, John W. 1991. "Conflict Resolution as a Political System." Pp. 71–92 in Volkan, Vamik D., Joseph V. Montville, and Demetrios A. Julius. *The Psychodynamics of International Relationships. Volume II*. Lexington, Mass.: D.C. Heath.

Burton, John W. (ed.) 1990. *Conflict: Human Needs Theory*. New York: St. Martin's.

Carmichael, Stokely, and Calvin V. Hamilton. 1967. *Black Power: The Politics of Liberation in America*. New York: Random House.

Cebulla, Andreas. 1994. *Urban Policy in Belfast: An Evaluation of Department of Environment's Physical Regeneration Initiatives*. Belfast: Department of the Environment for Northern Ireland, Central Statistics and Research Branch.

Center for Engineering and Planning. 1992. *Master Planning the State of Palestine: Suggested Guidelines for Comprehensive Development*. Ramallah, West Bank: CEP.

Center for Engineering and Planning. 1988. *Land Use and Master Planning Schemes for Towns and Villages in the West Bank*. Status Report. Ramallah: CEP

Central Community Relations Unit, Northern Ireland Office. 1995. *Community Relations Research Strategy 1995–1997*. 2nd edition. Belfast: CCRU.

Cheshin, Amir. 1992. "East Jerusalem—Policy vs. Reality." In Layish, Aharon (ed.) *The Arabs in Jerusalem*. Jerusalem: Magnes Press. Hebrew language.

Clark, W. A. V., and Eric G. Moore. 1980. *Residential Mobility and Public Policy*. Urban Affairs Annual Reviews volume 19. Newbury Park, Cal.: Sage.

Clarke, R. V. 1992. *Statistical Crime Prevention: Successful Case Studies*. New York: Harrow and Heston.

Coakley, John. 1993. "Introduction: The Territorial Management of Ethnic Conflict." Pp. 1–22 in Coakley, John (ed.) *The Territorial Management of Ethnic Conflict*. London: Frank Cass.

Coakley, John. 1992. "The Resolution of Ethnic Conflict: Towards a Typology." *International Political Science Review* 13, 4: 343–358.

Cohen, Ronald. 1978. "Ethnicity: Problem and Focus in Anthropology." *Annual Review of Anthropology* 7: 379–405.

Cohen, Stanley, and Daphna Golan. 1991. *The Interrogation of Palestinians During the Intifada: Ill Treatment, "Moderate Physical Pressure," or Torture*. Jerusalem: B'Tselem.

Community Development Centre, North Belfast. 1994. *Annual Report 1993–94*. Belfast: CRCNB.

Community Planning Weekend. Shankill, Belfast. 3–6 February 1995. Shankill Leisure Centre.

Compton, Paul, and John F. Power. 1986. "Estimates of the Religious Composition of Northern Ireland Local Government Districts in 1981 and Change in the Geographical Pattern of Religious Composition Between 1971 and 1981." *Economic and Social Review* 17, 2: 87–105.

Coon, Anthony. 1992. *Town Planning Under Military Occupation: An Examination of the Law and Practice of Town Planning in the West Bank*. Aldershot, U.K.: Dartmouth.

Cowan, C. 1982. "Belfast's Hidden Planners." *Town and Country Planning* 51, 6: 163–167.

Cropper, Stephen A. 1982. "Theory and Strategy in the Study of Planning Processes—The Uses of the Case Study." *Environment and Planning B*. 9: 341–357.

Cullen, Kevin. 1991. "Democracy Undone at Belfast City Council," *The Boston Globe*. May 4.

Daniszewski, John. 1996. "Israel to Let Settlements Grow in W. Bank, Gaza." *Los Angeles Times*. August 3, p. 1.

Darby, John. 1986. *Intimidation and Control of Conflict in Northern Ireland*. Dublin: Gill and Macmillan.

Davidoff, Paul. 1965. "Advocacy and Pluralism in Planning." *Journal of the American Institute of Planners* 31: 596–615.

Davis, Mike. 1990. *City of Quartz: Excavating the Future in Los Angeles.* New York: Vintage.

Dawson, G. M. 1984. "Planning in Belfast." *Irish Geography* 17: 27–41.

Dear, Michael, and Allen J. Scott (eds.) 1981. *Urbanization anu Urban Planning in Capitalist Society.* London: Methuen.

de Jong, Jan. 1994a. "What Remains? Palestine After Oslo." *News from Within* 10, 12: 3–14. Newsletter of the Alternative Information Center, Jerusalem.

de Jong, Jan. 1994b. "The Secret Map of Non-negotiable Jerusalem." *Challenge*, no. 28 (November–December).

Department of Economic Development (Northern Ireland). 1989. *Fair Employment in Northern Ireland: Code of Practice.* Belfast: DED.

Department of the Environment for Northern Ireland. 1995. *Making Belfast Work: Strategy Statement.* March. Belfast: MBW.

Department of the Environment for Northern Ireland. 1994a. *Belfast Residents Survey.* Belfast: DOENI.

Department of the Environment for Northern Ireland. 1994b. *Planning Bulletin.* DOENI: Town and Country Planning Service. Issue 4.

Department of the Environment for Northern Ireland. 1994c. *Making Belfast Work: Strategy Proposals.* April. Belfast: MBW.

Department of the Environment for Northern Ireland. 1993a. *Integrated Regeneration Strategy for Belfast.* Belfast: DOENI. (AU: Ester Christie and Bill Morrison.)

Department of the Environment for Northern Ireland. Department of Education. 1993b. *Springvale: Development of a Campus for the University of Ulster, Belfast.* Preliminary Evaluation. Private/confidential. April.

Department of the Environment for Northern Ireland. 1992a. *North Belfast Strategic Review.* Belfast: DOENI. Unpublished and confidential.

Department of the Environment for Northern Ireland. 1992b. *Development Scheme C.D.A. 110: Springvale.* Belfast: DOENI.

Department of the Environment for Northern Ireland. 1990a. *Belfast Urban Area Plan 2001.* Belfast: HMSO.

Department of the Environment for Northern Ireland. 1990b. Belfast Development Office. *Northgate Enterprise Park: A Development Concept for Inner North Belfast.* Interim Report. Unpublished. Internal circulation only.

Department of the Environment for Northern Ireland. 1989. *Belfast Urban Area Plan 2001: Adoption Statement.* Belfast: HMSO.

Department of the Environment for Northern Ireland. 1988. "Pre-Inquiry Response to CTA's Objections to the Draft BUAP." Pp. 187–221 in Blackman, Tim. 1991. *Planning Belfast: A Case Study of Public Policy and Community Action.* Aldershot, U.K.: Avebury.

Department of the Environment for Northern Ireland. 1987. *Belfast Urban Area Plan 2001. Draft.* Belfast: Her Majesty's Stationery Office (HMSO).

Department of the Environment for Northern Ireland. 1977. *Northern Ireland: Regional Physical Development Strategy 1975–95*. Belfast: HMSO.

Douglas, J. Neville. 1982. "Northern Ireland: Spatial Frameworks and Community Relations." Pp. 105–135 in Boal, Frederick W., and J. Neville Douglas (eds.). *Integration and Division: Geographical Perspectives on the Northern Ireland Problem*. London: Academic Press.

Douglas, J. Neville, and Frederick W. Boal. 1982. "The Northern Ireland Problem." Pp. 1–18 in Boal, Frederick W., and J. Neville Douglas (eds.). *Integration and Division: Geographical Perspectives on the Northern Ireland Problem*. London: Academic Press.

Dror, Yehezkel. 1989. *A Grand Strategy for Israel*. Jerusalem: Akademon.

Dumper, Michael. 1997. *The Politics of Jerusalem Since 1967*. New York: Columbia University Press.

Efrat, Elisha, and Allen G. Noble. 1988. "Problems of Reunified Jerusalem." *Cities* 5 (4): 326–332.

Efrat, Elisha. 1988. *Geography and Politics in Israel Since 1967*. London: Frank Cass.

Elazar, Daniel J. 1980. "Local Government for Heterogeneous Populations: Some Options for Jerusalem." Pp. 208–228 in Kraemer, Joel L. (ed.). *Jerusalem: Problems and Prospects*. New York: Praeger.

Elon, Amos. 1989. *Jerusalem: City of Mirrors*. Boston: Little, Brown and Company.

Environmental Design Consultants. 1991. *Belfast Peacelines Study*. Prepared for the Belfast Development Office. In conjunction with the Northern Ireland Housing Executive.

Eriksen, Thomas H. 1993. *Ethnicity and Nationalism*. London: Pluto Press.

Esman, M. J. 1985. "Two Dimensions of Ethnic Politics: Defence of Homeland and Immigrant Rights." *Ethnic and Racial Studies* 8: 438–441.

Esman, M. J. 1973. "The Management of Communal Conflict." *Public Policy* 21, 1: 49–78.

Esman, Milton J., and Shibley Telhami (eds.) 1995. *International Organizations and Ethnic Conflict*. Ithaca: Cornell University Press.

Etzioni, Amitai. 1968. *The Active Society: A Theory of Societal and Political Processes*. New York: Free Press.

Eversley, David. 1989. *Religion and Employment in Northern Ireland*. London: Sage.

Eversley, David, and Valerie Herr. 1985. *The Roman Catholic Population of Northern Ireland in 1981: A Revised Estimate*. Belfast: Fair Employment Agency.

Fair Employment Commission (Northern Ireland.) 1993. *Summary of the 1992 Monitoring Returns*. Commission.

Feldman, Allen. 1991. *Formations of Violence: The Narrative of the Body and Political Terror in Northern Ireland*. Chicago: University of Chicago Press.

Fisher, Ronald J. 1990. *The Social Psychology of Intergroup and International Conflict Management*. New York: Springer-Verlag.

Fitzduff, Mari. 1993. *Approaches to Community Relations Work*. 3rd edition. Belfast: NI Community Relations Council.

Forester, John. 1989. *Planning in the Face of Power*. Berkeley: University of California Press.

Frazer, Hugh, and Mari Fitzduff. 1994. *Improving Community Relations*. 3rd edition. Belfast: NI Community Relations Council.

Friedland, Roger, and Richard Hecht. 1996. *To Rule Jerusalem*. Cambridge: Cambridge University Press.

Friedmann, John. 1992. *Empowerment: The Politics of Alternative Development*. Cambridge, Mass.: Blackwell.

Friedmann, John. 1987. *Planning in the Public Domain*. Princeton: Princeton University Press.

Friedman, Steven. 1991. "An Unlikely Utopia: State and Civil Society in South Africa." *Politikon: South African Journal of Political Studies* 19, 1: 5–19.

Gabbay, Shoshana. 1994. *The Environment in Israel*. Jerusalem: Israel Ministry of the Environment.

Gaffikin, F., S. Mooney, and M. Morrissey. "Planning for a Change in Belfast: The Urban Economy, Urban Regeneration, and the Belfast Urban Area Plan 1988." 1991. *Town Planning Review* 62, 4: 415–430.

Gaffikin, Frank, and Mike Morrissey. 1990. "Dependency, Decline, and Development: The Case of West Belfast." *Policy and Politics* 18, 2: 105–117.

Gibbs, J. 1989. "Conceptualization of Terrorism." *American Sociological Review* 54: 329–340.

Gilbert, Paul. 1994. *Terrorism, Security, and Nationality: An Introductory Study in Applied Political Philosophy*. London: Routledge.

Gladdish, K. R. 1979. "The Political Dynamics of Cultural Minorities." In Alcock, Antony E., Brian K. Taylor, and John M. Welton (eds.) *The Future of Cultural Minorities*. London: MacMillan Press.

Goldsmith, William W., and Edward J. Blakely. 1992. *Separate Societies: Poverty and Inequality in U.S. Cities*. Philadelphia: Temple University Press.

Goldstein, Arnold P. 1994. *The Ecology of Aggression*. New York: Plenum Press.

Gorecki, Paul K. 1995. "Economic Implications of Peace." Paper presented at INCORE seminar, Belfast, February.

Grant, Joanne (ed.) 1968. *Black Protest*. New York: Fawcett World Library.

The Guardian (London: newspaper). February 13, 1995.

Guinier, Lani. 1994. *The Tyranny of the Majority: Fundamental Fairness in Representative Democracy*. New York: Free Press.

Gurr, Ted R. 1993. "Why Minorities Rebel: A Global Analysis of Communal Mobilization and Conflict Since 1945." *International Political Science Review* 14, 1: 161–201.

Gurr, Ted R. 1970. *Why Men Rebel*. Princeton: Princeton University Press.

Gurr, Ted R. 1968. "A Causal Model of Civil Strife: A Comparative Analysis Using New Indices." *American Political Science Review* 62: 1104–1124.

Gurr, Ted R., and Barbara Harff. 1994. *Ethnic Conflict in World Politics*. Boulder: Westview Press.

Gurr, Ted R., and M. Lichbach. 1986. "Forecasting Internal Conflict." *Comparative Political Studies* 9: 3–38.

Gutmann, Emanuel, and Claude Klein. 1980. "The Institutional Structure of Heterogeneous Cities: Brussels, Montreal, and Belfast." Pp. 178–207 in Kraemer, Joel L. (ed.) *Jerusalem: Problems and Prospects*. New York: Praeger.

Habitat International Coalition and the Palestine Human Rights Information Center. 1994. *The Palestinians' Right to Adequate Housing in East Jerusalem*. Expanded Version of NGO Written Statement for Agenda Item 8. UN Sub-Commission on the Prevention of Discrimination and the Protection of Minorities. 46th session. August.

Hadfield, Brigid. 1992. "The Northern Ireland Constitution." Pp. 1–12 in Hadfield, Brigid (ed.) *Northern Ireland: Politics and Constitution*. Buckingham: Open University Press.

Harb, Ahmed. 1994. "How Shall I Speak About Palestine?" *Birzeit University Newsletter* Number 25 (June), 10.

Harvey, David. 1973. *Social Justice and the City*. London: Edward Arnold.

Harvey, David. 1978. "On Planning the Ideology of Planning." Pp. 213–234 in Burchell, Robert W., and George Sternlieb (eds.) *Planning Theory in the 1980s: A Search for Future Directions*. New Brunswick, N.J.: Center for Urban Policy Research, Rutgers University.

Hasson, Shlomo. 1993. *Urban Social Movements in Jerusalem: The Protest of the Second Generation*. Albany: State University of New York Press.

Hasson, Shlomo, and Simon Kouba. 1994. "Local Politics in Jerusalem." Unpublished. Hebrew University: Department of Geography.

Heady, Ferrel. 1996. *Public Administration: A Comparative Perspective*. Fifth Edition. New York: Marcel Dekker.

Heller, Mark A., and Sari Nusseibeh. 1991. *No Trumpets, No Drums: A Two-State Settlement of the Israeli-Palestinian Conflict*. New York: Hill and Wang.

Hendry, John. 1989. "The Control of Development and the Origins of Planning in Northern Ireland." In Michael J. Bannon (ed.) *Planning: The Irish Experience 1920–1988*. Dublin: Wolfhound Press.

Hill, Moshe. 1980. "Urban and Regional Planning in Israel." Pp. 259–282 in Bilski, R. (ed.) *Can Planning Replace Politics? The Israeli Experience*. The Hague: Martinus Nijhoff.

Hillyard, P. 1983. "Law and Order." In J. Darby. *Northern Ireland: The Background to the Conflict*. Belfast: Appletree.

Hoffman, B. 1992. "Current Research on Terrorism and Low-Intensity Conflict." *Studies in Conflict and Terrorism* 15: 25–37.

Horowitz, Donald L. 1985. *Ethnic Groups in Conflict*. Berkeley: University of California Press.

Human Rights Watch. 1993a. *World Report*.

Human Rights Watch. 1993b. *A License to Kill: Israeli Operations against "Wanted" and Masked Palestinians*. New York: Middle East Watch.

Hutman, Bill. 1992. "At Least 10,000 Palestinians Live in Jerusalem Illegally." *Jerusalem Post: International Edition*. May 9, p. 5.

Hyman, Benjamin, Israel Kimhi, and Joseph Savitzky. 1985. *Jerusalem in Transition: Urban Growth and Change 1970's–1980's*. Jerusalem: Jerusalem Institute for Israel Studies and Institute of Urban and Regional Studies, Hebrew University of Jerusalem.

INCORE (Initiative on Conflict Resolution and Ethnicity.) 1995. *Program Information*. University of Ulster at Coleraine (Northern Ireland) and The United Nations University.

The Independent on Sunday (London: newspaper). March 21, 1993.

Innes, Judith E. 1992. "Group Processes and the Social Construction of Growth Management." *Journal of the American Planning Association* 58, 4: 440–453.

International Labour Office. 1977. *Meeting Basic Needs: Strategies for Eradicating Mass Poverty and Unemployment*. Geneva: ILO.

Isaac, Stephen. 1971. *Handbook in Research and Evaluation*. San Diego: EdITS Publishers.

Israel, State of. 1989. *Israel Lands Administration*. Jerusalem: ILA.

Israel, State of. Central Bureau of Statistics. 1984. *Census of Population and Housing 1983*. Jerusalem: CBS.

Jerusalem Municipality. 1997. *Statistical Yearbook 1996*. Jerusalem: The Jerusalem Institute for Israel Studies.

Jerusalem Municipality. 1994a. *Statistical Yearbook 1992*. Jerusalem: The Jerusalem Institute for Israel Studies. No. 11.

Jerusalem Municipality. 1994b. *East Jerusalem: Conflicts and Dilemmas— Urban Coping in the East of the City*. Prepared by Sarah Hershkovitz. Background Information for Lecture Day. April.

Jerusalem Municipality. 1994c. *Background Material for Discussion by the Ministerial Committee for Jerusalem Affairs*. 13 pp. unpublished.

Jerusalem Municipality. 1994d. *Municipality Services in the Arab Sector: Analysis of Needs and Solutions*. 4th draft. November 1994.

Jerusalem Municipality. 1986. *Development Plan for the Arab Sector*. City Planning Department, Planning Policy Section, Transportation Master Plan, Greater Jerusalem.

Jerusalem Municipality. 1984. *Statistical Yearbook*. Jerusalem: The Jerusalem Institute for Israel Studies.

Jerusalem Municipality. 1981. *The "Seam" Area: Planning Guidelines.* Jerusalem: Town Planning Department. Policy Planning Section.

Jerusalem Marketing Group. 1994. *Israel Business and Government Directory.* Jerusalem: JMG.

Kaminker, Sarah. 1995. "East Jerusalem: A Case Study in Political Planning." *Palestine-Israel Journal* 2, 2: 59–66.

Keane, Margaret C. 1990. "Segregation Processes in Public Sector Housing." Pp. 88–108 in Doherty, P. (ed.) *Geographical Perspectives on the Belfast Region.* Newtownabbey, NI: Geographical Society of Ireland.

Keating, M. 1988. *State and Regional Nationalism.* New York: Harvester and Wheatsheaf.

Keinon, Herb. 1997. "Heart of the Matter." *Jerusalem Post International Edition*, March 1, p. 8.

Kelman, Herbert C. 1990. "Applying a Human Needs Perspective to the Practice of Conflict Resolution: The Israeli-Palestinian Case." Pp. 283–297 in Burton, John W. (ed.) *Conflict: Human Needs Theory.* New York: St. Martins.

Kelman, Herbert C., and Stephen P. Cohen. 1976. "The Problem-Solving Workshop: A Social Psychological Contribution to the Resolution of International Conflicts." *Journal of Peace Research* 13, 2: 79–90.

Khalidi, Walid. 1993. *All That Remains: The Palestinian Villages Occupied and Depopulated by Israel in 1948.* Institute of Palestine Studies.

Kiernan, M. J. 1983. "Ideology, Politics, and Planning: Reflections on Theory and Practice of Urban Planning." *Environment and Planning B: Planning and Design* 10: 71–87.

Kimhi, Israel, and Benjamin Hyman. 1980. "Demographic and Economic Developments in Jerusalem Since 1967." In Kraemer, Joel L. (ed.) *Jerusalem: Problems and Prospects.* New York: Praeger.

Kimmerling, Baruch. 1983. *Zionism and Territory: The Socio-Territorial Dimensions of Zionist Politics.* Berkeley: Institute of International Studies, University of California.

Knaap, Gerrit, and Arthur C. Nelson. 1992. *The Regulated Landscape.* Cambridge, Mass.: Lincoln Institute of Land Policy.

Knox, Colin, and Joanne Hughes. 1994. "Equality and Equity: An Emerging Government Policy in Northern Ireland." *New Community* 20, 2: 207–225.

Korten, David C. 1980. "Community Organization and Rural Development: A Learning Process Approach." *Public Administration Review* 40, 5: 480–511.

Korten, David C. 1990. *Getting to the 21st Century: Voluntary Action and the Global Agenda.* West Hartford, Conn.: Kumarian.

Krishnarayan, V., and H. Thomas. 1993. *Ethnic Minorities and the Planning System.* London: Royal Town Planning Institute.

Krystall, Nathan. 1994. "Who Has the Right to Live There?" *News from Within* 10.7 (July): 9–13. Jerusalem: Alternative Information Center.

Krystall, Nathan. 1993. *Urgent Issues of Palestinian Residency in Jerusalem.* Jerusalem: Alternative Information Center.

Krumholz, Norman, and John Forester. 1990. *Making Equity Planning Work: Leadership in the Public Sector.* Philadelphia: Temple University Press.

Kubersky Committee of the Ministry of Interior of Investigating the Annexation of Territory East of Jerusalem. *Report of the Kubersky Committee.* 1992.

Kutcher, Arthur. 1975. *The New Jerusalem: Planning and Politics.* Cambridge, Mass.: M.I.T. Press.

Lapidoth, Ruth. 1992. "Sovereignty in Transition." *Journal of International Affairs* 45, 2: 325–345.

Lapidoth, Ruth, and Moshe Hirsch (eds.) 1994. *The Jerusalem Question and its Resolution: Selected Documents.* Dordrecht: Martinus Nijhoff.

Larson, Richard C., and Amadeo R. Odoni. 1981. *Urban Operations Research.* Englewood Cliffs, N.J.: Prentice-Hall.

Layish, Aharon (ed.) 1992. *The Arabs in Jerusalem: From the Late Ottoman Period to the Beginning of the 1990s—Religious, Social, and Cultural Distinctiveness.* Jerusalem: Magnes Press.

Levine, Marc V. 1990. *The Reconquest of Montreal: Language Policy and Social Change in a Bilingual City.* Philadelphia: Temple University Press.

Lijphart, Arend. 1977. *Democracy in Plural Societies: A Comparative Exploration.* New Haven: Yale University Press.

Lijphart, Arend. 1968. *The Politics of Accommodation: Pluralism and Democracy in the Netherlands.* Berkeley: University of California Press.

Livingstone, Stephen, and John Morison. 1995. "An Audit of Democracy in Northern Ireland." *Fortnight* 337 (supplement).

Longland, Tony. 1994. "Development in Conflict Situations: The Occupied Territories." *Community Development Journal* 29, 2: 132–140.

Loughlin, John. 1992. "Administering Policy in Northern Ireland." Pp. 60–75 in Hadfield, Brigid (ed.). *Northern Ireland: Politics and Constitution.* Buckingham: Open University Press.

Lovett, Tom, Deirdre Gunn, Terry Robson. 1994. "Education, Conflict and Community Development in Northern Ireland." *Community Development Journal* 29, 2: 177–186.

Lustick, I. 1979. "Stability in Deeply Divided Societies: Consociationalisation vs. Control." *World Politics* 31: 325–344.

McAdam, Doug, John D. McCarthy, and Mayer N. Zald. 1996. "Opportunities, Mobilizing Structures, and Framing Processes—Toward a Synthetic, Comparative Perspective on Social Movements." Pp. 1–20 in McAdam, Doug, John D. McCarthy, and Mayer N. Zald (ed.) *Comparative Perspectives on Social Movements.* Cambridge: Cambridge University Press.

McGarry, John, and Brendan O'Leary (eds.) *The Politics of Ethnic Conflict Resolution: Case Studies of Protracted Ethnic Conflicts.* London: Routledge.

McGivern, William. 1983. "Housing Development and Sectarian Interface Areas." In Murtagh, Brendan (ed.) *Planning and Ethnic Space in Belfast*. Occasional Paper No. 5. Centre for Policy Research. University of Ulster.

Masser, Ian. 1986. "Some Methodological Considerations." In Masser, Ian, and Richard Williams (eds.) *Learning From Other Countries: The Cross-National Dimension in Urban Policy-Making*. Norwich, U.K.: Geo.

Matar, Ibrahim. undated. "To Whom Does Jerusalem Belong?" Published in *Biladi: The Jerusalem Times*.

Matar, Ibrahim. 1983. "From Palestinian to Israeli: Jerusalem 1948–1982." *Journal of Palestine Studies* 12, 4 (summer).

Matthew, Sir R. H. 1964. *Belfast Regional Survey and Plan 1962*. Belfast: HMSO.

Matusow, Allen J. 1984. *The Unraveling of America: A History of Liberalism in the 1960s*. New York: Harper and Row.

Mayer, Robert R., and Ernest Greenwood. 1980. *The Design of Social Policy Research*. Englewood Cliffs, N.J.: Prentice-Hall.

Mazor, Adam, and Shermiyahu Cohen. 1994. *Metropolitan Jerusalem: Master Plan and Development Plan. Summary Document*. June.

Mazor, Adam, and Oren Yiftachel. 1992. "Israel 2020: A Long-Range Master Plan for Israel." In Golani, Yehonathan, Sofia Eldor, and Meir Garon (eds.) *Planning and Housing in Israel in the Wake of Rapid Changes*. Jerusalem: Ministry of Interior and Ministry of Construction and Housing.

Meehan, Maureen. 1996. "By-Pass Roads Destroy Hopes for Future Palestinian Autonomy." *Washington Report on Middle East Affairs* 14, 8: 8.

Ministry of Construction and Housing. Israel. 1992. *A City in Modiin*. Jerusalem: Ministry.

Mooney, S., and Gaffikin, F. 1987. *Belfast Urban Area Plan 1987: Reshaping Space and Society*. Belfast: Centre for the Unemployed.

Morley, David, and Arie Shachar. 1986. "Epilogue: Reflections by Planners on Planning." In Morley, David, and Arie Shachar (eds.) *Planning in Turbulence*. Jerusalem: Magnes Press, Hebrew University.

Murphy, A. B. 1989. "Territorial Policies in Multiethnic States." *Geographical Review* 79: 410–421.

Murray, Michael. 1991. *The Politics and Pragmatism of Urban Containment: Belfast Since 1940*. Aldershot, U.K.: Avebury.

Murtagh, Brendan. 1994a. *Ethnic Space and the Challenge to Land Use Planning: A Study of Belfast's Peace Lines*. University of Ulster, Jordanstown. Centre for Policy Research.

Murtagh, Brendan. 1994b. *Land Use Planning and Community Relations*. A report to the Northern Ireland Community Relations Council. University of Ulster.

Murtagh, Brendan. 1993. "The Role of the Security Forces and Peace Line Planning." In Murtagh, Brendan (ed.). *Planning and Ethnic Space in*

Belfast. Occasional Paper No. 5. Centre for Policy Research. University of Ulster.

National Advisory Commission on Civil Disorders. United States. 1968. *The Kerner Report*. New York: Bantam Books.

Neff, Donald. 1993. "Jerusalem in U.S. Policy." *Journal of Palestine Studies* 13, 1: 20–45.

Nelson, Arthur C., and James B. Duncan. 1995. *Growth Management Principles and Practices*. Chicago: American Planning Association.

Newman, O. 1975. *Design Guidelines for Creating Defensible Space*. Washington, D.C.: U.S. Government Printing Office.

Nordlinger, Eric A. 1972. *Conflict Regulation in Divided Societies*. Boston: Center for International Affairs, Harvard University.

Northern Ireland Census 1991: Belfast Urban Area Report. Belfast: HMSO.

Northern Ireland Community Relations Council. 1994a. *Fourth Report*. Belfast: NICRC.

Northern Ireland Community Relations Council. 1994b. *Symbols*. Belfast: NICRC, Cultural Traditions Group.

Northern Ireland Council for Voluntary Action. 1994. *The Implementation of Targeting Social Need*. Belfast: NICVA (Public Affairs Project).

Northern Ireland Council for Voluntary Action. 1993. *Twenty Years of Deprivation: A Comparative Analysis of Deprivation in the Belfast Urban Area Using Census Findings Published in 1991, 1981, and 1971*. Belfast: NICVA (Public Affairs Project).

Northern Ireland Housing Executive. Belfast Division. 1995. *Belfast Housing Strategy Review*. Belfast: NIHE.

Northern Ireland Housing Executive. 1994a. *Integration / Segregation: Preliminary Views and Approach*. Housing Policy Review Paper. Belfast: Integration/Segregation Group (NIHE).

Northern Ireland Housing Executive. 1994b. *Annual Report* April 1993–March 1994. Belfast: NIHE.

Northern Ireland Housing Executive. 1991. *Building a Better Belfast*. Belfast: NIHE.

Northern Ireland Housing Executive. 1990a. *The Housing Selection Scheme: Applying for a Housing Executive Home*. Belfast: NIHE.

Northern Ireland Housing Executive. 1990b. *Alliance North Belfast: A Case for Action*. Belfast: NIHE.

Northern Ireland Housing Executive. 1988. *Coping With Conflict: Violence and Urban Renewal in Belfast*. Belfast: NIHE.

Norton, Alan. 1983. "The Government and Administration of Metropolitan Areas in Western Democracies: A Survey of Approaches to the Administrative Problems of Major Conurbations in Europe and Canada." Birmingham, England: Institute of Government Studies, University of Birmingham.

O'Connor, James. 1973. *The Fiscal Crisis of the State*. New York: St. Martin's.

O'Connor, Robert. 1988. "Dateline Belfast: Government Officials Are Hoping That a New Plan Will Help Heal the City's Wounds." *Planning* 54, 10: 27–32.

O'Leary, Brendan, and John McGarry. 1995. "Regulating Nations and Ethnic Communities." Pp. 245–289 in Breton, A., G. Galeotti, P. Salmon and R. Wintrobe (eds.) *Nationalism and Rationality*. Cambridge: Cambridge University Press.

Osborne, Robert D., and Dale Singleton. 1982. "Political Processes and Behavior." Pp. 167–194 in Boal, Frederick W., and J. Neville Douglas (eds.) *Integration and Division: Geographical Perspectives on the Northern Ireland Problem*. London: Academic Press.

Palestine Human Rights Information Center. 1994a. *Recreating East Jerusalem*. Jerusalem: PHRIC. Written by Alison Brown and Jan de Jong.

Palestine Human Rights Information Center. 1994b. *Clever Concealment: Jewish Settlement in the Occupied Territories under the Rabin Government: August 1992–September 1993*. Jerusalem: PHRIC.

Palestinian Academic Society for the Study of International Affairs. 1995. *Diary (Calendar)*. Jerusalem: PASSIA.

Palestinian Academic Society for the Study of International Affairs. 1993a. *The Occupied Palestinian Territory*. Jerusalem: PASSIA.

Palestinian Academic Society for the Study of International Affairs. 1993b. *Annual Report*. Jerusalem: PASSIA.

Palestinian Central Bureau of Statistics. 1998. *Palestinian Population, Housing and Establishment Census—1997*. Web = www.pcbs.org.

Palestinian Economic Council for Development and Reconstruction. 1994. *Palestinian Emergency Development Program: The West Bank and Gaza Strip—A Brief Economic Overview*. A-Ram, West Bank: PECDAR.

Palestinian National Authority. 1995. *Judaization of Jerusalem: Facts and Figures*. Jerusalem: PNA Ministry of Information.

Palley, Claire. 1979. *Constitutional Law and Minorities*. London: Minority Rights Group.

Partrick, Neil. 1994. "Democracy Under Limited Autonomy." *News from Within* 10, 9: 21–24. Jerusalem: Alternative Information Center (newsletter).

Peace Now. 1997. *Settlement Watch—Report No. 9*. www.peace_now.org.

Pesic, Vesna. 1996. *Serbian Nationalism and the Origins of the Yugoslav Crisis*. Peaceworks paper no. 8. Washington, D.C.: United States Institute of Peace.

Polikoff, Alexander. 1986. "Sustainable Integration or Inevitable Resegregation: The Troubling Questions." In Goering, John M. (ed.) *Housing De-*

segregation and Federal Policy. Chapel Hill: University of North Carolina Press.

Poole, Michael. 1990. "The Geographical Location of Political Violence in Northern Ireland." Pp. 64–82 in Darby, John, Nicholas Dodge, and A. C. Hepburn (eds.) *Political Violence: Ireland in a Comparative Perspective.* Ottawa: University of Ottawa Press.

Project on Managing Political Disputes. 1993. *Practicing Conflict Resolution in Divided Societies.* Jerusalem: Leonard Davis Institute, Hebrew University.

Przeworski, Adam, and Henry Teune. 1970. *The Logic of Comparative Social Inquiry.* New York: Wiley.

Rawls, John. 1971. *A Theory of Justice.* Cambridge, Mass.: Harvard University Press.

Redpath, Jackie. 1991. "Power and the Protestant Community." In *Community Development in Protestant Areas: A Report on Two Seminars.* Belfast: Northern Ireland Community Relations Council.

Robson, Brian, Michael Bradford, and Iain Deas. 1994. *Relative Deprivation in Northern Ireland.* Policy, Planning and Research Unit. Department of Finance and Personnel. NIO. PPRU Occasional Paper #28.

Robson, Brian, et al. 1994. *Assessing the Impact of Urban Policy.* Department of the Environment. Inner Cities Research Programme. London: HMSO.

Rolston, Bill. 1992. *Drawing Support: Murals in the North of Ireland.* Belfast: Beyond the Pale.

Romann, Michael. 1992. "The Effect of the Intifada on Jewish-Arab Relations in Jerusalem." In Layish, Aaron (ed.) *The Arabs in Jerusalem.* Jerusalem: Magnes Press. Hebrew language.

Romann, Michael. 1989. "Divided Perception in a United City: The Case of Jerusalem." Pp. 182–201 in Boal, Frederick, and David N. Livingstone (eds.) *The Behavioural Environment: Essays in Reflection, Application, and Re-evaluation.* London: Routledge.

Romann, Michael, and Alex Weingrod. 1991. *Living Together Separately: Arabs and Jews in Contemporary Jerusalem.* Princeton: Princeton University Press.

Rose, Richard. 1976. *Northern Ireland: A Time of Choice.* New York: MacMillan.

Roseman, Curtis C., Hans Dieter Laux, and Gunter Thieme. 1996. "Modern EthniCities." Pp. xvii–xxvii in Roseman, Curtis C., Hans Dieter Laux, and Gunter Thieme (eds.) *EthniCity: Geographic Perspectives on Ethnic Change in Modern Cities.* Lanham, Md.: Rowman and Littlefield.

Rothman, Jay. 1992. *From Confrontation to Cooperation: Resolving Ethnic and Regional Conflict.* Newbury Park, Cal.: Sage.

Rothman, Jay, with Randi Jo Land and Robin Twite. 1994. *The Jerusalem Peace Initiative*. Project on Managing Political Disputes. Jerusalem: Leonard Davis Institute, Hebrew University.

Rowthorn, Bob, and Naomi Wayne. 1985. *Northern Ireland: The Political Economy of Conflict*. Cambridge: Polity.

Rule, James B. 1988. *Theories of Civil Violence*. Berkeley: University of California Press.

Russett, B., and H. Starr. 1989. *World Politics: The Menu for Choice*. 2nd ed. New York: Freeman.

Sack, R. 1986. *Human Territoriality: Its Theory and History*. Cambridge: Cambridge University Press.

Sack, R. 1981. "Territorial Bases for Power." In Burnett, A. and P. Taylor (eds.) *Political Studies from Spatial Perspectives*. New York: John Wiley and Sons.

Safdie, Moshe 1986. *The Harvard Jerusalem Studio: Urban Designs for the Holy City*. Cambridge, Mass.: MIT Press.

Said, Edward W. 1994. *The Politics of Dispossession: The Struggle for Palestinian Self-Determination 1969–1994*. New York: Pantheon.

Said, Edward W. 1993. "Facts, Facts, and More Facts." *Al-Hayat*, December 10.

Sandler, Shmuel. 1988. "Israel and the West Bank Palestinians." *Publius: The Journal of Federalism* 18 (2): 47–62.

Saunders, Peter. 1979. *Urban Politics*. Harmondsworth, Middlesex: Penguin.

Schiff, Zeev, and Ehud Ya'ari. 1990. *Intifada: The Palestinian Uprising—Israel's Third Front*. New York: Simon and Schuster.

Schmelz, U. O. 1987. *Modern Jerusalem's Demographic Evolution*. Jerusalem Institute for Israel Studies.

Schmitt, David E. 1988. "Bicommunalism in Northern Ireland." *Publius: The Journal of Federalism* 18 (2): 33–46.

Schroyer, Trent. 1973. *The Critique of Domination*. Boston: Beacon.

Schultz, R. H. 1991. "The Low-Intensity Conflict Environment of the 1990s." *Annual American Academy of Political and Social Science* 517: 120–134.

Seelig, Michael, and Julie Seelig. 1988. "Architecture and Politics in Israel: 1920 to the Present." *Journal of Architectural and Planning Research* 5 (1): 35–48.

Seliger, M. 1970. "Fundamental and Operative Ideology: The Two Principal Dimensions of Political Argumentation." *Policy Sciences* 1: 325–338.

Sennett, Richard. 1970. *The Uses of Disorder: Personal Identity and City Life*. New York: Vintage.

Shalev, Aryeh. 1991. *The Intifada: Causes and Effects*. Boulder and Jerusalem: Westview Press and Jerusalem Post.

Shankill Partnership Board. 1995. *Greater Shankill Regeneration Strategy*. As printed in *Shankill People*. February.

Sharkansky, Ira. 1993. "Policy Making in Jerusalem: Local Discretion in a Context that Favours Central Control." *Cities* 10, 2: 115–124.

Sharkansky, Ira. 1992. "Governing a City That Some Would Internationalize: The Case of Jerusalem." *Jerusalem Journal of International Relations* 14, 1: 16–32.

Shepherd, Naomi. 1988. *Teddy Kollek, Mayor of Jerusalem*. New York: Harper & Row.

Shehadeh, Raja. 1993. *The Law of the Land: Settlement and Land Issues under Israeli Military Occupation*. Jerusalem: Palestinian Academic Society for the Study of International Affairs.

Sibley, David. 1995. *Geographies of Exclusion: Society and Difference in the West*. London: Routledge.

Singleton, Dale. 1986. "Housing Allocation Policy and Practice in Northern Ireland." In Singleton, D. (ed.) *Aspects of Housing Policy and Practice in Northern Ireland 1984–1986*. Belfast: Queen's University.

Singleton, Dale. 1983. "Belfast Housing Renewal Strategy: A Comment." In Singleton, D. (ed.) *Aspects of Housing Policy and Practice in Northern Ireland*. Belfast: Queen's University.

Sisk, Timothy D. 1995. *Democratization in South Africa: The Elusive Social Contract*. Princeton: Princeton University Press.

Smith, Anthony D. 1993. "The Ethnic Sources of Nationalism." Pp. 27–42 in Brown, Michael E. (ed.) *Ethnic Conflict and International Security*. Princeton: Princeton University Press.

Smith, David J. 1987. *Equality and Inequality in Northern Ireland III: Perceptions and Views*. London: Policy Studies Institute.

Smith, David J., and David Chambers. 1991. *Inequality in Northern Ireland*. Oxford: Clarendon.

Smith, David J., and David Chambers. 1989. *Equality and Inequality in Northern Ireland 4: Public Housing*. London: Policy Studies Institute.

Smith, David M. 1994. *Geography and Social Justice*. Oxford: Blackwell.

Smith, M. G. 1969. "Some Developments in the Analytic Framework of Pluralism." In Kuper, Leo, and M. G. Smith (eds.) *Pluralism in Africa*. Berkeley: University of California Press.

Smith, Michael P. 1979. *The City and Social Theory*. New York: St. Martin's.

Smooha, Sammy. 1980. "Control of Minorities in Israel and Northern Ireland." *Comparative Studies in Society and History* 22 (2): 256–280.

Snyder, Jack. 1993. "Nationalism and the Crisis of the Post-Soviet State." Pp. 79–102 in Brown, Michael (ed.) *Ethnic Conflict and International Security*. Princeton: Princeton University Press.

Springfield Inter-Community Development Project. 1993. *Life on the Interface*. Belfast: SICDP.

Standing Advisory Commission on Human Rights. 1990. *Second Report on Religious and Political Discrimination and Equality of Opportunity in Northern Ireland.*

Stanovcic, Vojislav. 1992. "Problems and Options in Institutionalizing Ethnic Relations." *International Political Science Review* 13, 4: 359–379.

Stern, David I. 1992. "Population Distribution in an Ethno-Ideologically Divided City: The Case of Jerusalem." *Urban Geography* 13, 2: 164–186.

Stewart, A. T. 1977. *The Narrow Ground.* London: Faber and Faber.

Susskind, Lawrence, and J. Cruickshank. 1987. *Breaking the Impasse.* New York: Basic Books.

Sutton, Malcolm. 1994. *An Index of Deaths from the Conflict in Ireland 1969–1993.* Belfast: Beyond the Pale.

Sweeney, Paul. 1991. "From Veto to Achievement." In *Community Development in Protestant Areas: A Report on Two Seminars.* Belfast: Northern Ireland Community Relations Council.

Sweeney, Paul, and Frank Gaffikin. 1995. *Listening to People. A Report on the Making Belfast Work Consultation Process.* Belfast: Making Belfast Work.

Tarrow, Sidney. 1994. *Power in Movement: Social Movements, Collective Action, and Politics.* Cambridge: Cambridge University Press.

Thomas, Huw (ed.) 1994. *Values and Planning.* Aldershot: Avebury.

Thomas, H., and V. Krishnarayan. 1994. "'Race', Disadvantage, and Policy Processes in British Planning." *Environment and Planning A* 26, 12: 1891–1910.

Tilly, Charles. 1978. *From Mobilization to Rebellion.* Reading, Mass.: Addison-Wesley.

Tonge, Jonathan. 1998. *Northern Ireland: Conflict and Change.* London: Prentice Hall Europe.

Torgovnik, Efraim. 1990. *The Politics of Urban Planning Policy.* Lanham, Md.: University Press of America.

Touval, Saadia, and I. William Zartman (eds.) 1985. *International Mediation in Theory and Practice.* Boulder: Westview Press.

Trounson, Rebecca. 1997. "Violence Feared as Israel OKs New Housing." *Los Angeles Times*, February 27, pp. A1, A4.

Trounson, Rebecca. 1996. "3 Years After Rabin-Arafat Handshake, Process Endures." *Los Angeles Times*, September 13, p. A4.

Ulster Political Research Group. 1987. *Common Sense.* Belfast:

Upper Shankill Belfast Action Team. 1994. *Strategy Document 1994–97.* Belfast: MBW/BAT.

United Nations. 1996. *The Istanbul Declaration on Human Settlements.* Advance, Unedited Text. June 15. United Nations Conference on Human Settlements (Habitat II). Istanbul. June 3–14.

United Nations Population Fund. 1996. *Report on World Urbanization Done for Habitat II conference*. Website http:\\www.undp.org\un\habitat. June 15 advance, unedited text.

Weitzer, Ronald. 1995. *Policing Under Fire: Ethnic Conflict and Police-Community Relations in Northern Ireland*. Albany: State University of New York Press.

Weitzer, Ronald. 1990. *Transforming Settler States: Communal Conflict and Internal Security in Northern Ireland and Zimbabwe*. Berkeley: University of California Press.

Welch, David. 1993. "Domestic Politics and Ethnic Conflict." Pp. 43–60 in Brown, Michael (ed.) *Ethnic Conflict and International Security*. Princeton: Princeton University Press.

Whyte, John. 1990. *Interpreting Northern Ireland*. Oxford: Clarendon.

Whyte, John H. 1986. "How is the Boundary Maintained between the Two Communities in Northern Ireland?" *Ethnic and Racial Studies* 9, 2: 219–234.

Wiener, Ron. 1976. *The Rape and Plunder of the Shankill in Belfast: People and Planning*. Belfast: Nothems.

Wilkinson, Tracy. 1998. "Terror Against Israelis Ebbs, Changes Character." *Los Angeles Times*, October 21, pp. A1, A11.

Williams, Robin M., Jr. 1994. "The Sociology of Ethnic Conflicts: Comparative International Perspectives." *Annual Review of Sociology* 20: 49–79.

Wing, Adrien Katherine. 1994. *Democracy, Constitutionalism, and the Future State of Palestine*. Jerusalem: Palestinian Academic Society for the Study of International Affairs.

Wolfe, James H. 1988. "Cyprus: Federation Under International Safeguards." *Publius: The Journal of Federalism* 18 (2): 75–90.

Wood, D. 1991. "In Defense of Indefensible Space." In Brantingham, P. J., and P. L. Brantingham (eds.) *Environmental Criminology*. Prospect Heights, Ill.: Waveland.

World Bank. 1994. *Emergency Assistance Program for the Occupied Territories*. Investment Program. March. Washington D.C.: World Bank.

World Bank. 1993. *Developing the Occupied Territories: An Investment in Peace*. 6 volumes. September. Washington D.C.: World Bank.

World Bank. 1991. *Urban Policy and Economic Development: An Agenda for the 1990s*. Washington D.C.: World Bank.

Wright, Robin. 1993. "Ethnic Strife Owes More to Present than to Past." *Los Angeles Times*. Special supplement: The New Tribalism. June 8.

Yiftachel, Oren. 1995. "The Dark Side of Modernism: Planning as Control of an Ethnic Minority." Pp. 216–242 in Watson, Sophie, and Katherine Gibson (eds.) *Postmodern Cities and Spaces*. Oxford: Blackwell.

Yiftachel, Oren. 1992. *Planning a Mixed Region in Israel: The Political Geography of Arab-Jewish Relations in the Galilee*. Aldershot: Avebury.

Yiftachel, Oren. 1989. "Towards a New Typology of Urban Planning Theories." *Environment and Planning B: Planning and Design* 16, 1: 23–39.

Plans and Laws (selected)

Jerusalem

Allon Plan. 1969. Articulated in Allon, Yigal. 1976. "Israel: The Case for Defensible Borders." *Foreign Affairs* 55: 38–53.

Declaration of Principles on Interim Self-Government Arrangements between Israel and the Palestine Liberation Organization ("Oslo Agreement"). September 13, 1993.

Drobless, Matitiahu. 1978. *Master Plan for the Development of Settlement for the Years 1979–1983*. Jerusalem: The Jewish Agency.

The Five Million Plan. 1972. *Geographic Distribution Plan of Israeli's Population of 5 Million*. Jerusalem: Ministry of the Interior.

Gaza-Jericho Autonomy Agreement ("Cairo Agreement"). May 4, 1994.

Jerusalem Municipality. 1981. *The "Seam" Area: Planning Guidelines*. Jerusalem: Town Planning Department. Policy Planning Section.

Judea and Samaria: Guidelines for Regional and Physical Planning. 1970. Jerusalem: Planning Department. Israeli Ministry of Interior.

Master Plan of Jerusalem 1968. 1972. Jerusalem: Ministry of Interior.

Master Plan for the Settlement and Regional Development of Samaria and Judea, 1983–1986. 1983. Jerusalem: Israel Ministry of Agriculture and World Zionist Organization Department of Settlement.

Mazor, Adam, and Shermiyahu Cohen. 1994. *Metropolitan Jerusalem: Master Plan and Development Plan. Summary Document*. June.

Planning and Housing Law. 1965 and amendments. Jerusalem: Ministry of Interior.

Palestine Liberation Organization. Internal Department. 1993. *Economic Plan for 1994–2000*. Tunis: PLO. 2 volumes.

Partial Regional Master Plan. 1982. Amendment to Jerusalem District Regional Master Planning Scheme RJ/5 of 1942.

Partial Regional Scheme for Roads #50. 1991.

Settlement Division—The World Zionist Organization. 1981. *The One Hundred Thousand Plan*. Jerusalem: WZO.

Seven Stars Plan. Approved by Knesset 1990.

Sharon, Arieh. 1973. *Planning Jerusalem: The Master Plan for the Old City of Jerusalem and its Environs*. New York: McGraw Hill.

United Nations. *International Convention on the Elimination of All Forms of Racial Discrimination*.

United Nations. *Covenant on Economic, Social and Cultural Rights*.

Belfast

Building Design Partnership. 1969. *Belfast Urban Area Plan.* Belfast: BDP.

Department of the Environment for Northern Ireland. 1990. *Belfast Urban Area Plan 2001.* Belfast: HMSO.

Department of the Environment for Northern Ireland. 1989. *Belfast Urban Area Plan 2001: Adoption Statement.* Belfast: HMSO.

Department of the Environment for Northern Ireland. 1988. "Pre-Inquiry Response to CTA's Objections to the Draft BUAP." Pp. 187–221 in Blackman, Tim. 1991. *Planning Belfast: A Case Study of Public Policy and Community Action.* Aldershot, U.K.: Avebury.

Department of the Environment for Northern Ireland. 1987. *Belfast Urban Area Plan 2001. Draft.* Belfast: Her Majesty's Stationery Office (HMSO).

Department of the Environment for Northern Ireland. 1981. *Belfast Urban Area: Planning Statement and Progress Report.* Belfast: DOENI.

Department of the Environment for Northern Ireland. 1977. *Northern Ireland: Regional Physical Development Strategy 1975–95.* Belfast: HMSO.

Government of Northern Ireland. 1970. *Review Body on Local Government in Northern Ireland* ("the Macrory Report"). CMD 546. Belfast: HMSO.

Matthew, Sir R. H. 1964. *Belfast Regional Survey and Plan 1962.* Belfast: HMSO.

Northern Ireland Housing Executive. 1971– . *Annual Reports.* Belfast: NIHE

Northern Ireland Information Service. 1988. *Making Belfast Work: Belfast Areas for Action.*

The Planning (Northern Ireland) Order 1991. No. 1220 (N.I.). Belfast: HMSO.

Index